SPARTAN VICTΩRY:

THE INSIDE STORY OF

THE BATTLE FOR BREXIT

BY

THE RT HON MARK FRANCOIS MP

First published in the UK in 2021 by Kindle Direct Publishing
This edition published in 2021 by Kindle Direct Publishing
www.amazon.com/kdp

ISBN 9798484798391

Paperback printed and bound in Great Britain by Kindle Direct Publishing.
Hardback printed in Europe by Kindle Direct Publishing

For my great friend and fellow Parliamentarian,

the late Sir David Amess MP,

who taught me everything about how to be an MP

and, more importantly, why it still matters.

SPARTAN VICTΩRY:
The Inside Story of the Battle for Brexit

In Memoriam
Sir David Amess MP

This book, which is about the Battle for Brexit, was written during the Covid-19 inspired Lockdown and, after some editing, was originally due to be published in late October 2021. Around a week before the planned publication date, my greatest friend in Parliament, Sir David Amess MP, was cruelly taken from us, whilst carrying out one of his regular constituency surgeries, in Southend.

David himself was a Eurosceptic and a Brexiteer and he already knew well that I was writing this book. Perhaps ironically, he had published a (very good) autobiographical work of his own, entitled, *"Ayes and Ears: A Survivor's Guide to Westminster"* only a year or so previously. However, out of respect for David, I postponed the publication of Spartan Victory until after his funeral.

This book is primarily about what I call the "Battle for Brexit", of which David was a part but it already touched upon our earlier years together in Basildon, during the 1990s, when he was already the high-profile local MP (before transferring to Southend West) and I was a young Councillor, who one day wanted to follow in his footsteps, into the House of Commons.

Following his untimely death on 15th October, I paid tribute to him in a eulogy delivered in the House of Commons, the following Monday. A copy of that speech, taken from *Hansard* and about which some people have been kind enough to say some nice things, is now included in this slightly revised version of the book, at Appendix 8.

A copy of the "Prayer Card", which I placed in the Commons Chamber to keep Sir David's seat free during the tributes to him (rather as her Labour colleagues did for another of our fallen comrades, Jo Cox, in 2016) also appears at the top of this page.

This still remains, first and foremost a book about Brexit but I would also like to dedicate it to my friend Sir David Amess, without whom I would never have become a Member of Parliament in the first place and, thus, at least some of the events in this book might never have happened.

Rest in peace, David, my dear friend.

Mark Francois
Member of Parliament for Rayleigh and Wickford

Rayleigh, Essex
December 2021

Foreword

When I walked through Carriage Gates into the House of Commons almost two decades ago, no one in the world had ever heard of Brexit, or me. As a fresh faced and idealistic newly elected MP, who had just achieved a lifetime's ambition in being elected to the House of Commons, I had absolutely no idea of what was to happen to me. If you had told me at that time that I would one day help lead a rebellion against the Leadership of my own Party and indeed actively work to help oppose a sitting Conservative Prime Minister, I would have politely suggested that they lock you up for reasons of public safety.

It was not an easy journey to reach the House of Commons in the first place. Along the way I competed against John Bercow for the Chairmanship of the Federation of Conservative Students; helped David Amess defend the iconic marginal seat of Basildon in the 1992 General Election; fought against "Red Ken" Livingstone in Brent East at the following General Election; competed with Michael Portillo in the final to become the Conservative Candidate in the Kensington and Chelsea by-election; lost out to Hugo Swire in the final to become the Conservative Candidate in East Devon and then eventually had to defeat one Boris Johnson to become the successful Conservative Candidate in Rayleigh in 2001.

Nevertheless, the primary purpose of this book is to try and explain the great issues which were at stake in what I call the "Battle for Brexit", particularly between the EU Referendum of 2016 and our eventual departure from the European Union in January 2020. I have focused in some detail on the epic struggle that took place in Parliament during those three years or so, when it is not an exaggeration to say that the destiny of our nation hung in the balance.

This is the story of how a small group of Conservative MPs, having seized upon what was actually at stake, fought tenaciously to prevent a European Treaty being imposed upon them, which would effectively have kept us in the European Union in perpetuity, in complete defiance of the wishes of the British people, as expressed in the Referendum in 2016. It seeks to explain who were the "European Research Group" (ERG), who were the "Spartans" and what role did these groups of MPs play in that great Parliamentary battle and in the wider media as well.

Over the last few years, as an active protagonist for the Brexiteer cause, I have been called just about everything under the sun by a combination of political opponents, newspaper journalists, a rather weird man in a top hat and indeed innumerable people on Twitter. In a sense this is "my side of the story" – which you can now read and then judge for yourself.

This book is deliberately intended to seek to convey humour at times, in part to try and explain just how bizarre the life of a Member of Parliament can be in the 21st Century, caught between the hammer and anvil of increasingly demanding constituents on the one hand and an often deeply cynical media on the other.

In seeking to do this, the book also attempts to explain how Parliament works, and to give the reader "a look behind the scenes" of what really goes on in the Mother of Parliaments, to which almost three quarters of the population still bother to elect their representatives in a General Election. Some of these insights may not always be flattering but they are intended to be truthful and to help try and demystify some of what actually goes on at Westminster.

The book also seeks to explain how it was that our Parliamentary system – for all its faults – ultimately worked as intended, to help protect our liberty and our freedom when it was most certainly at stake. It hopefully also brings out how perilously close we came to having been locked into an antidemocratic institution – the European Union – forever.

If this book manages to achieve this objective, then it will certainly have been worth the trouble taken to write it. In any event, the Brexit debate will rage for years to come and no doubt be argued over by historians and academics for decades and perhaps even centuries thereafter.

So, for what it's worth, this is my version of events.

Mark Francois MP
Chairman of the European Research Group

Rayleigh, Essex
October 2021

Chapter 1: From Alcatraz to Westminster

Perhaps ironically for a future Conservative MP, I was born in what is now Jeremy Corbyn's constituency of Islington North, on the morning of the 14th August 1965.[1] The surname Francois is of Huguenot origin and, as far our family knows, our ancestors came across from France in the late 18th Century and, along with many other Huguenot emigres, settled in one of a number of clusters in North London, in what are now predominantly the Boroughs of Islington and Hackney.[2]

My fraternal grandfather, Matthew John Francois, fought in World War I as an infantry soldier in the Kings Royal Rifle Corps (KRRC) during which he was wounded. He later married a local girl, Rose, and they subsequently had four children: Harry, Reginald (Reg), Ernest (Ernie) and Florence (Flo). They were very much from working class North London stock and Reginald, my father, entered the world in 1925. He had a conventional working-class childhood and sometime after World War II broke out, he secured a job in an optics factory, helping to grind goggles which were used by RAF pilots. As such, he was in what was known as a "Reserved Occupation" and was exempted from conscription, because his work was considered vital to the war effort.

Nevertheless, in 1943, aged 18, he volunteered to join the Royal Navy and went through training at Lowestoft, before being posted to join a Royal Naval Patrol Service Minesweeper of the Western Isles Class, HMS Bressay (named after a small island in the Shetlands) in mid-1943. He was initially ordered to join his ship at Scapa Flow in the Orkney Islands, where his Minesweeping Squadron was based.

According to Naval records in the National Archive at Kew, HMS Bressay operated in and around the Orkney's helping to guard the major battleships of the Home Fleet for much of 1943 and early 1944, before she was sent south to Portsmouth in May of 1944, in order to participate in D-Day. On the 6th June 1944, my father, then aged only 19, and serving on a Minesweeper, was present on that momentous day when allied forces stormed ashore to help begin the liberation of Europe from Nazi tyranny. As a "Stoker", on what was still unusually a coal fired Minesweeper in those days, my father's job was to help keep the ship's furnaces well stocked with coal, which required you to be physically fit.

Reg was subsequently promoted to "Stoker First Class" and continued to serve on HMS Bressay[3] until he was demobbed in 1946 and transitioned back into civvy street. Not long afterwards he married a local girl, known as "Bunny" and they gave birth to a son, Brian, but unfortunately the marriage dissolved several years later.

Because of his service during the war, my father had learnt about boilers, engines and such like and so he then went through a number of jobs, a common feature of which was that they involved working with boilers, heating and ventilation. It was while doing such a job, in the maintenance department of the large Littlewoods signature store on Oxford Street in the early 1960s, that he was called upstairs to the kitchen area in Littlewoods' cafeteria, in order to mend a problem with their new dishwasher. The canteen supervisor who had made the call, was a beautiful young Italian girl named Anna Carloni, who as a result of this fateful chance, was several years later to become my mother.

Anna Carloni was born in Montellabatte, in North Eastern Italy in 1933. Her mother, my maternal grandmother, had been born Maria Salvi, to a relatively wealthy family. However, in her late teens she effectively eloped with a young agricultural equipment salesman called Gino Carloni, who lived in a house in Pesaro, on the Adriatic coast. Despite the opposition of her parents, they married and subsequently had five children of their own: Ada, Terenza (Renza), Valentino, Anna and then the youngest of the bunch, Carlotta (Carla).

In her 20's, Anna Carloni came to London, to work as an Au Pair for an Anglo-Italian family. Eventually Anna outgrew the job, but London was an exciting place in the 1960s and she decided she wanted to stay. Anna then got a job working in the cafeteria of Littlewoods' quite smart flagship store, which was on Oxford Street and being hardworking, was eventually promoted to Supervisor, to help manage the cafeteria.

When my father was called upstairs from the Maintenance Department to sort out their new dishwasher – which fortunately for me had been playing up – he was struck by how attractive Anna was and then proceeded in taking his lunch regularly in the cafeteria thereafter. In short, Reg spent the best part of six months unsuccessfully trying to chat Anna up and to persuade her to go out on a date with him.

Eventually, and largely in order to get rid of this grinning idiot, my mother reluctantly agreed to go out on a date one evening with Reg – on the strict understanding that this would be a one-off occasion and that he promised to leave her alone thereafter. It transpires that my father took Anna to a pub in North London, where, apparently, he spent every penny in his possession, got a bit tipsy into the bargain and then asked my mother if he could borrow some money in order to get the bus home! Confronted with such an unbelievably glamourous evening my mother was rather taken aback but of course Reg had to see her again, in order to refund her the bus fare.

After such an auspicious start, they inevitably fell in love. As mother was a Catholic and dad was a divorcee, a church wedding was out of the question, particularly in the 1960s and they therefore married at Islington Registry Office in 1965. Some months later they had a son, who they christened "Mark Gino Francois", incorporating the name of Anna's father. They were presumably blissfully unaware that they were christening a future Eurosceptic with such a pan-European name.

Life in Hanley Road

The young couple subsequently moved into a flat at 19 Hanley Road, off the Hornsey Road, in North Islington. They had few possessions, but a local furniture company called Andrews, based at Highbury Corner, were offering a deal that if customers purchased a certain amount of furniture, in return they would help them find lodgings in which to put it. It was via this arrangement that my parents came to rent a small three room flat in a converted Victorian house in Hanley Road. The flat was modest, with a bedroom, what we would now call a small kitchen-diner and a living room, with a linoleum floor. The television was of its time, with either 425 or 625 lines and a switch to enable you to convert from one to another. So, our first flat was not exactly Blenheim Palace but nevertheless, it was home.

Around a year after we moved in, my half-brother Brian, had met a young girl called Christine and they moved into a flat below us, in the same house. Dad and Brian were always close and although he had sometimes been quite hard-up for money, Dad had always made sure that Brian was financially provided for, when he was growing up as a young boy.

Two loving parents

Although our conditions were far from palatial, I was extremely fortunate to have two doting parents, who clearly loved me dearly. My father had not had much by way of a formal education in the 1920s and early 1930s but nevertheless, he taught me to read as a young boy with the aid of what we now know today as the "Thomas the Tank Engine" series of story books, which were written by the Reverend W Aubrey.[4] The books were actually being re-published at that time and my father would make a point of going to Hamleys, in Oxford Street, to buy each revised edition when it came out and would then read them to me at night and encourage me to learn to read the books myself thereafter. In the end, I almost learnt them all by rote and, by that device, learnt to read at a relatively early age.

My mother's English skills gradually improved as she lived in England for more years, but she retained to the end, the most marvellous set of malapropisms. For instance, if she bought a new piece of equipment (e.g. a new transistor radio) she would insist on reading what she called "the book of destructions" to tell her how to operate the bit of kit. Similarly, she would swear blind that we once bought a large item of furniture from MI5 and not MFI.

Moving out to the country

One evening in 1971, I remember my father explaining to me that we were going to leave London and move to a new town called Basildon, in Essex, which was "out in the country" to the East of London. Like any young child who has made friends at school I was reluctant to move but at the age of six I didn't exactly have a casting vote in the matter and so, with a sense of trepidation, I gathered together my belongings and prepared to head East.

I have lived in Essex ever since and have generally regarded myself as "London born but Essex bred" and have thus always felt something of an affinity for our capital city. In this, (although I had no idea of it at the time) I was to be in tune with many of my future constituents in Rayleigh, lots of whom have links, either first, second or third generation, harking back to London.

Nevertheless, despite my anxieties, moving "out to the country" was also something of an adventure, particularly when I was told that we were moving from a rather cramped flat to a brand-new house, with three bedrooms and a garden! So off we drove out of London, down the A127 London to Southend Arterial Road, to begin a new life in Essex.

Basildon New Town

In 1949, the post war Labour Government, led by Prime Minister Clement Attlee, passed the "New Towns Act", to create a number of new satellite communities in the home counties, surrounding London. The purpose of this initiative was essentially altruistic, to create, as its name suggested, a series of new towns to replace a large number of the slums in inner London, many of which had suffered heavy damage during The Blitz.

These new communities, to be built largely from scratch, were designed to have modern facilities, new homes and factories, parks and open spaces and to provide a much more civilised alternative for working class people, than the often cramped and sometimes even unsanitary conditions that their forebears had previously endured in the Capital. A number of these towns were created in a ring around London stretching from Bracknell in the West to Stevenage and Hemel Hempstead in the North, Crawley in the South and then two in Essex, one in Harlow in the North of the County and the second in Basildon, in the South.

Thousands of acres of land, much of which had previously been owned as small homesteads, were purchased by the Government, (via the newly established Development Corporations) for this reason, with Basildon New Town being centred on what had effectively been a small rural hamlet, with two more established villages, Pitsea to the East and Laindon to the West. A town centre was created in the 1950s onto which was then grafted a large industrial estate to the North of the town, which attracted a variety of national companies, from Ford (who built a large tractor manufacturing plant there), through Carreras, the cigarette makers and the defence and electronics conglomerate, GEC.

In order to accommodate the workers for these burgeoning new facilities, the Basildon Development Corporation built a number of large housing estates in the 1960s and early 1970s in Basildon, Pitsea and Laindon respectively. Families were rapidly moved out from London to populate these new estates, even while they were still being constructed.[5]

In our case, we moved into a new three bedroomed house on what was known as the "Five Links estate". This eventually totalled over a thousand properties, sub-divided into five areas, each one of which was named after a farm or homestead which had stood on the site, before the new houses were constructed. Our bit of the estate, which was quite close to Laindon Shopping Centre, was known as "Mellow Purgess" (named after a local dwelling, previously centred on that site) and comprised 166 houses/flats, as part of the overall total.

Welcome to "Alcatraz"

Our house, which we rented from the Development Corporation, but which was otherwise to all intents and purposes a "council house" was number 147 in Mellow Purgess and my parents regarded it very much as their new castle. There were six houses in our square with another square behind us and one in front of us as well. Dad parked his new car (a mark 2 Ford Cortina, which was coloured bright yellow and which my mother and I nicknamed the "Yellow Banana") in the car park on the edge of the estate.

I soon made friends with a young boy called Ian, a year younger than me who lived at 144 Mellow Purgess, in the next square along and I subsequently also befriended another boy called Colin, who lived at 66 Mellow Purgess, several squares distant and who went to my school.

The estate proved friendly and indeed won several architectural awards for its unique design, which, incredible though it may sound, was originally based on a Chelsea Mews concept. However, perhaps its greatest flaw was that part of the outside was ringed by four storey flats which, from a distance, gave a visual impression somewhat akin to a prison. Hence, while the estate was initially popular with those who moved on to it, many of the other locals in Laindon and across Basildon more generally rapidly ascribed it the nickname "Alcatraz". I personally regarded this as unfair but, rightly or wrongly, the name stuck and for people who have lived in Basildon for some years, the area is still known as Alcatraz to this day.

Nevertheless, we moved in and rapidly made ourselves at home. Dad, because of his gregarious nature (he was very much the "cheeky chappy" from London), soon made friends with many of the neighbours and we settled into what became a very happy, indeed close, community. My mother added her own Italian touch to the home, by paying for a small painted wooden sign entitled "La Nostra Casa" (which means, "Our Home" – not to be confused with the "Cosa Nostra" – which means the Mafia).

"Promise me something Son"

Sometime around my tenth birthday, Dad went into London to attend a reunion with some of his old Naval comrades. I would normally have been long to bed by the time that he returned home but, for some reason I can no longer recall, the Lord was kind and I stayed up late that night and was still awake when he got home. My father enjoyed a pint, but he was not by any means a heavy drinker, although when he came home that evening it was obvious that "he had had a sherbet or two".

Up to that point, I had tried to speak to my father several times about the role he had played in World War II but while he had often been willing to talk about amusing incidents, for instance the time he got "involved in a punch up with some American sailors in a pub in Portsmouth", he had always scrupulously steered clear of talking about combat. Many years later, when I became the Veterans Minister at the MoD and had an opportunity to speak to many World War II vets, I finally began to understand why. Essentially, for many Veterans who've done active service, and even seen some of their friends and comrades killed alongside them, it is simply too painful to talk about. Many of them metaphorically put these memories in a separate box and mentally turned the key and do not speak about such things openly again, even to their loved ones, until much later on in life, perhaps even when they are close to death.

Of course, at the age of ten, I was unaware of any of this, but I remember my father sitting down in an armchair and, to my amazement, he suddenly began to open up about what had happened on D-Day. He explained that having been in the bowels of the minesweeper stoking the furnaces, he heard the initial allied bombardment of the German positions begin at a little after 5:30am in the morning, when, as he put it, "the battlewagons really opened up". He said he had never heard a sound like it in all his life. He described it as a "cacophony" – quite a good word for a working-class lad – and said that it went on for quite some time to suppress the enemy defences.

By that time, the minesweepers had already performed their primary purpose having gone in hours before the allied assault, to sweep the approaches to the D-Day beaches, in order to clear them from mines, so as to allow the landing craft safe passage to the beachheads. I learnt many years later that the D-Day planners had been very concerned about the possibility of a combined German U Boat/E Boat counterattack on the allied bridgehead and therefore the planners had decided that once they had swept the approaches to the beaches, that the minesweepers would therefore be redeployed, on either flank of the Normandy bridgehead, to provide an advance screen, to give warning against any such German riposte. In the end this never happened but that is why my father was redeployed in the afternoon opposite Omaha beach, where the American's subsequently took very heavy casualties, as immortalised in the now famous movie *Saving Private Ryan*, starring Tom Hanks, which came out in 1998.

So, picture the scene, as I sat there as a ten-year-old boy, literally at my father's knee, completely spellbound as he painted a picture of what had happened on that fateful day. Of course, he never went ashore but, had the minesweepers not performed their vital role, neither would anyone else have either.

He didn't glory in any of it, far from it, he talked movingly about how many men must have been killed that day and the fact that he was lucky not to have been one of them. My father had always been a strong man, and I had never known him frightened about anything, I'd certainly never seen him cry but as he spoke,

I noticed that his eyes began to well up and that he developed a catch in his throat, something I had never previously witnessed in him before.

Then, with his by now liquid eyes, he turned to me and in a very earnest voice said something I have never forgotten. "Promise me something son" he said: "I want you to promise me something and mean it". For me this was really significant. My father brought me up to believe that you should tell the truth and not lie and that, in the old City saying, "your word is your bond" or, as he once said it to me in his own terms: "Son, your word is who you are". Similarly, he said it was one thing to agree to do something but if you used the words "*I promise*" then you were honour bound to do whatever it was. Therefore, you should never *promise* to do anything, unless you absolutely meant it.

And so, he said to me: "Promise me son, that when you grow up you will never, ever, take living in a free country for granted. All those men died so that we can live in a free country Mark, and you must promise me faithfully that you will never forget that". By now I was getting really quite upset to see my father looking like this and so, to calm him, I said: "I promise Daddy, I absolutely *promise* I will never take that for granted, as long as I live". "Good", he replied, seeming somehow reassured by my response. "That's good son, I am very pleased to hear you say that". After that point, which you might perhaps describe as the climax of the whole conversation, he said that he was feeling a little tired (and he admitted just a little bit drunk) and he had to be up early for work, so he thought that he should go to bed. I climbed the stairs after him and went to bed myself, fully resolved that having made this promise, which seemed very important to my father, I would never break it.

St Nicholas School – A "bog standard comprehensive"

In September 1976, in my recently purchased new school uniform, I walked through the gates of St Nicholas Comprehensive School in Laindon, in what would now be known as Year 7 but which in old money was the "First Year Seniors", to begin my secondary education. St Nicholas was, to use a phrase subsequently made famous by Alastair Campbell, every inch "a bog standard comprehensive",[6] whose unofficial mission statement was to prepare kids to work in the factories in Basildon New Town, or as secretaries or administrators in the offices and facilities that supported them.

I remember in assembly on our first day, we were told very clearly that there were 226 of us joining the school that morning. I have never forgotten that number and you might perhaps be curious to know how many of that 226 finally made it to university? The actual number was two. Less than one per cent of us. One was Barry Lemon, a very bright young kid with a penchant for mathematics whose father, David Lemon, was the Director of Studies at St Nicholas and the other one, was me.

Many of the teachers were hard working, but the school's ethos was pitifully weak, and it lacked any sense of clear ambition for its pupils. With some honourable exceptions, many of the staff were just going through the motions. After all we were just a bunch of working-class kids from a clutch of large Council estates, so why on earth should anybody waste their time on trying to get any of us into university?

There were no polished honours boards in the main hall, with the names of those awarded Oxbridge scholarships recorded in gold leaf, for posterity. There wasn't even a board in the first place. There was basically bugger all. I had a number of friends who were bright and fun and who could easily have benefitted from a university education – if it had ever practically been on offer. But the school made virtually no effort whatsoever to explain to its pupils what university could entail, indeed even what university was, and that sheer defeatism and chronic lack of aspiration for the pupils in their care is something I must admit I have felt angry about ever since.

Nevertheless, the school did have a track-record of producing musical talent. Some of the members of the pop band *Depeche Mode* were several years above me at St Nicholas, as indeed was *Alison Moyet*, who went on to achieve fame with *Yazoo* and as a solo artist in her own right. So, while we never got many pupils into Oxbridge, we did get a number of them on to *Top of the Pops*.

Whilst I lacked any musical talent whatsoever, I had been a fairly bright pupil at Junior School, and I had decided I would do my best to get on in life and therefore I applied myself to my studies as best I could. To help me, Dad did extra overtime for over a year in order to purchase a full set of *Encyclopaedia Britannica*, which was quite expensive in those days, in order to assist me with my studies. Many of my Sixth Form essays, written long before *Google* had even been conceptualised, were peppered with references to one volume of the *Encyclopaedia Britannica* or another. I will always be thankful to my parents, who did everything they practically could to nurture the reasonably bright kid they had been bringing up and to give him the best possible start in life, albeit from fairly humble beginnings.

As any young person will tell you, such support from your parents is priceless and it was only really because of that head start they gave me in life – right back to my father reading to me as a small child from the Thomas the Tank Engine books, that I ever had any chance of getting into Parliament at all. I will always be deeply, deeply grateful to both of them for everything they did in that regard.

Holidays in Pesaro

Ever since I was a bambino, each August my father would take a month's block annual leave and we would fly to Italy, to spend a holiday with my mother's Italian family, to whom dad was "Reginaldo" and I was ubiquitously "Marco Gino". To save on hotel bills we would stay at my Grandmother's (Nona's) home, in Pesaro, on a street just behind the seafront called "Via Pola". Most of the family lived in and around the town and my eldest aunt, Zia Ada, had married a local farmer named Gemino, who owned a lovely white painted farmhouse in the hills just above Pesaro, which we universally referred to as "The White House".

Some of my happiest childhood memories are of those holidays in Italy. In particular, I recall each summer attending a veritable feast at the White House, when the entire family – some thirty strong including all the cousins – would enjoy a meal that seemed to last an entire day. To the untrained eye, this must have looked like a scene from Francis Ford Coppola's *The Godfather* (but minus Marlon Brando).

At one such banquet my father got into a good-natured argument with Pino, Gemino's son, who declared himself "a communist", despite owning a large factory on the outskirts of Pesaro. As the evening wore on and the vino flowed merrily, this discussion became more intense, until close to midnight, my father, in his pigeon Italian, made an impromptu speech, showering the family in love, ensuring Pino of his deepest respect but the peroration of which was: "Vaffanculo la comunista!" – which brought the house down. At the end of this, Zio Ciccio (Renza's husband and very much a mild mannered, gentleman of the old school) sidled up to my father and whispered conspiratorially in his ear, "Bravo Reginaldo!".

In many ways my Italian relatives were straight out of central casting, a large, loving, extrovert Italian family, who readily accepted "Reginaldo" as one of their own – just as they did his son. For most Italian's, family trumps everything – career, fame and fortune, everything – and on that point, I often think they're right. In my experience at least, most Italians have some affection for "L'Englese". They are fond of our traditions, HM The Queen, tea at four o'clock and all the rest of it but they cannot understand why, compared to them, we are always so "uptight" about everything, from work to relationships. It might seem ironic to some that a future Eurosceptic would be so fond of his Italian relatives, but I always have been – and always will be.

Rudyard Kipling's "If"

When I was aged thirteen, my father gave me, as a present, a foolscap sized scroll, on which was inscribed a copy of Rudyard Kipling's famous poem, "If". The work, first published in 1910, took the form of a set of advice which the author had drafted for his young son, John, as guidance for how he should conduct his life. John Kipling, subsequently served in the Irish Guards and was killed at the Battle of Loos in 1915, but his father's immortal words (which were voted "Britain's Favourite Poem" in a BBC nationwide poll in 1995) live on.[7]

The poem begins with the words:

"If you can keep your head,
when all about you are losing theirs and blaming it on you
If you can trust yourself when all men doubt you,
But make allowance for their doubting too...."

And it memorably concludes:

"If you can fill the unforgiving minute
with sixty seconds' worth of distance run,
Yours is the earth and everything that's in it,
And – which is more – you'll be a Man, my son!".

My father explained to me that these were wise words and encouraged me to look after them – which I did. Moreover, he told me that if ever I was anxious or uncertain and for whatever reason he was not around to offer advice, then I should read the poem again and it would help me decide what to do. I put the poem away carefully to please my father, who despite his tough upbringing could be quite sentimental at times but privately thinking that I would probably never need to refer to it in quite the manner that he had suggested.

As it turned out, I was wrong.

"Dad...I want to be an MP!"

When I was very young, I didn't want to be a Member of Parliament, indeed I had no idea what such a thing was. What I did know however, was that my father had served in the Royal Navy in the War and as I was growing up, I decided I wanted to join the Army. I wasn't going to be an Admiral, but I was definitely going to be a General!

As a young boy I remember having a very badly glued together Airfix Spitfire hanging from my bedroom ceiling and I read a number of comics based on the War, like "*Commando*" and "*Victor*". However, as I got older, I moved on from cartoons to reading more seriously about the history of the Second World War and indeed the run up to it. In particular, I became absolutely fascinated by Winston Churchill, a man who had clearly seen all this coming and had done everything he could to warn people but who, initially at least, was not believed, indeed was written off as a troublemaker. Winston Churchill was a "Member of Parliament" and what was all that about? It turned out that he made quite incredible speeches in somewhere called the "House of Commons" and what was all that about too? Put simply, the more I read about all of this stuff, the more fascinated I became.

In particular, I was intrigued by the events of 1940, when Churchill became Prime Minister and Germany seemed about to invade the British Isles. His absolute determination not to surrender to Hitler but to fight on, however daunting the odds, made a lasting impression on me. The story has been brilliantly encapsulated in recent years by the film *The Darkest Hour,* for which Gary Oldman rightfully won an Oscar for his wonderful portrayal of Churchill. Nevertheless, as a young boy growing up in 1970s Britain I had to rely on books and mainly old news reel footage to comprehend what had really been at stake.[8]

When I was aged eleven, my mother took me to visit the Palace of Westminster and I remember sitting in the Strangers Gallery in 1976, looking down into the Chamber below and seeing these "Members of Parliament" talking about how best to run the country. I was dumbstruck. On the way out, I made a point of buying a postcard with a picture of the House of Commons on it from the Gift Shop and I still have that postcard in a box of keepsakes at home, to this day.

I can't remember exactly when I decided that this is what I wanted to do with my life, but I had worked out that it was the MPs and politicians who gave the General's the orders anyway and therefore if you really wanted to protect your country, it was even more important to be an MP, than it was a soldier. I never perceived myself as "a man of destiny" (as Churchill apparently did at a similar age)[9] but nevertheless I did, for whatever reason, have a "sixth sense" that one day my country would come under threat again and that, somehow, it was my duty to help resist this challenge, whatever it might be and howsoever it might manifest itself.

So, sometime around the age of thirteen, I remember having a conversation late one evening with my father when I told him; "Dad, I've decided what I want to do with my life, I want to become an MP". My father looked at me and smiled and said he was delighted to hear that was my ambition and moreover, if I really meant it, he would do everything he possibly could to help me.

To put this in context, this would have been in around 1978, in an era when MPs were regarded totally differently from the way they are today. There had been no "cash for questions", no "expenses scandal", and the media were still relatively deferential – certainly compared to how they are now. In those days, MPs, many of whom had fought in the Second World War, were still regarded as highly admired public figures, almost Lords of the Manor in their own localities and therefore to want to be one would have been regarded by most people as a laudable aim. It was certainly so for my father, who seemed delighted that this relatively bright kid sitting opposite him had decided, that one day, he wanted to serve his country in the House of Commons.

Losing Dad

A year later, my father was dead. It was made all the more painful by the fact that we never saw it coming. My father had led a tough life, much of it involving heavy manual labour (such as scrubbing out the inside of large industrial boilers, when they were down for maintenance) and, like many of his generation, he also smoked relatively heavily as well. He was easily a "20 a day man" and possibly more. My mother was also a smoker but less prolifically than Dad.

Reg suffered intermittently from epilepsy and was put on phenobarbitone, which in the 1970s was apparently the drug of choice for epilepsy sufferers. He also suffered badly with gallstones and then in 1978 was diagnosed as also suffering from Angina – the hardening of the arteries. He was put down for a triple heart bypass operation but, in those days, this was still a relatively rare procedure for which there was quite a waiting list. His operation was accordingly provisionally scheduled for some time early in 1980.

One afternoon in December 1979 he came home from an early morning shift at Shell and, as was often his practice, he had a nap on the sofa in the living room. There was nothing at all unusual about this except that in the early evening he looked slightly pale and said he was feeling tired and was going to go up to bed early. I vaguely remember having something important to do at school the following day, which was occupying my attention and so, I didn't really give it much of a second thought and just wished him goodnight. I then turned in later that evening, in the usual way. My father died of a heart attack in the small hours of the night, while I was still fast asleep.

Suddenly, in an instant, my comfortable world, of Laindon and school and all my friends was shattered. The wonderfully safe and secure existence, surrounded in love by two affectionate parents, had been torn apart, with absolutely no warning.

My mother appeared to take it very well at first and busied herself with making the necessary arrangements for the subsequent funeral. When my father was buried, my mother insisted on buying a double plot in the cemetery, so that one day she could be buried next to him and she even amended her very basic Will just in case the Italian family made any good-natured attempt to repatriate her. A large number of my father's work mates, all of them immaculate in suits and black ties, came to the funeral and the Reverend who conducted the service got my Dad's name wrong and referred to him a number of times as "Rob", rather than Reg. My father had such a quirky sense of humour that he probably would have found that funny in some way and because the Reverend was a man of God, no one had the gumption to interrupt him and so, we buried "Rob" and mourned him.

It was only some weeks later that it all really came out. The simple truth is that my mother and father were desperately in love and whilst they argued and rowed like any couple, there was a deep and enduring bond between the two of them, that had always seen them through thick or thin. I now see that the day that my father died, half of my mother died with him and she was never really the same from that day on. With hindsight, it would perhaps have been better if she had cried her eyes out at the time, but I think bottling it up didn't really help – if anything, quite the opposite.

Suddenly, there was just her and me, although my brother Brian was also wonderfully supportive, not least in helping to make all of the arrangements and being there on the day. Shell were also very empathetic and because my father had died as an employee of the company (although not literally at work) they provided a death grant of some £10,000 which my mother subsequently invested to buy 147 Mellow Purgess, virtually outright. This was slightly different from the "Right to Buy" vision that Margaret Thatcher had originally intended but, nevertheless, she had empowered people to buy their own Council houses and my mother took advantage of it accordingly when she could.

Christmas 1979 was awful. Although our next-door neighbours, David and Janet Munday, were absolutely wonderful in helping to try and comfort us, even inviting us next door for Christmas dinner, knowing that it was bound to cast a pall over their own family proceedings, for weeks I was inconsolable. I had always looked up to my father as a strong and loving Dad and suddenly, without warning, he was no longer there. The truth is, I still miss him every day.

My Mother's battle with Depression

Unfortunately, as Dad had died in the run up to Christmas, in the years that followed Mum often became very depressed around that time of year. I would dread the "clocks going back" and the advance of the dark nights, as almost without fail it meant that mother's condition would start to deteriorate, and she would suffer from clinical depression. So, from 14, I went from being a relatively bright student with two loving parents, to a young carer. I subsequently spent a number of Christmas days not at home or indeed next door with friends, but in the psychiatric ward of one institution or another, visiting my mother on Christmas Day. I still remember the mental health ward at Basildon Hospital, with its rather desultory Christmas bunting and a pathetic 3ft high, manky looking plastic Christmas tree, and my mother sitting beside it in a chair, hunched over and smoking a cigarette, clearly unwell.

Some years later when Richard Curtis' brilliant film, Love Actually was released, I went to see it at the cinema. It is in fact my favourite film, as I particularly love the way that Curtis manages to weave together the plots of so many different characters into one masterfully overlapping narrative. But there is one scene where a female office worker, whose brother is in a mental institution, interrupts her romantic evening, as she has to go round and spend Christmas eve with him on a psychiatric ward. The first time I went to see the film with a friend, my eyes welled up at that point, but I refused to say why.

That said, when mum was well, she was wonderful. Whenever friends came over to visit (which was frequently) she would, in a very Italian way, insist on feeding them – everything from the occasional snack to fully fledged dinners. My friends would often joke that even if you came to our house hungry, you never left that way. My mother was a warm-hearted Italian and always looked after me (and my school friends) as best she could.

I struggled through my O-levels and A-levels whilst trying to care for Mum. In fairness, she was not always ill, it was just the onset of winter months, with brutal regularity, when she would slide irresistibly downhill and often not really get back to her normal self until the Spring. All of my friends, Colin, Ian, Deano and the others knew about this and all were incredibly understanding, really just being there for me when I needed them to be.

One thing about being in this kind of situation is that it forces you to grow up very quickly, especially forty of so years ago, when we understood much less about mental illness than we now do today. Essentially, back then you had two pretty brutal choices: either grow up fast and learn to deal with it and all the complications it entails – or crumble. I wasn't going to do the second and so, in many ways, I was forced to do the first.

I remember some years later just outside the House of Commons after an argument with a colleague when he turned to me and said sharply: "You're a hard little bastard aren't you Mark?" In fairness to him, he never really had any idea why – but now perhaps you do.

Chapter 2: Battling Bercow at University

Despite mother occasionally being unwell, I studied hard for my O-levels and at the age of sixteen came out with ten good grade O-levels plus one CSE 1 in French, (which was to come in very handy when I sought a place at University, two years later). With these qualifications under my belt, I then transitioned to the Sixth Form at St Nicholas, for two years of A-levels, prior to applying to University.

Becoming a Tory

By this stage I was already certain that what I wanted to become one day was a Member of Parliament. I also, incidentally, wanted to marry Debbie Harry (along with just about every other hormonal adolescent male in my school) and also dreamt one day that I would fly on Concorde. Well, Concorde is no longer flying and Debbie Harry, whilst still attractive, was otherwise taken, so this left me with only one route to pursue.

By the time I was sixteen, however, I knew that I was instinctively a Conservative rather than a Socialist. My route to this had primarily been through the Defence issue, which I had been interested in since I was a small boy. By the early 1980s, Mrs Thatcher had swept to power in 1979 and was then opposed by a very left-wing Labour Party, led by Michael Foot. The Labour Party's position on Defence was unilateralist i.e. they believed that Britain should abandon its nuclear weapons, regardless of whether anybody else did or not. Foot had for most of his adult life been a member of the Campaign for Nuclear Disarmament (CND) and in the early 80's the Russians had deployed SS20 missiles to threaten Western Europe, to which NATO had decided to deploy American made Cruise Missiles as a response. It seemed to me that the Labour Party were idealistic but incredibly naïve and that the Soviet Union was based on a Communistic Dictatorship, where as we, for all our faults, were a democratic free country and I could not countenance supporting a political Party which seemed to me would put all of that at risk – especially given what I had promised my father.

Conversely, Mrs Thatcher's Conservatives had increased Defence spending, begun to re-equip the Armed Forces after years of relative decline and had stood up to the Soviet Union – and domestically to CND. Moreover, the early 1980s contained a hint of national renewal, with events as diverse as the storming of the Iranian Embassy in 1980 (by a previously unheard-of Regiment, called the Special Air Service or SAS) through to the "Botham Summer" of 1981, when Ian

Botham famously scored 149 runs to rescue a test match against the West Indies at Lords and then Bob Willis took 8 for 43 at Headingly, to win the next one as well.

We then saw the Falklands War in 1982, when the task force, ordered south by Mrs Thatcher following the Argentine invasion of some British affiliated islands few people had ever heard of, recaptured them successfully and in turn led to the downfall of a fascist military junta in Argentina into the bargain.[10] So, for me as a young man with an interest in strong defence, there really was no difficult decision about which political Party to support and the more I looked into the Conservative's economic policy, it seemed to me to make sense as well.

This was especially so when compared to Labour's policies, which at that time were heavily influenced by Tony Benn and included wholesale nationalisation – again something which seemed to me to be on one level altruistic but also hopelessly economically unrealistic at the same time. So, all in all, it was going to be the Conservative Party for me.

Moreover, if I was ever lucky enough to become a Conservative MP, then what I *really* wanted to be was a Government Minister, in which case, the only Department I was really interested in was the Ministry of Defence (MoD).

David Morris

When I took up my A-Levels in 1981, my plan was to concentrate on Economics and hopefully get a decent job in the City of London, to earn some money prior to becoming an MP. However, my plans were completely altered by a wonderful man called David Morris, who taught me History at A-Level, where the syllabus had a particular emphasis on the Tudors and Stuarts.

David Morris had a remarkable knack for bringing history to life. He brilliantly described the plots and intrigues of the Tudor Court, the challenges to Henry VIII and the constant threats against Elizabeth I, the lively events of the Reformation through to the Spanish Armada and so much else besides.

He was the sort of inspirational tutor that you really wanted to go out of your way to please. I remember sitting up late into the night on many occasions, working on my A-Level essays with the help of my trusted Encyclopaedia Britannica that my Dad had worked so much overtime to afford.

Softly spoken and with an engaging manner, "Mr Morris" led our small A Level class of around half a dozen with humour and a genuine zeal for the subject. To him, it was very important for us to understand our country's fascinating history, if we were ever to have any hope of shaping its future, in whatever capacity.

Even the presence in our A Level history class of the stunning Vanessa Hawkins, was not enough to distract me from the subject as taught by Mr Morris (well, most of the time anyway).

Because of David Morris I finally elected to concentrate on History, rather than Economics, and I never looked back. Unfortunately, some of the teachers at St Nicholas School had relatively low aspirations for their pupils but David Morris was completely the opposite. He always believed that young people should be encouraged to achieve to the best of their ability and he certainly brought out whatever ability there was in me – something for which I will be ever grateful.

My first Election

My political convictions were put to the test in the Summer of 1983, when Mrs Thatcher called a General Election. Whilst she fought the national campaign against Michael Foot's Labour Party, our politics teacher decided to run a parallel election in the Sixth Form and, perhaps inevitably, I became the Conservative Candidate while my fellow "Joint Head Boy", Barry Lemon, whose father was a socialist, stood for Labour. I remember we had a Hustings in front of our Sixth Form colleagues, canvassed them and did our best to represent our two points of view. At the end of the campaign, the result of my first ever election contest was as follows:

Election for Nicholas School Sixth Form, Mock General Election June 1983

Mark Francois	Conservative	28
Barry Lemon	Labour	26
Peter Seward	SDP Liberal Alliance	5
Conservative Majority		2

Interestingly, to teach us about alternative voting systems, our politics master also decided to run a parallel election under a variant of proportional representation, by which I lost by one vote – and I have been against PR ever since.

So, with this election victory to my name, I also saw the new Parliamentary constituency of Basildon captured by a very young Conservative MP, called David Amess. His election had been a surprise to a lot of people, including many of the pollsters, who had regarded Basildon New Town – which basically comprised a small amount of middle-class housing but massively outnumbered by a large number of working-class Council estates – as being solid Labour territory.

However, Mrs Thatcher's robust Manifesto – accompanied by a higher take-up in Basildon of her "Right to Buy" policy than almost any other town in Britain – had helped to secure David Amess' election to Parliament at the tender age of 28.[11] Having seen what he had been able to achieve only inspired me to try harder myself.

Off to Uni

I worked hard at my A Levels and eventually came out with A's in History and Economics and, perhaps ironically, a B in Politics (although I did also manage a Distinction at S level in History too). I applied to read History and Economics at Oxford, but was unsuccessful. However, like many other "Oxbridge rejects" in my day, I did manage to secure a place at Bristol, in this case to read History under Professor John Vincent, who acted as something of a mentor during my three very enjoyable years there, from 1983 to 86.

On my first full day at Bristol, in September 1983, I went along to the Freshers Fayre, where all of the various university clubs and societies lay out their respective stalls to attract newly arrived students into their ranks. I joined the Bristol University Conservative Association (BUCA) in the morning and the Officers Training Corps (OTC) in the afternoon.

Joining up

In a period when the Berlin Wall was still in existence, the OTC was based at the old Artillery Grounds on Whiteladies Road. I subsequently joined the infantry sub-unit (as I wanted the physical challenge) and then had a fun three years, attending drill nights on Wednesday afternoon/evenings and spending around one weekend a month (or sometimes more) training, usually on Salisbury Plain. As part of this stint, I spent a fortnight in 1984 in West Germany on "Exercise Lionheart", the British Army's largest reinforcement exercise since WWII.

After graduating from Bristol in 1986 and having been commissioned as a Territorial Army (TA) infantry officer, I moved onto King's College London, to study for an MA, transferred to London OTC and then subsequently joined my local TA infantry regiment, The Royal Anglians, as a junior officer when I returned to Essex. I eventually transferred onto the Reserve Officers list (RARO) after the fall of the Berlin Wall, when the Cold War, at least as we had known it for several decades, appeared to be coming to an end.

The Student's Union

As a Member of BUCA, I used to regularly attend meetings of the Bristol University Student's Union, which took place in a large hall called the Anson Room in the Student Union building in Clifton. The Student's Union elected its own officers, who were effectively put on a one-year sabbatical and then given a salary whilst they ran the Student Union's affairs, and we were of course affiliated to the wider National Union of Students (NUS).

After heated debates in the Anson Room, the protagonists from various sides would then retire upstairs to the Student Union's Nelson Mandela Bar (we had a Nelson Mandela Bar before Nelson Mandela House was created in the popular television sitcom, *Only Fools and Horses*) where often the debate would continue but generally convivially, over a pint or four of heavily subsidised beer. I made many friends during my first year in BUCA and resolved at the end of my first year that when we came to the BUCA Annual General Meeting, I might even perhaps have a crack at the Chairmanship.

Lembit Opik

In my second year, I subsequently stood for election as Chairman of BUCA and to my surprise and delight, was narrowly elected. It was then my duty to lead the charge against the University Labour Club and indeed the Socialist Workers Society in the debates that followed in the Anson Room. The whole situation was made much more interesting by the election in the same year of one Lembit Opik (later to become a high-profile Lib Dem MP) as the Student Union President.

Unusually, Lembit was not elected on any of the Party slates that normally secured candidates to the officer positions in the Union but rather he founded his own society called "Philosophers in Social Sciences" (or PISSOC for short and the clue was in the name). This was what you might call a cross-party organisation, whose objectives were essentially more Dionysian than political, indeed I can remember being in the bar late one night and watching Lembit literally drain the slops bucket, almost to its last drop.

This rather clever coup worked very well and so I often found myself debating in the Anson Room not just with the Leaders of the Labour Club but also with Lembit as well. Thus, began a friendship which was to be reignited when he was subsequently elected to Parliament in 1997 as the MP for Montgomeryshire and I followed him into the Commons several years later.

Lembit, whose heritage is partly Estonian, achieved a very high media profile when he began dating one of two Romanian pop singers, known as "The Cheeky Girls", whilst still an MP. When Lembit began going out with the first Cheeky Girl, he mentioned to me one evening that her sister had been complaining that she couldn't find a boyfriend and suggested that the four of us should go out on a double date. As Lembit was forever in the tabloids or magazines such as *Hello* or *OK* because of his relationship with Cheeky Girl 1 (which unfortunately ended in tears), I decided that discretion was the better part of valour and turned down his generous offer.

Professor John Vincent

John Vincent was the Professor of History at Bristol University and headed up the History Department in the time that I was there in the mid-1980s. At the time, Bristol was very much a left-wing University, with a student body that advocated a "No Platform Policy for racists or fascists" which roughly translated meant, they didn't like allowing anybody to speak who was in anyway even vaguely right-wing.

As John Vincent had a regular column in *The Sun* newspaper, and often used historical examples in support of the Thatcher Government, he was something of a hate figure for the left in Bristol and on a number of occasions, including support from the Bristol branch of the Socialist Workers Party, they attempted to burst into his lectures and interrupt the proceedings. On one occasion I remember being involved in something of a rugby scrum in the entrance to the lecture theatre, as the hard left attempted to burst in and stop him from teaching us about the history of our own country.

John was an accomplished historical author in his own right and wrote a number of very well received books particularly about Victorian politics (he was a great expert on Gladstone) and he was very much an academic and indeed political mentor of mine in the time that I was at University.[12] I have had the great pleasure of receiving a number of encouraging hand written notes from him down the years, not least during the trials and tribulations of Brexit.

John Vincent sadly passed away in 2021. Because of Covid-19 restrictions I was unable to attend his funeral and pay my respects to his widow, Nicolette, in person. Nevertheless, perhaps I can atone for that in some way by paying tribute to him here. He was a truly exceptional man – and a good friend.

FCS (The Federation of Conservative Students)

In my second year at Bristol, I succeeded in being elected as the Chairman of BUCA. Following this, I was encouraged to go to the "next rung up" in student politics and become involved in the Federation of Conservative Students or FCS for short.

In many ways, the FCS was a mirror-image of the NUS, in that it too was a highly political organisation, but one of the right, rather than of the left. In my second year, I was elected to the National Executive of the FCS, as one of only a few moderates on that body. At the time, the Federation of Conservative Students was dominated by the Libertarian faction (known colloquially as the "Libs") who had nothing to do with the modern-day Liberal Democrats but who believed very much in the freedom of the individual, rather than the state. For some Members of this faction (but by no means all) this was taken as far as arguing that the state should have absolutely no control whatsoever over the lives of the individual – up and to including the decriminalisation of hard drugs, such as heroin.

The Opposition to the Libs within the FCS comprised of a variety of groups from what might be called traditional One Nation Conservatives, through more Social Conservatives and a group known as the "Party Faction" who essentially identified themselves as Party loyalists. However, to the Libs, their opponents were derided collectively as "the Wets", in reference to the patrician One Nation Tories who tended to oppose Mrs Thatcher in Cabinet. In those days, "the Libs" outnumbered "the Wets" in FCS by a margin of approximately two to one, whereas in the wider Conservative Youth Movement outside the Universities and Colleges, the more widely recognised Young Conservatives (or YC's), the boot was arguably on the other foot.

At the 1985 FCS Annual Conference at Loughborough University, which was attended by some 400 delegates, there was a rather riotous party which caused some damage in one of the student accommodation blocks, which had been hired out for the conference. Conservative Central Office subsequently conducted an inquiry, the results of which were essentially inconclusive, but nevertheless FCS was effectively put on notice by the Party hierarchy that such "hijinks" were unlikely to be tolerated much further into the future.[13]

Francois Vs Bercow

Unfortunately for me, most of the meetings of the FCS Executive took place on weekends when I also had training commitments with the OTC, which I tended to put first, as coming from the minority faction and being heavily outnumbered on the FCS Executive, there seemed to be relatively little point in turning up in the first place. However, the 1986 conference was scheduled to take place at Scarborough in Yorkshire and the emerging candidate for the libertarian faction was an extremely articulate young politics student from Essex University, named John Bercow. It was always likely that Bercow was going to win the election at Scarborough but nevertheless, his opponents began casting around for a candidate to undertake something of a suicide mission, in order to take John Bercow on in the autumn. The headquarters of the Wets as it were, was the Oxford University Conservative Association (OUCA) and on a drizzly, windy Saturday morning in January 1986, I found myself sitting in a café opposite Bristol bus station when a senior student from OUCA was due to come down by coach from Oxford, to talk about the situation in FCS. The name of that student was Nick Robinson.

Over coffee in this rather weather-beaten café, Nick asked me to become in effect the moderate's candidate at the forthcoming Scarborough Conference, which in the end, I reluctantly agreed to do. In fairness to myself, I knew there was absolutely no hope of winning, but I was opposed to some of the extreme views of some of the Libertarian's and felt that someone ought to take them on and whilst I'd rather it was someone else, in the end Nick told me it was basically me or nobody, so it had to be me.

Once it became apparent that I was going to run against the Lib's rising star, I was derided as "a Wet" throughout the Tory Student movement and by the time I got to the Scarborough Conference that autumn, I had been nicknamed the "Member for Bristol Niagara". Indeed, at the very rumbustious hustings that then took place, as I got up to speak, on an obviously prearranged signal, Lib supporters in the first three rows put up umbrellas as if to emphasise my "wetness".

The hustings themselves were an extremely lively affair. I was challenged by the Libs for having failed to attend any of the Executive meetings, to which I retorted that I had been serving my country in uniform and I had never apologised to any lefty for doing so and was damned if I was going to start now! At this point, I seem to remember there was uproar in the hall of over 300 Tory students.

When it came to John's speech, he attacked me from start to finish and I particularly remember him describing me as "intellectually knee high to a grasshopper". When it was my turn to reply, I was equally robust. In truth I cannot remember precisely what I called him in return, but it was less than flattering. Of course, little did I know at the time, in what was a very charged atmosphere, amidst a pretty packed hall of Tory students, that I was effectively taking lumps out of the future Speaker of the House of Commons.

When the votes came to be cast the result was as follows:

Election for the Chairmanship of the Federation of Conservative Students - 1986

John Bercow	Libertarian Candidate	197
Mark Francois	The "Wet" Candidate	123
Libertarian Majority		74

Nevertheless, I still believe I may have won some grudging respect from some of my FCS contemporaries, including some rather well-known names today, such as (Sir) Robbie Gibb (who was Communications Chief for Theresa May when she was PM) and indeed, Dougie Smith (who now works for Boris Johnson at No 10).

John Bercow

John Bercow was born the son of a North London Taxi Driver and studied politics at Essex University. We became rivals in Conservative student politics but the animosity that we shared at that time was never really carried on into later life.

When he became Speaker some years later it is probably fair to say that John became one of the most controversial Speaker's in living memory, certainly among many of my Conservative colleagues. He was, to use popular parlance, "a bit marmite". Some Tory MPs admired him, whilst others plainly hated his guts.

Personally, John always treated me fairly and would often call me at Prime Ministers Questions if I were to stand. He loved reminding the Chamber about our battles many years ago in FCS (to the point where on one occasion I had a word with him afterwards and said: "I don't mind the ribbing John, but they've heard it so many times now, that you've got to come up with a better joke!") In truth, I think we enjoyed a sort of uncanny love/hate relationship, dating back to our days in FCS.

However, privately, John certainly had a magnanimous side to him and could actually be very kind to colleagues. Therefore, even though we crossed swords a number of times over Brexit, for instance when I sometimes challenged his procedural decisions over Amendments and such like, there was never any deep enmity between us and even a few days before he retired in the Chair, I was able to say to him, tongue-in-cheek: "Mr Speaker, speaking as one midget to another, I wish you a very happy retirement".

In 2021, John Bercow announced that he had joined the Labour Party, thus having come full circle, from his early days as an ardent Thatcherite in his youth – and one opposed by the "Tory Wet" Mark Francois.

Whatever one thinks of John Bercow – and opinions certainly vary – he will certainly go down in history as one of the most outspoken and controversial Speakers of modern times.

King's College London

It was still my plan at that stage to try and earn some money in the City, before seeking to enter the House of Commons and so I went for a number of interviews on the Milk Round and managed to secure a future job working as a Graduate Trainee on the Lloyds Bank Graduate Development Programme.

All of my friends told me that I was too much of a maverick to work for a bank but nevertheless, at the age of 21, no one can tell you anything and so I ploughed on with my nascent banking career, save that I had asked if they could defer the job offer for one year, as I was very keen to do the MA course in War Studies at King's College London.

War Studies at King's

In September 1986 I was sitting at the back of the old lecture theatre in the King's College building in The Strand when the Head of the Department, Professor Lawrence Freedman (now Sir Lawrence Freedman) entered the theatre to give his opening address to the class of 1986/87. He spoke softly but with authority and I can still recall his opening words, which were as follows:

"Good morning Ladies and Gentlemen, as the Head of the Department, I am delighted to welcome you to King's for our one-year MA programme, which I hope you will enjoy. Now, perhaps we should start as we intend to go on. We call this the Department of War Studies because we study war, not conflict or tension but war, in which people get killed, sometimes unfortunately, very many of them. If you would really prefer to study peace, personally I have no problem with that – but go to Bradford instead".[14]

Sitting at the back of the hall, I remember thinking "Wow, if the rest of this year is like this, I am *really* going to enjoy this!" and so it transpired. Sitting in the Student Union bar a couple of weeks later, I got chatting to another student called Joe Baynes, who had served as a Platoon Commander in the Regular Army and then gone on to read History at Reading before joining the one-year MA at King's. When I asked him how he had afforded it, he told me that he had been very lucky, because there was only one Economics and Social Research Council (ESRC) grant for students on that course and he had beaten some other guy from Bristol to win it!

Joe and I subsequently became great friends and remain so to this day. Interestingly, another of the students in that year group, with whom Joe and I became acquainted, was Christopher Mackenzie Geidt, another former Army Officer, who subsequently went on to become a very accomplished Private Secretary to HM The Queen and now sits as a cross bench Peer in the House of Lords.

Suffice to say, King's College London was a rather different institution in the 1980s from the ultra-liberal one it has become today.

Sir Lawrence Freedman

Sir Lawrence Freedman is one of the foremost strategic experts in modern Britain. A grammar school boy, he studied at several universities, including Oxford, before eventually joining the respected Department of War Studies at King's College London in the early 1980s.

Lawrence Freedman was commissioned to write the British Official History of the 1982 Falklands War, which he subsequently published in 1986, including a number of accurate criticisms about weaknesses in the conduct of an otherwise ultimately successful campaign, including the intelligence failures which contributed to it arising in the first place.

He has also written about a whole range of other conflicts, including the Cold War, the Cuban Missile Crisis and the Vietnam War. He has received a veritable plethora of academic accolades, plus a Knighthood in 2006 and elevation to the Privy Council in 2009.

Given this distinguished background, he was also made one the members of the controversial Iraq War Inquiry in 2009 (which I had voted in favour of, in 2003). However, in view of the heavy politics surrounding the report, not least the heated debates surrounding Tony Blair's legacy, I think Lawrence found this a more aggressive experience than perhaps he was previously used to in the world of academia.

When he subsequently published a major book entitled "Strategy: A History" (Oxford University Press) in 2013, as one of his former students, I went along to the book launch at King's College to support him and purchase a copy (in which he duly wrote something nice). I thought it was typical of Lawrence that on the front cover, instead of something obvious for a book on this subject, like perhaps a chess board, he chose a photograph of a Trojan Horse instead.

Sir Lawrence Freedman's Wikipedia entry points out that when he was awarded the Chesney Gold Medal by the Royal United Services Institute (RUSI) for a lifelong contribution to the study of Defence and international security, the citation included the following observations:

"As the Cold War ended, Professor Freedman was one of the prime movers in the growing debate about European security arrangements, as well as the new and emerging threats of terrorism and failed states".

However, It also states:

"...Under his supervision, generations of students, as well as officers in Her Majesty's Armed Forces learnt about the changing nature of war and Britain's military history".

I am very proud to say that I was one of them.

In the Autumn of 1987, having graduated from Kings, I began a full time job working for Lloyds Bank on their graduate development programme. I commuted into London and was based at their branch at Leadenhall Street in the heart of the City of London, almost directly opposite the relatively new Lloyds Insurance Building nearby. Lloyds Bank's philosophy, which made some sense, was that graduate trainees, who we were told were being groomed for future roles in senior management, should begin life on the shop floor as it were, by working in a branch and getting to know the basics of banking at ground level.

In addition to working during the week, I was enrolled for the Institute of Bankers (IoB) exam programme, which also involved a day-release scheme, studying at college in Walthamstow on Wednesday afternoons. Everyone at the bank seemed very welcoming and also included a number of people that lived in Basildon and commuted into Leadenhall Street branch every morning.

5 ROYAL ANGLIAN (Volunteers)

In addition to starting a new full-time job I transferred to my local TA Infantry Regiment, the Fifth Battalion of the Royal Anglian Regiment (Volunteers) – or 5 ROYAL ANGLIAN (V) for short. As a young Second Lieutenant, I was assigned to Number 1 Company, based at Vange Camp on the eastern edge of Basildon, just off the A127. Vange, just outside Pitsea, was in some ways the most earthy part of the whole of Basildon, with a large amount of public sector housing, people on pretty modest incomes and with a considerable variety of social problems.

The TA centre at Brickfield Road in Vange (which today is now a modern housing estate) essentially comprised a number of old World War II Nissan Huts with an armoury and a mess. The TA soldiers, many of whom worked in local factories or were self-employed, attended drill nights for training on Wednesday evenings and then would go away at least one weekend a month for more intensive training, often at the Stanford Training area (STANTA) near Thetford Forest in Norfolk. I was made the Officer Commanding (OC) Vange Camp, with Company Headquarters in Braintree, north of Chelmsford, whilst the Battalion's Headquarters was at Peterborough in Cambridgeshire.

If the balloon had gone up, our Battalion's war role, was to defend a key bridge in the First British Corps (1 BR Corps) rear area in West Germany, at a town called Rinteln, where there was, at that time, also a large British military hospital.

The bridge was what was known in military parlance as a "reserved demolition" which meant that it was our job to defend the bridge so that friendly forces could transit across it but, if the Russian's were ever to advance to the point of capturing the bridge, friendly forces would retreat onto the home bank and we would then blow it up, having received the code word from the Corps Commander (a Lieutenant General). The bridge would thus be mined for rapid destruction just in case – hence the term "reserved" demolition.

However, our Commanding Officer (the 'CO') was a hard-charging type, who was absolutely determined that 'our' bridge would never fall into enemy hands, under any circumstances. During a Battalion study weekend, on a Sunday morning (after a pretty heavy night in the Officers' Mess the night before) he turned to the assembled officers in his Battalion and said the following: "Right Gentlemen, (it was the late 1980s and we were all male officers) I am sure you are all familiar with the concept of the Fog of War,[15] in which messages get jammed, despatch riders fail to get through and confusion reigns accordingly. In order to avoid such a situation, as your Commanding Officer, let me give you my 'final order' now, on a sunny Sunday morning, in the peaceful heart of the English Countryside".

"If we ever have to do this bloody thing for real, if at any point one single Soviet or Warsaw Pact soldier so much as sets a foot on the approach road to our bridge, let alone the bridge itself, at that point – regardless of whether we have the General's codeword – the senior surviving officer in the Battalion will immediately blow the fucking thing to kingdom come!"

"Is that perfectly clear?" [Absolute silence] "Thank you Gentlemen – lets go to lunch!"

I enjoyed having a platoon of soldiers under my command, which provided a variety of challenges, including on one occasion having to appear as a character witness at Billericay Magistrates Court, when one of my privates had run another motorist off the road after they had cut him up. Suffice to say, that was a challenging morning but, nevertheless, I managed to help keep him out of jail!

I very much enjoyed my time with the Battalion, which took up at least one weekend a month and sometimes a lot more than that. It's important to remember the context; in those days the Berlin Wall was still up, the British Regular Army numbered a quarter of a million men and women and the Territorial Army, or the TA as it was widely known, was another 75,000 on top, providing a combined strength of the Army, both Regular and Reserve, of almost a third of a million. There were no active operations in Iraq or Afghanistan and, in effect, we trained for one scenario only – which was World War III. This often involved preparing to fight in a nuclear, biological or chemical environment (NBC) and meant that we spent a fair time in training wearing special chemical proof suits, which were charcoal lined, and every soldier would carry a respirator in order to protect you against chemical weapons. We took our role seriously – because we thought there was a reasonable chance that we might one day have to do it for real, although fortunately events turned out differently. Nevertheless, if it had ever come to it, I hope that we would have given a good account of ourselves, in Defence of all we believed in – at least until we blew the bloody bridge to smithereens!

Switching Roles

After a short sojourn at Lloyds Bank, I began to reluctantly admit that my friends had been right after all. I had been recruited on the milk round with tales of rapid advancement to a senior position within one of Britain's major high street banks, but it soon became apparent that the word "rapid" had been highly exaggerated and that it was going to take very many years to work my way up the ladder in what was still a very Conservative institution, with a small c. The bank was, at least at that time, pretty traditional and there was a premium on conformity. For someone who has always had a bit of a maverick streak to his character, I soon began to realise that this was definitely not for me.

When I mulled it over, I realised that I was obviously very interested in politics, bored rigid working for a bank and thought that actually a job in public relations or the related field of public affairs might be far more interesting. Besides, it might also help me to make some contacts which might eventually assist me in becoming an MP, which was still very much my ambition. So, I wrote off to a dozen or so such companies in the field and, unbeknownst to me, in one of those companies someone had resigned on the same day that, by sheer chance, my letter (in a pre-email era) had physically landed on their doormat.

I subsequently went for an interview and was offered the job shortly thereafter, which I gladly accepted and then handed in my resignation to the Manager at Leadenhall Street. He was in no way surprised and said he'd been expecting it, as he'd been able to sense that I already had itchy feet. His parting words as I went out of the door were, "Absolutely no hard feelings Mark, and I hope you do well in life – but if you go one penny overdrawn without permission, I will hammer you!".

The Road Forks

So, in early 1988 I took up a job with a public affairs company based near St James' Park Tube Station. Things were also changing in other areas as well. On moving back to Basildon, I had joined the local Conservative Association and had been briefly involved in the 1987 General Election campaign, helping mainly to deliver leaflets to electors.

In 1989, the Langdon Hills branch of the Basildon Association, which covered the ward in which I lived, invited me on to their Branch Committee and some months later asked me to stand as the Conservative Candidate for Langdon Hills at the forthcoming local elections, the following May. At that time, I was working hard in London, and commuting to and forth each day on a highly unreliable rail line, plus attending TA drill nights on a Wednesday evening and doing something like one in three weekends with 5 ROYAL ANGLIAN. I realised that it wouldn't be practically possible to do all three and therefore I was going to have to choose.

My decision was made easier when the Berlin Wall came down in late 1989, and the Soviet grip on Eastern Europe rapidly began to collapse. Suddenly, the threat of World War III seemed to recede and therefore, I decided to hand back my kit at 5 ROYAL ANGLIAN and transfer on to the long term Reserve list (then known as RARO) which meant that I would still be liable for call up in a national emergency, but I would no longer be an active member of the TA.

Fortunately, the balloon never did go up as it were, the Soviet system collapsed under the weight of its own inherent contradictions and we never did have to fight the Soviet's in a World War, against a nuclear armed opponent. My military service lasted seven years, both as an Officer Cadet and then as a Junior Officer but in that time, I was never mobilised for operations, never saw active service and have no medals, as I never earned any. Nevertheless, to this day, I do have an unerring respect for those who have been on active service, in whatever theatre they have served.

Nonetheless, Service in the military did teach me a number of qualities which I think would stand anyone in good stead in a political career, not least the importance of thorough planning and preparation and the need to work as a team, in order to achieve common objectives. In fact, of the current House of Commons of 650 MPs, over 30 of them (overwhelmingly, but not exclusively, Conservative), have Served in the Armed Forces prior to coming into Parliament, either Regular or Reserve and indeed some MPs, such as Penny Mordaunt still undertake an active role in the Reserve Forces, on top of their Parliamentary duties as well. I still have my Queen's Commission, signed by Her Majesty and it is something I will always remain proud of.

Instead, I decided to concentrate on politics thereafter, with the hope of getting on to Basildon District Council, as a stepping stone to eventually becoming an MP. As it turned out, Basildon, particularly in the 1990's, was a very exciting and rumbustious place in which to learn your political trade.

Chapter 3: Working with David Amess – The Basildon Years

Politics in Basildon

The geographically large Basildon constituency was captured by the Tory MP, Harvey Proctor, as part of Mrs Thatcher's victory in the 1979 General Election. There were then subsequent boundary changes in the early 1980s which divided the seat in two. The old constituency was effectively divided by the A127 Southend arterial road. To the north was the middle-class town of Billericay (made famous in Ian Drury's song "Billericay Dickie", which contains the line "I'm a Billericay Dickie – and I'm doing very well") and the commuter town of Wickford (which was not immortalised in a song by Ian Drury). South of the A127 lay the new town of Basildon, with its eight predominantly urban wards, including the town centre, the big industrial estate to the north of the town and many large Council estates that ringed them.

In the early 80s Boundary Review, the constituency was effectively divided along the A127 to produce what many would have regarded as a safe Conservative Seat in the north, named Billericay and comprising mainly the towns of Billericay and Wickford and thus creating a second seat of Basildon itself, comprising largely the new town to the south. It was widely considered that this represented a "one all draw" as Billericay would likely be a Conservative safe seat and Basildon would be the same for Labour.

However, in 1983 a young and dynamic Tory Councillor from Newham, David Amess, surprised all the pundits and actually won the constituency of Basildon, in Margaret Thatcher's post Falklands landslide. So amazed was Amess to win that he had only written a concession speech, where he intended to go down fighting after his defeat had been announced. Instead, when he was tipped off a few minutes before the declaration that he had won, he had to dash into the toilets and compose a victory speech at barely a few minutes notice.

Whilst this proved a tremendous victory for the Basildon Conservative Association, they were still faced by Basildon District Council, which covered both constituencies and had a number of Conservative Councillors in the north in Billericay and Wickford, but which was still dominated by the far larger number of Labour Councillors in the new town to the south. Indeed, when David Amess won the new Basildon Parliamentary seat in 1983 there was not a single elected Conservative Councillor anywhere within it.

Basildon District Council had been created by the Walker reforms in the early 1970s and had never been run outright by the Conservative Party since its inception.

Moreover, the Council had become a notoriously left-wing example of Labour in local Government. The Council existed on a high tax and spend model, and there were "Nuclear Free Zone" signs on most of the main roads leading into the Basildon District. The Council's Leader, John Potter, often made a point of turning up to Council meetings with a copy of the Morning Star under his arm, just to drive home Labour's dominance of the local area.

Candidate for Langdon Hills

The Langdon Hills ward, in the north western corner of Basildon new town, was in some ways a microcosm of the divide between the two larger constituencies that made up the Basildon District. The ward was divided in two by a railway line. On one side of the railway line was Laindon Shopping Centre, which was a bit of a 1960s concrete jungle and two large Council estates – the "Alcatraz" estate that I lived on and, directly across the road, the "Siporex" estate, which took its name from a Swedish rapid build system, that had been used to construct it, a few years before Five Links (Alcatraz) was built. The walls of Siporex houses, were built of "aerated concrete". The best way to describe this is as being akin to Aero chocolate bars, which were made up of chocolate, with air bubbles inside. Siporex was similar, in that it was made up of concrete but containing air bubbles, which over the years often tended to crack.

As a result, many of the houses suffered from bad cracking and other maintenance problems and very few people ever exercised the Right to Buy them, which Mrs Thatcher had provided from 1979 onwards. Conversely, quite a few people on Alcatraz had bought their houses, just as my mother had done after Dad had died. Siporex, with hardly any owner occupiers at all, was one of Labour's absolute heartlands in Basildon.

On the other side of the railway line was another smaller Council estate called the Langdon Hills estate but the remainder of the housing in the area was all private, much of it built by property developers after the Second World War. There was thus a kind of unwritten rule between the two Party's regarding the Langdon Hills ward, i.e. the Conservatives would canvass the private sector housing and Labour would canvass the Council estates and whoever got more of "their" voters out to the polls on the day was the winner.

However, as I lived on the "Labour" side of the railway line, and had grown up on Alcatraz, it seemed perfectly legitimate to me to abandon this so called understanding and to campaign and canvass as hard as I could across the entire ward, including the three Council estates as well.

However, 1990 was the year that Mrs Thatcher famously introduced "the Community Charge" (popularly, or rather more unpopularly, dubbed "the Poll Tax"). This new system of asking people to pay local taxes based not on the value of a property but on the number of people that lived in it, proved highly controversial. Nevertheless, it did have the benefit of allowing you to make very clear comparisons between the level of Poll Tax in one borough and another and whether or not people were getting value for money. In London, the Conservative's classically exploited this by highlighting Tory Wandsworth, with a very low level of Poll Tax with neighbouring Labour Lambeth, with one of the highest levels in the country. We managed to do the same in juxtaposing the very high Poll Tax in Labour-run Basildon, with comparatively low Poll Tax in Tory managed Southend (which was the first local authority in Britain to outsource its refuse collection service, in the early 1980s).

Despite this, 1990 was an extremely challenging year to be a Conservative Candidate anywhere, and this was certainly true in Langdon Hills. The problem was compounded by the fact that my opponent was a Labour incumbent, Councillor Chris Webb, who was popular locally and lived on the Siporex estate and thus enjoyed a considerable personal vote from that locality.

Despite this, I canvassed the whole ward actively but, in those days, people would often put small, coloured posters in their windows in order to indicate which Party they supported (something which relatively few people still do today). When I went out canvassing on the Siporex estate with my loyal Agent, Sandra Hillier, this ironically saved us a great deal of time, because there were so many A5 red posters with the name of Chris Webb tucked into kitchen windows that we only bothered to canvass the doors without them.

I put out some quite punchy literature comparing Basildon's Poll Tax to that in Southend and the poor local services which we received in return but, despite having fought a fairly high-profile campaign, when it came to the count at the Towngate Theatre, I was defeated.

An election count in Basildon was a bit of a mixture of the Last Night at the Proms and a football match. Whilst the votes were actually counted in the recently constructed new Town Hall (known as the Bas Centre, or to us local Tories as "The Kremlin") they were then announced in the Towngate Theatre next door.

By some tradition, which appears to have been lost in the mists of time, the Labour Party and their activists would always populate the stalls of the auditorium, whereas the Tories would be in the middle and upper circles above.

When my result was read out in the Towngate Theatre, I had lost by just 78 votes, as follows:

Basildon District Council Election for the Langdon Hills Ward – 3rd May 1990

Mark Francois	Conservative Candidate	1,973
John McDougal	Green Candidate	188
Chris Webb	Labour Candidate	2,051
Joe White	Liberal Democrat Candidate	289
Labour Majority		78
Turnout		49.9%

Sandra Hillier

Sandra Hillier (nee Hyland) was the Chairman of the Langdon Hills Branch committee, which I joined after returning from university. Under electoral law in Britain, when a candidate stands for election – from a local Councillor to a Member of Parliament – they nominate an "election agent" to run the campaign and oversee the compliance with any legal technicalities, from making sure that literature is correctly printed (and not libellous!) and that the campaign complies with all other electoral requirements.

Sandra Hillier was my first ever election agent, when I stood as the Conservative candidate for the Langdon Hills ward in 1990. In what was a very challenging year for the Conservative Party, she went out canvassing with me, night after night, as well as encouraging me throughout the campaign. Candidates, especially new candidates, are traditionally rather nervous in the run-up to polling day and Sandra calmed my anxieties and kept me focused on the task in hand.

Although I was narrowly unsuccessful in 1990, she stood by me and volunteered to run my campaign again the following year, when, surrounded by an excellent campaign team, we turned a narrow defeat into a stunning victory in 1991.

I have stayed in touch with Sandra and her husband Stephen down the years (they now live in Dorset) and have always referred to her affectionately as "my first agent". It was Sandra Hillier who really set me off on my political career, for which I will be forever grateful.

Because I had fought a fairly punchy campaign – and then lost – the Labour Party taunted me mercilessly at the count. As I was standing up in the dress circle, from the stalls below, there were shouts of "Where's Francois now then?" and a few things slightly spicier than that as well.

I had worked very hard for months and was desperately disappointed not to win but the fact that Labour actively took the mickey meant that by the time I got home that evening, I was utterly determined to win the seat next year. Because Basildon Council elects "in thirds" this meant that the 14 wards each had three Councillors, so there would be another opportunity to fight exactly the same ward again, a year later.

A week afterwards, I wrote a thank you letter to all the activists who had assisted in the campaign (a copy of which I still have) in which I said the following: "The turnout was a previously unheard of 49.9% and this, combined with our standing in the polls was just too much for us to overcome. However, our support nationally is beginning to recover, and I do not think we will see anything like the same protest vote again in May 1991. I am confident that if we work equally hard again, we can win Langdon Hills next year. Prepare for battle!"

"It's Councillor Francois to you!"

I was rapidly readopted by the Langdon Hill ward to be their candidate the following year and I spent the next year campaigning like a man possessed. Along with Sandra and my small team of helpers, we canvassed the entire ward of some 9,000 electors again from top to bottom – twice!

Again, we put out some punchy literature highlighting the difference in the level of Poll Tax between Basildon and Southend and we also ended up on the side of the angels in protesting against a proposed Tesco superstore in the private part of Langdon Hills, which many residents were deeply against, but the Labour Council was minded to approve. Residents Against Tesco Superstore (RATS) helped me in my campaign, not least because the Labour Party behaved very arrogantly about the planning proposal.

When it came to the count in Basildon a year later, the result was somewhat different. This time, after a year of extremely hard work, with a highly motivated team of helpers, the result was as follows:

Basildon District Council Election for the Langdon Hills Ward –May 1991

Mark Francois	Conservative Candidate	2,550
Paul Kirkman	Labour Candidate	1,658
David Jones	Liberal Democrat Candidate	459
Conservative Majority		892
Turnout		52.03%

So, a year later, I fought exactly the same ward, on exactly the same boundaries and turned a Labour majority of 78 into a Tory majority of 892. Now it was my turn to crow at the count. After the result had been read out, I leant over the balcony of the circle in the Towngate theatre and bellowed at the socialists below, "Hello, do you remember me? Last year you were asking, 'Where's Francois now?', well I'm here again Basildon Labour Party, but now it's Councillor Francois to you!".

We also gained several other seats that evening, which meant we were now within striking distance of achieving majority Conservative control of Basildon District Council, for the first time ever, in the elections in May 1992. However, as the previous General Election had been in 1987, it seemed likely that we could be combining this battle with a General Election as well. Faced with this prospect we made our plans accordingly.

Mutual Aid Officer

In anticipation of the forthcoming General Election, Conservative Central Office invited constituencies to appoint "Mutual Aid Officers" (MAO's) to help co-ordinate the flow of mutual aid across constituency boundaries, in particular so that safer Conservative seats, could provide volunteers to help defend critical marginals, of which Basildon, which David Amess had successfully defended again in 1987, was now a classic example. I was appointed the Association's Mutual Aid Officer and was asked to attend the Association Executive, which is in effect the Board of the local Party, that oversees all of its activities across the constituency.

On the first occasion that I went to the Executive, I was advised by Sandra to, "Keep quiet for the first few months and see what goes on before you say anything". In the end I lasted about 45 minutes. The main item for discussion that night was whether or not the Association could afford to purchase a computer, in order to help us prepare for the forthcoming General Election.

After having heard the arguments batted back and forwards for nearly an hour, in exasperation I put my hand up and, when called, I suggested that this was a critical seat which the Conservative Party had to hold at all costs, if we were to prevent the Labour Leader, Neil Kinnock from becoming Prime Minister and instead keep John Major in Downing Street. I then suggested that given this, it might be an idea if the Association came into the 20th Century particularly as we were gradually moving towards the end of it. When I was challenged on how we would get a computer and indeed any software to go on it, I said I would solve the problem – which indeed I did.

We managed to purchase a computer relatively modestly, but the difficulty was the software programme. Such stuff was still pretty nascent, and the package being offered by Central Office at that time was relatively expensive to a point where the Association were reluctant to purchase it. Fortunately, I was friends with a computer programmer called Phil Coley, who lived in the neighbouring constituency of Castle Point and who basically helped design a Polling Day programme from scratch, which we then installed on the computer and which saw us through the 1992 General Election. I also began to build links with neighbouring Associations in South Essex in order to try and co-ordinate a flow of mutual aid to help us in the run up to the inevitable General Election campaign.

As part of this, I also joined up with an organisation called "Conservative Fight Back", which comprised groups of Conservatives from most of the very left-wing boroughs in London. At that time, the so called "Loony Left" were running a number of boroughs in London on very left-wing principles, of which perhaps the best known examples were "Red Ted" Knight's administration in Lambeth but also other very left-wing Labour boroughs like Camden and Tower Hamlets as well.

Overarching all of this was "Red Ken", the left-wing Labour Leader of the pan-metropolis Greater London Council (the GLC). In many of these boroughs the Conservative Party held only a handful of seats and were akin to something of a resistance movement behind enemy lines, similar in some ways to Conservative Associations at university in the heyday of the National Union of Students. It seemed to me that as we faced a very left wing administration in Basildon, our colleagues in London were obvious soul mates, and so we established a system whereby I attended Conservative Fight Back Meetings as our Mutual Aid Officer and when there were by-elections in London, some of our activists would travel in from Basildon to help out and then they would return the complement by travelling out to Basildon later on. We thus established a system of give and take between ourselves and some of the London Conservatives which was to stand us in very good stead in the battle which lay ahead.

David Walsh

County Councillor David Walsh was one of my greatest friends in politics, before he sadly passed away from a heart attack several years ago. Tall, dark and good-looking, "with a twinkle in his eye", David came from Scottish/Irish descent and lived life to the full as a great bon viveur.

I signed him up as a Member of the Conservative Party, one evening when we went out canvassing on the Alcatraz Estate and we became very good friends thereafter.

Although he had worked for many years as a successful insurance broker in the old Lloyds of London, he had also seen a lot of life and had a great knack of correctly judging both people and situations. I helped him get elected to Essex County Council and, in turn, he assisted me in winning my seat on Basildon Council.

One Saturday evening, after a rather long Langdon Hills Ward Committee meeting, we retired to The Joker public house in Laindon, when a wedding reception was in full swing. There was a disco blaring in the upstairs bar as we stood at the bar downstairs, quietly sipping our pints. David turned to me and said softly: "This whole place is about to kick off massively in about fifteen minutes". When I asked him how he knew, he simply replied: "I can just sense it Mark".

About 12 minutes later, a shriek broke out from the upstairs bar, followed by the sound of a punch being thrown and someone coming tumbling down the stairs into the main bar. The "victim" then picked up a barstool and charged back upstairs, presumably seeking retribution. Something akin to a massive bar brawl, reminiscent of a spaghetti Western, then broke out all around us, as we continued quietly drinking, whereupon Dave leant across the bar and whispered: "I'm obviously losing my touch Mark, I was three minutes out!".

The Battle for Basildon in 1992

As well as seeking to take control of Basildon District Council, we also faced the challenge of seeking to hold David Amess' seat as the MP for Basildon at the forthcoming General Election. David had won by 1,379 votes in his shock election victory in 1983 and had increased his majority to 2,649 votes in 1987 but that still only represented just over 5% of the total vote, so the seat remained a classic marginal.[16] Moreover, in those days (but not now) Basildon had become traditionally the first marginal seat to declare on General Election night – partly because the officers who ran the Council made it a point of pride to conduct the count very quickly. This meant, in effect, that the whole nation would be looking to Basildon on General Election night, as the first indication of who had won and whether or not the Labour Leader, Neil Kinnock, had succeeded in replacing the Conservative's John Major as Prime Minister.

Labour were only too aware of this and during Council meetings, they would constantly taunt us that time was running out and that they were going to win the Parliamentary seat when the General Election finally arrived. We were equally determined to stop them dead in their tracks and so, as early as 1991, we began a process of seeking to doorstep canvass as much of the eight urban wards that made up the Basildon constituency as possible, prior to the General Election campaign commencing in earnest. This was no small task, as there were over 30,000 homes that we had to cover across the constituency, with pretty limited resources.

In practical terms, this took the form of a Tuesday night canvassing team, which I led and which would take turns in going out and canvassing key parts of each of the eight wards, one week at a time. The other critical members of the team were County Councillor David Walsh, who had won the County Council division of Westley Heights (which included my own Langdon Hills ward) back in 1991.[17] Dave was a tall, good looking man, always immaculately dressed who worked as an Insurance Broker at Lloyds. He came from a large family, was quick witted and was always on hand with a joke or a wise crack whenever the occasion demanded it. Alongside him was my other great friend, Stephen Horgan, who worked as a Senior IT Specialist in the City for Lloyds Bank. Steve was in many ways the antithesis of Dave, he was a tee-totaller, quite serious at times, a black belt in Jujitsu and was usually seen in a pin striped suit, even out canvassing in the evenings. The three of us became colloquially known in the Association as "the Three Musketeers" as we were such close friends. Added to this motley crew was David Shields, a former RAF Policeman turned Security Consultant, Kevin Blake, a part time Football Referee and worker in an Engineering Firm and Simon Smith, a young 18-year-old student and Member of the Young Conservatives, who clearly enjoyed coming out with us once a week. Along with a handful of other volunteers, we made it our mission to canvass as much of the constituency as we possibly could.

Meanwhile, battle continued in the Council Chamber, which is where I learnt my rather robust debating style. Discourse in the Chamber was, shall we say, rather direct. In fact, Basildon was once described to me by a friend as: "the only local authority in the United Kingdom, where, at Council meetings, the Councillors actively heckle the public gallery!". Indeed, there was considerable cut and thrust in debate, not least as by that time, given our gains in the 1991 elections, the Labour Party were only continuing to run the Council on the Chairman's casting vote. Thus, we were threatening to capture the Council while, in turn, Labour were threatening an asymmetric victory to take the Parliamentary seat.

Basildon Conservatives

The Basildon Conservative Association during the 1980s and early 1990s were probably among some of the most ardent campaigners in the Conservative Party.

Comprised mainly, but by no means exclusively, of working class Thatcherites, living in a New Town created by post-war socialist idealism, to our Labour opponents we were not just Tories but "class traitors" to boot. The Basildon Labour Party could cope with "Tory toffs" from Billericay venturing into the New Town to campaign against them but what they simply couldn't get their head around was that people like myself, David Walsh and Steve Horgan (the Association's "Three Musketeers") all of whom lived on the Five Links Council estate, could possibly support Conservative principles whilst coming from essentially working class backgrounds.

The Basildon Labour Party, many of whom began as old style socialists in the East End of London, were then joined, if not supplanted, by a new cadre or younger, more-left wing activists, almost exclusively with public sector backgrounds.

These would-be class warriors never really understood the transformative power unleashed by allowing working class families to purchase their own Council houses or buy shares in major national corporations like British Airways, British Telecom or British Gas – and thus gain a greater economic stake in society for them and their loved ones.

Once David Amess broke the mould by surprisingly capturing the new Basildon constituency for the Conservatives in 1983, British society then underwent a series of convulsions, from the 1984-85 Miners Strike, through market liberalisation via "Big Bang" in the City in 1986 and then the series of major privatisations referred to earlier, but the Basildon Labour Party always struggled to keep pace.

While they constantly claimed to represent "working class people" (despite often having relatively comfortable middle-class backgrounds themselves) they never remotely comprehended the genuine aspirations of said people to strive to do better for themselves and their children.

That lack of understanding of the hopes and dreams of the electorate by his opponents is, I believe, at least partly why David held the seat successfully three times, in 1983, 1987 and 1992 respectively.

At grass roots level, the battles for control of Basildon Council were equally hard fought. A political scientist might perceive them, perhaps with some merit, as a genuine "ideological struggle" between Thatcherite Tories on the one hand and hard-left socialists (some of them were proper Marxists) on the other.

For us, however, it was simply a battle to win control of the community in which we lived and, as we saw it, try and improve the lives of the people who lived there, by concentrating more on repairs to Council properties and damaged pavements and less on opposing the Right to Buy and promoting nuclear free zones.

"What's an Ann Summers Party?"

We went out regularly on those Tuesday nights, in all weathers, armed with our canvass cards, a few leaflets and a Membership book and we made a point of inviting any staunch Conservative supporters we encountered to join the Conservative Party – which a number of them did, on their doorsteps. Ironically, on one night we were canvassing my own estate of Alcatraz in the pouring rain, but despite the awful conditions, we signed up four Members that night – perhaps because people felt sorry for us!

There was also considerable room for humour. For instance, when we had finished canvassing, we would normally clock off a bit before 9:00pm and go to whichever pub we were nearest to when we concluded. One evening Dave Shields tried to excuse himself, which was very unlike him, so when we pressed him on the reasons for his absence, he slightly sheepishly admitted: "My wife Georgina's been to an Ann Summers party this evening and I'm quite keen to get home and see what she's bought". "What's an Ann Summers party?" enquired the young Simon Smith. To which David Walsh, who had that marvellous ability to keep an entirely straight face, even when he was talking the most absolute rubbish, turned to Simon and explained as follows: "Well Simon, it's a bit like a Tupperware party but with a religious theme. So, there's a sort of sale of religious artefacts and icons and stuff like that". "Oh, that's funny", replied Simon, "I never figured my mother for religious, but she's been to quite a few of those parties over the last few years".

As we canvassed, we came across a number of voters who were reluctant to vote Conservative but who clearly did not want Neil Kinnock as their Prime Minister. We marked those people down with a special "Q" Code (for "Question Mark" on the Coley system) because we figured the way that those waverers decided to vote would have a material impact on the final result. As it turned out, we got that one right.

The 1992 General Election

Eventually, the General Election was called for April 1992 and the campaign began in earnest. There was tremendous interest in Basildon (for the reasons explained earlier) and numerous national journalists came down to test the water and try and predict what the outcome was likely to be. David Amess was an absolutely inspirational candidate, always leading from the front, and going out canvassing tirelessly three times every day, in the morning, afternoon and evening respectively.

Unfortunately, David also had a habit of going into pubs in order to canvass electors, something which Dave Walsh and I persistently tried to advise him against, as we both took the view that people don't like being pestered by politicians when they simply go out for a drink. On one occasion in the Flying Childers pub, having been given a pretty stark warning by the publican that, "It's all going to kick off in here massively in about two minutes", we managed to get David out of the pub just before a major public order situation occurred. In fact, I remember Dave Walsh's blunt advice to the candidate as follows: "David, if you don't leave this bloody pub right now, neither Mark or I are going to visit you in A&E in the morning".

David also had a campaign battle bus with a specially prepared jingle, "Vote, Vote, Vote for David Amess – he's the only one for me!" By the end of the campaign, I would almost wake up in the middle of the night with this jingle running around my head.

"Labour's Tax Bombshell"

The Labour Party made a major tactical error during the campaign, when their Shadow Chancellor, John Smith, published a Shadow Budget, showing the areas in which an incoming Labour Government would boost public spending and, crucially, which taxes they intended to raise in order to pay for it.[18] Their thinking appeared to be that in being candid with the electorate about their plans to "tax and spend" they would somehow win the respect of the voting public.

As it turned out, their gambit backfired spectacularly. I remember commuting into work at the time on the old "Misery Line" into Fenchurch Street and noticing the passenger opposite me avidly reading his Daily Mail and then frantically punching figures into a pocket calculator. When I politely enquired what he was doing he replied: "I'm working out how much these Commie bastards are going to cost me if they win in a fortnight's time!"

The Tory Party Chairman, Chris Patten, responded with a striking campaign entitled "Labour's Tax Bombshell", with a poster of an enormous bomb, to emphasise the devastating taxes that Labour were about to unleash on the British electorate, if they emerged victorious at the forthcoming election.

This targeted approach really hit home and out on the doorsteps wavering voters increasingly gave two reasons for not voting Labour – namely "Kinnock" and "tax". In the final few days of the campaign, our canvas returns, which were inputted into the computer every night by a dedicated activist named Liz Frost,[19] showed a definite hardening of the Conservative vote – probably just enough for us to hold the seat.

Polling Day 9th April 1992

When it came to polling day itself, we had tellers on virtually every polling station to keep a record of which of our supporters had voted and then a team in each of the eight wards to run round and remind our supporters who hadn't yet cast their ballot, to go to the polling stations and vote (what is known in the trade as "Knocking Up").

We worked our socks off that day. When I briefed the knock-up teams personally in the morning, I told them to concentrate in particular on the 3,000 or so wavering "Q's" on our knock-up lists, and to drive home mercilessly the threat of Neil Kinnock and high taxes on the doorsteps that evening. We were certainly blessed by a marvellous headline in *The Sun* which famously declared: "If Neil Kinnock wins today, will the last person to leave Britain please turn the lights out". When the polls finally closed at 10:00pm, we then went off to the election count, which was held at the old Festival Hall. I will never forget that count as long as I live.

Each Party is allowed a certain number of scrutineers who oversee the count (then undertaken by Bank Tellers hired in for the process) to make sure that all of the votes are correctly allocated to each Candidate. The votes were counted into 50s and then collated in small empty ice cream boxes, each containing 1,000 votes, which were then assembled on a large table at the centre of the hall. So, by counting the number of ice cream boxes for each side, you could effectively keep track of the running total. When the count was concluded, we were all anxiously peering at the table in the centre and trying desperately to count the ice cream boxes but, having done it several times, we consistently came out with 22 for each side and a rumour swept round the hall like wildfire, which was one word long: "Recount!" After over a year (in fact nearer two) of punishing hard work the thought of having to sit through a recount was almost too much to bear. At just that point the Returning Officer called out, "Are there any more votes to be counted?" After what seemed an agonising silence, from the far end of the hall one of the Council officers stood up and said "Yes, sorry, just a second" and then walked over to the central table with two more ice cream boxes full of votes. You could have heard a pin drop. As he put them down on the central table, one of my colleagues, Danny Lovey, exclaimed "They're both Blue!", followed by a few seconds of absolute pandemonium, as we realised that we must have won.

When it came to the Declaration itself, the Labour Chairman of the Council, whose name ironically was Councillor Marks (not quite Marx) read the result out as if he had ashes in his mouth. "David Anthony Andrew Amess – the Conservative Candidate – 24,159 votes. John Potter – the Labour Party Candidate – 22,…", you never heard the rest, it was basically blanked out by a loud yell, as every Tory in the hall went bananas. The count was being broadcast live and apparently an even louder cheer went up at Conservative Central Office at Smith Square, Westminster, when they realised that if we had held Basildon, John Major must have won the General Election – and so it turned out to be.

To add insult to injury, David had produced a number of small A6 size calling cards with his photograph which we had used during the election campaign and Simon Smith had mischievously brought a stock of them to the count. By the time that the desperately dejected Labour activists got back to their cars, they found a smiling visage of David Amess tucked behind the windscreen wiper of every single Labour vehicle. To say that this went down badly with our defeated socialist friends, would be an understatement – they were bloody furious – and you could hear the torrent of expletives right across the large car park.

After two years of being ritually taunted by our Labour opponents that we were going to be "slaughtered" in Basildon come the General Election, we held an uproarious victory party at my mother's house in Mellow Purgess, with a number of John Potter posters, which I had managed to liberate from dejected Labour voters, placed strategically around the house, including one in the downstairs loo!

Stephen Horgan

My other great political friend from Basildon days was Stephen Horgan, who in many ways was the complete opposite of David Walsh. A senior IT Manager for Lloyds Bank, Steve didn't smoke or drink (his favourite tipple was Diet Coke), he normally went out canvassing in a pinstripe suit and he was also a martial arts blackbelt to boot.

If David Walsh was the "funny man" then Steve was the "straight man" and as the three of us became really close friends, we were nicknamed "The Three Musketeers" by the other Members of the Basildon Conservative Association.

On one occasion in the early 1990s, Steve and I both went after work straight to Hackney, to provide mutual aid for the Hackney Conservatives on the evening of a local by-election. The Committee Room to which we had been asked to report was difficult to find and so we popped into a local pub – both in suits and Barbour jackets – to seek directions. After nobody wanted to engage with us, the Publican appeared, told us where to head for and offered us both a free drink, as "it's always nice to see you fellas in here". I whispered: "they think we are coppers Steve, just drink your diet coke politely and then let's go".

Steve succeeded me as a Conservative Councillor for Langdon Hills and subsequently stood for Parliament in the North of England but was unfortunately unsuccessful. Tragically he was then diagnosed with a rare blood cancer and passed away only a few months later, and a few years after David Walsh, while still only in his late 30s. At Steve's funeral, one of our Councillors turned to me and said: "This is terrible Mark – and now you're the only Musketeer left!" By this time, I had become an MP, but I will never forget either of my fellow Musketeers and all they stood for.

As well as letting off steam after two years of extremely hard work, there was also another purpose to all our carousing – to keep spirits high for the next battle only a month later, our chance to capture outright control of Basildon Council for the first time ever.

Reflecting on the results a few months later, a chastened Guardian Columnist, Alan Rusbridger, wrote: "If some of our leading political pundits and psephologists had spent a little less time in the Garrick and a little more time in Basildon, there would have been far fewer red faces on the morning of April 10".[20]

For the record, the result in Basildon in April 1992 was as follows:

David Amess	Conservative Candidate	24,159
John Potter	Labour Candidate	22,679
Geoff Williams	Liberal Democrat Candidate	6,963
Conservative Majority		1,480
Turnout		79.77%

Operation Basildon Storm

Although we had helped David successfully defend his seat – seemingly against all the odds – there was now one further challenge, which was to try and achieve Conservative majority control of Basildon District Council (for the first time since its creation) at the local elections a month later.[21] Protagonists on both sides were pretty exhausted by this stage, but our tails were up, whereas the Labour Party, who had honestly expected to win Basildon quite comfortably, were clearly massively dejected.[22] Part of our success was due to an extremely accurate canvass and the fact that we had some three thousand or so "Q's" marked on our computer and these were the people we had focussed in on particularly when we undertook the knock up on the night. Logic suggested that these voters would also be critical in the local elections as well.

So, we set out for a further month of door knocking in what I christened "Operation Basildon Storm". The challenge we had was that Basildon Council had 42 Councillors, so you needed 22 for a majority. At the time, Labour had 21 seats, the Conservatives 17 and the Liberal Democrats 4, with the Labour Party only surviving on the Chairman of the Council's casting vote. In order to take control of the Council we needed to win another 5 seats to take us to 22. Rightly or wrongly, a number of the officers who worked for the Council at that time were very left-wing and I remember bumping into one of the Directors of the Council, ironically also named Mark, in a local nightclub, called "Time", about two weeks before polling day. To be fair, he had had a few to drink by this stage of the evening and so he delighted in telling me that the officers had done their own private analysis and they thought we might end up with 19 seats, or even 20 at a pinch but there was no way we would get to 21 and certainly not 22.

I replied, partly based on my experience of fighting Langdon Hills first time around, that it was often usually a good idea not to call the result of an election until you actually knew how the people had voted – and I would see him at the Towngate Theatre on the night.

The reason for his confidence (well, arrogance really) was that in order to take control of the Council, we would have to win some Labour wards in the New Town that we hadn't won in living memory. One of these was Vange, where David Shields was our candidate, and I was acting as his Election Agent. Whatever happened in Vange, no one seemed to believe that we could ever storm the Labour bastion of Fryerns – their absolute heartland, including the large industrial estate and some of the toughest Council estates in Basildon.

"I'm on the Game love, like me mum!"

Arguably the roughest Council estate in the whole of Basildon New Town in the early 1990s was not Alcatraz or even Siporex but "Craylands", a maze of low-rise blocks with back alleys, with high unemployment and myriad social problems. Nevertheless, buoyed up by our success at the General Election we invaded this previous Labour fortress with the aim of trying to capture the ward, which as one of our team said to me: "has been represented by Labour since the Romans left Britain". On one occasion a bridge nearby the estate, which overlooked a main road, had been draped with a blanket bearing the celebratory slogan: "Happy 30th Birthday Grandma!"

On one such visit we were canvassing a row of houses and just about to move onto the next one when a car drew up. I shouted to my colleagues "you go ahead, I'll just catch this one" only to be confronted by a young but rather tarty girl getting out of her car. When I tried to canvas her, she seemed irritated and told me she had been up all-night working. Trying to keep the conversation going, I enquired as to what she did for a living, which drew the sharp retort: "I'm on the Game love, just like my mum, and I don't vote for nobody, so piss off!"

As part of our campaign, we used the computer to produce personally addressed letters to Conservative supporters (and "Q's") in every ward in Basildon and I remember going round to our committee room in Fryerns the day before polling day, only to see several thousand of these neatly stuffed in their envelopes but still waiting to be delivered. A number of the Members of our Fryerns branch were getting on a bit in years and, frankly, they were exhausted, as they told me pretty bluntly when I popped in. I empathised and then said: "Look, I know we are all absolutely knackered, myself included, but we pulled off an amazing result in the General Election and we now have the opportunity to do something even more incredible. Think how we'd all feel tomorrow night at the count if, after all this work, we'd fallen short by only one seat? If we can just give this one last push, there really is a chance that we could take this Council once and for all. I'll take 500 of them and do them all myself if you guys will do the rest?". At that point, the senior Member of the branch looked me in the eye and said: "Alright Mark. We will do this for David Amess and for you, but we've never, ever, won Fryerns, so I hope to God you're right".

When it came to the count that night, the atmosphere was electric. The reaction on the doorsteps when we'd gone round systematically knocking up had been warm and there appeared to have been quite a healthy turnout at the polling stations, even in the Labour heartlands, so it's true to say that we were optimistic. Something incredible then happened. We won Fryerns East (including Craylands) by nearly 100 votes. At that point the most unbelievable cheer went up in the Towngate Theatre because we all instinctively knew, in an instant, that if we had won in Fryerns, we must have taken the entire lot – which is exactly what happened.

There were 14 wards up for election on Basildon District Council that night and we won 15 – because there was a double header by-election in Billericay East that evening, and it would have been rude not to have won that one as well. By the end of the evening, we didn't have 20 seats or 21, or even 22, but 26! We were euphoric and I remember bumping into the same Council Officer, Mark, walking down the stairs as he was walking up and I looked him straight in the eye and said: "You're quite right, Mark, we didn't end up with 20 or even 21, in the end, did we?".

The look of anguish on his face was almost indescribable and, of his own volition, he was flicking through the appointment's pages of *The Guardian* pretty promptly thereafter. Perhaps unsurprisingly, he soon secured an even better paid job, with another left-wing Labour Council, somewhere else.

Result of the Local Elections for Basildon District Council – May 1992

State of the Parties on May 1991		State of the Parties on May 1992	
Labour	21	Labour	13
Conservative	17	Conservative	26
Liberal Democrats	4	Liberal Democrats	3
Labour Majority	0	Conservative Majority	10
(Chairman's Casting Vote)			

Under New Management

We took control of the Council the following morning and had appointed a team of senior Councillors by lunchtime. David Amess turned up with a large placard saying, "Under New Management" which we were all photographed underneath. By the end of the evening, mysteriously, all of the nuclear free zone signs on the roads leading into Basildon had disappeared.

In short, we had held the iconic seat of Basildon in the General Election and then captured the Council from Labour to boot, only one month later. This was no small achievement and was due to the incredible hard work of a whole range of people, with David Amess at the zenith.

We immediately set about a programme of reforming Basildon Council, dropping its hard-left ideology and concentrating on the priorities of local residents instead. Amongst other things, we managed to persuade the Department of the Environment to provide us with a substantial grant to completely redevelop the defective Siporex estate and replace it with traditional housing but to a modern design. The new estate christened "Church View" (because you can see St. Nicholas Church on the hill from there) was a massive improvement on its predecessor. As a result of reducing bureaucracy, we also managed to reduce Basildon's "poll tax" and return to local residents some of their own hard-earned money.

At the count on the night a massively dejected Labour Party, huddled together in the stalls of the Towngate Theatre, attempted a derisory chorus of "The Red Flag". After two years of extremely hard work, the 200 or so Conservative Councillors and activists in the Towngate Theatre took exception to this and Labour were rapidly drowned out by an impromptu rendition of "Land of Hope and Glory". I recall a couple of chaps who had come down from the north of the county to help out on the night, who were perhaps not used to the rather rumbustious scenes at a Basildon count. I well remember because the two of them were standing next to me at the time and one turned to his friend and said, "What on earth is going on Brian?", to which his chum replied: "Look, Tarquin, I know it's a bit different to what we're used to in Braintree, but for goodness sake man, just sing!".

It is probably true to say that we were bad winners in that we celebrated massively on the night and then made a point of rubbing Labour's nose in it in the Council Chamber at every possible opportunity thereafter – for about a year. The defeated Labour Council Leader, John Potter, who had also been their unsuccessful candidate at the General Election took particular exception to the way that we used to wind him up in Council meetings. On one occasion, in the middle of my speech he stood up and exploded, "I'm damned if I'm going to listen to any more of this rubbish, I'm off to the toilet". To which I retorted: "That's good to hear Councillor Potter, because that's the only motion you'll be passing tonight!".

Some people have commented on the fact that I do have a fairly robust debating style in the House of Commons – well now you know where it came from.

"Do you play bridge?"

We also attempted to help out in neighbouring local government by-elections closer to home in Essex, particularly on polling day, when we often offered to help the local Association to "knock up".

On one such occasion we offered to help out in a by-election for a normally safe Conservative Ward on Southend Council. However, it transpired that we had been given incorrect details of where the Committee Room that we were supposed to report to, was actually located. In those days the polls closed at 9pm for local elections and of course there were no mobile phones, so by 7pm we resolved to head off to the Association Headquarters at Iveagh Hall in Leigh Road, to seek accurate directions.

When David Walsh and I arrived at Iveagh Hall (with Steve Horgan and David Shields still in the car outside, with the engine running) we rushed in, only to find a bridge evening in progress. When we enquired if anyone could re-direct us to the by-election, we were addressed by a charming lady of advancing years in the following terms: "We don't know anything about a by-election Dear, but we're playing bridge and we're a couple of players short. Do either of you play bridge by any chance?"

At that point we decided to finally admit defeat and set off for the nearest pub that we could find. However, we had been given advance tickets to the by-election count at the Civic Offices and duly turned up, only to discover that the Conservative candidate had narrowly triumphed, by just a handful of votes. We were then thanked profusely for coming over from Basildon and helping to bring about the victory and invited to another pub to celebrate our no doubt invaluable contribution to such a tight win. We all looked at each other briefly and, deciding that it would all take too long to explain anyway, we quietly followed our new found comrades to the bar.

Incidentally, many years later someone else asked me quite unexpectedly whether or not I played bridge – but that is perhaps a different story for another book altogether.

The ERM and Black Wednesday

We continued on a roll after the victory in Basildon and a few months later we went up to Harlow, to assist in a by-election there. Essentially it was our Tuesday night canvass team that made the journey and whilst we were out knocking up on a Council estate in Harlow, we met the local Labour Party coming the other way. The Labour Party obviously didn't recognise us, and the Leader of their gang shouted across the road, "You're not from round here, what are you lot doing here?", to which Dave Walsh shot back: "Oh we're from Basildon mate, we're here tonight because where we come from, there's nothing left to win!".

Ironically, despite our bravado, when we got to the count in Harlow Town Hall that night, it was extremely close. The Returning Officer called the three election agents over (but the acoustics in their Council chamber are good and you could hear what he said from some distance away). He turned to the Conservative Agent and said; "On the first count, I have your candidate ahead by one vote. Would you like to request a recount?". To give him credit, the Tory Agent scratched his bearded chin thoughtfully and then replied laconically, "Erm no, I think I'm fine with that thank you". After three recounts we were declared the winner – literally by one vote. The only time I have ever seen that in an election count in person, before or since.

However, our fortunes, and indeed that of the entire Conservative Party began to change in September 1992, when we were famously ejected from the Exchange Rate Mechanism (ERM) on what, according to your point of view, became known as Black (or White/Golden) Wednesday. In essence, the Major Government had pursued a disastrous policy of attempting to shadow the Deutschmark within the European Exchange Rate Mechanism, which had led to the UK pursuing artificially high interest rates for far too long, with many businesses collapsing and people losing their homes due to increasingly high mortgage rates, as a result. On Black Wednesday there was a run on the pound and the Government famously increased interest rates from 10-12% in the morning and then again from 12-15% in the afternoon – a rise of 5% points in one day, which had never occurred previously in peace time.[23]

Ironically, my old school friend Deano was by now working in a Dealing Room in the City and I remember his subsequent description of what happened. When the Bank of England increased its base rate, then known as Minimum Lending Rate (MLR) from 10-12% in the morning, there was absolute pandemonium in the dealing room, with dealers screaming down phones as they attempted to cover off their various positions. Conversely, in the afternoon, when it was announced that MLR had been increased from 12-15%, this announcement was met with a stunned silence.

One of Deano's colleagues on his desk turned round to him and said: "Well, that's it then, they'll never keep that up, they'll be out of the sodding ERM by tonight", and so it proved. The Chancellor, Norman Lamont, with his young special advisor, (one David Cameron, in the background) famously walked down the Treasury steps and said that after a "difficult day" on the financial markets, "the UK would be temporarily withdrawing from the ERM".[24] Mercifully we never re-joined and once we no longer had to maintain artificially high rates to shadow the Deutschmark, as the pro-European's in the Cabinet like Ken Clarke and Michael Heseltine had avidly believed we should, interest rates then fell back rapidly and the economy finally began to recover. However, there is no doubt that Black Wednesday seriously damaged the Conservative's reputation for economic management, and we began to slip back in the polls accordingly.

However, this was compounded by Norman Lamont's Budget in 1993. The public finances had been in some difficulty and so, Lamont as Chancellor, decided that he had to raise taxes across the board, both direct and indirect, including large increases in VAT.[25] However, part of the Tory's successful General Election campaign less than a year earlier had been to warn the country about the very severe tax increases that would take place if Labour were to come to power. Yet here we were, less than a year on, effectively imposing a whole massive set of tax increases – exactly what we had warned the country against and assured them would come to pass if Labour were allowed to win.

In the eyes of the public, rather than those who dwell in the Westminster village, at that point we effectively became liars. We had done exactly what we told the British people the other lot were going to do if they won and then, having been victorious, we then dropped the "tax bombshell" ourselves instead. However, pressing the economic necessity, to the average man in the street, this was completely unforgiveable, and we were then punished accordingly. It is my belief that, combined with Black Wednesday several months earlier, from that point onwards, our credibility as a Government and John Major's Premiership, was effectively shot to pieces.

Although it is only anecdotal, by sheer coincidence we had a by-election in the Labour heartland of Fryerns which was ongoing when the Budget was announced. Even though this was Labour's back yard in Basildon, given the results of nine months earlier, up to that point, our canvass returns were very good, and it seemed that the result would be a nip and tuck a fortnight later. However, as soon as the Budget was announced our canvas returns completely collapsed and our canvassers were met with open hostility, on door after door.

I well remember speaking to one elector who, when I asked him whether he was going to vote Conservative, responded as follows:

"I voted for you lot 'cause you told me that if Labour won, they were going to tax me up to the eyeballs. And now you've won, you've done exactly the same thing anyway. I don't care what you try to say to me son, you're a bloody liar, now get off my sodding doorstep before I really lose my temper. Just piss off!".

We were subsequently slaughtered in the Fryerns by-election in a ward when he had triumphed only nine months previously. Again, whatever the economic necessity of the Budget, it was a political disaster and from then on it was only a matter of time until the electorate sought retribution and the Major Government was finally wiped out at the polls.

<table>
<tr><td colspan="3">Result Fryerns Central Ward,
May 1992</td></tr>
<tr><td>Candidate</td><td>Votes</td><td>Share</td></tr>
<tr><td>Stuart Allen (Conservative)</td><td>1,828</td><td>46%</td></tr>
<tr><td>Rachel Bolt (Labour)</td><td>1,644</td><td>42%</td></tr>
<tr><td>John Smith (Liberal Democrat)</td><td>459</td><td>12%</td></tr>
<tr><td>Conservative Majority</td><td>184</td><td>4%</td></tr>
<tr><td>Turnout</td><td></td><td>46%</td></tr>
</table>

<table>
<tr><td colspan="3">Result Fryerns Central Ward,
April 1993 By Election</td></tr>
<tr><td>Candidate</td><td>Votes</td><td>Share</td></tr>
<tr><td>Paul Kirkman (Labour)</td><td>2,574</td><td>68%</td></tr>
<tr><td>Phil Turner (Conservative)</td><td>870</td><td>23%</td></tr>
<tr><td>John Smith (Liberal Democrats)</td><td>334</td><td>9%</td></tr>
<tr><td>Labour Majority</td><td>1,604</td><td>42%</td></tr>
<tr><td>Turnout</td><td></td><td>43%</td></tr>
</table>

The Maastricht Treaty

This situation was only made worse by the civil war in the Conservative Parliamentary Party over the Maastricht Treaty. In 1992, Prime Minister John Major had signed Britain up to the Treaty of Maastricht, a major milestone in the integration of the European Institutions. Amongst other things, Maastricht turned what had been the European Economic Community (the EEC) into the European Union (the EU) which many people argued was a further steppingstone towards the creation of one Federal European Superstate (just as the advocates of the

European Project has always envisaged). The Maastricht Treaty also facilitated the creation of a single European currency, which ultimately became known as "The Euro". Although Major had negotiated an opt out from the Euro, so that the UK could retain the Pound Sterling, and also an opt out from what was known as the "Social Chapter" (a whole raft of social and employment legislation, more popular on the continent) it was still a major step forward in the direction of a European State. As such, it proved unpopular with a number of Conservative MPs, which was a problem for the Government as each EU Member State had to ratify the Treaty via its own constitutional mechanism, which in our case meant via an Act of Parliament.

Thus, began over a year of Parliamentary trench warfare within the Conservative Party, made more difficult as the Conservatives, post Black Wednesday and Lamont's Budget, lost one by-election after another, even in traditional Tory heartlands.[26]

"The Maastricht Rebels" as they became known were led by determined and principled Tory MPs such as Michael Spicer and Bill Cash, who consistently voted against the Bill to ratify the Treaty, which itself took many months to go through the House of Commons. The divisions in Parliament, which at times became very acrimonious, were in some ways a harbinger of what was to follow in the bitter arguments over Theresa May's Withdrawal Agreement some years later.

The Maastricht Treaty was also divisive among the Conservative Party in the country (often referred to in Conservative circles as the "Voluntary Party" i.e. those grassroots Members of the Party who are neither MPs or Peers, or Party Officials).

It seemed to me, as a young Conservative Councillor aged 27, that despite the opt outs, particularly on the single currency, we were still seeding too much power to the European institutions at the expense of our own Parliament. Moreover, John Major's Government, which was overwhelmingly pro-European in nature, with the so called "Big Beasts" of Michael Heseltine and Kenneth Clarke close to its centre, was absolutely adamant that they would not permit a Referendum in the United Kingdom to test whether or not this fundamentally important Treaty actually had public support. Indeed, Ken Clarke famously boasted that he had never even read it![27]

"God Save the Danes!"

I had an opportunity to air my strong reservations about Maastricht at the Young Conservatives Annual Conference, which that year took place just up the road from Basildon, in Southend-on-Sea. There was a very lively debate between those in the YC's who were pro-European or instinctively loyal to John Major and young Euro-sceptics, who were very fearful of what Maastricht would actually mean for the sovereignty of the United Kingdom. I remember speaking passionately in that debate, vehemently against the Maastricht Treaty and in particular about the fact that it was being rammed through without a Referendum. Just prior to the Conference the Danish people had rejected Maastricht which led to many Conservative MPs signing an Early Day Motion calling for a "Fresh Start" in the Government's approach to Europe.[28] This had filtered down to the YC Conference and I still remember to this day my peroration, which was: "God save the Queen Chairman. God save the Danes – and may the Danes yet save us from ourselves!". To my genuine amazement this was met with a spontaneous standing ovation in the hall, incorporating cheering and clapping of a type which I was unused to, even in the rumbustious atmosphere of Basildon politics.

On the way out of the hall, I bumped into a formidable lady named Dawn Bayman, who was the Party's Senior Agent for the Eastern Region (including Essex) and who was personally very close to John Major and thus something of a "power in the land" within the Party. It is probably fair to say that she was not entirely enamoured of my speech. She fixed me with a steely glare and said: "That was a very interesting speech Mark, I would be happy to report it back to the Prime Minister. Remind me, how exactly do you spell your surname?". To which I replied: "It's F-R-A-N-C-O-I-S and don't forget the cedilla under the C! Good afternoon to you Mrs Bayman". Thus, for the first time in my life and after nearly a decade as a Party Member, I had suddenly become a Tory rebel.

Eventually, the Treaty was brutally rammed through the House of Commons by the Major Government, ultimately by the use of a "Vote of Confidence" by which Major threatened to call a General Election if the rebels did not bow to his will.[29] Several books have been written about this extremely acrimonious time in Parliament but, whichever view one might take of the Maastricht Treaty, it is true to say that the divisions within the Conservative Parliamentary Party only magnified the sense in the eyes of the public that the Conservatives, after four terms in office, had been there for too long.[30]

On the doorsteps under Major

In the subsequent County Council elections in May 1993, the Conservative candidates up for election that night were virtually annihilated. The so called "Tory Shires", proved to be anything but and by the end of the night, the Conservative's had lost control of every single County Council in the country, bar Buckinghamshire, which contained some of the most affluent parts of the United Kingdom and has an extremely strong Grammar School tradition to boot. Just about everywhere else, Tory candidates were mown down like infantry at Passchendaele, as the electorate vented their anger on the Tories for economic mismanagement and blatantly breaking their word on tax.

Norman Lamont, despite administering this strong economic medicine, partly at the PM's behest, had by now been sacked by Major as Chancellor and replaced by the Europhile Ken Clarke. Lamont famously summarised the whole situation when he subsequently described Major's Government as being: "in office, but not in power".[31]

In the following sets of local elections, in 1994 and 1995, it only got worse, in fact much worse. Canvassing on the doorsteps in those years was a bloody nightmare. Time and again electors, even in very affluent properties, let alone on Council estates, were slamming the doors in the faces of Tory canvassers, so disillusioned were they by John Major and his hopelessly divided Government. Indeed, by 1995, in local Government, the Conservative's held Buckinghamshire County Council, very few London Boroughs like Wandsworth and Westminster and less than a dozen other Council's across the entire United Kingdom. Literally thousands of Tory Councillors, irrespective of their personal track records in local Government, were wiped out as the electorate expressed their disdain at the ballot box, at what they saw as a tired and failing Conservative Government. By 1994 our majority on Basildon District Council had been reduced and the tables were now turned on us and we ran the Council precariously on the Chairman's casting vote. More by accident than design, I was appointed as the Group's Whip for that year and it was my responsibility to help make sure that we had 21 candidates present at every Council meeting. I'm pleased to say that we never actually lost a vote during that period although on one occasion we had to yank one of our Councillors off a cruise in the Mediterranean and fly him home from the nearest Port, in order to attend an Emergency Council meeting the following night. I was the one who had pleaded with his family to get him back, so when he turned up hot foot from Stansted Airport on the night – and then one of the Labour Councillors failed to attend anyway – the look on his face is something I prefer to forget, even to this day.

Joining the Carlton Club

The other significant thing that happened to me in that period was that I applied to join the Carlton Club, the Conservative Party's own club in the heart of St James'. The sponsor for my application was David Amess MP, who had promised to do this as a thank you for all the hard work I had done in helping him to defend Basildon in the General Election. My seconder was an old friend, Paul Green, a successful Wandsworth Councillor who I had met through Tory circles a few years ago.

The Carlton Club was originally founded by the Duke of Wellington in the mid-19th century and had beautiful premises on Pall Mall. It was in the original club that the fateful decision was taken by Tory MPs to break from Lloyd George's Liberals in 1922, from which the "1922 Committee" of Conservative backbench MPs still takes its name. Unfortunately, the old clubhouse was destroyed by German bombing in WWII which led to the club moving to its current premises at 69 St James', only a few hundred yards away from the original site.

In the 19th century the club was the equivalent of Conservative Campaign HQ (CCHQ) today and was the nerve centre of the Conservative Party in their great battles against the Whigs and latterly the Liberals. By 1992 the Carlton no longer performed any Headquarters role but was still something of an important power centre within the Conservative Party and so, I thought that it would be a good idea for an aspirant Tory MP to apply for membership.

In those days, some three decades ago, would be Members were invited to have lunch with two Members of the so called "Scrutiny Committee" – to ensure that you were the right sort of "Chap" to join the club. I therefore remember quite a pleasant lunch with two congenial senior Members who, in fairness, wanted to understand my commitment to the Conservative cause – as well as ensuring that I didn't eat my peas with a knife. Somehow, I managed to sneak in below the radar and passed this test and I am glad to say that I have been a Member of the Carlton ever since.

For many years, the Carlton Club, which at that time was all-male, was wrenched by arguments over whether or not to allow women to join as Members. I remember speaking in favour of such a change and going "co-ed" at one Extraordinary General Meeting on the subject, with, among others, Michael Portillo looking on. Eventually, under William Hague's Leadership, we finally wore the diehards down and women were finally admitted as full Members in their own right, with, I am glad to say, many having joined since.

The club today is in good heart and enjoys a broad social mix and indeed has a very lively junior branch as well.

Having managed to get elected on to Basildon District Council, become Vice Chairman and then Acting Chairman of Housing, I decided that perhaps it was now time to start thinking about trying to find my first Parliamentary seat to fight. I was already a Councillor, now it was time to start thinking about becoming an MP. However, that meant surmounting the not inconsiderate challenge of getting onto the Party's Approved Candidates List (which I managed to do, with David Amess acting as my nominated sponsor). I also applied for a vacancy to become the Prospective Parliamentary Candidate (PPC) for Brent East in North West London, not that far away from where I was born in Islington.

In reality, I only applied to Brent East to gain some interview experience and never expected, for one moment, to be selected as the candidate. However, when I got through to the final round of the selection process, held in a church near Gladstone Park, one of the other candidates was suffering heavily from the flu and the other was incredibly nervous, so more by process of elimination than any else, they eventually plumped for me! Thus, almost by accident, I gained an opportunity to stand for Parliament and follow in the footsteps of my great friend, David Amess.

(Sir) David Amess

Sir David Amess was my oldest and greatest friend in politics. Growing up in the heart of East London, he began his political career as a very young Councillor in the London Borough of Redbridge, before scoring a stunning victory to capture the new Parliamentary seat of Basildon, as part of Mrs Thatcher's landslide General Election victory in 1983.

David famously "put Basildon on the map", not least by relentlessly mentioning the New Town at every possible opportunity in the House of Commons, particularly at Prime Minister's Questions, when the Tory backbenchers would join in the sport and roar him on!

David and I first met, when I was briefly involved in the 1987 General Election, freshly back from university, but he helped me get elected on to Basildon Council in 1991 and, in return, I ran his canvas at the 1992 General Election. David subsequently sponsored me to join the Tory Parliamentary Candidates List in 1995 and acted effectively as my mentor when I was first elected to the Commons in 2001.

In the mid-1990s, the Parliamentary Boundary Commission conducted a Review, which included tearing the original Basildon constituency, compromising the eight, relatively compact Basildon New Town wards apart, effectively in two. The result was to merge the northern part of the New Town with Billericay, to form a "Basildon and Billericay" constituency and the southern element with parts of Thurrock, to form "South Basildon and East Thurrock (or SBET for short).

With his old constituency, which he had already successfully fought three times now having been dismembered, David switched to Southend, to replace the retiring MP, Paul Channon and was successfully elected as the new MP for Southend West in 1997. This led some ill-informed critics to malign David for having undertaken the "chicken run", to a supposedly safer seat. However, this overlooks that his old seat had effectively disappeared as a result of the boundary changes. Moreover, if David really had been a chicken, he would surely have sought to move prior to the 1987 General Election and certainly before the 1992 contest, when just about every political pundit in the land was telling him he had no hope of holding his Basildon seat. Nevertheless, he stood his ground and won in 1992, against all the odds. So, to paraphrase Churchill: "Some chicken, some neck!"

In both Basildon and later Southend, David served as an absolutely exceptional constituency MP. He developed a strong reputation as both a conscientious and extremely empathetic constituency MP. Although he was clearly capable of Ministerial Office, he never sought to climb the greasy pole of political advancement. Rather, his great priorities were his family, his strong Catholic faith and working for his constituents.

As good friends for some 30 years I was absolutely delighted when David was knighted by HM the Queen at Windsor in 2018. As he told our local paper, The Echo; "as a boy from the East End of London, I never dreamt of being knighted by the Queen, in a castle".

David was a staunch Monarchist, a Patriot, a Thatcherite Conservative and also a committed Eurosceptic. He had campaigned strongly for Leave back in 2016 and was a subsequent supporter of the European Research Group, attending a number of its gatherings, especially during the climax of the Battle for Brexit in 2019/20. When the Government delayed our originally planned departure from 29th March 2019 he told the Commons: "I am Leaving the European Union anyway, even if the rest of you are not!"

In mid-October 2021, after four decades of selfless public service as an MP, Sir David was cruelly taken from us when he was attacked at one of his regular constituency surgeries; a senseless act which shocked the entire country. I subsequently paid tribute to him in the House of Commons and I have taken the liberty of reproducing that eulogy at Appendix 8 of this book, so I will not repeat all of that here.

Suffice to say, he was quite simply the best bloke I ever knew and I have dedicated this book to his memory accordingly.

Chapter 4: Beating Boris to Get a Seat

In 1995, much to my surprise, I was selected to become the Conservative Party's Prospective Parliamentary Candidate (PPC) in the North West London seat of Brent East. My opponent, the incumbent Labour MP, was the high-profile left-winger, Ken Livingstone, a former Leader of the Greater London Council (the GLC). I had only really applied to the constituency to get some early interview experience but, to my surprise and delight, they unexpectedly selected me to take on "Red Ken".

Livingstone was obviously a very well-known figure, with a national profile and in contrast I was a total unknown. Nevertheless, we soon established a regular canvass team, which in this case went out on Monday nights with the aim of canvassing as much of the constituency as possible, before the General Election was called. We had at least one advantage in this, in that Brent East was a relatively compact geographical area, including a great deal of terraced housing, varying from the relatively spacious middle-class areas of, Brondesbury, Mapesbury and Cricklewood, to long rows of Victorian terraced houses in and around Willesden Green, finally complemented by six twenty-storey GLC tower blocks in Carlton Vale.

My old University chum Michael Halcrow, who at that time had a flat in Acton, used to drive over to meet us in the Con Club for a drink on Monday nights and then take me back to stay in a spare room at his flat in Acton on Monday evenings, before I went back into work on Tuesday morning. We would thus go out canvassing for two hours on a Monday and then retire to the Willesden Green Con Club to share our respective tales from the doorstep.

However, it was during the Hustings in the 1997 General Election campaign itself, that Ken Livingstone said something which I have never forgotten. He told the audience: "As a Member of Parliament, a General Election is an opportunity for you to commune with your 68,000 employers, and to listen to what they are trying to tell you whilst you are asking them to renew your contract, to continue working on their behalf". Even though politically Ken and I were chalk and cheese, I have always remembered this, because it seemed to me a very good summation of the role of an MP – that they are employed by their constituents to represent them – and not the other way around. I have always sought to bear this in mind in all the years that I have subsequently served in the House of Commons, so if we didn't agree on much else, on this one matter at least, I think Ken Livingstone really had a point.

Red Ken

Ken Livingstone was born in Lambeth, South London, in 1945. He was elected on to the old Greater London Council (GLC) in the 1970s and seized control of the council in a carefully configured internal Labour coup in 1981.

For the next five years, he was a constant thorn in the side of Mrs Thatcher's Conservative Government and was given the sobriquet 'Red Ken' by the tabloid press, for his support for left-wing causes, from CND to sympathy towards Sinn Fein.

Following the abolition of the GLC in 1986, Ken turned his attention to Parliament and secured the nomination as the Labour Candidate for Brent East at the 1987 General Election.

However, he never really flourished in the House of Commons in the way he had at County Hall (including being famously denied a Parliamentary office by the Labour Whips, for almost a year).

When the incoming Blair Government recreated a pan-London Government, the Greater London Authority (GLA) and the post of a London-wide Mayor, Livingstone switched again and was elected – and then re-elected – as the new Mayor of London in 2000 and 2004.

A bon viveur, restaurant critic and notable raconteur, 'Red Ken' was arguably the highest profile local Government politician in Britain for over two decades. When I fought him as the Tory 'Sacrificial Lamb' in 1997, his profile in Parliament had diminished, relative to his days of leading the GLC but he still courted controversy, not least due to his ongoing sympathy for the Irish Republican cause.

Nevertheless, his point about an MP having 68,000 "employers", is one that has lived with me ever since and is also one that many other MPs would, in my opinion, do well to remember.

The 1997 General Election

The 1997 General Election campaign was, quite frankly, miserable from a Conservative point of view. John Major's Government was by now tired and bitterly divided by heated disputes over the Maastricht Treaty (see Chapter 8) and most Conservative MPs and activists sensed privately that, after 18 years in power, the Conservatives were almost certainly heading for defeat.

Moreover, the Labour Party by this stage was led by a young, outwardly charming and charismatic Leader in Tony Blair, who many formally Tory voters found unthreatening as a potential Prime Minister. Philip Gould, in his brilliant book about how Labour came to power entitled, "The Unfinished Revolution" explained that while Blair's public mantra was famously "Education, Education, Education", in private he and his team used the alternative slogan of "Reassurance, Reassurance, Reassurance".[32] They succeeded brilliantly in persuading Mr and Mrs Middle Class, living at 1 Acacia Avenue, who had never previously voted Labour in their life, that he was an unthreatening, moderate, Labour Leader offering a fresh start to Britain, after nearly two decades of what had become in the end, tired and bitterly divided Tory rule. It was against this background, with Labour at one point scoring over 50% in one national opinion poll,[33] that I put on my Blue rosette and proceeded to traipse up and down the back streets of Kilburn and Willesden Green, seeking Conservative support. To say that this was a character-building experience doesn't really do it justice. For instance, one night in the winter, just a few months prior to the Election, I was out canvassing a long terraced street called Dartmouth Road, just off Willesden Green High Road. It was a dark and cold evening and I was on my own.

As I began at the top end of the road, it started raining gently and as I worked my way down it, the rain increased in intensity, so that by the time I approached the bottom it was raining so heavily that the water was dripping off the tip of the barber cap that I had been wearing to try and keep dry. However, for some reason I became absolutely determined to get to the end of the road, even though the canvass card that I was attempting to record my results on was turning into papier mâché in my hands. About four doors from the end, I knocked on a door to be confronted by an extremely large man – six foot three if he was an inch – standing in his doorway in a white vest and clearly unimpressed in having been disturbed on a winter's evening, at what by then was about 8:30pm. He took one look at me and bellowed; "Who the bloody hell are you?", to which I replied with the first thing that popped into my head: "Good evening sir, I'm a wet Tory" (something I have not often been accused of since). To give the man his credit, he replied in kind when he said, "Oh you must be that Tory candidate bloke, well I'll give you this son, you've obviously got a sense of humour, but Arsenal are on the telly so do me a favour and bugger off!".

For some reason the ten minute walk back to the Willesden Green Con Club for a hot toddy in the bar seemed to last about an hour and I remember sitting there on my own thinking, "What on earth am I doing here? The Government are extremely unpopular, I am up against a nationally renowned Labour MP, I've gone out on my own and got soaked to the skin and even when it comes to polling day, I know that I am going to get slaughtered anyway, so what's the point?!". Anyone who has ever fought a Parliamentary seat will have felt like this at some point and this particular evening just happened to be my turn.

In total, including the period of the General Election itself (which to make matters worse was a much longer General Election campaign than usual) I fought Ken Livingstone in Brent East for a total of around 26 months, both as the PPC and then as the official, fully fledged candidate, once the Election was called. During those two years, I and my team did not manage to knock on every door in Brent East – but we must have come pretty close. We also leafletted the entire constituency during the General Election and laid on a number of street stalls and other campaigning events as well. Nevertheless, the national picture was extremely depressing and all of us knew in our heart of hearts, that we were going to lose the General Election – the only question was by how much.

Tony Eastman

Tony Eastman was the Association Chairman for most of my tenure as the Conservative Prospective Candidate/Candidate Brent East.

Tony was a doughty campaigner in the Conservative cause. Often accompanied by his great friend, David Benetar, he would be out night after night, either campaigning on the doorsteps or at some Party meeting or other.

Tony was also an absolutely staunch Eurosceptic and a firm opponent of the Maastricht Treaty, which he regarded as ceding too much power to the emergent European Union.

After I moved on from Brent East, Tony Eastman remained involved and helped campaign for David Gauke, my successor as the Conservative Candidate in Brent East in 2005. When Tony sadly passed away several years ago, both David Gauke and I attended his funeral.

The Faxes from the Bunker

I remember one morning, around a week prior to polling day, being alone in the Association Office, with my redoubtable association Chairman, Tony Eastman. The then Conservative Party National Chairman, Brian Mawhinney, in an effort to maintain morale, had been sending out a message around once a week to all

Party activists, attempting to tell them that the campaign was actually going very well. These became affectionately known in our Association as "Mawhinneygrams", and they came through on the old fax machine, one of those that contained a paper roll within it, and which would chug away quite loudly when a fax was coming through. That morning, I remember we had been out leafletting and had come back to the Con Club for lunch and were just collating some more leaflets for the afternoon delivery, when the fax machine suddenly burst into life.

When it had finished coughing and spluttering, Tony tore the fax off and handed it to me. In essence, the message which was entitled, "Dear Conservative Colleague", reported that the campaign was going extremely well and that some of the canvass returns from the marginal constituencies were among the best that we had ever seen. It implored us all to make one last great effort in order to secure John Major a record fifth term in office for the Conservative Party. Tony turned to me and said, "What do you make of this Mark?", to which I replied: "Chairman, of course if you and I were in front of the rest of the Association we would have to maintain morale. However, as I have come to respect you over these last two years and we are alone, I interpret this message to mean three things: One: Berlin will never fall. Two: Our great counter attack across the Oder River, begins at 05:30 tomorrow morning and Three: We will break the will of the enemy to resist with the use of the terror weapons and fight on to ultimate victory". Tony looked at me wistfully and said, "As a Conservative candidate, do you really think you should be talking like that?", to which I replied, "Oh come on Tony, we both know it's completely hopeless, Major is utterly useless, the Party is going to be completely massacred next week and all we can possibly do is fight our little corner of the battle, as effectively and loyally as we can". He looked at me again for a moment and said, "Of course, you are right Mark, that's all that we can do and for whatever its worth, we will do it together".

After a long-drawn-out campaign, we worked hard on Polling Day to persuade as many Conservative voters as we could to go to the polls, but it was clearly hopeless. Again and again people we had down as Conservative supporters made excuses for why they couldn't go and vote that day, and many had difficulty looking me in the eye. I had already steeled myself on the way to the count, which was at Brent Town Hall, that I was going to lose but even I had not really anticipated the scale of the absolute massacre that the Conservative Party was about to suffer that night. The one thing that cheered me up was the thought that while I knew I would lose in Brent East, and although my friend Stewart Jackson, would also lose next door in Brent South, then at least Sir Rhodes Boyson, who was an extremely popular local MP, would hold on in Brent North and that was something that we could celebrate at the count, if nothing else.

The polls closed at 10:00pm and I went back to the small flat in Neasden that I had rented for the campaign and got changed into a suit before turning up at the Town Hall at around about 11:30pm. While I was looking out for my Chairman, a marvellous man named Tony Eastman, I spied a small, solitary figure sitting on his own at the far end of the hall with his head in his hands. When I walked a little closer, I realised it was Sir Rhodes Boyson and I suddenly thought, "Oh my God, he must have lost too".

It turned out that Rhodes had got there early and as soon as he had seen the first ballot boxes opened from his constituency, which he had represented for over 20 years, he instinctively knew that he had been defeated. His Agent was anxiously peering over the ballot papers but the look on Rhodes' face said it all. He knew.

It only got worse as the evening wore on. In Basildon, the Election result had been conducted on its own as it were, but in Brent all three Parliamentary constituencies were being counted simultaneously, side-by-side, on very long tables in the middle of the large auditorium that was built into the Town Hall building. Off to one side was a bar and I remember at one point an almost primeval scream emanating from the bar, followed by a Labour supporter rushing into the middle of the hall and yelling at the top of his voice, "We've got Portillo!". In this he was signifying the defeat of a star of the Tory Cabinet, Michael Portillo, who had just lost his seat elsewhere in North London, in Enfield Southgate. Portillo, at that time a Thatcherite and the darling of the Tory Right, was considered a potential future Tory Prime Minister and the joy of the Labour activists at his defeat was unalloyed. Nevertheless, by the early hours of the morning, it was clear that the Conservative Party, under the hapless leadership of John Major, had suffered one of the worst electoral defeats in its entire history.

I was always meant to lose, as indeed was Stewart Jackson, but Rhodes Boyson had been an extremely hard working and dedicated constituency MP for two decades – but even that didn't save him from the complete electoral Tsunami which engulfed my Party that night. At one point in the middle of all the commotion, I remember standing on my own in a corner of this cavernous hall, almost in a kind of temporary out of body experience, and thinking to myself, "How on earth did it ever come to this?".

For the record, my result in Brent East in the 1997 General Election, was as follows:

Brent East Parliamentary Constituency General Election – 1997

Ken Livingstone	Labour Candidate	23,748
Mark Francois	Conservative Candidate	7,866
Ian Hunter	Liberal Democrat Candidate	2,751
Sean Keeble	Socialist Labour Candidate	466
Andrew Shanks	Pro Life Candidate	218
Miss C Warrilo	Dream Party Candidate	120
David Jenkins	NLP Candidate	103
Labour Majority		15,882
Turnout		45%

In the end, I had managed to keep the swing from Conservative to Labour down to under 15%, which statistically was one of the better results in London that night. Nevertheless, such was the scale of our defeat that arguing about a few percentage points either one way or another in terms of the swing to Labour was really completely irrelevant.

In short, we had been slaughtered and Labour had been swept to power. As I packed up my flat in Neasden, and prepared to hand back the keys, I remember wondering how many years it would take the Conservative Party to recover from such a catastrophic defeat?

The eventual answer being, quite a few.

Brent East Conservatives

Like their earlier counterparts in Basildon, the Conservatives in Brent in the mid-to-late 1990s were pretty passionate campaigners as well.

In the 1980s the London Borough of Brent, in North-West London, had won a reputation as one of the most "Loony Left" Boroughs in the capital, indeed anywhere in the country.

A highly ethnically diverse community, the Labour politicians who ran Brent in the 1980s were already obsessed with the politics of race and identity, long before it became fashionable in political circles elsewhere.

Conversely, the Conservatives in Brent, while paying due regard to these issues, won control of the Borough by campaigning very effectively over a number of years on "pavement politics", such as very high rates, poor domestic repairs, dirty streets and dreadful administration at the Town Hall.

Drawing lessons from well-established Conservative Boroughs, such as Wandsworth and Westminster, the Tories in Brent, led for a number of years by the dynamic Bob Blackman (now the Conservative MP for Harrow East) set about driving radical change in Brent – and they controlled the Council when I was fighting Ken Livingstone in the Brent East constituency.

The Brent East Conservatives were probably a bit more diverse, both ethnically and socially then their Basildon counterparts alongside whom I had first learnt to campaign. Nevertheless, they took their politics equally seriously and were prepared to go out in all weathers to fight for the cause in which they believed.

While most of the Conservative held wards in Brent were in the slightly leafier Brent North constituency, held by the long-standing Conservative MP, Sir Rhodes Boyson, in Brent East, with it's much more urban feel and Labour majority, there was much more of a feeling of "fighting behind enemy lines" – which engenders a certain doughty camaraderie all of its own.

The small but active Association, led by an inspirational chairman in Tony Eastman, never stopped fighting for their cause, despite the seemingly endless setbacks in the dying years of the Major administration, as eighteen years of Tory Government came to a crushing defeat in 1997. It took real guts to put on a blue rosette and go out canvassing in places like Willesden Green and Kilburn in the mid-1990s, but the Association were still up to it, even though, in our heart of hearts, we already knew that the outcome was utterly inevitable.

The Kensington and Chelsea By-Election

I thus returned to Essex to lick my wounds and spent the best part of a week working in the garden, primarily painting the garden fence. Perhaps my one consultation in all of this, was that I asked Karen, the beautiful young girl from Basildon Conservative's that I had started going out with, to move in with me in my home in Langdon Hills (which I had bought several years previously) and I was delighted when she consented and moved in a few days later. Although I now had a live-in partner, with whom I was very happy, I no longer had a Council seat and had just been slaughtered in a Parliamentary one. It seemed like it was going to be a very long haul indeed to get into the House of Commons, not least as the Conservative Party had been reduced to a rump of 165 MPs, out of a total of some 650, (barely a quarter of the House). The sky looked very dark indeed and it was clearly going to take quite a while to realise my ambition of becoming an MP.

One opportunity unexpectedly presented itself in 1999 when a by-election was caused in Kensington and Chelsea, by the sudden death of the sitting Tory MP, the flamboyant Alan Clark. Mr Clark was a great admirer of Margaret Thatcher, a determined foe of Michael Heseltine and famously wrote a hilarious set of diaries, (a copy of which I still have in my bookcase to this day). [34] Alan Clark's death meant the Conservative's had to pick a candidate to fight the forthcoming by-election and, partly out of devilment I applied – and rapidly found myself in the final round!

In the end, there were four candidates in the final. Michael Portillo, Derek Conway (himself a former MP), [35] Warwick Lightfoot, a K&C Councillor and extremely bright Treasury Special Advisor and yours truly. I gave my speech and answered questions from the audience but both they and I knew that I was never going to win. Nevertheless, both Karen and I were treated very generously, and I received a warm round of applause at the end – almost as a sort of consolation prize.

At the end of the evening, to the surprise of absolutely nobody, it was announced that Michael Portillo had been overwhelmingly selected as the Conservative Candidate for the forthcoming by-election. The results themselves were never read out but, by sheer good fortune from my point of view, a journalist on *The Times* newspaper, who was also a Member of the Association and therefore entitled to be present in his own right, wrote up the selection meeting the following morning and, for reasons best known to himself, wrote in his column that I had come second. (Ironically, in a conversation years later with one of the K&C Officers, they told me that they couldn't remember exactly the order of voting, but if anything, they thought that I had probably come third). Nevertheless, thanks to this journalist I was suddenly "the man who had come second to Michael Portillo", and as a result, my hit rate in obtaining interviews in other good Conservative seats around the country went up accordingly.

Michael Portillo

Michael Denzil Xavier Portillo is perhaps one of the most dynamic Leaders the Conservative Party never had. He famously lost his Enfield Southgate seat in the early hours of Friday morning, during the 1997 General Election, which led to the memorable question: "Were you up for Portillo?" He later won the 1999 Kensington and Chelsea by-election handsomely, which allowed him to re-enter Parliament, but he was clearly affected by his experiences.

Initially a staunch Thatcherite, by the time that he stood for the Leadership of the Conservative Party in 2001 he had clearly been "on a journey" that created a more socially Liberal politician, which unsettled many of his more traditional supporters in the Parliamentary Party.

This in turn led to him missing out on the postal ballot run-off among Voluntary Party Members (eventually between Iain Duncan Smith and Kenneth Clarke) by literally just one vote, in the final qualifying ballot among MPs.[36] If just one more Tory MP had voted for Portillo instead of IDS, he would probably have defeated Ken Clarke among the Party's Membership, chiefly because of the Europe issue and would then have gone onto become Leader of the Conservative Party and perhaps one day, even Prime Minister. Thus, can political careers sometimes hang literally, on a single vote.

Several years earlier in 1995, as Defence Secretary, he had got into hot water at the Conservative Party Conference for his so-called "Who Dares Wins" speech, wherein he evoked the famous motto of the SAS in urging Tory representatives in the hall to fight for a victory over Labour, whenever the General Election was to occur. I remember this well, as speaking as the PPC for Brent East (and by a prior arrangement, via Portillo's Parliamentary Private Secretary, my friend, David Amess) I had effectively acted as Portillo's "warm up man" earlier in the debate.

During my speech, I rather enlivened the audience by telling them that "I must confess Mr Chairman, that I do sometimes get just a little bit cheesed off at being lectured by French and German politicians that we, in Britain, are not doing enough to help build a free and independent Europe, when if it hadn't been for us – Perfidious Albion – there wouldn't be a free and independent Europe!.."

However, unusually for Conference, the debate ran slightly ahead of time and so they squeezed in one further speaker from the floor, who was the new PPC for Maidenhead, one Theresa May. As I came off the platform and she replaced me, we nodded briefly to each other, as it was the first time that we had ever met.

Who knew?

Hunting for a seat

I was subsequently interviewed in a number of seats, including in Huntingdon (John Major's previous constituency) but as soon as I revealed that I had been an opponent of the Maastricht Treaty, that was that. As I had ideally wanted an

Essex seat, I was delighted when I managed to get into the final for the Castle Point constituency in South Essex. Ironically, the other two candidates on the night were the previous Conservative MP, Bob Spink (later of UKIP), Philip Hollobone, an absolutely passionate Eurosceptic – even then – and me. So, as somebody quipped on the night, I was the "left-wing candidate" in the final! However, the members selected Bob Spink. I also managed to reach the final in East Devon, where I lost out to former old Etonian, and Guards Officer, Hugo Swire.

Vacancy in Rayleigh

Almost anyone who has finally made it into the House of Commons will probably tell you, perhaps with a drink or two inside them, that at some point whilst hunting for a seat, they got so fed up with the whole process that they very nearly threw in the towel. For instance, I know one good friend, who subsequently became a Cabinet Minister, who had lost in *nine* finals before finally being selected for a relatively safe seat in Surrey.

Perhaps my one great consolation during this period was that I had asked Karen to marry me (I actually proposed to her overlooking Galway Bay in Ireland) and she had consented, so we had arranged to be married in our local parish church, back in Langdon Hills, in the summer of 2000. So, having accepted that I probably wasn't going to get a good seat to fight in this particular electoral cycle, and that I would probably have to wait for the following General Election in 2005/6, we then settled down to concentrate on planning our wedding.

One evening in March 2000, completely out of the blue, I came back from a trip to London to find a voicemail message on my answer phone from someone in the Rayleigh Conservative Association, privately alerting me that earlier that evening the sitting Conservative MP, Michael Clark, had unexpectedly announced at the Association Annual General Meeting, his decision to stand down at the forthcoming General Election. This meant they would obviously need to select a new candidate to fight the seat and moreover would probably want to do it quickly. Not only was this an Essex constituency (about 15 minutes down the A127 from where we were living in Langdon Hills), but it also had the added attraction of having a very healthy Conservative majority of 10,684 over Labour, in 1997. Moreover, in 1992, when we had been busy defending Basildon, Michael Clark had come over to help out in David Amess' campaign, before being re-elected in his own seat (then named Rochford) by just over 21,000 votes.

I have always tried to steer clear of using the term "safe seat" (partly because of what Ken Livingstone had taught me and also because it implies that you are somehow taking the electorate for granted) but nevertheless, most political commentators would have regarded Rayleigh as a Conservative safe seat and, as well as being a beautiful part of the country, and located moreover in my home county of Essex, it was therefore definitely a prize worth having.

However, one significant problem was that when the Rayleigh Association agreed their timetable for the interviews, the first round, which was to be held at Renouf's Hotel in Rochford, was set slap bang in the middle of our honeymoon, in Canada. We therefore had to take an acid decision about whether or not I would fly back from Canada or, alternatively, we would honeymoon somewhere else or, perhaps, I would even have to pass up the whole opportunity in its entirety. In the end, Karen was very understanding, and we agreed to switch the honeymoon from Canada to Norfolk – which would enable me to travel backwards and forwards to Rayleigh far more easily. However, this is just one example of how, right from the very beginning, politics continually got in the way of our marriage.

The Legend of the Boris interview

In the end, around 160 wannabe candidates applied for the plum vacancy in Rayleigh and, as with other Associations, a Selection Committee was formed to help sift through all the applicants and to conduct the initial round of interviews. One of the other candidates who applied was the then Editor of *The Spectator* magazine, one Boris Johnson. Even to this day, Members of my Association still tell the legend of Boris' interview, which, as ever with this extraordinary man, was completely different from everyone else's.

What actually happened was that the Selection Committee decided to interview around 20 people, spread across a weekend. Boris and I were on separate days, so our paths did not cross. In the event, he was interviewed on the Saturday and I was on the Sunday. However, even in those days, Boris was something of a name (though of course nothing compared to now) and the local paper, *The Echo*, reported that Boris Johnson had been called for an interview by the Rayleigh Conservative Association and that he was due to arrive in a Rolls Royce.[37] This was completely untrue. On the day, Boris came down from London on the train and disembarked at Rochford station, for the less than 10-minute walk to the hotel. However, perhaps fortunately for me, on that day there was freak weather and Boris was ingulfed in a shower of almost neo-biblical rain, so that by the time he got to the hotel, without a raincoat or even an umbrella to protect him, he was, quite literally, soaked to the skin. The Association Members took pity on him and managed to find him temporary access to a room, where he was handed a large towel and given an opportunity to dry off as best he could. Nevertheless, as there were multiple candidates, in order to keep to the timetable, he was eventually told that he would have to go through to make his speech. When Boris walked into the room to meet the Selection Committee, he was apparently still dripping water from the ends of his cuffs and his famous mane, having been dried roughly with a towel, had risen up to make him look like something out of the Lion King.

He then proceeded to give (as you would expect) an extremely humorous speech but one in which he barely referred to the constituency at all. His speech was followed by 20 minutes of questions, the first one of which was, "Mr Johnson, what is your opinion of PPG3?". For the record, PPG3 stood for the old Planning Policy Guidance Note 3, issued by the then Department of the Environment, which governed the touchy subject of when you could and could not build in the Green Belt.[38] To this day, the whole issue of development remains the greatest local political issue in the constituency and was thus of obvious interest to the Members of the Selection Committee, many of whom served either on Rochford District Council, or the higher tier Essex County Council, or in some cases, both.

To this question, Boris famously replied, "Yup, erm, PPG3. Seminal. Fundamentally important to everything that the modern Conservative Party is trying to achieve…Never heard of it!". This was met with some hilarity by the Selection Committee, but as they proceeded to ask him subsequent questions about planning and indeed other issues relating to the constituency, it rapidly became apparent that not only did he barely know where he was, he had done absolutely no research about the constituency whatsoever and had effectively turned up with a generic speech and hoped to bluff his way through. Luckily for me, the Selection Committee weren't having any of it, and, although they clearly found him very amusing, he never progressed to the second round.

Conversely, when I turned up on the Sunday morning, having served on Basildon Borough Council and indeed as Vice Chairman and even Acting Chairman of the Housing Committee, I did indeed know what PPG3 was and was thus able to give a fairly comprehensive answer. Also, as I had lived in the county since the age of six, I knew quite a lot about Essex and indeed a fair bit about Rayleigh and I therefore had some intuitive understanding of what the Selection Committee might be interested in. In addition, the Chairman of the Selection Committee, Hilton Brown, very sportingly mentioned to the Committee that I had interrupted my honeymoon to attend the interview. Therefore, Boris never got through, the first round, whereas I did. I have teased him about this a number of times down the years – which perhaps explains why I do not serve in his Cabinet and most probably never will!

I made it to the final, which took place at the Mill Hall Arts and Events Centre in the centre of Rayleigh, with something like 100 or so Association Members present. I was up against two other candidates, one of whom worked for an Investment Bank in London and the other of whom had been a speech writer for William Hague, the Leader of the Conservative Party, a point he played upon mercilessly during his speech.

By this stage, I had decided that this was the seat I really did want to represent in Parliament, and I threw my heart and soul into preparing for the final. Not only did I do a whole bunch of additional research on the constituency, I actually rehearsed my speech ten times – including three full "dress rehearsals" in my best suit, on the morning itself, before delivering it. After the speech and questions, the Association also added in a "Question Time" type panel at the end, which was chaired by the Association Chairman, Mr Hilton Brown.

After the Members had voted, I still remember vividly the moment when Hilton Brown walked in to the "Green Room" next door, went up to the first candidate and smiled, walked on to the second and did the same and then walked up to me and said: "This has been an extremely difficult choice as we had three excellent candidates before us this afternoon. But in the end, only one person can be the winner and I'm delighted to tell you, Mark, that it is you. Congratulations, you are now our Prospective Parliamentary Candidate for this constituency at the General Election".

Candidate

Karen and I were married on the 30th June 2000, at St Mary's Church in Langdon Hills and with all our friends and family moved on to a reception at Orsett Hall. I remember it as a very joyous occasion at which a number of my Italian relatives, including Zia Carla, Zia Ada's daughter, Lena, and my cousin, Michele, were present. Indeed, I attempted a small part of my groom's speech in Italian, to thank them for making the effort to be present to share in the day. We subsequently moved into a home in Rayleigh, in the run up to Christmas 2000 and I began in earnest to plan for the forthcoming General Election, which seemed increasingly likely to be held the following year.

The 2001 General Election

Even though I had effectively inherited a majority of over 10,000 votes from Michael Clark, given what had happened to the Tory Party in 1997, and also that, at that time at least, Tony Blair remained a relatively popular Labour Prime Minister, I took absolutely nothing for granted and fought the constituency as if it were a marginal seat.

We did a great deal of door knocking and leafletting and I attended a public hustings at Holy Trinity Church in Rayleigh at which the other candidates were present. The key Conservative campaign in the 2001 General Election was "Keep the Pound" which was led enthusiastically by William Hague, the Tory Leader.

Nevertheless, as I knocked on door after door, it gradually became apparent that the electors, in 2001 at least, did not see William as a potential Prime Minister. I don't know whether it was something to do with his hair, his accent or the baseball cap that he had unfortunately been photographed in a couple of years previously, but, whilst Tony Blair still very much "looked the part" as a Prime Minister, at that time at least, William Hague did not.

Had he been the Tory Leader some years later, for instance after his very accomplished stretch as Foreign Secretary, under David Cameron, the result might have been completely different but, in 2001, William Hague was a hard sell, although I continued to defend him to the end.

On Polling Day itself, the result in the Rayleigh constituency was as follows:

Rayleigh Parliamentary Constituency General Election – 2001

Mark Francois	Conservative Candidate	21,434
Paul Clark	Labour Candidate	13,144
Geoff Williams	Liberal Democrat Candidate	6,614
Colin Morgan	UK Independent Candidate	1,581
Conservative Majority		8,290
Turnout		61%

At the election count on the night, I thanked my campaign team for their extremely hard work and was given a note by the Returning Officer, confirming that I had been formally elected to the House of Commons, to serve as the new Member of Parliament for Rayleigh. So, after all those years of striving, I was finally to be sent to Westminster to serve as an MP – a lifetime's dream was about to come true.

That weekend a letter arrived at home from the Conservative Chief Whip, James Arbuthnot MP, congratulating me on my election and inviting me to attend the House of Commons for a meeting at 9:30am the following Tuesday, in Committee Room 14 of the Palace of Westminster, to begin my induction as a Conservative MP.

It was thus that I went up to the House of Commons, for the first time since my visit with my mother aged 11, to begin a Parliamentary career. When I walked through the main entrance at Carriage Gates for the first time, I had absolutely no idea whatsoever of the dramas which would unfold and even less of an inkling that I would one day be intimately involved in some of them.

Hilton

W H Brown (or "Hilton" Brown as he is universally known) is something of a local political legend in South Essex and has undoubtedly been the bedrock of the Rayleigh Constituency Conservative Association for well over two decades. A canny Scot, he moved south decades ago to work as a senior manager for the Royal Bank of Scotland in the City of London (when, as he likes to say: "It was still a proper bank").

Hilton is widely respected throughout the constituency, even by his political opponents. A stickler for the rules, he has served as the Association Chairman on several occasions over the last twenty years and still continues to serve to this day, as the Association's popular President.

As far as I know, Hilton has never sought public office himself (other than perhaps at the Caledonian Club, of which he is an active Member) but he has put in literally thousands of hours in helping other Conservative's to be elected, from local Councillors to Members of Parliament. For this considerable effort, he was given a special lifetime achievement award by the Conservative Party, several years ago.

Hilton has also been my successful Election Agent at six General Elections, and we have evolved a practice where we swap our best guess of the eventual result in respective sealed envelopes on polling day and then open them at the count that evening to see who was closest.

I habitually lose this competition and indeed on one occasion Hilton correctly predicted the Labour vote across the constituency to within three votes of the eventual total, of slightly over 10,000!

However, back in 2000 Hilton chaired the initial Selection Committee and then the final Association General Meeting at which I was officially selected to become the Conservative Candidate for Rayleigh. He has thus played a pivotal role in my political career for over 20 years, for which I am extremely grateful.

Finally, Hilton is one of the straightest, most reliable and dependable men I know, unflappable in virtually all circumstances – except perhaps when his beloved Glasgow Rangers are playing Celtic.

Chapter 5: Into Parliament and Working for George

A Dream Come True – Welcome to Big School

I have often likened going to the House of Commons as a newly elected MP to that transition that you make when going from Junior School to Senior School in your youth. Suddenly, you are in the middle of a big building, where everyone appears to be in a hurry and knows exactly where they are going, except for you. There are all sorts of rules and procedures you have to assimilate very quickly and there are a bunch of sometimes gruff prefects – called the Whips Office – to tell you off if you get it wrong. It is indeed a great deal to take in, particularly as the job begins on day one.

Your constituents start contacting you right from the moment that you arrive and there is no opportunity to "play yourself in" as in cricket. The fact that you are brand new is not the most important thing in the mind of a constituent, who tells you they urgently need your help, particularly when they add that they just voted for you to boot!

The first thing that newly elected MPs do in the Chamber of the House of Commons is to assemble as part of the whole House, in order to elect the Speaker, under Standing Order No. 1. In this case, the incumbent Speaker, Michael Martin, an avuncular Scottish Labour MP, was standing for re-election, which is formally proposed by the "Father of the House" (the longest continually serving MP)[39] and in this case, Michael Martin was reappointed as Speaker unopposed. Once the Speaker is appointed, his next duty is to ensure that each individual MP takes the Oath of Allegiance to Her Majesty, under his watchful eye, sitting in the Speaker's Chair.

Maiden Speech – Against the EU Treaty of Nice

In addition, another major hurdle I had to overcome (like any new boy or girl) was making my Maiden Speech. This is quite a psychological hurdle as it represents the first time you have ever spoken in the House of Commons. Previously, Members would often wait many months before making their Maiden Speech in the House, wanting to spend a lot of time in the Chamber to better understand the dynamics of the place and in order to prevent embarrassment by piling in too early as it were. However, given our sparse numbers in the Commons, only 166 MPs, of which the newbies now made up almost 20%, we were encouraged by the Whips to make our Maiden Speeches as soon as we felt able, so that we could actually be of some use to the wider Party in subsequent debates.

By this stage, I was not an out and out Eurosceptic *per se*, but I had campaigned strongly to Keep the Pound and I was certainly wary of the growing power of what had become the European Union over the everyday lives of the people of the United Kingdom. I therefore chose to make my Maiden Speech in the debate on the Ratification of the Treaty of Nice, a subsequent Treaty following on from Maastricht and Amsterdam, which further enhanced the power of the European Institutions.[40]

After quite some preparation, I delivered the speech on the 4th July 2001. In accordance with Parliamentary tradition, I furiously rubbed one of the feet of the statue of Winston Churchill standing in Member's Lobby, guarding the entrance to the House of Commons. The tradition is that new Members making their Maiden Speech, rub Churchill's foot, in the hope that some of his great oratory will rub off on them when they come to speak. Realistically, however, the ambition of most MPs at this point in their career is not necessarily to deliver something along the lines of Churchill's historic "We shall never surrender" speech in June 1940,[41] but merely to survive the ordeal in one piece. This is certainly where I set the bar that afternoon as I walked into the Chamber.

As it turned out, there were two other Conservative MPs who had also elected to make their Maiden Speeches on that day, Mark Prisk and Mark Hoban, so we were rapidly nicknamed, Mark 1, Mark 2 and Mark 3. For want of any better way of working out the order of speaking, they decided to call us in alphabetical order and so I went first. If I am honest, I think the two minutes before I stood up to deliver that speech was probably the most frightening experience of my life.

And then the moment came. Speaker Martin turned to me and called, "Mr Mark Francois". He also indicated to the House that this was a Maiden Speech, which means by tradition that no one attempts to intervene or interrupt your remarks. In Parliamentary terms, this is the one free run that you ever get and so I decided to make the most of it.

A Maiden Speech, like Roman Gaul, is traditionally divided into three parts. In one part of it, by way of introduction, you describe your constituency to the House of Commons and say how lucky you are to represent it. I did indeed feel very lucky to represent Rayleigh, so this was no problem. Secondly, you mention your predecessor and pour praise upon them, even if they were an opponent you have just defeated and deep down you actually hated their guts. In my case, this most certainly did not apply as I had a deep respect for Michael Clark, who had represented the constituency with distinction for 18 years and had been exceptionally friendly to me ever since I was adopted as the candidate. So, I was very happy to say nice things about Michael and indeed his very popular wife, Valerie, as part of my remarks. In the third part of the speech, you are meant to at least genuflect to whatever the topic is that the House is supposed to be debating that evening, so at this point, I actually mentioned Europe.

In essence, my argument was that when the British people had voted in the Referendum in 1975, they had voted to remain in a "common market" and that since then the European Institutions had massively expanded their power over the UK, in each case doing so without a Referendum and therefore, in my opinion, not really enjoying proper public consent to do so.

In fact, I went on to prophecy that if this process continued, there would eventually be trouble ahead:

"I am in favour of enlargement of the European Union in principle, but not at any price. I have an affection for the Republic of Ireland; I proposed to my wife Karen while overlooking Galway bay. The next time I visit, I would like to congratulate the people of that country on their sagacious decision to vote against the Nice treaty, and by such a clear margin.

Whatever the views of any Member of the House on the European issue, when a country as traditionally pro-European as the Irish Republic votes against a European treaty, that should, at the very least, give us all pause for thought. I confess that I was not quite old enough to vote in the British referendum in 1975, but I believe there was no real practical discussion of a federal Europe or of abandoning our currency. *The British people were essentially told that they were assenting to a free trade area—a common market—and that is what they endorsed in 1975. The further we move from that position, the greater the risk that we shall exhaust their patience on all things European.* We are an historically tolerant people, and we are willing to negotiate and co-operate, but we will not be subsumed by a foreign Superstate that ignores our traditions and undermines our laws".[42] (emphasis added).

I also made a point of mentioning my father and his Service in World War II, a thing I had promised myself I would always do, if and when I was eventually elected to Parliament. In total the whole ordeal lasted around ten minutes or so and when I sat down at the end, I experienced the most amazing feeling of relief. I had not wowed them in the aisles, but neither had I cocked it up and those around me told me that it had been a very fair opening innings, which was really all I was seeking to achieve. I sat through the debate and listened to Mark Hoban and Mark Prisk deliver two very good Maiden Speeches before finally retiring to the Terrace and opening a bottle of Champagne with Karen and the rest of her family, to celebrate my survival. As I was walking out of the Chamber, on the way to meet them, I remember one of the Door Keepers winking and saying to me: "Well done, Mr Francois, Sir. Go and enjoy a drink, you've earnt it".

Oral Questions – Remember Rule One!

Once you had made your Maiden Speech, you were then eligible to ask an Oral Question of Ministers from a Government Department, at Departmental Question Time. Each Parliamentary day begins with the Speaker's Procession, followed by Prayers conducted by the Speakers Chaplain ("the Padre") and then up to an hour of Questions to Ministers of a Government Department. The Department's rotate on a regular cycle and normally each Department has an Oral Question session around every four to five weeks. My first Oral Question was to the Home Office, about anti-social behaviour in Rayleigh.

The Home Secretary that day was the Labour stalwart, David Blunkett MP,[43] and as Question 7 was drawing to a close, I was sitting in my place running through in my head the question that I was about to ask – which, corny though I know it sounds, I had rehearsed in front of the bathroom mirror several times the night before. Just as I was playing this through in my mind, the fellow newbie to my left said: "You've got the next question, haven't you?", to which, distracted, I replied "What?". He repeated his enquiry, "You've got the next question, haven't you? Question 8?". "Yes", I said, slightly irritated, "Why?". "Remember Rule One of all political life", he said. "What?" I responded. "Remember Rule One of all political life". "What's that?", I said. "Don't fuck it up", he quietly replied, so as not to be overheard by the microphones in the Chamber. At that instant, Speaker Martin called me, and I stood up and said, "Number 8 Sir". When the Home Secretary gave his reply, I then bobbed up to complain about anti-social behaviour in Rayleigh on a Friday night and what on earth were the Government doing about it? I sat down having opened my account in this regard and turned to my interlocutor and said, "How was that?". "Fine", he said, "I think that went well. By the way, I know who you are. You're Mark Francois, because your name's on the Order Paper. But we've not really met yet – my name is George Osborne". Thus, did I first meet a future Chancellor of the Exchequer.

The Kundan Group

Just as at school, it is natural to make friends in the first instance with the other new kids in your class, so in Parliament you naturally make friends with the fellow Members of your intake – because you are all effectively in the same boat. A small group of us became friends and got into the habit of going out for dinner to a somewhat downmarket Indian restaurant at the junction of Horseferry Road and Millbank, called "The Kundan".[44] This was by no means a "political dining club" in the classic mould, such as the Blue Chips or the '92 Group,[45] rather this was merely a bunch of newly elected MPs going out for a curry and a gossip and a chance to swap experiences.

The six members of that group were, Mark Hoban and Mark Prisk (alongside whom I had made my Maiden Speech), Chris Grayling, Paul Goodman, a Scottish Tory MP called Peter Duncan and myself. Down the years, a number have left Parliament for one reason or another and today only Chris Grayling and I remain. Nevertheless, back in 2001, we all became firm friends, and our paths were to criss-cross on numerous occasions in the years ahead.

The CFI trip to Israel – With Boris and George

As well as your constituency duties, and your duties in the House of Commons, you will sometimes be invited to be part of an overseas delegation, to visit another part of the world. There are a whole series of All Party Parliamentary Groups (APPGs), one for seemingly just about every country on earth, whose job is to improve Parliamentarian's understanding of their country and what it has to offer. Unsurprisingly, each one of these nationally related APPGs attempts to put forward the best possible image of its respective country. In addition, there are some related organisations which attempt to lobby MPs in accordance with their nation's objectives.

One such group is the Conservative Friends of Israel (CFI) which for many years has sought to lobby Conservative MPs on behalf of the state of Israel. As part of this, they have helped to organise a number of delegations down the years to visit Israel and they have been particularly good at seeking out newly elected Conservative MPs in order to try and explain to them Israel's point of view. Early on in my first term in Parliament, I was invited to visit the state of Israel by the Director of CFI, Stuart Polak (now Lord Polak of Hertsmere).[46] Their choice of invitees on this trip was interesting, and the other three politicians going with me were, Theresa Villiers (at that time still an MEP, before she became the MP for Chipping Barnet in 2005), an up and coming Tory backbencher named, George Osborne (he of "Rule One") and another well known, Tory backbencher, even at that stage, called Boris Johnson. The four of us thus set off to spend the best part of a week in Israel, as guests of the Israeli Government.

While we were there, an event took place which I will never forget. At that stage, Boris had not yet flown out (he joined us later) but Theresa, George and I were sitting in a restaurant in Tel Aviv, waiting to meet an Israeli academic who was an expert in suicide bombings. Deeply ironically, whilst we were waiting to meet him, suddenly the mobile phones of all the entourage around us started to go off, all at the same time. Clearly something serious had happened and a couple of minutes later our guide explained to us, in sombre terms, that unfortunately a suicide bombing had just taken place in the old market, in downtown Tel Aviv; that the suicide bomber had died and that apparently a number of other civilians had been badly wounded. He then asked us if we wanted to go and visit the site of the bombing but made the point that if we wanted to go, we would have to go there and then. He also cautioned us that by the time we got there, the media would probably have been alerted and it was possible that they would be on site.

As our Israeli host said quite bluntly: "Look, this is entirely up to you but if you really want to understand what goes on in this country, we will take you there, but you have to decide right now". We then went into a quick huddle and decided that if our purpose in visiting Israel was to find out what was really going on for ourselves, then we felt obliged to go. We accordingly piled into the minibus and were driven at high speed down to the old market area. We got out of the bus about 100 yards short of the incident and then managed to weave our way through the tightly located market stalls (which were rather akin to wooden cabins but with a tarpaulin roof) until we finally got to the stall where the bomb had gone off. I will never forget the sight that greeted us. There was essentially a large black hole in the ground where the bomber, a 16-year-old boy from Ramallah on the West Bank, had been standing when he detonated his explosive vest. Most of the rest of the kiosk was badly charred and already there were specially trained Jewish volunteers in high-vis vests, standing on ladders, putting small pieces of the innocent victims into specially designed plastic bags.

In the midst of this, running down the alleyway between the market stalls came, Orla Guerin, the Middle East Correspondent of the BBC, who had indeed heard what had happened and who then realised that there were three British politicians at the scene. Suddenly the camera lights were turned on and a microphone was shoved under our chins and Orla Guerin asked the three of us what we thought this development meant for peace in the Middle East?

While I was desperately thinking of something to say, George essentially took command of the situation, looked into the camera, and said extremely calmly that whilst this was clearly a tragedy, it in no way was likely to contribute to a long-term solution of the problems in the Middle East, which could only ultimately be achieved by peaceful negotiation, on the basis of a two-state solution. Orla then proceeded to effectively interview George for the next five minutes (which was apparently then broadcast back home on Newsnight that evening). Theresa also chipped in, whilst as far as I can remember, I was too taken aback by the whole tragic incident to have very much to contribute. I remember being struck at the time not just by how horrific the whole sight was but also how incredible coolly and calmly George dealt with the whole thing, including handling what could otherwise have been an extremely difficult interview. All the media training I had done to that date had not really prepared me for what I saw in front of me, but George dealt with it extremely professionally and I think it was perhaps at that moment that I began to realise that this young man was marked out for higher things.

We were subsequently joined several hours after the incident by Boris, whose old journalistic instincts had clearly kicked in and who said that he was determined to try and get to Ramallah to interview the mother of the deceased suicide bomber. The Israeli authorities were adamant that because of the bombing the West Bank had been placed into lockdown, Ramallah especially, and that there was no prospect whatsoever of Boris getting through.

Nevertheless, true to his word, a large white land rover turned up at our hotel during breakfast the following morning, with the words "Press" emblazoned down the side and Boris leapt in and drove off with some media friends in an attempt to conduct his interview. In the end, the West Bank was indeed locked down and Boris never got anywhere near Ramallah, but despite being on a CFI organised trip, he had endeavoured to try and understand the issue from a Palestinian point of view as well. Nevertheless, that incident cast a bit of a shadow over what was otherwise an extremely interesting trip to arguably one of the most fascinating countries on earth.

On a slightly more light-hearted note, a couple of days later we were taken to inspect the "security wall", used to divide parts of Israel from the wider West Bank. In fact, at that time at least, much of the wall was still under construction and so much of the barrier actually comprised a wire fence, albeit one packed with sophisticated sensors and overseen by a myriad of CCTV cameras.

We were shown into a command centre, which included banks of TV screens, closely monitored by Israeli soldiers doing their National Service. It was stressed to us how extremely sensitive the fence's sensors were, to try and prevent any security breaches. Following our briefing, we were promptly taken outside to inspect the fence in person, whereupon Boris suddenly took it upon himself to perform an impromptu test of the system. He grabbed the fence and started shaking it, whilst exclaiming: "So what happens if I do this then?"

As we looked on in horror, about one minute later, a jeep containing four Israeli soldiers, armed to the teeth, came hurtling over the ridge and an Israeli Sergeant leapt out and bellowed: "Who grabbed the bloody fence?!" to which the other three of us bravely replied: "He did!" Boris has always had a bit of a mischievous streak and it was certainly on display that afternoon – and even what could only be described as a stern bollocking from an Israeli NCO didn't seem to dampen it materially. However, judging by the initial outraged expression on the Sergeant's face, Boris was lucky not to have been shot – in which case the recent history of the United Kingdom would have been rather different!

Whatever view one takes of the Middle East issue, which is undoubtedly complex, I still think George's instinctive response was right. Ultimately, the issues of the Middle East, including Israel and the fate of the Palestinians on the West Bank, and in Gaza, will only be resolved by peaceful negotiation rather than by force, and I very much hope that one day, such a peaceful outcome may yet come to pass.

"The Chief Whip wants to see you!"

A few months later, I was sitting in the Chamber with my now good friend and Kundan dining partner, Mark Hoban, when one of the Conservative Whips, Dr Julian Lewis, came into the Chamber and asked us both if we were waiting to speak in the House. When we both confirmed that we weren't, we were just in there to get the feel of the debate, he replied, "Good, in that case, the Chief Whip wants to see both of you right now". Rather startled I enquired, "What about Julian?" To which he replied: "The quicker you get yourself down there, the quicker you'll find out!". Being called to see the Chief Whip was not always a good sign and was rather akin to being called into the Headmaster's Study at school. Sometimes this would be to receive praise, but often not and so it was, with a sense of trepidation that brother Hoban and I made our way down to the Opposition Chief Whip's office, just off Members Lobby. By the time that we emerged, we had both been promoted to the Opposition Whip's Office!

House of Cards – Into the Tory Whips Office

The following morning, at 11:00am, I presented myself at the Conservative Whips Office, alongside my friend Mark Hoban and also Angela Watkinson, the Member of Parliament for Upminster and also a Member of the 2001 intake, who was the third newbie to be invited to join the Whips Office. We thus entered into one of the inner sanctums of Parliament. The Whips Office is very much the "Operations Room" of the House of Commons, and it is the job of the Whips to keep the whole show on the road and to try and organise matters, such that procedure in Parliament runs as smoothly as possible, whilst also seeking to ensure that both Government and Opposition have their say.

Serving in the Whips Office is the most marvellous apprenticeship for learning about how Parliament really works. I have likened it to friends to standing behind the theatre curtain in a theatre and seeing how the scenery is moved around and the ropes and pulleys are exercised, in keeping the whole show going out on stage. You learn a lot about the finer points of Parliamentary procedure and have an opportunity to work with experienced Shadow Ministers or Ministers and to learn from them along the way.

Each Whip is normally assigned to support one or more Departmental teams, and as the Junior Whip I was given a relatively gentle start by being assigned to the Shadow Department for Culture, Media and Sport (DCMS Team). There is a strong spirit of camaraderie in the Whips Office – and a considerable degree of banter – and I soon learned that the only way to survive was to give as good as you get. Nevertheless, there was a real sense of being part of a team effort, particularly as we were hopelessly outnumbered in the Chamber by the Labour Party, who were guaranteed to win almost any vote by a substantial majority.

Home Affairs Whip – and dealing with Cameron

After some six months in the Whips Office, Iain Duncan Smith carried out a reshuffle, which had been partially pre-empted by John Bercow's resignation from the Front Bench (over his opposition to Iain Duncan Smiths' policy on gay adoption). As a result of this, I was "bumped up" within the Whips Office and moved to a more demanding role as Home Affairs Whip. This was important, because part of Tony Blair's legislative programme was to be "tough on crime and tough on the causes of crime" and this involved quite a large number of complex Bills, such as Criminal Justice Bills, relating to Home Office matters. As the Home Office Whip, it was my job to keep the Shadow Front Bench team, led by the Shadow Home Secretary, Oliver Letwin, informed of any intelligence about the likely progress of this legislation, so that Shadow Ministers could allocate their time accordingly and prepare to debate the relevant Bills, both in the Chamber of the House of Commons and in more detail upstairs, in Committee, sometimes for months at a time.

At one time, I was also David Cameron's personal Whip and when I denied him an afternoon off to attend a Carlton TV Board meeting (because he'd only asked me that morning) he was furious! However, he subsequently asked me for time off to attend a medical appointment for his disabled son, Ivan, which I granted without question – and said if he ever needed further time off for that reason, I would do whatever I could to help. In return, he wrote me a charming note. Even then, you could sense that this highly articulate new MP was going to ascend the greasy pole – in fact, within just three years, he was to become the new Leader of the Conservative Party.

George joins the Whips Office

In addition, the Office was joined in this reshuffle by a new Junior Whip, George Osborne. The Opposition Whips Office in the House of Commons is basically one big, long thin room, and the desks were organised with the two most junior Whips sat right at the back and then moving in ascending order to the Deputy Chief Whips own office, at the top of the room (with the Opposition Chief Whip in their own separate office round the corner, just off Members Lobby). I therefore spent the next six months, basically sharing a desk with George Osborne, during which time we became relatively good friends, both learning how to operate as Whips and sharing confidences about some of our colleagues along the way.

George was one of the most "political" MPs I had ever met, with a very alert mind and a constant fascination for why senior politicians behaved in a particular way. George was forever asking me "Why do you think they've done this?" or "What do you think motivated X or Y to do that?" and we would often debate these questions in hushed tones, at the far end of the Whips Office.

IDS

Iain Duncan Smith, a former Scots Guards officer first elected to Parliament in 1992 is known almost universally at Westminster by his initials, "IDS". He first came to prominence early on, as a new Member of the 1992 intake who was prepared to join the Maastricht Rebellion, against John Major's Bill to ratify the Maastricht Treaty.

Other 1992 "newbies" who joined this cause included Bernard Jenkin and John Whittingdale (all three of whom still remain in the House of Commons, almost thirty years on).

The son of a WWII Spitfire pilot, "Smithy" Duncan Smith, IDS has always held strong views on the European issue, which is one of the reasons why, having beaten Michael Portillo by just one vote to reach the final of the 2001 Conservative Leadership Contest, IDS went on to defeat the more experienced but Europhile Kenneth Clarke convincingly in the postal ballot of Members of the Voluntary Party.

However, from the word go, it was clear a number of Conservative MPs, centred around the former Whips Office during the battles over Maastricht, were reluctant to accept his authority, despite IDS having been clearly elected by the wider Party Membership. This led to something of a whispering campaign against his Leadership from the outset, which culminated in the 2003 Conservative Party Conference where he was confronted with claims about alleged irregularities in the running of his Parliamentary office – all of which subsequently turned out to be completely untrue.

Nevertheless, this smear, combined with temporary poor poll ratings against Tony Blair, contributed to IDS losing a Vote of Confidence among Conservative MPs (in which I was one of the few remaining Members of the Whips Office to vote for him).

Whereas some MPs might well have descended into a long sulk at this misfortune, IDS instead rapidly dusted himself off and effectively reinvented himself as a campaigner for social justice, helping to found the think tank, the Centre for Social Justice (CSJ) and spending time investigating real life conditions in some of the most deprived estates in Britain, including the notorious "Easterhouse Estate" in Glasgow.

When the Conservatives returned to Government, albeit in Coalition under David Cameron, this knowledge was put to good use when IDS returned to the Cabinet as Secretary of State for Work and Pensions, during which time he oversaw major reform of the welfare system, culminating in the introduction, after some delays, of Universal Credit, which superseded Gordon Brown's extremely complicated system of tax credits – a system so fiendishly complex that often many of the officials administering it could barely understand it, let alone their clients.

During the Battle for Brexit, IDS remained one of the most prominent members of the European Research Group, although as a former Party Leader, quite understandably perhaps, he always retained some sympathy for the plight of Theresa May.

IDS became Chairman of Boris Johnson's successful Leadership campaign in 2019 but was not rewarded with high office thereafter. Nevertheless, he still remains one of the most influential backbenchers in Parliament, as well as being an absolute gent.

Separation and divorce

When I was first elected in mid-2001 I could not have been happier. I had a job I had always dreamed of, a lovely wife, a decent home and what I hoped was a bright future ahead of me. However, politics does have a way of taking over your whole life if you let it and, as it were, I "dived into the swimming pool headfirst" without a thought of the knock-on effect on those around me. When a marriage breaks down it is always a sad thing and I don't think it would be appropriate in these pages to go into detail about what happened but, suffice to say, that I didn't afford Karen anything like the time and attention that I should have done. Remember, we had even had to reschedule our honeymoon because of the first interview in Rayleigh and then the summer after I was elected, we weren't able to take a proper holiday either, because I had become so absorbed in the Iain Duncan Smith Leadership campaign around the country. Working in the Whips Office can be extremely intense – and it certainly was at that time – and I see, with hindsight, that Karen tried to tell me on a number of occasions she was feeling neglected, but the truth is, I was so self-absorbed in what I was doing, I didn't really hear what I was being told, until it was too late. As a result, Karen and I separated in the spring of 2003 and we eventually divorced fairly amicably in 2006.

Mum dies

2003 was a very rough year for me because of the separation and, the following year, I received another severe blow when my mother, Anna, died of a heart attack, aged 70. The truth is that despite my pleading with her to do otherwise, mother continued to smoke, regularly for many years and eventually this did considerable damage to her lungs. She was diagnosed with Chronic Obstructive Pulmonary Disease (COPD) and eventually succumbed to a heart attack. So, aged 39, I buried my mother, next to her beloved husband, Reg, as she had always desired, in the same plot. One thing I remember is that my father's old employer, Shell, who had a rather paternalistic network which kept an eye on Shell pensioners such as mum, sent a representative to my mother's funeral, 25 years after my father had died in their employ. I have never forgotten that kind gesture and I have been grateful to the company ever since.

Michael Howard becomes Leader

Following Iain Duncan Smith's resignation, a full blown Leadership contest was averted when Conservative MPs, perhaps influenced by the bruising events of the previous few months, rapidly rallied behind Michael Howard, the former Home Secretary, as a Leader behind whom they could unite, in order to fight what was likely to be a General Election within the next 12-18 months.[47] Micheal was an extremely experienced politician, with a keen lawyer's mind and represented a very steady hand on the tiller. He soon carried out a reshuffle to form a new Opposition Front Bench, as a result of which I found myself moving from the Whips Office to the Shadow Treasury team under the new Shadow Chancellor, Oliver Letwin.

Working for George – Shadow Treasury Minister

So, in 2004 I moved on from the Tory Whips Office to join the Shadow Treasury team, headed up by Oliver Letwin as Shadow Chancellor with the rapidly promoted George Osborne, as Chief Secretary to the Treasury (responsible for scrutinising public spending in particular). As the junior member of the team, I was the Shadow Economic Secretary, responsible for indirect taxation (VAT, Customs Duties etc).

My only real economic background up to that point was a Grade A in A-level Economics and three months or so very junior experience as a graduate trainee in the City with Lloyds Bank. Nevertheless, I was now expected to lock swords with Ministers at HM Treasury, who would, of course, be supported by the full panoply of the Civil Service.[48]

In order to help me do this I cast around for a new researcher, with an economic background, and I subsequently appointed a young man called Christopher Howarth, who like me, had served in the Territorial Army in his youth but also had a legal training and had worked as an accountant for KPMG.

I owe Chris a great deal of gratitude for helping to get me through my years on the Shadow Treasury team as a Shadow Treasury Minister, assisted by a number of other experts who were sympathetic to the Party. For instance, the first time I had to do a mini debate about a piece of secondary legislation relating to VAT, to help brief me, Central Office sent over a bright young accountant on the Candidates List, called Karen Bradley (who some years later was to become the Secretary of State for Northern Ireland).

The 2005 General Election

Eventually in 2005, Tony Blair called a General Election, his third as the Leader of the Labour Party. By now a lot of the shine had begun to wear off the Blair Premiership, not least because of the great national controversy over the decision to go to war in Iraq in 2003. The Labour Party had been deeply split by this decision, including the fact that Blair had failed to secure a second UN resolution in favour of military action. However, as we now know, he had effectively already promised George Bush "I will be with you, whatever".[49]

Nevertheless, right or wrong, the whole controversy over what became the Iraq War had continued to rumble on and so Labour went into the 2005 General Election, ahead in the polls but by nothing like the massive margins that they had enjoyed in 1997 or in 2001.[50] In the event, the Conservative Party put up quite a good fight, by focusing on a few key issues, which appeared to resonate with at least parts of the electorate including law and order, immigration and Europe and this time, the Labour majority was cut to less than 70.[51] In Rayleigh I was fighting to be re-elected for the first time and, just as in 2001, I fought it as it if were a marginal seat.

Locally, after a hard-fought campaign (in which we also provided a lot of mutual aid for Jackie Doyle-Price, the Conservative Candidate in highly marginal Thurrock) the results in the Rayleigh constituency were as follows:

General Election Result for the Rayleigh Constituency, 2005

Mark Francois	Conservative Candidate	25,609
Julian Ware Lane	Labour Candidate	10,883
Sid Cumberland	Liberal Democrat Candidate	7,406
Janet Davies	UKIP	2,295
Conservative Majority		14,726
Turnout		64.2%

I was very pleased to increase the Conservative majority from slightly over 8,000 in 2001 to nearly 15,000 in 2005, although having only been an MP for four years, the truth is that the bulk of the credit for this must go to the improvement of the Party's fortunes nationally, compounded with a great deal of hard work by my local Party activists, and only a relatively small amount could be attributed to me.

Nevertheless, as any MP will tell you, it is always rewarding to be re-elected to Parliament for the first time, thus demonstrating that your constituents have been prepared to support you again, after having now seen you in action for several years as their local MP.

Cameron becomes Tory Leader

A few months later, Michael Howard announced his decision to stand down as Leader of the Conservative Party, in order to facilitate a Leadership election, which would allow the leading contenders to lay out their stall at the forthcoming Party Conference in October.

The "breakthrough candidate" was the young and charismatic, David Cameron, who like me was a Member of the 2001 intake and who was offering a more liberal variant of Conservatism to MPs and the Party's Membership. Cameron's campaign manager was his close friend, the Shadow Chief Secretary, and second in command of our Treasury Team, George Osborne.

The story of how David Cameron won the Conservative Party Leadership is a book in itself and is brought out well in his recent memoir "*On the Record*".[52] In fact, it was the most incredible coup, orchestrated by a very tight knit group of friends, almost all of whom had served together with David Cameron, some years previously in the Conservative Research Department (CRD). The old CCO in Smith Square did not have a modern open plan layout but rather the CRD included a long corridor on which individual members of the Department were based. If you walked down that corridor in the 1990s, you would have seen a series of names on the door including George Osborne, Ed Lewellyn, Kate Fall, Ed Vaisey and others, all of whom were key adherents to "Dave" as they would refer to him in private and who made up an exceedingly well organised campaign team, with George co-ordinating their activities in support of their candidate.

Cameron played a blinder at the Party Conference when, rather than the traditional speech from a podium, he addressed the Party Conference, without notes, in a relaxed and confident speech which he had learnt word for word, (including rehearsing it thoroughly in his hotel room at the Conference itself). Cameron took the Conference by storm, whereas his main rival, David Davis' speech never really got off the runway.

For my own part, I resolved to vote for Dr Liam Fox, a Eurosceptic Thatcherite, whose political instincts were perhaps closest to my own but, unfortunately, Liam was knocked out in the earlier rounds of the contest. I then remember receiving a phone call from George who told me "not to sod about" and to join the Cameron campaign, which by this stage was gathering considerable momentum. After a further conversation with George, I did come out for Cameron, along with a number of other former Fox supporters, as the contest narrowed down to Cameron vs Davies, in a postal ballot of Conservative Party members around the country.

Nevertheless, when Sir Michael Spicer eventually announced the result, David Cameron was pronounced the Leader of the Conservative Party by 134,446 (68%) to 64,398 votes (32%), an emphatic majority of over 2:1, and thus his eleven-year reign as Tory Leader began.[53]

George becomes Shadow Chancellor

One of Cameron's first acts as Tory Leader was to appoint his long-term friend and Campaign Manager, George Osborne, as Shadow Chancellor of the Exchequer, meaning that he now headed up the team in which I served.

A little time thereafter, I was also promoted to become the Shadow Paymaster General, effectively the number three in the team, concentrating on taxation issues and shadowing Dawn Primarolo, the MP for Bristol South, affectionately known throughout the House of Commons as "Red Dawn". (She acquired the nickname because when she entered the House of Commons in 1987, it had been very much as a left-wing firebrand although she moderated and moved to the centre as her career evolved and she was now one of Gordon Brown's most trusted lieutenants in the Treasury).

Like me, Dawn did not have a formal economic background, but she had a reputation for sheer hard work and what she didn't know instinctively, she often learnt by rigorous application. We were subsequently to cross swords on a number of occasions both in the House of Commons and upstairs in Committee on the Finance Bill, but I seem to recall it was always good natured. Whilst working on George's Shadow Treasury Team, I occasionally also came up against Ed Balls.

Ed Balls

Edward (Ed) Balls, a former *Financial Times* journalist, was elected as the Member of Parliament for Normanton (later Morley and Outwood) in 2005. Even before his election to Parliament, Ed Balls had already made a name for himself as a prominent and powerful Special Adviser to Gordon Brown, the Chancellor of the Exchequer.

Once elected to Parliament, he was rapidly promoted with the support of his mentor, and soon became a junior Minister at HM Treasury, still working for his master but now as Economic Secretary to the Treasury. He also married fellow Labour MP, Yvette Cooper.

We once very amusingly caught Ed out during a Finance Bill debate on the floor of the House, after Philip Hollobone had remembered chasing him for a vote many years previously during the election of officers for the Oxford University Conservative Association (OUCA). Based on Philip's "testimony", when we challenged Ed in the Commons that he had gone effectively to a private school (Nottingham High School) and then joined the Conservative Party at Oxford, he was visibly embarrassed – and blurted out that he had actually joined all three Political Parties as a student, in order to listen to all of the visiting speakers![54] The whole stunt was rounded off nicely when a new member of the 2005 intake, one David Gauke, intoned that although he too had been to Oxford, he never bothered to join OUCA, because he regarded it as: "full of lefties on the make".

Ed famously lost his seat in the 2015 General Election to the Conservative candidate, Andrea Jenkyns (who would later go on to become a 'Spartan' in 2019). To his credit, Ed didn't sulk about this, and went on to develop an alternative career as an academic and TV personality, perhaps most famously when he appeared in Series 14 of the BBC's *Strictly Come Dancing* and proved popular with the voting public – surviving until week 10 – relatively late on into the competition.

In any event, Ed is one of the few politicians in history to have a day named after him. On 28th April 2011, he accidentally tweeted just his name – Ed Balls – which led to much merriment on Twitter and the subsequent creation of "Ed Balls Day" – which I have even seen commemorated on posters on the London Underground. If only for this reason, we have not heard the last of Ed Balls.

As Shadow Paymaster General I was now primarily responsible for direct, rather than indirect taxation, focusing mainly on the big taxes, such as income tax and National Insurance. Working alongside Christopher Howarth, we did a lot of research into the length and complexity of the UK tax code, eventually managing to demonstrate that we had the second longest tax code in the world, beaten only by India. On a wider point, by this stage we were, as a Team, gradually beginning to achieve some traction in warning the world about the significant amount of borrowing that was being undertaken by the Chancellor, Gordon Brown.

George

Although some of my Brexiteer friends might not thank me for saying it, George Osborne is one of the most capable politicians I have ever met. Political to his fingertips, I believe it was a loss to the House of Commons, when, following the end of David Cameron's Premiership, George stood down from Parliament at the 2017 General Election.

A good leader, generally cool under pressure and with a wicked, even impish, sense of humour, he tended to engender strong loyalty from those who worked for him, be they politicians or staffers. A fellow Member of the 2001 intake, George and my paths crossed on a number of occasions, in the Opposition Whips Office, when I worked for him on the Shadow Treasury Team and then, latterly, when I was Shadow Europe Minister – and was frequently in meetings with George, David and William on European Policy.

George had opened his account as Shadow Chancellor impressively, when he tore into the then Chancellor, Gordon Brown, in response to Brown's Autumn Statement in 2005. I also witnessed him reacting incredibly calmly under pressure in response to Brown's 2007 Budget, which outwardly appeared to reduce income tax by 2p in the pound (which he had achieved by sleight of hand in abolishing the 10% tax rate for the lower paid). George brilliantly summarised this as "it's not a tax cut, it's a tax con!" and won the resultant media war which followed.

On one occasion George kindly came to speak as Guest of Honour at my local Association's gala dinner. My neighbours' kids had asked to meet him beforehand, which eventually resulted in George dressed in Black Tie, bouncing on the trampoline in their back garden (to the utter amazement of my other neighbours, in their own back garden next door).

In the end, we obviously parted company over the 2016 EU Referendum, when George, who apparently pleaded with David Cameron not to hold the Referendum, became a leading member of the campaign to Remain. He retained his pro-EU views when he left Parliament and went on (amongst other posts) to become Editor of the *London Evening Standard*.

We still disagree over Europe – and probably always will – but one way or another, I have a funny feeling that we have not yet heard the last of George Osborne.

Things can change fast in this job

By 2007, I had been working on the Treasury team for three years, been promoted and felt that I enjoyed a good working relationship with George and his two special advisers, Rupert Harrison and Matt Hancock (the latter of whom had been recruited from the Bank of England and was extremely bright but didn't take any trouble to hide it). I had learnt to hold my own on economic matters in the House of Commons Chamber, even on points of technical detail and now had three Finance Bills under my belt. Thanks partly to all the great support from Christopher Howarth, I now felt relatively comfortable in the role and was actually quite enjoying myself.

However, politics has a way of throwing surprises at you, and I was in a pub in London one Saturday afternoon, when I received a call from Ed Llewellyn, David Cameron's Chief of Staff, telling me that Graham Brady had just resigned as the Shadow Europe Minister (due to a dispute over Grammar Schools) and that I had just been promoted to take his place and that moreover, William Hague was waiting to see me. When I asked when, Ed replied: "Now" and thus I switched from the Shadow Treasury Team to the Shadow Foreign Affairs Team in the midst of one pint and suddenly found myself dealing not with budgetary matters but rather with the vexed issue of Europe.

Chapter 6: Working for William –
and Fighting the Lisbon Treaty

Having spent a very enjoyable three years working for one of the Tory Party's brightest stars, George Osborne, following my phone call with Ed Llewellyn in a pub, I suddenly found myself working for another star in the Conservative firmament, William Hague. William was, and still is, an extraordinary man. He first came to national prominence at the Conservative Party Conference in 1977 when he gave a barnstorming speech as a 16-year-old, warning the Conference about the dangers of continued socialist rule in Britain [55] By the time I went to work for him in 2007, he was one of the most senior members of the Shadow Cabinet and, perhaps along with George, one of the few people who possessed sufficient authority to persuade David Cameron when he was wrong.

Some months later, George was to deliver his own barnstorming speech at the Conservative Party Conference, when he famously dared Gordon Brown (who had taken over as Prime Minister some months earlier when Tony Blair resigned in June) to bring on the General Election that many people in the media had been predicting he would call. In his speech to the Conference, George announced something which we had been mooting privately in the Shadow Treasury Team for a while, which was effectively to raise the threshold for Inheritance Tax to £1 million. I remember being in the hall at the Conference, no longer part of his team but having seen rumours in the press that morning that he was going to announce it, and I recall sitting in the audience, willing him to utter the words. When he did, the hall erupted, with representatives perhaps instinctively sensing that this would give us a weapon with which to fight Labour, if the election were actually called.

In his rallying speech to close the Conference, David Cameron then effectively "called Brown out" and invited him to declare the election, stressing that the Conservative Party was ready to fight. The combined effect on the media was electric and indeed to some extent on the public as well and on the Friday, 5th October, *The Guardian* of all newspapers published a poll under the headline "Cameron Bounces Back" that showed Labour and the Conservatives neck and neck on 38% each.[56]

In the end, Gordon Brown famously ducked calling an election and earned the temporary nickname "Bottler Brown" (which was even commemorated by Wetherspoons, with a number of Bottler Brown beermats, one of which I still have as a memento in my office in Parliament today). Despite this, however, the

Conservative Party still faced a number of considerable challenges, not least what to do about the vexed issue of Europe, a topic which had divided the Party for years.

As the Shadow Europe Minister, I now had the pleasure of having day-to-day oversight of this policy, reporting to William as the Shadow Foreign Secretary and then, through him, to David Cameron as Party Leader. One aspect of this challenge was that when he stood for the Leadership of the Conservative Parliamentary Party back in 2005, David Cameron had famously pledged to take Conservative MEPs out of the main centre right grouping in the European Parliament, known as the European People's Party (or EPP) because it was effectively pledged to create a Federal Europe.[57] To the wider public, most of whom didn't even know the name of their MEPs anyway, this might have seemed a rather esoteric argument but, within the Conservative Party, including particularly the Parliamentary Party, it was seen as an iconic issue about whether or not we were truly prepared to resist the march on the continent towards a Federal Europe.

The European "Project"

Following the end of the Second World War a number of politicians on the European continent became convinced that the only way to prevent Europe ripping itself apart in future was to effectively merge the often-competing Nation States into one, supranational, Federal State. To advocates of this idea, which was often openly discussed on the continent, this was known colloquially as "The Project" and indeed the Treaty of Rome, signed in 1957 which created the original European Economic Community (EEC) had pledged its signatories to seek "Ever closer union" and thus in fairness the desired end state was, arguably at least, in plain sight even from the word go.[58]

Many would contend that when Ted Heath took Britain into the EEC in 1973, he knew full well that this was the desired outcome of The Project. However, realising that the British people were unlikely ever to sign up to such an enterprise, he and his allies were very careful to conceal from them their true intent. As the journalist Hugo Young, hardly a diehard Eurosceptic, subsequently outlined in his book about Britain's relationship with Europe, *This Blessed Plot,* during the debates in Parliament concerning joining the European Community, Heath's Minister's consistently downplayed the loss of sovereignty that would result from membership.

"Ministers did not lie, but they avoided telling the full truth. They refrained from stating categorically that the law of the European Community would have sovereignty over British law. This was a conscious, much deliberated choice. The Bill did not contain, as it might have done, a clause stating in terms the general rule that Community law was to be supreme".[59]

While some of Heath's sternest detractors have argued that he essentially took Britain into the European Community on a lie in 1972/3, it is probably true to say that he took us in, at best, on a half-truth. The UK's inclusion in "The Project", was very skilfully disguised by constantly stressing the economic – rather than political – objects of joining.

In any event, Harold Wilson's incoming Labour Government, which narrowly won two successive General Elections in 1974, was so divided on the European issue that they agreed to hold a National Referendum in 1975, on the question of whether or not the United Kingdom should remain in the EEC.

Harold Wilson, as Prime Minister, let it be known that he was in favour of staying in the EEC but that, he would otherwise take no active part in the Referendum campaign – although he pledged to implement the decision of the Country, whatever it might be. In the 1975 Referendum, most mainstream politicians, even including Margaret Thatcher, argued that we should remain within the EEC.[60]

Only relative outsiders at either end of the political spectrum, such as Enoch Powell of the Conservative Party and Tony Benn in the Labour Party, actively opposed this, arguing that the intent was ultimately to create a European Superstate.[61] The overwhelming opinion of the media and the wider British Establishment was that such a threat was exaggerated. The British people were repeatedly told that the EEC was essentially a free trade agreement and therefore that we would be voting to remain a part of what was repeatedly characterised as the "Common Market". The British, who have historically been free traders, at least since the days of Cobden and Bright, thus unsurprisingly voted to remain in the EEC in 1975, by a majority of slightly over two to one.[62]

All might have remained well had things halted at this stage. However, over time, the advocates of The Project dreamt up one Treaty after another, all of which had the effect of moving the Nations of Europe incrementally in a Federal direction. The Maastricht Treaty of 1992, which famously divided the Conservative Parliamentary Party so bitterly, turned the European Economic Community (EEC) into the European Union (the EU), and laid the foundations for the creation of a European Single Currency, which eventually became the Euro.[63]

Further European Treaties, of Amsterdam and of Nice (the latter of which I had opposed in my Maiden Speech) moved the European Union in an increasingly Federal direction; every time without any further Referendum in the UK.

Then, in 2005, the advocates of the European Project produced "The European Constitution". By this stage, Europe already had a Parliament, an Anthem (Ode to Joy), a Flag (the twelve golden stars on a blue background), was moving towards one currency and was now, under the European Constitution, to effectively have a Foreign Minister and a President of the European Union, thus adding even more of the trappings of a State. However, the ambitions of the Federalists were temporarily blunted when the Constitution was unexpectedly rejected, in Denmark and in France.[64]

In Britain, this was becoming a serious argument in the run up to the 2005 General Election, with the Conservatives under Michael Howard running hard against the idea. However, Tony Blair effectively diffused the issue by promising a Referendum to the British people, if ever we were to sign up to the Constitution, which would then have to be ratified by Parliament as well (just as Maastricht and the other Treaties had been). Nevertheless, aware of this and determined to prevent any individual Nation State from defying the unanimity that would be required for such a Treaty to pass, the advocates of a Federal Europe then ditched the European Constitution, only to bring it back, barely a couple of years later in almost entirely unaltered form but now re-christened as the "Treaty of Lisbon".

Despite having some Eurosceptics in his Government, such as Ed Balls, Gordon Brown, reluctantly signed up to the Treaty of Lisbon and agreed that Parliament should be asked to ratify it, by passing the requisite legislation, the European Union (Amendment) Bill.[65]

In order to get around Blair's promise of a Referendum, Brown and his Labour Government sought to maintain the fiction that the Lisbon Treaty was different from the European Constitution, even though reading the two proved very clearly, that in their effect, the complete opposite was true.

Indeed, the cross-Party European Scrutiny Committee of the House of Commons, chaired by the veteran Eurosceptic Bill Cash, examined both documents in great detail and unambiguously concluded that they were "substantially equivalent".[66] In late 2007 the Bill to ratify the Lisbon Treaty came before the House of Commons and William, as the Shadow Foreign Secretary and I, as the Shadow Europe Minister and effectively his Deputy, set about preparing for the extensive debates that were likely to take place over the Treaty and its contents.

The Lisbon Treaty itself stretched to some 300 pages of A4, written in a form of legalise in which EU bureaucrats specialise. I duly read the Lisbon Treaty that summer, whilst on holiday with my girlfriend, Haley, in the Dominican Republic. I must have looked a bit out of place, sitting on a sun lounger with a long drink, with the large Treaty document (it was about an inch thick) a series of highlighting pens and post-it notes, scribbling notes in the margin as I worked my way carefully through the voluminous text. This was hardly the sort of classic holiday novel that you might expect to read by the pool, whilst on vacation with your girlfriend.

Although I have no formal legal training, I was still basically able to follow the legalese in the documents and when I got back to Britain, I made a point of consulting a number of legal experts, on the details of the text, to understand exactly what they meant. In short, however, the Lisbon Treaty was a significant further step towards a Federal European Government, not least by creating a post of the "President of Europe".

Debating the Lisbon Treaty

After some months of preparation, we arrived at the actual debates on the European Union (Amendment) Bill. During the Second Reading, William delivered a brilliant speech, (which you can still view on YouTube if you search for "William Hague/President of Europe") in which he mercilessly taunted the Labour Party about the prospect of Gordon Brown's arch-rival, Tony Blair, who was rumoured to be angling for the job of European President envisaged in the Treaty, actually getting the post.

I worked with William on this speech, along with Christopher Howarth and William's Special Adviser, Denzil Davidson, (although I have to say that all of the gags in that wonderful oration were William's).

At one point in his speech, with David Cameron sitting on one side of him in the House of Commons, George Osborne on the other, and me sitting next to Cameron, William presaged the motorcade of the President of the European Union sweeping into Downing Street, to the consternation of the Prime Minister, Gordon Brown.

As William mischievously put it:

"We can all picture the scene at a European Council sometime next year.
Picture the face of our poor Prime Minister, as the name of "Blair" is placed in nomination by one President and Prime Minister after another:
The look of utter gloom on his face,
The nauseating, glutinous praise oozing from every Head of Government,
The rapid revelation of a majority view, agreed behind closed doors when he was, as usual, excluded.
Never would he regret more no longer being in possession of a veto:
The famous dropped jaw almost hitting the table, as he realises there is no option but to join in
And then the awful moment when the motorcade of the President of Europe sweeps into Downing street.
The gritted teeth and bitten nails:
The Prime Minister emerging from his door with a smile of intolerable anguish;
the choking sensation as the words, "Mr President", are forced from his mouth.
And then, once in the Cabinet room, the melodrama of, "When will you hand over to me?" all over again".[67]

William had the whole House in fits. Cameron was laughing his head off, George was slapping his thighs and even David Miliband, the Foreign Secretary (never a great fan of Brown's anyway) was quite openly laughing throughout this section of the speech. Nevertheless, despite a brilliant Parliamentary oration (which quite deservedly subsequently won *The Spectator* magazine's Speech of the Year)[68] when the bells finally rang, Labour simply used their majority to bulldoze the Bill through its Second Reading.

We then moved on to spend 14 nights in the House of Commons debating the elements of the 300-page Treaty in detail. As is the way in these things, William had done the Second Reading and as his Deputy, it then fell to me to debate the specific details of the Bill and the Lisbon Treaty night after night.

In order to make our task more interesting, Bill Cash, if anything the father of the Eurosceptics in Parliament even then, tabled several hundred Amendments to the Treaty. I well remember Christopher and I sitting in my office, sometimes well after midnight, trying to keep track of the numerous different, often highly complex, Amendments to the Bill, of which Bill Cash's seemed to outnumber all of the others put together.[69]

Nevertheless, despite a lot of tremendously hard work, as we ploughed our way through the debates night after night, it soon became apparent that we could not so much as alter a single punctuation mark in the Treaty itself. Parliament had effectively been reduced to a rubber stamp, for a Treaty that we had had virtually no role in drafting and which it was practically impossible to amend but by which we would be legally bound, once ratified, by all EU Member States, all the same.

Trying to force a Referendum on Lisbon

If it was not possible to defeat or even amend the Lisbon Treaty, then the only other way to stop it was to force the Government to concede a nationwide Referendum on whether or not to ratify it. As the ever-stubborn Gordon Brown made it very clear that he did not intend to bow to public or media pressure on this issue, the only remaining option became to try and force an amendment through the House of Commons – not to alter the Treaty itself but to mandate a Referendum on it instead. Moreover, there was a sense of urgency about all this, as once the Bill was passed and the Treaty was ratified (and the other EU nations had done likewise), the Treaty would become effective under international law and it would then be too late to change it. Once that stage had been reached (and by now the Czechs were virtually the only other country still to ratify)[70] then the only way to nullify the effects of the Lisbon Treaty would be to Leave the European Union itself, which back in 2008, seemed a virtual impossibility.

As the debates on the Bill's Committee Stage wore on over several weeks (the 14 nights allocated were not consecutive) I spent hours with Christopher pouring over the division lists, constantly calculating and re-calculating whether there was *any prospect at all* of defeating the Government and forcing a plebiscite. I kept copious notes of what MPs said in each debate, assisted of course by *Hansard*, always on the look-out for any non-Tory MPs who might be inclined to vote for our referendum amendment, which had been earmarked for the final day of the fourteen.

I also had several secret discussions with Labour Eurosceptics, led by Ian Davidson, the feisty Labour MP for Glasgow South West, who privately suggested that up to two dozen Labour MPs might just be prepared to defy their three-line whip and back a Referendum – but only if they believed we had a realistic chance of winning. As Ian put it to me bluntly: "We're not going to die on the barbed wire for nothing Mark!". So that meant it all came down to the Liberal Democrat's. If they could somehow be persuaded to back a Referendum amendment at the end of the Committee Stage, then a combination of them, the Conservatives, the Democratic Unionist Party from Northern Ireland (the DUP) and Ian Davidson's Labour Eurosceptics could defeat Gordon Brown's remaining Labour MPs – but only just.[71]

Instead, in order to avoid this dilemma, Nick Clegg's largely Europhile Liberal Democrats had (ironically) adopted the position of rejecting a Referendum on Lisbon, in favour of a full up In/Out Referendum on European membership itself. They had developed this stance without any real conviction whatsoever and as a matter of sheer tactical expediency to get them off the hook over Lisbon, whereas their 2005 General Election Manifesto had called for a referendum on the European Constitution – but said nothing about an In/Out vote instead![72]

"We're not bloody talking to that lot!"

When I served for three years as David Cameron's Shadow Europe Minister, most of the key decisions on European policy were taken, in theory, by the Conservative Shadow Cabinet. In practice, however, they were taken by four politicians: David Cameron as Leader of The Opposition; George Osborne as Shadow Chancellor (and Cameron's principal *consiglieri);* William Hague as Shadow Foreign Secretary – and me, the Shadow Europe Minister and very much the most junior of the four. For completeness, when the topic of the meeting was Europe, we were usually joined by Cameron's ever faithful and highly efficient Chief of Staff, Ed Llewelyn, and William's Europe adviser, Denzil Davidson (who later went on to work for Theresa May in No 10). Andy Coulson, Cameron's communications chief, (who incidentally had attended Beauchamps High School in Wickford) also joined us when discussing media handling.

Around halfway through the Committee Stage of the Ratification Bill, I made a verbal presentation to this Group on the chances of defeating the Government on a Referendum amendment, several weeks hence. I went through the various mathematical permutations in detail, including my private discussions with Ian Davidson but summed up by saying that the crux of it all, was what the Lib Dem's were going to do. I admitted that, given their generally pro-European views it was a long shot but, nevertheless, I recommended that we should seek to open highly confidential negotiations with Nick Clegg, on whether there might be any circumstances in which they might be prepared to contemplate working with us, to inflict a truly historic defeat on Gordon Brown's Labour Government.

After I had concluded, you might have been forgiven for thinking that I had just advocated the slaughter of the firstborn. Cameron in particular was adamant that: "We're not talking to that bloody lot" and that we would not become beholden to the Liberal Democrat's for help in defeating the Lisbon Treaty, or indeed for anything else thank you very much. The whole idea was rapidly dismissed – at which point any realistic hope of forcing a Referendum effectively disappeared.

Given all of this – and the literally months of preparatory work and secret discussion with Labour MPs it had entailed – you can perhaps understand why I allowed myself a wry smile when, barely two years later, David Cameron launched his "Big, Generous Offer" to Nick Clegg and his Lib Dem MPs, to form a formal Coalition Government and make Cameron Prime Minister. When it suited his purpose (but in fairness, the country's too), Cameron was clearly not quite so reluctant to talk to "that bloody lot" after all.

The Referendum Amendment

Because this was a Constitutional Bill, i.e. one that altered our constitutional arrangements, because of the transfer of further powers to the EU, the 14 nights in Committee Stage were conducted not in a Committee Room but in the Main Chamber, on the Floor of the House of Commons. The tradition is that a Bill with major Constitutional implications is treated in this way, so that any MP can participate in the debate and move amendments, not just those allocated to a much smaller Committee, which sits separately in a Committee Room upstairs, (as in say, the bulk of the Finance Bill). Throughout this period, the Conservatives had campaigned, including in the national media, for a Referendum to be held on the Treaty, if it were not ratified by the time that we came into Government.

Indeed, on one occasion, I remember visiting the old *News International* Headquarters at Wapping, with William, to brief Rebecca Wade, the then Editor of *The News of The World*, on what was wrong with the Lisbon Treaty and why they should oppose it. As we walked down the long halls at the *NOTW* Headquarters, which they shared with *The Sun*, they had a large number of famous front pages blown up on the wall, as if in large poster format. These ranged from "Gotcha" (the famous *Sun* headline in the Falklands War when we sank the cruiser General Belgrano) through to, unfortunately, one of William done up as a parrot, hanging upside down from a perch just prior to his speech as Leader to the Conservative Party Conference, with the headline "It's a Dead Parrott". I remember William grinning as we walked past this poster, but it never threw him off his stride. When we got down to Rebecca's office, at the far end of the building, we were told to wait because she was dealing with a serious editorial problem at their sister paper, *The Sun*. When we were eventually ushered in, she apologised and said, "I'm terribly sorry William, we normally only use Page 3 models who haven't had work done but there's been an accusation today that one of our models had a boob job several months ago, so I've spent the whole afternoon dealing with a major tits crisis!". You really couldn't make it up.

Fortunately, our briefing still appeared to have been worthwhile, as we did receive considerable support from *The Sun* and indeed from a number of other right-wing newspapers in opposing the Lisbon Treaty but, nevertheless, Gordon Brown ploughed on regardless. However, he was so torn by his actions that he organised to sign the Lisbon Treaty privately, out of sight of the cameras and away from all the other Leaders of the EU.[73]

The Government had deliberately arranged the timetable of the Committee Stage to leave our Amendment, calling for a Referendum on Lisbon, to the final day of the 14. The day before, I remember being contacted by a very anxious Bill Cash who pleaded with me to go and see him. Although Bill and I are now great friends, it would not be untrue to say that during the period of this Treaty, he nearly drove me mad.

In fairness to Bill, he was self-aware and when I went to see him, he readily conceded that it must have sometimes been difficult to deal with him but, nevertheless, he said that he had been up to look at the latest Amendments in the Public Bill Office and someone else had tabled an Amendment which was likely to trump ours when it was selected. In other words, we wouldn't get the chance to lead the argument for a Referendum but somebody else would. Bill pleaded with me to take his advice and to alter the drafting of our Amendment, along the lines he suggested, to make sure that we actually lead the debate. After rapidly consulting with William, this is exactly what I did and – true to his word – Bill was right (as he often is on European matters) and thus, fortunately, our Amendment was eventually selected to lead the critical debate, the following day. Our Amendment (with Bill's suggested change) called for a Referendum of Lisbon, in the following terms:

"The other provisions of this Act come into force if an affirmative answer has been given to the question asked in a Referendum held in accordance with section [Referendum] and any legal challenge made under an order made under that section has been disposed of by the court or courts in question."[74]

Sir Bill Cash

By historical coincidence, William (Bill) Cash was born on 10th May 1940, the same day on which Winston Churchill famously became Prime Minister. Like my father, Bill's father, Paul Cash MC, served on D-Day and subsequently in Normandy but he was unfortunately killed only a few days later, when Bill was barely four years old.[75]

Bill was first elected to Parliament in a by-election as the MP for Stafford back in 1984. (By another coincidence, David Cameron subsequently fought the seat of Stafford in 1997 but lost out during the Blair Landslide). Bill Cash switched to the nearby seat of Stone in Staffordshire at the 1997 General Election and has represented that constituency in the House of Commons ever since.

Bill really came to prominence during the acrimonious debates over the Maastricht Treaty in the early 1990s, when he was a fierce opponent of John Major and one of the undisputed leaders of the Tory Maastricht rebels. The late Teresa Gorman's book, "*The Bastards*"[76] acts as a very readable summary of that whole battle and, interestingly, includes an appendix showing the voting record of all the Maastricht rebels, a few of whom, like Bill, Iain Duncan Smith and Sir Bernard Jenkin, still serve in the House of Commons, today. The rebels are ranked by how often they voted against the Government or abstained on key votes relating to Maastricht and unsurprisingly, Bill's name is literally at the top of the Eurosceptic league table, of 47 then MPs.[77]

A constitutional lawyer by training, Bill is an absolutely forensic advocate, able to quote whole sections of UK and European law from memory. A founder member of the ERG after Maastricht, during the subsequent debates over Lisbon, he harried both the Labour Europe Minister, Jim Murphy and occasionally me as his Shadow as well. However, I think that I gradually earned his respect when he realised how passionately I opposed the Lisbon Treaty too.

During the subsequent debates over Theresa May's so-called Withdrawal Agreement, more than a decade later, Bill was an absolute stalwart and the Chairman of the so-called "Star Chamber", which played a crucial role in scrutinizing the Attorney General's legal advice on how the WA would operate, if adopted. Bill, now aged 81, is also the "Grandfather of the House", the oldest MP still serving, yet he remains a very active member of the ERG.

In view of his long and dedicated service as a Parliamentarian, even most of his diehard opponents did not begrudge his thoroughly deserved Knighthood, to become Sir William Cash in 2014.

"You're summing up Mark!"

Given the critical importance of this Amendment, William led-off for HM Opposition and made a brilliant case for why the British people should be allowed to vote specifically on such a further transfer of power to Brussels.[78] Because this was an Amendment rather than a Second Reading debate, Labour were allowed to respond and then lots of MPs would be allowed to contribute, before William, as the mover of the Amendment, would have a few minutes at the end to summarise his case, before the question was put to the vote.

However, about halfway through the debate, William suddenly turned to me and said, "Jim Murphy wants to have a summing up speech for the Government". I was slightly taken aback and said: "Well that's highly irregular. He's already had his go William and so you should sum up for us at the end in the normal way". "No", said William, "Given the immense importance of this, I think the Government should be allowed to sum up their case too". "Well, you're the boss", I replied "as long as you get to speak last". "No Mark", he said: "I've already spoken, you've worked on this for months and I think you should sum up for us instead". Suddenly, an icy chill ran down my spine. "But William", I remonstrated, "I don't have any prepared speech and the vote is barely three hours from now". "Well", replied William, "in that case, I suggest you get cracking. I'm off for a bowl of soup!".

So, there I sat, in the Chamber of the House of Commons, suddenly about to give the most important speech of my life to date, with not so much as a scribbled note in front of me. I asked one of our Whips to sit at the Despatch Box, nipped out at the back and rapidly rang Christopher and Denzil to explain what have happened and told them to get working on something as fast as they could. As a backup, I started jotting down a number of bullet points on a sheet of paper, but as the clock ticked down, I could feel my blood racing faster and faster as the thought dawned on me, that after literally months and months of highly detailed preparation, often late into the night, I might effectively have to do this final, crucial, speech off the cuff!

Mercifully, Denzil and Christopher worked heroically, and a speech arrived about 20 minutes before I was finally due to stand up. I scanned through it and made a few modifications of my own and then, when Labour's Europe Minister, Jim Murphy had finished summarising for the Government, I had around 10 minutes to have the last word.

By this stage, the House was absolutely packed, and the atmosphere was truly electric. Despite having been a Shadow Treasury Minister before and as Shadow Europe Minister, I'd spoken night after night on the Treaty in the Commons, I had never before given a speech of such importance, during a set-piece Parliamentary occasion like this. This was a highly-charged House of Commons event, with many people watching at home on television and – with less than three hours' notice – the boy from Alcatraz in Basildon was summing up! However, the Lord was kind, as eventually my nerves fell away, and I got into my stride.

As well as castigating the Government for refusing the people a chance to decide this vital issue of national Sovereignty, I also had a real pop at the Liberal Democrats too, for going along with it all, by abstaining in the critical vote, in the following terms:

"Tonight, we are taking an important decision for our country, so what are the Liberal Democrats going to do? What is the party of Lloyd George, Asquith and Gladstone going to do tonight when the future of our country is in the balance? They are going to go and hide in the toilets because they do not have the guts to vote on the question either one way or the other! And it is the Liberal Democrats who promise us a new politics, a politics of change. If that is all they have to offer, they should go back to the starting board and start again".[79]

Summarising our case against the Lisbon Treaty, as already rejected in its original form as the European Constitution by other European Member States, including France, but which had been revived and was now before the House of Commons, I argued passionately:

"The two documents are the same. The Council mandate of the intergovernmental conference 2004 brought forward almost all the same innovations. That is how it was done. The European Scrutiny Committee said that the two were substantially equivalent and Valéry Giscard d'Estaing summed it up perfectly when he said:

'Public opinion will be led to adopt, without knowing it, the proposals that we dare not present to them directly...All the earlier proposals will be in the new text but will be hidden and disguised in some way.'

In the latest poll, 88 per cent. of the British people wanted a Referendum. This House collectively, and all parties, gave their word that they would have it. We dishonour this place if we do not keep that promise. We say: let the promise be kept, let the question be put, let the Commons retain its honour in the eyes of the public, and let the people decide!"[80]

I sat down to loud cheers from the Conservative benches behind me, jeers from the Labour benches opposite and scowls from the absolutely furious Lib Dem off to my left. Incidentally, it never occurred to me, at any point during this speech, that within two years we might be in a Coalition Government with the Liberal Democrats and the people that I was now calling everything under the sun, might have a role in determining my future. In other words, I never saw the Coalition coming! All I cared about that night was doing everything I could to persuade the House of Commons, including Labour and Lib Dem MPs, to effectively break ranks and give the British people the final say on whether or not to ratify the Treaty. In the event, I failed.

Although around a dozen Lib Dems did indeed break their own Three-Line Whip and vote with us for a Referendum (including, very honourably a number of Lib Dem Frontbenchers who subsequently had to resign)[81] only a few die-hard Labour Eurosceptics eventually voted with us and the outcome was that the Government defeated the Referendum Amendment by 311 votes to 247 (a comfortable Government Majority of 64). At this point, it was obvious that the Government would also win the subsequent vote on the Third Reading of the Bill and so all the tension rapidly bled out of the situation. I remember later that evening being absolutely disconsolate that I had not somehow been able to persuade the House of Commons to vote for a Referendum, something in which I passionately believed.

However, William was kind enough to comfort me and explain that he didn't think he could have done any better either (although I'm sure he could) and that most MP's minds were already made up before they even went into the Chamber that evening and thus no amount of oratory was going to swing more than a handful of them. So, given Labour's majority (and lacking official Liberal support) our task was almost hopeless from the start. Nevertheless, he assured me that we had put up a very good fight and that we would continue to campaign for a Referendum, as long as the Treaty was not ratified by the time we came to power – in which case, under International Law, it would then effectively be too late to do anything about it.

William

William Hague is one of the most accomplished politicians of his generation. A largely self-made man, successful author with a beautiful and intelligent wife and a strong intellect himself, assisted by his great friend, Michael Ashcroft, he helped keep the Conservative Party alive after it's crushing 1997 defeat under John Major. William once humbly described his Leadership to me in the following terms: "Someone had to do the nightshift Mark – and it just happened to be me".

He went on to become a distinguished Foreign Secretary in his own right and even defied Enoch Powell's dictum that: "Ultimately, all political careers end in failure"[82], by bowing out on his own terms in 2016, while he was back in the Cabinet and still very much at the top of his game.

He was also a pleasure to work for – as long as you weren't late! He has legendary, almost metronomic timekeeping skills (which is partly why his civil servants loved him) but the greatest sin in William World was to be late for a meeting. On one occasion I got stuck on the phone with a very difficult constituent who simply refused to stop talking.

In the end, I finished the conversation as politely but firmly as I could and dashed round to William's office, to arrive just slightly over five minutes late. William's body language soon told me he was less than impressed with my imprecise punctuality – and, on a point of honour, I was never late for any meeting with him again.

I have been told by some others that I do a reasonable impression of William. However, I came unstuck one afternoon when his staff brought me through a draft press release and asked me to approve it. Putting on my best William voice I said: "Well, this looks fine to me, but given that it touches on a sensitive area of the Party's policy, I think we should run it pass the boss first, just to make absolutely sure that it meets with his approval". Whereupon a voice behind me said softly: "Oh that's alright Mark, I've already approved it!" At this point, I was all set to return to my office and clear my desk, when he quietly confided in me: "Actually Mark, that's one of the better impersonations I've heard down the years".

By campaigning so strongly to "Keep the Pound", for which he was ridiculed in the Liberal media at the time, he also effectively deterred Tony Blair from trying to take Britain into the Euro, until the Party was sufficiently recovered to fight off the threat completely. Although he subsequently campaigned to Remain in the 2016 Referendum, in my opinion, the Conservative Party undoubtedly owes William Hague a great debt, particularly for helping to keep it alive from 1997 to 2001, following Tony Blair's absolute landslide victory.

My Epiphany, "We've got to get out of this!"

In the end, the Czech's, who were the last to hold out against the Treaty, eventually caved in and it was formally legally ratified and deposited in Rome, thus bringing it into effect under International Law and representing yet another ratchet towards a Federal European Superstate. I had spent months and months and innumerable late nights preparing to fight this beast, only to realise that Parliament had effectively been completely neutered and reduced to the level of a rubber stamp. I remember saying to Christopher over a drink after it was all over, "This is absolutely bonkers, we've got to get out of this! It doesn't matter who people vote for in a General Election, if this process continues, we'll soon be part of a European Superstate, and the entire House of Commons will merely be reduced to the status of a glorified Parish Council".

That, in effect, was my epiphany. It was the Lisbon Treaty and the debates surrounding it which finally convinced me that The Project was remorseless, genuine reform was a pipe dream and that we either had to Leave the European Union, or eventually surrender any remaining ability to govern ourselves.

When I entered Parliament in 2001, if it came to Europe you could have put me under the heading, "Remain and Reform" but after Lisbon I was convinced that we had to Leave, although at that stage, even within the Conservative Party, this was a love that dare not speak its name. Interestingly though, Labour so misjudged the mood of the people in ramming Lisbon through without a Referendum (just as, in fairness, John Major had done over Maastricht too) that it began to change the climate of public opinion in the United Kingdom, whereby more and more people began to question the growing influence of the EU over our lives. It wasn't just what they had done, it was the *way* that they had done it and it's interesting that it was following on from Lisbon that you can really track the rise of the United Kingdom Independence Party (UKIP)[83] who ultimately had a significant influence (but not the only influence) in persuading David Cameron to announce what eventually became the In/Out Referendum of 2016. So, ironically as it transpired, in ramming the Lisbon Treaty through the House of Commons in 2008, although the Federalists might have won the battle, in the end, it contributed materially to them ultimately losing the war, in the UK at least.[84]

Leaving the Federalist European People's Party – The EPP

As well as all the battles over Lisbon, as the Shadow Europe Minister, David Cameron had charged me with fulfilling his pledge to take our MEPs out of the EPP and to form a new Eurosceptic grouping within the European Parliament. The story of how I managed to achieve this (aided by a small number of sympathetic MEPs) and creating an alliance across a number of EU nations to consolidate it, is probably a book in itself and so I will leave the detail for another day.

Suffice to say, that after two years of incredibly early starts to get up and jet around much of Europe, (particularly Eastern Europe), I finally managed to amass sufficient MEPs from the required seven European Nations to form a new Group in the European Parliament. All this was achieved despite concerted efforts from the EPP – who were determined not to allow any break away

Eurosceptic Grouping in the European Parliament to be created – to foil us at every turn. Nevertheless, in June 2009, we successfully launched the European Conservatives and Reformists Group (the ECR) in the European Parliament including British, Czech and Polish MEPs and one each from Belgium, Hungary, Latvia, and Lithuania. (Thus, complying with the requirement to have seven constituent nations represented in any new Group).

Despite many predictions at the time that this Group would not survive more than a few weeks, it eventually grew to become the third largest grouping in the European Parliament, surpassing the Liberal (ALDE) Group and even the Green's Group and, at one stage at least, being numerically behind only the EPP and the Party of European Socialists (PES). In some ways, leaving the EPP was the first "crack in the dam" of our eventually Leaving the European Union – but it was only achieved after a tremendous amount of hard work and in the face of fierce resistance behind the scenes, much of it from within our own Conservative ranks.

GVO

Without doubt, I would never have succeeded in executing my orders to take the Conservatives in the European Parliament out of the European Peoples Party and into a newly created Eurosceptic Grouping, without the staunch support of Geoffrey Van Orden MEP.

Like me, Geoffrey Van Orden (or 'GVO' as he is almost universally known) was a former Army officer, although while I had only been a Territorial, he had served as a Regular, including distinguished service in some very challenging environments. Tall and perfectly spoken, he had married a lovely girl named 'Fanny' and rose to the rank of Brigadier, before going into politics under John Major's Premiership and succeeding in becoming elected as an MEP for the East of England region (including my own county of Essex).

To make the whole challenge of leaving the EPP even more interesting, a number of the MEPs in the British Conservative delegation were strong believers in 'The Project' – and thus adamantly opposed to Cameron's instinct to quit the EPP. This even extended, in some cases, to actively conspiring with the EPP to seek to scupper the entire idea. Throughout this whole extremely difficult process, with more enemies than friends, GVO was my most steadfast ally, and, while I was eventually rewarded with promotion to the Shadow Cabinet, he received no such endorsement, despite working tirelessly for two years to make Cameron's promise to his Party a reality.

I remember on one occasion, during a highly secret midnight meeting with our Czech and Polish allies, in a former Communist complex, in a wood in the middle of nowhere in Central Poland (honestly), him encouraging me that, however bizarre this all seemed – it would eventually come good – and so it proved.

Thank you, Geoffrey, we could never have left the Federalist EPP without you!

Into the Shadow Cabinet

Although this development passed most of the public by (who really cared which Grouping our MEPs sat with in the European Parliament anyway?), within the Conservative Parliamentary Party this was considered as something of a triumph for Cameron – particularly as it had already been tried twice before and failed[85] – and David Cameron was absolutely delighted. On the back of this, he promoted me to the Shadow Cabinet, still as the Shadow Minister for Europe but now with Shadow Cabinet Rank. This was a considerable promotion and now I found myself sitting literally at the top table of the Conservative Party, whilst still working for one of the three most senior Members within it (and arguably, indirectly, for Cameron too).

During Shadow Cabinet meetings, held usually in the Shadow Cabinet Room in the Palace of Westminster, I was very much the new boy and would sit at the far end of the table, next to Oliver Letwin, who at one time gave me a very nice bottle of vintage port, as a thank you for travelling down to Dorset, to address his recent Association Dinner on the subject of our Europe policy.[86] It was very exciting to witness Party policy being debated at the highest level and Cameron was a very effective Chairman of debate. Everyone was allowed to have a say if they wanted but only if you had a substantive intervention to make and there were no points at all for chiming in sycophantically just to say, "moi aussi".

In reality, the key players in that 2009 Shadow Cabinet remained David Cameron, George Osborne and William Hague. Most of the critical decisions were taken by these three and their senior staffers, in Cameron's office in the Norman Shaw North building, elsewhere on the Parliamentary estate. In truth, most Party leaders rely on a trusted "inner circle" of senior politicians and strategic advisers, (indeed Margaret Thatcher and Tony Blair were little different)[87], and Cabinet/Shadow Cabinet is now largely for show, a forum in which the Leader seeks to bind in the rest of their senior team, to whatever policy decision they are advocating. This was how Cameron ran the Shadow Cabinet and everyone in the room knew it. I rarely piped up at all, unless asked about some matter directly relating to Europe. Nevertheless, during one meeting on a hot afternoon my mind started to wander, and I confess I couldn't help pinching myself that this lad from Alcatraz was now a member of the Shadow Cabinet, of one of the principal political Parties in the world.

As it turned out, my time in the Shadow Cabinet was to be brutally short lived, because only a few months later Gordon Brown eventually called a General Election, which many in the Conservative Party hoped that we might actually win.

The 2010 General Election

By 2010, Labour had been in power for 13 years, and just as the Conservative's had been after 18 years, they were beginning to look like a tired and divided administration. Gordon Brown, a rather dour individual, did not possess any of the charisma, humour or breadth of communication skills of his predecessor, Tony Blair, and moreover had presided over a vast increase in public spending, to the point where, by the time of the 2010 General Election, the Government was spending over £156 billion a year more than it was bringing in in taxation. The outgoing Chief Secretary to the Treasury, Liam Byrne MP (the Minister who is supposed to control public spending) famously left a note on his desk in the Treasury for his incoming successor, which said; "I'm afraid there is no money. Kind regards and good luck!".[88]

Against this background, David Cameron's Conservatives went into battle and confounded many of the pollsters and media pundits by managing to take a number of Labour seats, but not quite enough to form an absolute majority, in the House of Commons .

For my own part, as a Member of the Shadow Cabinet, during the campaign I was dispatched on tour around the country to visit marginal seats and to help raise the profile of Conservative candidates in their local media. I spent over a month criss-crossing the country, accompanied by Christopher Howarth, armed with an almost unique rail pass (paid for by the Party, not the public) at a cost of around £600 a week, but which allowed you to travel on virtually any train in the United Kingdom, other than the Eurostar or the Gatwick Express. On one occasion we were in Scotland using this ticket when the ticket inspector explained that in many years of working on the railway, he'd never seen one of these tickets, other than on his initial training course.

I spent most of the days mid-week in that campaign travelling around the country with Chris, helping our candidates in marginals and, in return, I was able to campaign in my own seat at weekends. The Boundary Commission had conducted a review of Parliamentary boundaries a couple of years previously, which had led to the creation of an additional seat in Essex, because of the rapidly increasing population. The net effect of this locally, was that I lost the town of South Woodham Ferrers and some very picturesque surrounding villages in the Hanningfield's, Ramsden Heath and Downham, and in order keep the numbers up, I was given Wickford, from the old Billericay constituency, instead.

The name of my seat thus changed from Rayleigh to Rayleigh and Wickford. One by-product of this is that Wickford is part of the Basildon Borough Council area and thus if re-elected, I would in effect be inheriting an area under the local authority on which I had begun my political career, as a young Councillor in the early 1990s.

When the votes were counted on General Election night, the result in the new Rayleigh and Wickford constituency was as follows:

General Election Result for the Rayleigh and Wickford Constituency, 2010

Mark Francois	Conservative Candidate	30,257
Susan Gaszczak	Liberal Democrat	7,919
Mike Le Surf	Labour Candidate	7,577
John Hayter	English Democrats	2,219
Timo Callaghan	UKIP	2,211
Andrew Evenett	BNP	2,160
Conservative Majority		22,338
Turnout		69%

On a personal level, I was delighted at this outcome as my majority had increased again and now stood at slightly over 22,000, putting Rayleigh and Wickford firmly in the top dozen or so of the "safest" Conservative seats in the country. As well as a great deal of hard work by my local Association and their campaign team, this result had been assisted by the fact that the Liberal and Labour votes were almost perfectly divided. Nevertheless, it was a very healthy majority, whichever way you cut it.

Unfortunately, we did not fair quite as well across the nation as a whole and eventually we were 8 seats short of an overall majority. In the end, the Conservatives won 307 seats, the Labour Party won 258, and the Liberal Democrats surged to 57 seats in the House of Commons, their best performance in decades. The Liberal Democrats had done very well, not least as a result of a stunning performance that Nick Clegg delivered in the first of the Leader's televised debates early on during the campaign, which boosted their poll rating considerably (this also partly explained why the Liberals eventually came second in my own seat as well).

So, by the time I got back from my count at about 3:30am on the Friday morning and turned on the television, it was apparent that Labour had lost but it was not yet clear who had actually won!

Chapter 7: Working for Her Majesty

About three days prior to the 2010 General Election, I had been travelling on a train with Christopher when I received a telephone call on my mobile from William Hague. He asked me what time my count was likely to declare the result on Friday morning and I said from past experience, I guessed it would come in somewhere between 3:00-4:00am. William said his might be similar but that, in any event, he wanted me to get as much sleep as I could and then to present myself looking bright and breezy on the steps of the Foreign Office, at 9:00am on Friday morning. His intent was clear, "If we win this thing Mark, then you and I are going to walk into the Foreign Office on Friday morning and let them know they're under new management". I remember telling William enthusiastically that nothing would please me more and we rounded off the call by wishing each other luck. When I told Christopher (who was hoping to get a job as a Special Adviser in the Department if we won), he was equally buoyed up by the suggestion.

Of course, when Friday morning finally dawned, I was not standing on the steps of the Foreign Office but rather sitting at home in Rayleigh, much like everybody else, wondering what on earth was going to happen next? I was still in the Shadow Cabinet and so I was subsequently involved in several conference calls, to discuss what we might do now.[89]

David Cameron was obviously disappointed that we hadn't won outright but he argued very strongly, that morally at least, Gordon Brown had lost but warned us that we might end up in a bidding war with Labour in an attempt to form some kind of Coalition with the Liberal Democrats, in order to give us a majority in the House of Commons. He said that he would do his best to reach out to Nick Clegg, who was clearly buoyed up, having done far better than almost anyone had expected in the General Election, and who was now well aware that he effectively held the balance of power, as "kingmaker".

Cameron's "Big Generous Offer"

Gordon Brown could do the maths as well and seemed equally determined to try and remain in Government, albeit with Lib Dem support. He authorised his negotiating team, including his key lieutenant, Ed Balls, to enter into discussions with Clegg and the Lib Dem Leadership, to try and come to suitable terms.[90] David Cameron, when he became aware of this, decided that we had to reach out substantially to the Liberal Democrats in order to try and seal the deal before Labour beat us to the punch.

Cameron then launched his "Big Generous Offer" to Clegg and the Liberal Democrats involving the prospect of a Referendum on Electoral Reform.[91] As you might expect, this caused some disquiet in the Shadow Cabinet but, nevertheless, Cameron argued persuasively that if we were unable to do a deal with the Liberal Democrats, he feared Gordon Brown would offer them just about anything anyway in order to remain in No 10.

In the end, terms were struck, and I remember attending the Shadow Cabinet Meeting where we were briefed on the outlines of the deal. As well as offering the Liberal Democrats a Referendum early in the Parliament on proportional representation, it had been agreed that we would bring in a "Fixed Term Parliament Act", to regulate the timing of the General Election to only once every five years, unless in exceptional circumstances. Apparently, the Liberal Democrats had been keen on this to ensure that we would not seek to collapse the Coalition when it suited us. David Cameron then handed over to Oliver Letwin, to explain how such an Act would work in practice.

From memory, there were only three of us in the Shadow Cabinet who expressed reservations against it, who were Liam Fox, Theresa Villiers and myself.[92] We attempted to warn that this was a major constitutional precedent and there might well be times when a Conservative Prime Minister, for one reason or another, would want to go to the country and being bound to a five-year timetable was a dangerous precedent to set. Nevertheless, Cameron was clearly determined to get his deal with Clegg approved and as a powerful personality in the Cabinet, he effectively drove it through there and then, with obviously pre-arranged support. Whatever any of our individual reservations, this was now going to be the deal, like it or lump it.

The Coalition is formed

David Cameron and Nick Clegg accordingly formed a formal Coalition, and famously held a press conference in the Rose Garden in Downing Street, to tell the nation of their plans to Govern in the national interest. Principle among this were measures to reign in public spending, in order to prevent a collapse in economic confidence, given the fact that Labour had virtually run out of money (as evidenced by Liam Byrne's infamous note).

Although there had been a temporary "Lib/Lab pact" under Jim Callaghan in the mid-to-late 1970s, this had not been a full-blown Coalition as such and in fact one had to go back to the Second World War, when Churchill formed a Government of national unity, to find an example of a full-blown Coalition.

Therefore, in terms of living memory at least, we were all to some extent in unchartered waters.

Because of the length of time that the Coalition talks took, even after David Cameron was invited by HM The Queen to become Prime Minister, with Nick Clegg as his Deputy, it still took some time to flesh out all the appointments in the Cabinet, let alone the junior Ministers, further down the food chain. All of those who had been Minister's in Opposition were therefore left hanging for over a week whilst the two-Party Leaderships haggled, in effect, over who was going to get what.

I thus basically sat in my office for a week, waiting for the phone to ring. I attempted to hold my nerve but eventually one day, I had just about had enough of this (as indeed had lots of other Shadow Minister's in a similar position) and I resolved that I was finally going to ring my boss, William, in order to try and find out what the hell was going on. Ironically, about an hour later, the phone rang but rather than William, it was George. He explained to me that, unfortunately, I wouldn't be going to the Foreign Office after all but that one of the challenges faced by the new Government would be forming a Coalition Whips Office, in which Conservative and Lib Dems Whips would have to work together. The Chief Whip would be Patrick McLoughlin, and apparently Patrick had asked for me to be one of the Senior Whips in his new team.

Although I had enjoyed my time in the Whips Office, this was by no means what I had in mind and it would be true to say that I was pretty unhappy at the prospect, having been dreaming about a senior position in one of the great Departments of State. George well understood my disappointment and hinted that I would be made a Privy Councillor to help cushion the blow. He then said: "Listen, I know you're not happy with this, but Patrick has specifically asked for you and he's going to need your help. Just do this and I will look after you. Don't stand on your honour, Mark. Please just take it and make the best of it and David and I won't forget it". In the end, I didn't stand on my honour and they didn't forget it.

The new arrangement was something of a Venn diagram. In essence, there would be a Conservative Whips Office, with Patrick McLoughlin as Chief, John Randall as the Deputy, and me as number three. There would also be a Liberal Democrat Whips Office, with Alastair Carmichael as the Lib Dem Chief Whip. The two would then overlap to come together and form a "Government Whips Office", with Patrick as the overall Government Chief Whip, Alastair Carmichael as one Deputy Chief Whip and John Randall as the other, whereas I would be in effect the number four and the Operations Office for the Whips Office, overseeing day to day activities, including tactics in the Chamber.

In addition, by tradition, three Senior Government Whips also hold titular positions in the Royal Household, namely the Comptroller, the Treasurer, and the Vice Chamberlain. In practical terms, this means that they are present for certain ceremonial occasions, including Royal Garden Parties but the Vice Chamberlain also acts in effect as the Queen's messenger to Parliament, so it was made plain to me that while my day job was acting as Ops Officer for the Whips Office, I would also find myself working for HM The Queen at times as well. As George had hinted, I also had the additional privilege of being made a Privy Councillor too.

Patrick McLoughlin

Patrick McLoughlin (now Lord McLoughlin) has never been what you might call an archetypal Conservative politician. Born in Staffordshire in 1957 both his father and grandfather before him were coal miners and he followed in the family tradition, working at the Littleton Colliery in Cannock in the 1980s. However, despite being a Member of Arthur Scargill's National Union of Mineworkers (NUM) like most Staffordshire miners, McLoughlin continued working during the prolonged and highly controversial Miners' Strike of 1984-85. At the 1984 Conservative Conference he achieved a standing ovation when he pointed out that he was still a working miner.

Two years later, Patrick McLoughlin narrowly won the seat of West Derbyshire by barely 100 votes in a by-election caused by the retirement from politics of the liberally minded Tory, Matthew Paris. Patrick held several junior Ministerial posts in the years that followed but it was in the Conservative Whips Office that he really made his name.

Patrick McLoughlin was appointed a junior Whip by John Major in 1995 and he then served continuously in the Whips Office for seventeen years, rising through the ranks to become Deputy Chief Whip under William Hague in 1998 and then eventually Chief Whip under David Cameron in 2005, a post he then retained for seven years before becoming Secretary of State for Transport in 2012.

I served under Patrick as a Whip both when he was Deputy and later Chief and the man was a natural Whip to his fingertips. He combined a deep knowledge of the Conservative Parliamentary Party and the myriad of characters within it with the no-nonsense attitude of a former pit Shop Steward. A fierce Party loyalist, with an in-depth understanding of Parliamentary procedure, he was not exactly known for suffering fools gladly and sometimes errant Backbenchers were put right, at close range as it were.

However, he also possessed a compassionate side for any colleagues who were in difficulty, even if those outside the Office rarely saw it.

If I learnt whatever Whipping skills I might possess from anybody, it was probably from Patrick McLoughlin, who was the rock of the Tory Whips Office for many years. Even on highly pressurised days, of which were there were quite a few in the Whips Office, he would simply say something like "we are in for an interesting time in the House of Commons today".

Patrick was made Party Chairman by Theresa May when she became Leader in 2016 but was replaced in that role by Brandon Lewis by the time that the Battle for Brexit reached its height in 2019-20. He was subsequently Knighted, and then made a Life Peer in 2019, when he left the House of Commons after some 33 years as an MP. His ascent from a coal mine to the House of Lords is living testimony to the social mobility that a career in politics can facilitate and the fact that it is not solely the preserve of those from privileged backgrounds, or "the big horses on the hill".

Vice Chamberlain of HM Household

Essentially, the job of Vice Chamberlain involved three specific duties. Firstly, to act as the Queen's messenger to Parliament. In practical terms this meant that there were a number of public appointments, such as, for instance, the Chairman of the Electoral Commission, which were in practice recommended by Parliament but still officially required the Sovereign's Assent prior to their commencement. In such cases, I would therefore have to go to Buckingham Palace (or wherever Her Majesty was staying) with the relevant documents which she would then be requested to sign. Thereafter, my job was to march into the House of Commons, in morning dress and read out the brief message from Her Majesty, confirming the appointment. This meant, in effect, that I would have a private audience with The Queen several times a year.

Secondly, the Vice Chamberlain was responsible each day that Parliament sat (other than occasional Fridays) for preparing what was known as the "Royal Message". This is a one-page summary despatched at 6:00pm each evening, informing Her Majesty of any important events that had taken place in Parliament that day. When being briefed on this by her courtiers in more detail, I was encouraged not to write a comedy sketch but to occasionally put in any light-hearted events, for instance if Dennis Skinner had one of his usual rants at the Prime Minister[93], as I was told The Queen enjoyed things slightly out of the ordinary in the Royal Message, which she would read through faithfully, every evening before dinner. As someone new to the job, I said to one of the courtiers, that given the recipient of this product, I would take the duty very seriously in any event, but nevertheless, just as a guide, could they tell me whether or not The Queen, with all the other State papers she had to read, tended to just glance through this, or did she read it very carefully? The reply which came back was as follows: "Oh no, Mark, she reads it very carefully indeed. After all, it's her Parliament and she's keen to know what goes on in it. If you think we're kidding, just wait a couple of months and one evening include some paragraph about what Micky Mouse said to Donald Duck in the Chamber – and then see what happens!". This more than made the point and I never had the courage to test the theory. I therefore took that job very seriously indeed, not least as it was subsequently explained to me that The Queen would sometimes draw on the content of these messages when she was having her regular weekly audience with the Prime Minister, normally on either Tuesday or Wednesday evenings.

The third duty was to act as a "hostage" during the State Opening of Parliament. This is a tradition going back hundreds of years, based on the fact that at the end of the Civil War, Parliament executed Charles I. Therefore, on the day of the State Opening, Her Majesty would travel in a formal procession to Parliament, change into the State Robes, and then deliver what is known as the "Queen's Speech" (outlining the Government's legislative programme for the year ahead). Given what had happened to Charles the First, Monarchs had learnt to take no chances and thus, by tradition, when The Queen went to Parliament, an MP would be sent the other way to Buckingham Palace, to be held as hostage to ensure the Sovereign's safe return.

In the event, this turned out to be quite a pleasant captivity. It began in the morning with a cup of coffee and a shortbread biscuit and, shall we say, conditions improved as the day wore on and besides you were able to watch the whole ceremony on a large flat screen television, in a rather comfortable room in the Palace. Part of the work of the Vice Chamberlain, in particular the content of each Royal Message, is quite rightly confidential but, suffice to say that it was both a pleasure and a privilege, to work for HM The Queen for the best part of two years.

Off to the MoD

In the Autumn of 2012, David Cameron announced a reshuffle of the Government, again in coordination with the Liberal Democrats. Both David Cameron and George Osborne knew full well that my lifelong ambition had been to serve as a Minister in the Ministry of Defence and in the end, they kept their word and gave me my chance.

Although I was sad in some ways to leave the Whips Office, because there is a great sense of team sprit there and it was wonderful to be part of it, I must confess I was also delighted to be told that I was being reassigned to the Ministry of Defence as the Minister for Defence Personnel, Welfare and Veterans (Min DPWV or sometimes just "Min Vets" for short). This is something which I had wanted since being a boy really, and so, it was with great delight that I tidied my desk in the Whips Office and then eagerly walked up Whitehall into Main Building, the Headquarters of the Ministry of Defence.

"I want the Geniums!"

A little while into my tour as Min Vets, I received a briefing on the medical support that the Department provided to Armed Forces personnel who had been wounded in the campaigns in Iraq (known in MoD speak as Operation Telic) and Afghanistan (Operation Herrick). When I asked about the prosthetics that our severely wounded personnel were issued, I was told that they were given a product called the "C Leg". When I enquired how, for example, this compared with what the American's gave their seriously wounded, there was some slightly uncomfortable shifting of seats in the room. When I pressed the point, I was told that the American's gave their wounded a product called "The Genium", but that they were *extremely* expensive and probably over specified for what was really required. That didn't impress me one bit. As far as I was concerned, if a soldier in Afghanistan had lost his legs whilst out on patrol against the Taliban, he deserved the best prosthetic that money could buy – and moreover I was certain that if I walked down Rayleigh High Street and asked my constituents, that 99 out of 100 would agree with me. "Right then", I said, "I want the Geniums, whatever it costs!". Thus, began a nine-month battle against the MoD's internal bureaucracy (of which some of the medical bureaucracy is the most conservative, with a small c, of the lot) in order to try and obtain these new advanced prosthetics. In doing so, I discovered that I had a powerful ally in Bryn Parry, the Chief Executive of Help for Heroes.

As Min Vets, part of my job was to liaise with all the main military charities in the United Kingdom, ranging from the largest and best known, such as the Royal British Legion and Help for Heroes, through the individual service charities such as the Army Benevolent Fund (now known as The Soldiers Charity) through to others such as Combat Stress, who specialise in dealing with mental health issues of ex-service personnel.[94]

Bryn Parry was a bit like me, a maverick. Whereas most military charities were run by retired two or three star Generals (or their Service equivalents), Bryn Parry had been a Captain in the Infantry, who had established something of a reputation during his career for being prepared to challenge authority, when he thought that it was wrong. Having left the forces but stayed in touch with a friend who had been wounded on operations, he and his wife resolved to undertake a bike ride in order to try and raise several thousand pounds towards the cost of building a swimming pool at his rehabilitation centre for wounded Veterans. This initial bike ride, which raised several thousand pounds, then evolved into Help for Heroes, one of the most successful military charities in British History, which to date has raised well over a quarter of a billion pounds to help assist wounded personnel.[95]

When I mentioned the prosthetics issue to Bryn, he explained that he too had been railing against the system and he also wanted to see the Geniums issued to wounded personnel but had come up against a brick wall of bureaucracy, much as I had. He told me that the only British Serviceman ever to be issued with a pair of Geniums was Corporal Daralangui, a Commonwealth soldier, who had been given a pair of Geniums to allow him to better compete for his country in the Paralympic Games. However, the Corporal was still serving in the Army. At that point, I hit on an idea. The Prime Minister, David Cameron, was due to visit Help for Heroes' premier recovery centre, at Tedworth House in Wiltshire, some weeks hence. I was down to accompany him on the visit as Veterans Minister and Bryn mentioned that Corporal Daralangui had in fact been a patient at Tedworth House in the past. We therefore rapidly hatched a plan to try and win Prime Ministerial support.

When the Prime Minister went to visit, I went with him and we began our tour at "The Tin Hut" in Tidworth, which was an old, corrugated tin building that Bryn Parry had been given by the Army, after months of nagging them for some premises to help his new charity get off the ground.[96] They made a point of sitting the PM at what was originally Bryn's desk, and he was fated by Help for Heroes staff who still worked there, who rapidly queued up to have selfies with him. In my view, David Cameron always had something of an affection for the Armed Forces, and therefore, he was, perhaps unsurprisingly, obviously pleased to be given this kind of reception.

I then got into the Prime Ministerial car and had an opportunity to brief him on the relatively short drive down to Tedworth House. I used the time to best effect and explained to him the issue about the Geniums and why they were so much better than the C Leg but that we were having trouble getting some in the MoD

134

establishment to approve their issue and getting the Treasury to pay for it. When we got to Tedworth House, we then took the Prime Minister on tour and he had an opportunity to meet a number of Veterans, one of whom just happened to be Corporal Daralangui. Noticing his artificial legs, the Prime Minister enquired what they were, and the Corporal then explained that he'd been very fortunate to be given a pair of Geniums. The Prime Minister took the bait and asked him why these were so much better than the other leg and the Corporal then went on to explain it far better – as a user of the product, than I or indeed Bryn (both of whom were looking on) could possibly have done. I confess, that we never fully explained to the Corporal what we were up to, but, clearly speaking from the heart, he turned out to be a brilliant salesman, nonetheless.

Towards the end of the visit the Prime Minister then had to do a rather difficult interview because we had not done well in some local elections and, as he usually did, he undertook a quick preparatory session in a private room with his staff where they fired some questions at him, as a rehearsal, before he went out to meet the cameras. I chose my moment carefully. As he came out of the room with a camera crew just setting up in the gravelled courtyard of Tedworth House, I asked if I could have a quick word. "What is it Mark?", he said, understandably slightly irritated: "I've got to go and do this bloody interview". "Yes, Prime Minister, I know that but it's very important". "What Mark?", he said. "Prime Minister, you've got *The Sun* Military Awards (the Millie's), coming up in a couple of months' time. How would you like to stand up and announce that every wounded soldier from Iraq and Afghanistan who needs artificial limbs, will be given the Geniums, the best prosthetic that money can buy?" He looked at me and said: "Yes Mark, that's a very good idea, just do whatever you have to do to make it happen and if anybody argues, send them to me!" "Thank you, Prime Minister", I said, "Good luck with your interview".

At the end of the visit, I then travelled back separately to London and went straight into the Ministry of Defence and called a meeting of senior officials where I delighted in telling them that the Prime Minister himself had just *directed* us to make sure that we would issue all our seriously wounded who would benefit from it, with Geniums and that he wanted the MoD to prepare the announcement. A few months and six and a half million pounds from the Treasury later, we were ready to make the announcement, not at the Millie's as it turned out but at the Armed Forces Rehabilitation Centre at Hedley Court.

By this stage I had been working on this project for the best part of nine months, and so I was absolutely delighted to be told, the night before, that the Secretary of State, Philip Hammond, would be coming down to Hedley Court to make the announcement instead, but he would be grateful if I could accompany him, "in case there were any technical questions". In fairness, I would not be the only junior Minister in history ever to have worked hard on a project, only to have had their Secretary of State take the credit at the last moment. This is perhaps the classic *cri de coeur* of junior Ministers down the ages.

In any event, what really mattered was not who stood in front of the cameras that day and took the credit but the fact that the Geniums would be issued to those who really needed them. Some months later, I saw a video of one of our wounded soldiers from Afghanistan in the gym on a treadmill, jogging successfully in a pair of Geniums. If I never achieve anything else in my life – I achieved that, and in many ways, it was worth coming into politics just to make that one change. This is an example of where being a Minister, despite all its frustrations, can actually be a force for good.[97] It's a well-worn cliché that people want to come into politics to "make a difference" but, on this issue at least, I actually did.

Min AF – "The best job in Government"

In the autumn of 2013, following a further reshuffle, I was again promoted, this time within the MoD itself, to become the Minister of State for the Armed Forces, ubiquitously known throughout Whitehall as Min AF. Minister of State for the Armed Forces is sometimes referred to as "the best job in Government". In essence, that is because you get to spend a lot of time with members of our Armed Forces – in many ways the best of the best – and also to play with much of the highly sophisticated kit, but without all the onerous responsibilities of the Secretary of State. If, like me, you had been interested in Defence since you were a small boy, this really was a dream job.

Within the Ministry of Defence, Min (AF) has responsibility for Operations, so for instance, I took over the day-to-day Ministerial responsibility for the final few months of the drawdown of British Forces from Afghanistan, a highly complex process which was being planned and orchestrated from Permanent Joint Headquarters (PJHQ) at Northwood, near the end of the Metropolitan Line, on the Northwest outskirts of London.[98]

During my time as an MoD Minister, I visited our troops in Afghanistan on two occasions. Firstly, as Min Vets to lay a wreath on behalf of the Government on Remembrance Sunday, at the UK Brigade Headquarters at Lashkar-gar and secondly, to visit British Forces in Kabul and at Kandahar in 2014.

Operation Gritrock

In 2014, we successfully conducted the drawdown from Afghanistan, some months earlier than had been widely anticipated. Fortunately, due to some excellent staff work by the military planners at PJHQ, we managed to depart from our main Garrison at Camp Bastion, virtually without incident and fly most of our people home before the Taliban had really woken up to what was happening. We only left behind several hundred troops, who were no longer intended to participate in direct combat, but who were tasked to help train the Afghan Army and provide security, mainly in Kabul, instead.

However, no sooner had this challenge been accomplished, than within a few months we began to receive reports of a breakout of the highly contagious Ebola virus in Sierra Leone, one of the poorest countries on earth. The UK Government mounted a major response, led by the Department for International Development (DFID), with considerable support from the Ministry of Defence. Within the MoD, this effort was codenamed "Operation Gritrock" and, as Min AF, I was assigned Ministerial oversight of this endeavour.

In the end, after months of a combined international effort, the disease was eventually beaten back. As part of our deployment, I had the privilege of visiting out troops in Sierra Leone, including at a rapidly constructed field hospital on the outskirts of the capital, Freetown. I was overawed by the courage of our personnel, especially our medical personnel, who despite very thorough training, still took considerable risks to combat this highly contagious disease, something they succeeded in doing without any of our personnel becoming fatally infected (although we did have a couple of near misses).

We have seen again more recently, the important contribution of the Armed Forces during the battle against Coronavirus, helping to ensure the supply of Personal Protective Equipment (PPE) to hospitals and other facilities and also helping to set up mobile testing centres around the country, so that key workers and others can be tested to see whether or not they have contracted the virus.

This role as the "Department of last resort" is a fundamental part of what the Ministry of Defence does, and therefore it was a great honour to serve as a Minister in that Department – something I will always be proud of and never forget.

In the spring of 2015, we all knew that a General Election would shortly be in the offing and of course, after the election would follow a further inevitable reshuffle.

By this stage, I had served in the Department for nearly three years (which is quite a long stint for an MoD Minister in recent times) and so I began to suspect that whilst I would merrily have served in that Department for years, perhaps the time was coming when the Prime Minister might let someone else have a go. I think perhaps the military had sensed the same and I remember following a service for the Fallen in the Afghanistan campaign at St Paul's Cathedral, I was detailed to be part of a receiving line for the two princes, William and Harry at a reception for attendees of the Service, focusing mainly on military Veterans, to be held at the Headquarters of the Honourable Artillery Company, in the City of London.

Whilst waiting for the Royal Party to arrive, a General who I had much enjoyed working with turned to me and said: "Well, Minister, I must say it's been very interesting working with you these past few years". "Thank you General", I replied, "that answer sounds like it could cover a multitude of sins, what do you mean by it?". "Actually Minister, to be frank, there have been occasions when you've driven us all mad with your incessant demands to do this or that on behalf of the Armed Forces. But at the end of the day, we all put up with it because we all knew without exception, that your heart was absolutely in the job, so whatever happens now, it's been a pleasure working with you".

I must say, there are worse things to be told by a Three Star General and its true, my heart had been in it and I hope that whether it be a Veteran now walking around on a pair of Geniums or perhaps one of our personnel who came back safely from Sierra Leone, that I might have at least done some small good, whilst I had the privilege of serving in what I still believe to be the greatest Department in Government.

Adele and the "A Team"

When my first PA, the redoubtable Anna Tolchard, told me that she and her husband were planning to semi-retire down to their native Devon, she kindly offered to keep assisting me, by helping part-time with some of my constituency correspondence.

This was just a temporary arrangement – which lasted for over a decade. (The French have a saying which roughly translates as: "Nothing endures quite like the provisional" and in this case it turned out to be absolutely true).

However, this left an obvious void as I would need a new PA, based at Westminster.

138

Anna kindly agreed to help me with recruiting her successor and we decided that she would sift the CVs and conduct the initial interviews and try and find three good candidates, from whom I could pick, with her advice, the winning candidate.

As word got out that I was looking for a new PA, a strange thing began to happen. A number of the other secretaries on our corridor "just popped by" to mention that a young lady named "Adele" who had previously worked on the same floor for Bob Walter MP, had apparently applied and that she would be really very suitable for the role.

After this had happened for the fourth time in as many days, I asked Anna who this lady was and was told that she, too, had received similar advice from her counterparts and had in fact already earmarked Adele as one of the potential candidates.

A fortnight later, sitting in my office with Anna, I was awaiting the arrival of this superwoman when a quiet, unassuming young lady calmly walked in. She was reserved, bordering on shy and it was initially a bit difficult to get answers out of her. However, once we turned to how she saw the role and dealing with constituents she came alive and by the time that the interviews were concluded both Anna and I agreed that she was the stand-out candidate. That was almost fifteen years ago.

Since that time Adele has been my loyal PA and later Office Manager as well. She married a charming Frenchman, and they have a lovely son, who has a passion for football.

When Adele departed on maternity leave, I asked my recently appointed researcher, Alexandra Rich (Alex) to step up and act as my PA while Adele was away, which she did flawlessly. Adele is as organised as a Swiss watch but, it turns out, that if Adele metaphorically came from Berne then Alex came from Zurich. She did a terrific job and then stood back, without rancour, when Adele returned as my full-time PA around a year later.

When I became a Minister at the MoD, I had a full time PA, Adele; a part time correspondence/constituency secretary, Anna and a full-time researcher, Alex. I christened these three formidable ladies "The A Team", which also went down very well with my local Association back home.

Adele is not avidly "political" and certainly not an ardent Brexiteer. What she is, however, is a thoroughly professional team player and someone who manages to cope with a demanding boss without losing her cool, or her subtle sense of humour either.

One morning when I was a Minister, and three things had already gone skewwhiff by breakfast, I came into my Westminster office and whingeingly exclaimed: "Just for once, just once, I would like to have an uneventful, normal day!" To which she calmly replied: "This is a normal day Mark; they're all like this!" So, Minister – 0, PA – 1, extra time not required!

During the Battle for Brexit Adele was pretty unflappable. I think she probably let out a small sigh every time I headed off to Millbank to do another media round, as the emails, either for or against, usually started flowing in (and, in a few instances, flooding in) shortly afterwards. She dealt with all of this with good grace. There is an old saying, that "good help is hard to find". I believe that's true but excellent help is even better.

The 2015 General Election

Despite many commentators saying that it would only last a matter of months, the Conservative/Liberal Democrat Coalition actually held together for the best part of five years, until a General Election came to be held in the summer of 2015. By this stage though, the Coalition had effectively started to break down, perhaps based in part on the Lib Dems anger at having lost the AV Referendum but also due to other disputes such as reform of the House of Lords and proposed changes to Electoral Boundaries. In essence, the increasingly awkward marriage was already heading for the divorce courts by the time that the election was finally called.

During the General Election, one of the issues that absorbed the pundits greatly was what effect, if any, the United Kingdom Independence Party (UKIP) would have in denying the Conservatives a possible overall majority. Back in South Essex, this was very much a live issue and in constituencies such as neighbouring Castle Point, it was very much a Blue/Purple battle i.e. a struggle between Conservatives vs UKIP with the Labour Party and the Liberal Democrats trailing a poor third, or worse.

In the end, to the surprise of many, David Cameron and the Conservatives won the 2015 General Election outright, albeit with a narrow majority of just 12 seats.

The Liberals however, suffered a crushing defeat and went back from some 57 seats down to only as many as eight. Locally in Rayleigh and Wickford we achieved a very satisfactory result, which was as follows:

General Election Result for the Rayleigh and Wickford Constituency, 2015

Mark Francois	Conservative	29,088
John Hayter	UKIP	11,858
David Hough	Labour	6,705
Linda Kendall	Independent	2,418
Mike Pitt	Liberal Democrat	1,622
Sarah Yapp	Green Candidate	1,529
Conservative Majority		17,230
Turnout		69%

I had thus been re-elected with a still quite substantial majority and about which I was obviously very pleased. Nevertheless, the General Election had been extremely hard work, during which I had had to campaign in multiple constituencies, as well as trying to fight my own campaign in Rayleigh and Wickford and maintain my responsibilities as an MoD Minister (because even though there is a General Election, the Government still has to continue in the meantime, until a new Government is elected).

In particular, my time at the Ministry of Defence had been quite intense, having to deal with everything from the drawdown from Afghanistan, through to helping deal with the floods in the West Country in early 2014, through to Operation Gritrock and overseeing the Department's fight against the Ebola virus in Sierra Leone.

Off to DCLG

When the Government was reformed after the election, David Cameron now had a small working majority in the House of Commons which gave him the political authority to reshuffle his Cabinet pretty much however he liked. I remember he called me into No 10 and said: "Mark, I know how much you love the MoD, so I feel in some ways I'm taking a fish out of water here but nevertheless, you've served in Local Government before and I want you to go over to the Department for Communities and Local Government to support the new Secretary of State, Greg Clarke".

I had not really been in DCLG all that long when the EU Referendum campaign began in earnest in the Spring of 2016 and, alongside all other Ministers and indeed other MPs, I was effectively forced to take sides (see Chapter 8).

However, I do remember the Ministers and civil servants at DCLG as being highly committed to what they were doing, including trying to support Local Government through a very challenging period of austerity.

Nevertheless, when David Cameron, who had effectively led the Remain campaign, lost the Referendum and resigned, to be replaced quite rapidly as Prime Minister by Theresa May, I did not really expect to survive yet another reshuffle. I remember saying to a close friend at the time, "I think my number's finally up this time" – and so it proved to be.

Back to square one – Life as a Backbench constituency MP

Although I knew David Cameron and George Osborne well, I enjoyed no such personal relationship with Theresa May. She had been elected four years before me, as part of the 1997 intake and although I had dealings with her whilst at the MoD (for instance during anti-terrorist exercises when she was Home Secretary) there was no real affinity and so, I was not surprised to be dropped from her Government in the reshuffle, shortly after she won the Conservative Leadership in 2016.

Besides, having now served on the Front Bench, both in Opposition and in Government for very nearly fifteen years without a break, I was pretty exhausted, so when the call came through from Gavin Williamson, her new Chief Whip, telling me that, unfortunately, I would be leaving the Government, I did not protest. If anything, the main feeling I remember at the time was one of relief.

No more 18-hour days, no more Red Boxes full of challenging submissions requiring rapid approval, no more being constantly pestered by well-meaning civil servants, even on Sunday evenings, no more "hospital pass" media interviews, attempting to justify some unpopular policy either. Instead, a chance to stand back a bit and refocus on the primary task of being an MP, to work for the employers who elect you in the first place, as Ken Livingstone had pointed out to me, all those years ago.

I have always enjoyed the role of a local Member of Parliament, so, having greatly enjoyed my time in Government, especially at the MoD, but having left the front bench in 2016, I was quietly resolved to just concentrate on being a good constituency MP for the rest of my Parliamentary career, however long that might still be.

And then somebody mentioned Europe....

Chapter 8: Vote Leave and the 2016 EU Referendum

The issue of Europe is one that has divided the Conservative Party for almost five decades. As a Party we have been arguing over it even before Ted Heath took us into the European Economic Community in 1973. As Jacob Rees-Mogg has reminded me on several occasions, even the vote to join the EEC led to a split in Tory ranks with those who already had doubts about surrendering Sovereignty, voting against it at the time.[99] The Labour Party were also officially opposed to joining the EEC but a number of pro-European Labour MPs, such as Roy Jenkins and Shirley Williams (some of whom were later to break away from Labour and form the Social Democratic Party, or SDP in the 1980s) defied the Labour Whip and helped Heath carry his Motion to join the EEC over the line by just eight votes, in 1972.[100]

The Evolution of Conservative European Policy – From Heath to Cameron

When the UK subsequently joined the EEC in January 1973,[101] the make-up of the Conservative Parliamentary Party was overwhelmingly pro-European in nature. In many ways, this was very understandable. The House of Commons in the early 1970s still contained a considerable number of MPs who had fought in the Second World War (Ted Heath included) and many of them saw the EEC and further European integration as a way of preventing such a major conflagration ever breaking out on the European continent again. Being "pro-European" was therefore very much the orthodoxy of the time, so much so, that in the 1975 Referendum on whether or not the UK should remain within the European Economic Community, even Margaret Thatcher campaigned for a "Yes" vote (i.e. to stay in) and was famously photographed in a colourful jumper, emblazoned with a number of European national flags, as part of the Yes campaign.[102]

However, once in Downing Street, Margaret Thatcher became increasingly concerned at the growing power of the European Institutions and what she saw as their continuing attempt to impinge upon the everyday life of ordinary Britons, via policies such as the Common Agricultural Policy, the Common Fisheries Policy and even the administration of Value Added Tax (VAT). In 1988, Mrs Thatcher gave her famous "Bruges Speech" in which she warned that: "We in Britain have not worked so hard in order to roll back the frontiers of the state, only to see them re-imposed upon us at a European level".[103]

It was bitter arguments over Europe – combined with the unpopularity of the Community Charge (rapidly dubbed the "Poll Tax") – that eventually led to Margaret Thatcher's departure from office in 1990. She had fallen out with the ardently pro-European Michael Heseltine over the future ownership of the Westland Helicopter company, when he famously stormed out of Cabinet in 1986.[104] She then fell out with other pro-European members of the Cabinet, including her Deputy Prime Minister, Sir Geoffrey Howe, as well as fighting running battles with her formidable Chancellor, Nigel Lawson, about Britain's membership of the Exchange Rate Mechanism (the ERM).[105] Even by her fall in 1990, the bulk of the Conservative backbenches were more instinctively pro-European than Eurosceptic.

Margaret's successor, John Major, then famously assented to the Maastricht Treaty, which led to the European Economic Community evolving into a new entity, the "European Union" (or EU), which increasingly possessed the trappings of a state. Perhaps most controversially, the Maastricht Treaty presaged the creation of a single European currency (later to become The Euro) and Major's Government remained deeply divided about whether or not to eventually abandon the Pound Sterling and join the single European currency instead, once succinctly summed up by John Major as "wait and see". During the bitter battles over the Maastricht Treaty in Parliament, Major also faced a minority of Eurosceptic Cabinet colleagues, including John Redwood, Michael Portillo and several others, who, in an off the record moment at the end of an interview, he famously described as "the Bastards".[106]

By 1995 such was the division in the Conservative Party over the European issue that Major directly challenged his critics to "put up or shut up". This led to a Leadership Election against John Redwood, who coined the slogan "No Change, No Chance" but which Major comfortably won, by 218 votes to 89.[107] However, significantly at that stage, only Conservative MPs were allowed to vote on the Leader, and it was not until the 2001 Leadership Contest that ordinary Conservative Party Members were given the final say.

Major's divided and exhausted Government was nevertheless overwhelmingly defeated by Tony Blair's incoming new Labour administration in 1997 (pretty much as Redwood had predicted two years earlier). As the new Prime Minister, Blair then came under strong pressure from his European neighbours to commit the Labour Government to joining the Euro. However, he too had Cabinet opponents to this idea, led by his powerful Chancellor, Gordon Brown, surrounded by strong allies such as his Special Advisor, Ed Balls and his influential press aide, Damian McBride. The Conservative Party under William

Hague, still reeling from its crushing electoral defeat, nevertheless put strong pressure on Blair not to join the Euro, after it was officially launched on 1ˢᵗ January 1999, amidst considerable pomp and ceremony and accompanied by the EU anthem, "Ode to Joy".[108] A combination of internal Labour opposition and external Conservative and media pressure successfully managed to dissuade Blair, who was inclined towards joining the single currency, to risk it and certainly not to do so without a Referendum.[109] Although the Conservative Party was again heavily defeated in the 2001 General Election under William Hague, his "Keep the Pound" campaign, which was at the centrepiece of the Tories 2001 election pitch, again succeeded in helping to deter Blair from chancing it. As William said several years later at a conference at the Royal United Services Institute (RUSI), which I attended: "We campaigned to Keep the Pound – and indeed we have kept the Pound – so at least we won on that one, if nothing else".[110]

By this stage, the Conservative Party's policy on the single currency had become a touchstone for the Party's wider policy on Europe as a whole. Under William Hague, in a compromise with his influential, pro-European Shadow Chancellor, Kenneth Clarke, it was agreed that the Party's policy would be not to join the single currency, for at least a Parliament. William Hague's successor as Tory Leader, Iain Duncan Smith, hardened this policy to opposition to joining the single currency as a matter of principle; a position which was also maintained in turn by his successor as leader, Michael Howard. By the time that David Cameron took over as Conservative Leader in 2005, the Conservatives still remained opposed in principle to joining the single currency with David Cameron's additional commitment that he would withdraw his MEPs from the pro-Federalist European Peoples Party (the EPP) in the European Parliament, something which we successfully achieved, with me as the Project Manager, in 2009.

"We shall not let matters rest there" (WSNLMRT)

Shortly after becoming Conservative Leader, David Cameron, whose great ally was his Shadow Chancellor, George Osborne, invited William Hague to "come out of retirement" and become his Shadow Foreign Secretary. William agreed and then led the Opposition to yet another European centralising Treaty, the Lisbon Treaty with me acting as his deputy as Shadow Europe Minister (see Chapter 6). We had campaigned hard to try and persuade Gordon Brown to hold a Referendum on the Lisbon Treaty, but he resolutely refused, knowing that he had sufficient votes in the House of Commons to ram the Treaty through, with a much larger majority than Major had ever enjoyed over Maastricht some 16 years previously.

However, David Cameron, in an article in *The Sun*, famously offered a "cast iron guarantee" that an incoming Conservative Government would hold a national Referendum on the Lisbon Treaty, providing that it had not been Ratified by the time that we came into power.[111]   Unfortunately, most commentators and members of the public only heard the first bit of the sentence and not the second and therefore there was great disappointment when the Treaty was eventually Ratified, and Cameron announced that, unfortunately, a Referendum would no longer be possible, as the Treaty was now effectively binding in international law.

Nevertheless, during the subsequent debates in Parliament, when taunted by the Labour Party on what the Conservatives would do, William Hague shot back that if we came to power and the Treaty had already been Ratified then, "We would not let matters rest there". He said this during a debate on the Foreign Affairs portion of the Queens Speech on 6th November 2007 and at the time, most commentators missed it, except the BBC's then Political Editor, Nick Robinson, who realised immediately that William had said something really significant.[112]

When I spoke to William afterwards, I asked him what exactly he meant by it to which he replied, that he hadn't worked out a detailed policy, he was just determined that if they did manage to ram the Treaty through without a Referendum, "they won't get away with it Mark" and that we would have to respond in some way or other.[113]   We therefore spent several months and numerous meetings trying to work out exactly what our response would actually mean, to "We shall not let matters rest there" (or WSNLMRT). I spent much time with William, his Special Advisor, Denzil Davidson and my own Researcher, Chris Howarth, chewing over the options for what this riposte might actually comprise. After endless internal debate, I took Denzil and Chris out to a pub just off Sloane Square one evening and in an upstairs bar told them: "Right, we're not leaving this pub until we have an actual plan to put to William on Monday".

In the end, on 23rd January 2008, David Cameron finally unveiled the basis of what "We shall not let matters rest there" actually meant.[114] The centrepiece of this was a "Referendum Lock", not to have a referendum on Lisbon but to ensure that if ever any subsequent European Treaty were negotiated, which transferred further powers from Westminster to Brussels, this could not be ratified unless first endorsed by the British people in a Referendum. There were several other aspects to "We shall not let matters rest there" but the Referendum Lock was undoubtedly the central element and became the centrepiece of our European policy, in the subsequent 2010 General Election.[115]

The resultant Coalition Government, with the highly pro-European Liberal Democrats, meant that David Cameron was keen to downplay the European issue, as it was potentially very divisive within the partnership. In the end, all the crunch policy decisions were taken by four men, David Cameron, George Osborne, Nick Clegg and his right-hand man, Danny Alexander (Chief Secretary to the Treasury under George) in what became known across Whitehall as "the Quad". Given the pressing economic crisis which the Coalition Government had inherited from Gordon Brown, the last thing the Quad wanted to do was to spend endless hours debating European policy.

However, the 2010 General Election, in which the Conservative Party had made numerous gains, saw the entry into Parliament of a considerable number of more Eurosceptic Conservative MPs, such as Steve Baker, Conor Burns, Zac Goldsmith, Priti Patel, Dominic Raab and one Jacob Rees-Mogg among others, and so the pressure from the Conservative Backbenches on David Cameron to do something muscular about Europe only intensified, rather than waned. Indeed, in 2012, 73 Conservative MPs voted for an Amendment calling for a Referendum on Britain's Membership of the European Union (although the Amendment itself was poorly drafted and talked about a Referendum with three questions rather than a straight "In/Out" choice, which is one of the reasons why it did not garner further support). I thought personally that a three question Referendum was practically unworkable and so I didn't vote for it either. However, this action gave notice that despite Cameron's famous dictum that "the Conservative Party should stop banging on about Europe" the issue still aroused strong passions among many Tory MPs and was clearly not going to go away.[116]

The rise of UKIP

The United Kingdom Independence Party (UKIP) was founded originally as the "Anti Federalist League", a minor Eurosceptic Party established in London by the historian, Alan Sked, in 1991.[117] It changed its name to UKIP in 1993 but, as a Eurosceptic movement, it was overshadowed in the mid-1990s by the rival "Referendum Party" which had been organised by the Financier, Sir James Goldsmith, (father of the future Tory MP, Zac Goldsmith) and which stood a number of candidates against John Major's Conservatives in the 1997 General Election. Jimmy Goldsmith himself stood against one of Major's great allies, David Mellor, in Putney in that year and arguably took sufficient right-wing votes to contribute to Mellor's defeat.[118]

However, the Referendum Party was subsequently dissolved sometime after the 1997 General Election and UKIP effectively took up the mantle of an outwardly

Eurosceptic Party, and one committed to Leave the European Union. In essence, the clue was in the name. In the 1999 European Elections, UKIP won 3 seats, with 6.5% of the national vote.[119]

However, the real driving force behind UKIP as a national entity was Nigel Farage, a City Dealer from Kent, who was one of the Party's wannabe MEPs, who was first elected to the European Parliament in 1999 and who then became UKIPs Leader in 2006. Farage had a great knack for publicity and for "saying what others were thinking but dared not say". He was unabashed about taking on the British Establishment and their fellow travellers in the media and did not shy away from giving often controversial interviews about the growing power of the European Union and the risks of large-scale immigration into the United Kingdom. The accession of the so called "A8" Eastern European nations to the EU in 2004 did indeed presage over a million Eastern Europeans coming to the UK in a relatively few years and Farage proved very adept at highlighting the pressures on national infrastructure and public services that was caused by this spike in immigration (albeit, that many of those incoming immigrants actually worked extremely hard and no doubt contributed to the growth of the British economy following their arrival). Nevertheless, in the 2004 European Elections, UKIP won 12 seats.

Following their subsequent, Post Lisbon Treaty success in the 2009 European Elections (where they won over 2 million votes and secured 13 MEPs), UKIP gradually began to stand candidates in local elections as well and in a number of cases actually managed to get UKIP councillors elected. More worryingly from a Conservative point of view, they often challenged the Conservative Party directly for the allegiance of right-wing voters, and in the 2010 General Election, some defeated Conservative candidates argued that UKIP candidates had almost certainly cost them their seats.[120]

David Cameron once famously described UKIP as "...a bunch of... fruitcakes and loonies and closet racists mostly", which led to a furious reaction from Nigel Farage and indeed from some elements on the right of the Conservative Party, who felt that insulting UKIP and its supporters (many of them former Conservatives) was not the best way to deal with the electoral challenge that they posed.[121] As the Coalition Government began to run into trouble on a variety of fronts, pressure grew on David Cameron as Prime Minister to offer an In/Out Referendum on Membership of the European Union – in order to address the electoral threat from UKIP and also to settle the increasingly vexed question once and for all.

Cameron's Bloomberg Speech

After much internal debate among his inner circle in Downing Street, in January 2013, Cameron made an audacious move when in a speech at Bloomberg, he effectively committed a future majority Conservative Government to holding an In/Out Referendum on Britain's Membership of the European Union. The key passage of Cameron's speech announced:

"It is time for the British people to have their say. It is time to settle this European question in British politics.

I say to the British people: this will be your decision.

And when that choice comes, you will have an important choice to make about our country's destiny.

I understand the appeal of going it alone, of charting our own course. But it will be a decision we will have to take with cool heads. Proponents of both sides of the argument will need to avoid exaggerating their claims.

Of course, Britain could make her own way in the world, outside the EU, if we chose to do so. So could any other Member State.

But the question we will have to ask ourselves is this: is that the very best future for our country?

We will have to weigh carefully where our true national interest lies".

It was difficult in some ways for the Liberal Democrats to object to this as, ironically, during the debates on the Lisbon Treaty some five years previously, they had argued themselves for an In/Out Referendum – albeit purely as a device to avoid committing to a Referendum on Lisbon at the time. Therefore, to some extent, even despite their disquiet within the Coalition at this development, they were effectively hoist by their own petard.

Much has already been written about what finally persuaded David Cameron to take this fateful decision.[122] At this time, I was serving in the Ministry of Defence and so effectively had no input into the matter one way or another – and so in many ways, I was just as surprised as anybody else. There has since been a rather polemic debate into what led Cameron to make this move. Some would argue that it was solely external pressure from UKIP, led by a very proactive Nigel Farage, that persuaded Cameron that if UKIP were not to spoil any chance he had of winning a subsequent General Election outright, he would have to promise this Referendum, in order to try and neutralise the UKIP threat. Conversely, others in the Conservative Party might argue that it was concerted internal pressure from Backbench MPs, such as Bill Cash, Peter Bone, Philip Davis and others, who finally persuaded Cameron that the only way out of his European Dilemma was to offer a definitive plebiscite.

My own view on this is that both sides are right, and it was, in fact, a combination of the two, although the precise percentages are difficult to quantify definitively. In simple terms, it was the external pressure from UKIP, combined with the internal pressure from the Conservative Backbenches, plus a few Eurosceptics within Cameron's own Cabinet, echoed in the right-wing elements of the media, that finally led him to conclude he would be unable to break out of the Coalition and win a General Election in his own right, unless he were to offer an In/Out Referendum first.

When pressed on how he would vote in any such Referendum, Cameron hinted that he would vote for Britain to stay in the EU but stressed that he would respect the decision of the people, whichever way it went.

In 2014, David Cameron subsequently campaigned very successfully in the Referendum on Scottish independence, in which he and his allies delivered a significant blow to Alex Salmond's Scottish Nationalist Party (SNP) by winning a vote that Scotland should remain part of the United Kingdom by a margin of 55% to 45%.[123] This double-digit victory, for which Cameron had campaigned extremely hard, no doubt emboldened him and those around him that a similarly energetic campaigning performance could win any subsequent In/Out Referendum on the EU as well. The In/Out Referendum pledge was thus included in the Conservative's 2015 General Election Manifesto in the following unequivocal terms:

"For too long, your voice has been ignored on Europe. We will: give you a say over whether we should stay in or leave the EU, with an in-out referendum by the end of 2017".[124]

Therefore, over several decades, the Conservative Party's policy on Europe had shifted very significantly in a Eurosceptic direction. It had evolved from one of joining the European Economic Community under Ted Heath (who many people believed secretly dreamed of a Federal Europe, but dared not say so at the time); to one of advocating the Maastricht Treaty without a Referendum and leaving open the possibility of joining the single currency under John Major; to opposition to joining the single currency for a Parliament under William Hague; to opposition in principle to joining the single currency under both Iain Duncan Smith and Micheal Howard and then, to a "Referendum lock" and, eventually, to offering an In/Out Referendum under David Cameron.

If plotted as a spectrum, this illustrates how very far European policy had evolved in the Conservative Party over the 43 years between joining the EEC in 1973, to the Referendum on whether or not to Leave what had then become the EU, in 2016.

Fig 1. Conservative Party Policy on Europe 1973 - 2016

"Pro-European"							"Eurosceptic"
1973	1992	1997	2001	2003	2005	2013	2016
Heath	Major	Hague	IDS	Howard	Cameron	Cameron	Cameron
Britain Joins the EEC	Wait and see on single currency	"Keep the Pound" Don't join the Euro for a Parliament	Against joining the Euro in principle	Against joining the Euro in principle	Anti-Euro & leave the EPP	Promises In/Out Referendum	EU Referendum Announced for 23rd June 2016

The In/Out Referendum is called

To the surprise of many political pundits, David Cameron won the 2015 General Election with a small but workable majority of 12 seats, the first outright Conservative General Election victory since John Major's 23 years previously. Then, with the momentum of both the Scottish Referendum and the General Election wins behind him, he took a decision to tackle the European issue head on, relatively early on in the new Parliament. Accordingly, on 20th February 2016, Prime Minister David Cameron announced that an In/Out Referendum would take place on the 23rd June 2016, to effectively settle the question of Britain's future relations with Europe once and for all. As he told the House of Commons:

"But with the special status this settlement gives us, I do believe the time has come to fulfil another vital commitment this government made – and that is to hold a Referendum.

So, Mr Speaker, I am today commencing the process set out under our Referendum Act to propose that the British people decide our future in Europe through an in-out referendum on Thursday 23rd June".[125]

David Cameron is a Politician who has always worn his heart on his sleeve. Whether it was forcing reluctant Members in his Party to accept the validity of gay marriage, or indeed his very active campaigning in the Scottish Referendum, he has never been one to shy away from a fight. Whereas in the 1975 EEC Referendum, Harold Wilson as Prime Minister let it be known that he favoured remaining in the EEC but then effectively took little further part in the campaign, promising the British people that as PM, he would execute faithfully whatever decision they came to; Cameron conversely decided from the outset that rather than "remain above the fray" he would campaign wholeheartedly for Britain to Remain in the European Union.

Reputedly, George Osborne warned his friend Cameron in the strongest possible terms that he should not have consented to an In/Out Referendum and that it could one day destroy his Premiership. Nevertheless, Cameron was obviously convinced that a combination of his energy and commitment, with the weight of the Government machine, a supportive media and the full weight of the British Establishment behind him, could successfully carry the day.[126]

With the consent of the Electoral Commission, who were detailed to oversee the Referendum, it was agreed that the question to be posed on the ballot paper would be as follows:

"Should the United Kingdom Remain a Member of the European Union or Leave?".

This was a very straightforward question and had the effect of gradually polarising the country into two distinct camps, "Leave" and "Remain".

The £9m Government Booklet

Parliament subsequently passed an Act, the EU Referendum Act 2016, to effectively set the "Rules of Engagement" under which the forthcoming Referendum would take place. This mandated that each side would have one officially nominated campaign, with each having an equal budget of up to around £7 million to spend on persuading the British public of its case.[127] However, before the spending limit kicked in, the Government rushed out an A5 14-page colour booklet to every household in the United Kingdom entitled: "Why the Government believes that voting to Remain in the European Union is the best decision for the UK". The printing and delivery of this booklet cost in the region of £9 million and it could be argued that this gave the Remain campaign a significant head start. Either way, page 13 of the booklet was headed: "A once in a generation decision".

It went on to say:

"The Referendum on Thursday 23rd June is your chance to decide if we should Remain in or Leave the European Union. The Government believes it is in the best interests of the UK to Remain in the EU.

This is the best way to protect jobs, provide security, and strengthen the UK's economy for every family in this country – a clear path into the future, in contrast to the uncertainty of Leaving".

However, crucially, for the debates that were to follow, it then famously said the following:

"This is your decision. **The Government will implement what you decide**". (Emphasis added).[128]

That commitment from the Government, in a booklet sent to every household across the UK prior to the vote, could not have been clearer. The language was concise and unambiguous and gave a direct promise to the voters that the Government would implement the decision of the people. This was to be a material consideration in what subsequently happened after the votes had actually been counted, (especially after the people of the United Kingdom had the temerity to reject the Government's very expensive advice).

Taking sides

At first glance, the Referendum was hardly a fair fight. Pitched on the side of Remain were the four established political Parties in Britain, the Conservatives, the Labour Party and the Liberal Democrats – whilst in Scotland, the Scottish Nationalist Party were also very firmly in favour of Remaining in the EU. This position was also supported by almost the entire British Establishment from the Confederation of British Industry (the CBI), through to the Trade Union Congress (the TUC), the BBC, SKY, and a number of national newspapers ranging from *The Times* through to the *Guardian*, *Independent* and the *Mirror*.

Ranged against this was what came to be known as the officially nominated "Vote Leave" campaign, which had no single individual leader, but had the support of a number of prominent Cabinet Ministers plus obviously UKIP and a few national newspaper titles, including the *Daily Telegraph*, the *Daily Mail*, the *Daily Express* and *The Sun*. Whilst the Eurosceptics therefore enjoyed some support in the popular press they were heavily outnumbered in the broadcast media, whose leanings (whatever their official position) were clearly overwhelmingly in favour of Remain. As just one example, according to the Think-tank *Civitas*, in 10 years leading up to the Referendum, the BBC's flagship *Today* programme on Radio 4 (whose output *Civitas* scrutinised in detail) had given just 4% of its airtime on the issue of Europe to Eurosceptic commentators, the other 96% had been given to people who were pro our relationship with the EU, a "pro-European ratio" of over 19:1.[129]

For Politicians, this was clearly a binary decision. Although a few MPs (such as the future Speaker of the House, Sir Lindsay Hoyle) went through the campaign without wishing to publicly declare a position, either for Leave or Remain, the vast bulk of MPs decided that they had to fight publicly for one cause or the other. For Ministers, this was something of a challenge as the normal rules of collective responsibility meant that Ministers would be expected to adhere to the Government's official line, i.e. to campaign for and vote for Remain.

However, in 1975, Harold Wilson had allowed his Ministers to campaign on either side of the EEC Referendum without having to resign and people within the Government seized on this precedent. In particular, Chris Grayling, the Transport Secretary in the Cabinet, did other Eurosceptic Ministers a massive favour when he went to see Cameron and effectively threatened to resign if the Prime Minister did not grant similar leave for Ministers to campaign on whichever side their conscience dictated.[130] David Cameron subsequently announced that whilst he would obviously prefer Minister's to campaign and vote for Remain, he recognised that some had long-standing reservations about our relationship with the EU and therefore he would consent to allowing Ministers to campaign to Leave, without having to resign. At this time, I was still a Minister at the Department for Communities and Local Government and therefore, I too had to decide on which side of the battlefield to plant my flag.

Believe it or not, despite the fact that I had always been a Eurosceptic I did not take the decision lightly, or without some forethought. I genuinely tried to weigh up both sides of the argument but in the end, it seemed to me inevitable, that if Remain were to win this Referendum, then all further resistance to European integration would effectively be steamrollered very rapidly, and the United Kingdom would effectively become co-opted as a wholehearted part of "The Project" which would lead, ineluctably, to us becoming part of a Federal European State. There was no way on earth that I could campaign for that and so, after first weighing it up, I resolved very clearly in my own mind that I would declare for Leave and campaign accordingly.

If I am honest, I thought we were going to lose. It seemed to me that the odds were stacked so heavily against us (the Government's booklet not withstanding) and such was the power of the broadcast media – almost all of whom were privately in favour of Remain – that there was very little way that we could win. Nevertheless, I felt that even if this turned into some 21st Century "Charge of the Light Brigade" it would be important to go down fighting, because there was a great principle at stake. In effect, this was going to be a battle for the destiny of our country, and we had to fight wholeheartedly, even if the odds were tilted heavily against us. After all, our forebears had fought battles in the past and still triumphed against all the odds and so, perhaps there was still a chance that we might somehow do the same as well.

I remember being at home on Sunday evening when the phone rang and on the other end of the line was the then Chief Whip, Mark Harper (someone whom I have always admired and got on well with) who politely enquired if I had decided how I was yet going to campaign in the Referendum? I told the Chief that, having thought it over, I was going to vote and campaign for Leave and I was very unlikely to change my mind. The Chief Whip took it well and told me, without rancour, that the Prime Minister would obviously be disappointed, but he was never rude or angry at any point (if you know Mark Harper, that's just not his style). When I reminded him that the Prime Minster had said that Ministers with a long-standing conviction could support the Leave campaign and that I had made my Maiden Speech 15 years ago against the growing power of the European Institutions and did that count as evidence of a "long standing conviction", the Chief politely took the point. He wished me well in the campaign – but not too well – and we parted on good terms.[131] Shortly after this private conversation, I then publicly announced that I would be supporting the Leave campaign.

In the end, there were just over a dozen or so of the roughly 100 Ministers in Government who came out for Leave. In the first rank, as it were, were prominent members of the Cabinet, including Michael Gove, Chris Grayling, Penny Mordaunt, Priti Patel, Theresa Villiers and John Whittingdale. Cameron had apparently been counting on both Gove and Boris to campaign for Remain and was reportedly very disappointed on both counts.[132] I remember the media scrum outside Boris' house in London as they waited for him to come out onto the pavement outside and finally declare his decision. In the event, he told the waiting press scrum: "I will be advocating vote leave – or whatever the team is called, I understand there are a lot of them – because I want a better deal for the people of this country, to save them money and to take back control. That is really what this is all about".[133]

Some people have criticised Boris Johnson for his hesitation and even the fact that, given his strong journalistic background, he reputedly wrote two op-ed pieces, one arguing the case for Leave and one arguing for Remain. Critics have seen this as a sign of indecision. However, Winston Churchill, when faced with a dilemma would apparently sometimes take a piece of paper and draw a line down the middle of it and mark one column as 'plus' and the other 'minus' and then list the advantages and disadvantages of a given course of action, as a method of helping him to decide what to do. As a journalist, I think this was Boris' equivalent of Churchill's subdivided piece of paper. Nevertheless, via whatever method he came to this decision, he eventually told the world that he would campaign to Leave and then kept his word, to considerable effect.

I was very much in the second tier of junior Ministers who came out to campaign for Leave, including Steve Baker, James Duddridge and myself. Although none of us enjoyed anything like the prominence of Michael Gove or Boris Johnson, it did demonstrate that this was not just an issue about which Cabinet Ministers felt strongly but that it also filtered down through the lower Ministerial ranks as well. Even though we were heavily outnumbered by Minister's who campaigned for Remain, I can report in all honesty that I can never remember any member of the Government being rude to me, at least at that time, about my decision. I think by that stage most people had already worked out where I stood on the European issue, that my Ministerial career would probably be destroyed afterwards once Remain had (inevitably) triumphed and so basically left me to get on with it.

As someone who had come into Parliament already wary about the growing power of the European institutions and had helped lead us out of the EPP, it was the Lisbon Treaty that had convinced me that, one day, we would have to Leave the European Union, although when the Treaty was Ratified in 2008, it never occurred to me, for a single moment, that such an opportunity would present itself within just another eight years.

The Referendum Campaign

A great deal has already been written about the EU Referendum campaign of 2016, with one of the best summaries undoubtedly being Tim Shipman's tour de force, "*All Out War*" (William Collins (2016). Channel 4 subsequently produced a drama entitled "*Uncivil War*." which highlighted Dominic Cummings, brilliantly portrayed by Benedict Cumberbatch, as a driving force behind the official "Vote Leave" campaign, to persuade us to Leave the European Union.[134]

This may well be true, not least as Cummings has a reputation as a formidable campaigner. However I believe the eventual result was an incredible team effort between experienced politicians, pollsters and skilled campaigners at the national level, combined with some extremely hard grass roots campaigning, as people from a variety of political backgrounds – or indeed in many cases, absolutely none at all – took up not arms but leaflets and posters and actively went out into High Streets and onto doorsteps up and down the United Kingdom, to quite passionately make the case for leaving the European Union. (Unbeknownst to me at the time, my future partner, Olivia, was one of them).

From my own point of view, I had relatively little interaction with the national campaign and was only in and out of Vote Leave Headquarters at 3 Albert Embankment, just across the river from Parliament, on a handful of occasions. I spent most of the Referendum campaigning around Essex and in particular in my own local constituency of Rayleigh and Wickford, alongside a coalition of the local Conservatives, plus UKIP (including a Mr John Hayter, my opponent at the 2015 General Election), several other UKIP Councillors, a handful of Independents and some people from other grass roots Eurosceptic organisations, such as Leave.EU. In addition to the official literature and posters produced by the Vote Leave campaign I decided that as the local MP I should nail my colours firmly to the mast and therefore paid for a two-sided A4 leaflet headed: "Why I'm backing Brexit by Mark Francois MP", which was then printed and distributed across the constituency by members of our impromptu, cross-Party coalition. The opening paragraph of my leaflet read as follows:

"Dear Constituents,

You may remember receiving an expensive taxpayer funded Government leaflet recently about the forthcoming EU Referendum on Thursday June 23rd. It is of course your democratic right to vote whichever way you choose but I have funded this leaflet to try and give the other side of the story and to explain to my constituents why I am voting to Leave the EU. I believe there are three key reasons for doing this:"

I then summarised them as taking back control of our own country, seeking value for money and reasserting control over our own borders. At the bottom of the front page, I added the following passage:

"In summary, I want to live in a democracy, where we take back control of our own borders, elect our own Government and make our own laws. We in Britain have a once in a lifetime opportunity to secure this in June – and I very much hope that we will take it".[135]

I further amplified the case on the back of the leaflet, with a photograph of me shaking hands with Boris in New Palace Yard of the House of Commons, with Big Ben (before it was surrounded in scaffolding) in the background. In the end, aided and abetted by my excellent Chairman and Constituency Agent, Hilton Brown and many local volunteers, we managed to get over 30,000 of these leaflets printed and delivered through virtually every door in the constituency, prior to Polling Day. We also went out and manned stalls in the High Streets in order to hand out literature and try and persuade people to vote Leave. I threw myself into the campaign with gusto, although I still privately thought that the odds were very much against us winning.

Project Fear

I think the first real inkling I had that we might actually win was when I heard my former boss, the Chancellor, George Osborne, on the *Today* programme effectively threatening the British people with a "punishment Budget" if we were to vote to Leave the EU. He further predicted that in such a scenario, three things would rapidly follow. Firstly, the economy would dive into recession. Secondly, unemployment would soar by over half a million in short order and thirdly, that house prices would collapse by 18% (how the Treasury calculated this and why they made it 18% and not 19%, 20% or 25% I don't know but nevertheless, 18% it was).[136] I remember sipping my morning coffee and putting my tie on as George made this broadcast and thinking, "My goodness George, you've just made the most fundamental mistake". Both George and I had read history at university and one thing that runs as a golden thread through British history is that you cannot bully us. Many have tried and all have failed. The British are an inherently reasonable people, often far more patient than many of their counterparts, but there is a point beyond which they simply will not go. And what sounded like a blatant attempt to bully or frighten the British people to vote to Remain in the EU, seemed to me to be a fundamental error on behalf of the Remain campaign – and so it pretty much proved to be.

In fact, thankfully, the whole Remain campaign was something of a disaster. It was hampered by squabbles about who was really in charge and the fact that the Labour leader, Jeremy Corbyn (an instinctive Eurosceptic for most of his political life) consistently failed to rally Labour voters to the Remain banner. Reportedly, he agreed time and again to undertake national media performances in support of Remain, only to pull out at short notice – a point clearly highlighted in the subsequent Channel 4 documentary.[137] In addition, the Remain campaign produced very few positive reasons at all for Remaining in the European Union. The crux of their campaign was aimed at the alleged economic consequences for the ordinary family of Leaving the EU, filled with portents of doom about economic disaster and rising unemployment if the British people were to display the temerity to vote to govern themselves. This barrage of doom-laden scaremongering, willingly amplified by ardent Remainers across the broadcast media, rapidly became characterised as "Project Fear", which almost certainly worked to the Government's disadvantage, as many voters who perhaps might not have been stirred by more traditional arguments over sovereignty, simply reacted adversely against shameful attempts to bully them, by their own Government.

The introduction of President Obama into the Remain campaign was a further example of this trait. Whilst many at No 10 almost hero-worshipped Obama as an extremely articulate and empathetic Democratic President, they seemingly failed to calculate the adverse reaction that would follow an American President, intervening in a British Referendum. When he famously implied that if Britain voted to Leave the EU, we would effectively go to the back of the queue when seeking to negotiate a trade deal with the United States,[138] many in No 10 were absolutely delighted and thought that his intervention would be decisive. However, for someone sitting in a pub in a depressed northern town, this intervention was less than entirely persuasive. Again, and again, the Remain campaign attempted to play on people's fears, whereas the Vote Leave campaign appealed more to hope, as Dominic Cummings' character says in the Channel 4 documentary: "They're going to appeal to their heads – whereas we're going to appeal to their hearts".[139]

"Hang on, we could win this!"

It was really with about a week to go, that I finally began to believe that we had a chance of winning. Almost everyone that I spoke to in my constituency told me that they were going to vote Leave. To begin with I put this down as something of a "Essex microclimate" as the county has historically always been one of the most Eurosceptic in the UK. Nevertheless, I started ringing other pro-Leave MPs in other parts of the country, including the North, the Midlands and the West Country and many of them reported exactly the same phenomenon – that they were having trouble finding anybody who would *publicly* admit to voting Remain. All the pundits had said that London would vote overwhelmingly to Remain (as indeed proved to be the case) but I was finally beginning to believe that the weight of opinion outside of the M25 had begun to shift decisively towards voting Leave, and that, perhaps, on the night, we might just somehow snatch it.

I remember subsequently going to the local count at Clements Hall Leisure Centre in Hawkwell on the evening of June 23rd, hoping against hope that we might somehow have done it and being there when the first result came in, from Newcastle, at around midnight. The result showed a narrow victory for Remain (but narrower than many of the commentators had been predicting). A friend from Vote Leave HQ, then texted me and said: "Sunderland will be in within a few minutes and that should really tell us how we're getting on. If we win in Sunderland, we're going to do this thing!". I mentioned this to the other people in the hall, including the UKIP activists with whom we had been working for weeks and this led to great excitement. I remember one of them saying: "Mark's got the inside track, and he says that if we win Sunderland, we've done it". Anyway, a few minutes later the Sunderland result came through and it did indeed show a clear majority to Leave. In some ways, this was analogous to the Tory victory in Basildon back in 1992, when "those in the know" realised that it must have meant the Conservatives had won the General Election. Similarly, once the Sunderland result came in, those in the know on both sides suddenly realised that, incredibly, Vote Leave had won.

This was particularly embarrassing for Andrew Cooper (now Lord Cooper), David Cameron's private pollster who had apparently rather arrogantly texted the Vote Leave Headquarters immediately after the close of poll to tell them, with some fanfare, that Remain had won by a clear margin of at least 10 points. The reply from Vote Leave was along the lines of, "Let's just wait and see shall we" and it wasn't long before those in Downing Street realised that Cooper was horribly mistaken, and the game was up.[140]

I remember leaving the count in the small hours, to travel back home and put the television on, in order to witness a series of results flood in, which only confirmed the trend. Famously, at around 5:00am in the morning, David Dimbleby, the Anchor-man for the BBC's results programme, declared, "That's it. We're out!". At this point, elated but also exhausted, I decided to go to bed, unaware that the Prime Minister was about to announce his resignation only several hours later, while I was still asleep. For the record, the result of the 2016 EU Referendum was as follows:

EU Referendum Result – 2016

Leave	17,410,742
Remain	16,141,241
Leave Majority:	1,269,501
Turnout	72.2%

So, against all the odds, against the advice of the four main political Party's in the United Kingdom, against the wishes of the overwhelming majority of what might be called the "British Establishment", including vast numbers of journalists in the electronic media, and despite the determined efforts of "Project Fear", the British people actually voted for democratic self-Government and their right to decide their own destiny after all.

David Cameron

Even though he campaigned actively for Remain, I always regarded David Cameron to be quite a good Prime Minister, who had gone into No 10 in 2010 in extremely difficult circumstances. Moreover, he had always treated me decently and had allowed me my life's ambition, to become a Minister in the Ministry of Defence.

Perhaps for this and a combination of other reasons, I was one of 84 Conservative MPs who dispatched a private letter on the eve of the Referendum, pleading with Cameron not to resign if the result went against him.

A number of adverse commentators have since accused David Cameron of effectively "abandoning his post", because the country had come up with a result that he didn't like. Nevertheless, I suspect he felt he simply had no choice. Rather than attempt to remain "above the fray" much as Wilson had done in 1975, he decided instead to wholeheartedly enter the contest and campaign passionately for the Remain outcome, in which he ultimately believed. Given that this course of action had been clearly defeated by the British people – by a majority of over 1.2 million votes – he probably felt that he had no other option but to announce his resignation.

Politicians being the way that they are, this of course led to immediate speculation about who would become his successor. Cameron had, in effect, been the leader of the Remain campaign (not least because of the repeated absences of Jeremy Corbyn) but, this time around, all his energetic campaigning had not succeeded, as it had done in previous General Elections and indeed in the Scottish Referendum as well. This was one question on which the British people decided not to agree with him, and this is perhaps the thing for which he will best be remembered (his recent embarrassments over his relationship with City Financier Lex Greenshill and his company, Greenshill Capital, notwithstanding).

Personally, I believe that that would be a mistake. David Cameron took over the Premiership in near impossible circumstances and, strongly supported by George Osborne and indeed with the help of the Liberal Democrats in the Coalition, dragged the country back from the brink of economic catastrophe and helped put the public finances back on an even keel – albeit having to take some extremely painful and difficult decisions in the process. For that, he still deserves at least some credit in my view, Greenshill or not.

Nevertheless, with Cameron having abruptly resigned, as the old saying goes, "Politics abhors a vacuum" and so a number of Leadership campaigns rapidly got under way to secure his replacement, some much faster than others. Unlike in previous years, I did not really become actively involved in any one of these campaigns, as I was just content that we had actually won the Referendum and were now going to Leave the EU. However, I admit I did vote for Theresa May in the first ballot of Conservative MPs (whereas ideologically as it were, I might have been expected to vote for Andrea Leadsom, but I had some reservations about her relative lack of experience). In the end, Leadsom's campaign effectively imploded after a disastrous interview with *The Times* newspaper, in which she highlighted the fact that Theresa May did not have children whereas she did. I believe that this was a genuine mistake and was not meant in a malign manner but, nevertheless, the press reaction to her remarks was so vitriolic that she was effectively forced to withdraw from the contest, leaving Theresa May as the only candidate standing and thus obviating both the need for an extended campaign and for the election to finally be decided by Conservative Members around the country. [141]

There was therefore no runoff and no final postal ballot. Her Majesty the Queen called Theresa May to Buckingham Palace on 13th July 2016 and she subsequently emerged from the door of No 10 Downing Street and promised a new Government based on making: "Britain a country that works for everyone". Famously, in an interview shortly thereafter, she declared that: "Brexit means Brexit", although she was vague on the detail of how precisely this was to be achieved.[142] In many ways this was a harbinger of what was to follow – although most of us did not realise it at the time.

Chapter 9: The ERG and the Road to Chequers

The European Research Group (the ERG) was founded by Michael Spicer MP, in 1993, following the highly divisive debates in Parliament over the Maastricht Treaty. Michael Spicer, the MP for Mid Worcestershire, had acted as the de-facto Chairman of the so-called "Maastricht Rebels", who consistently voted against John Major's attempts to Ratify the Maastricht Treaty in the House of Commons. Aided by other prominent Eurosceptics such as Bill Cash (the MP for Stone in Staffordshire) and Richard Shepherd (the MP for Aldridge Brownhills), Spicer and his rebels fought a running guerrilla war in Parliament for over a year, in a determined attempt to prevent the Bill to Ratify the Maastricht Treaty from reaching the Statute Book. However, in the end, having had to resort to the threat of calling an early General Election, John Major eventually managed to get his Bill through, although on some occasions succeeding by only very narrow margins and, on one crucial division, winning by literally just one vote.[143]

The creation of the ERG

After the bitter travails of Maastricht, Michael Spicer resolved to create a standing group of Eurosceptics, who could continue the battle at Westminster against the creation of a European Superstate and, particularly, to ensure that if there were ever to be another Parliamentary battle akin to Maastricht, then Conservative MPs would have the best possible research and arguments at their disposal. In addition, as EU documents often tended to be written in long-winded, highly bureaucratic, and legalistic language, a key role of the ERG was to scrutinise and decipher the true meaning of such documents, so that British MPs, who might have to vote on them on behalf of their constituents, could understand what they really meant and thus the true implications of their votes, either one way or another. Thus, the "European Research Group" was formed, as a pooled research service, with a bright Oxbridge graduate named Daniel Hannan (later to become a highly prominent MEP) as its first researcher.[144]

In its early years the ERG had a very low profile and was probably known to only a handful of people outside of the Westminster village. It produced extremely worthy, though sometimes rather dry research papers, often specialising in the finer aspects of EU organisation or European law, but with a readership not exactly matching that of *The Sun* newspaper.

I was tapped on the shoulder in 2001, following my Maiden Speech against the Treaty of Nice, and it was suggested that as I clearly was Eurosceptic minded, I might be a natural candidate to join the ERG. I accordingly signed up in the autumn of 2001, without any idea whatsoever of what this would one day lead to. Down the years a number of other Eurosceptic MPs joined the ERG's ranks, including (perhaps surprisingly to some people) the newly elected MP for South West Hertfordshire in 2005, one David Gauke, who joined the ERG and was rapidly appointed as its Treasurer, shortly thereafter. However, the ERG continued to maintain a relatively low profile, although it did produce a number of valuable research papers that I drew upon in my role as Shadow Europe Minister when I was debating the Lisbon Treaty in 2008/2009.

The ERG has had a number of Chairmen down the years, but it was really when Steve Baker, the MP for Wycombe (and successor in that seat to my old friend, Paul Goodman) took the Chair in November 2016, that he really began to raise the group's profile. Steve, who had served as an Engineering Officer in the Royal Air Force, concentrating on the Jaguar Ground Attack Aircraft and then later on the Tornado Fighter Bomber, was an Electronic Engineer by trade, who at one point had worked on programming the Tornado to carry nuclear weapons in the event of World War Three. Steve put his technical capabilities to good use and radically improved the ERG's own internal communications, for instance establishing several WhatsApp groups so that senior members of the group could communicate internally. Steve began to raise the organisation's profile in the media, and he had also been a very effective member of the Vote Leave campaign, in 2016, prior to taking the Chair of the ERG later that year.

Under Steve's Chairmanship, the prominent Eurosceptic backbencher, Jacob Rees-Mogg, was appointed Deputy Chairman of the ERG and I was invited to become one of several Vice Chairman of the Group. However, in addition to the official "Officers" of the ERG, the group's ranks were swelled by a number of long-standing senior Backbenchers, including Maastricht Veteran Bill Cash, another leading Maastricht rebel, Iain Duncan Smith (a previous Leader of the Conservative Party), Bernard Jenkin (Shadow Defence Secretary under Iain) and Owen Paterson, a former Northern Ireland Secretary under David Cameron. The ERG also enjoyed the support of John Redwood (who had challenged John Major for the Leadership in 1995), Theresa Villiers (also a former Northern Ireland Secretary) and a number of prominent members of the House of Lords, including Lord Lamont, Lord Lilley, Viscount Ridley and Baroness Meyer.[145]

The Lancaster House Speech

To begin with, as a group the ERG was obviously delighted with the outcome of the Referendum and were initially reassured by Theresa May's statement of intent that "Brexit means Brexit" although, much like everyone else, we were keen to know what the details of that would actually comprise.

However, in the latter part of 2016, despite her having become Prime Minister and enjoying a narrow but workable majority in the House of Commons, Theresa May came under increasing criticism for failing to lay out any kind of detail or road map for how the United Kingdom would Leave the European Union. In addition, she had still chosen not to trigger the formal Exit Mechanism from the EU, known as Article 50 (see below).

Partly in response to these criticisms, on the 17th January 2017, Theresa May gave a major speech at Lancaster House in London, setting out in broad terms the kind of future relationship that she envisaged between the United Kingdom and the European Union.

The Lancaster House speech, as it became known, was initially well received, not least by the European Research Group, as it heralded a future between the UK and the EU, based on free trade to our mutual economic advantage. As Theresa May argued in her speech:

"Our vote to leave the European Union was no rejection of the values we share. The decision to leave the EU represents no desire to become more distant to you, our friends and neighbours. It was no attempt to do harm to the EU itself or to any of its remaining Member States. We do not want to turn the clock back to the days when Europe was less peaceful, less secure and less able to trade freely. It was a vote to restore, as we see it, our parliamentary democracy, national self-determination, and to become even more global and internationalist in action and in spirit.

We will continue to be reliable partners, willing allies and close friends. We want to buy your goods and services, sell you ours, trade with you as freely as possible, and work with one another to make sure we are all safer, more secure and more prosperous through continued friendship.

You will still be welcome in this country as we hope our citizens will be welcome in yours. At a time when together we face a serious threat from our enemies, Britain's unique intelligence capabilities will continue to help to keep people in Europe safe from terrorism. And at a time when there is growing concern about European security, Britain's servicemen and women, based in European countries including Estonia, Poland and Romania, will continue to do their duty.

We are leaving the European Union, but we are not leaving Europe.

And that is why we seek a new and equal partnership – between an independent, self-governing, Global Britain and our friends and allies in the EU".[146]

The direction envisaged at Lancaster House seemed to be very much in the spirit of the Referendum result, with the United Kingdom becoming an independent Sovereign State, trading with the EU but not being bound by its decisions or its regulatory framework for the future. Unsurprisingly, this went down well with Eurosceptics and was well received in the Conservative leaning elements of the media. For instance, the *Daily Telegraph* flatteringly drew comparison with Margaret Thatcher's 1984 demand for "our money back" as a rebate.

Whereas *The Daily Mail's* verdict on the speech was: "Steel of the new Iron Lady". On the day Theresa May said Britain WILL quit the single market, she put Cameron's feeble negotiations to shame with an ultimatum to Brussels that the UK will 'walk away from a bad deal'".[147]

Leaving the EU – Article 50

On the back of the apparent success of the Lancaster House speech, the Prime Minister then gave notice of her intention to trigger Article 50, to begin the formal process of the United Kingdom Leaving the European Union.

The Lisbon Treaty, for all its faults, had included a mechanism by which States could voluntarily opt to Leave the European Union. When Lisbon was consolidated into the other European Treaties, this became Article 50 of the Treaty on the Functioning of the European Union (or Article 50 TFEU, for short). In essence, Article 50 stated that if a country wished to Leave the European Union, it had to give notice in writing to this effect, which would trigger a period of two years during which the Member State wishing to Leave could negotiate its subsequent relationship with the remainder of the EU.

The key passage reads as follows:

ARTICLE 50
TFEU

"A Member State which decides to withdraw shall notify the European Council of its intention. In the light of the guidelines provided by the European Council, the Union shall negotiate and conclude an agreement with that State, setting out the arrangements for its withdrawal, taking account of the framework for its future relationship with the Union. That agreement shall be negotiated in accordance with Article 218(3) of the Treaty on the Functioning of the European Union. It shall be concluded on behalf of the Union by the Council, acting by a qualified majority, after obtaining the consent of the European Parliament".[148]

Theresa May subsequently gave notice of her intention to trigger Article 50 on 20[149] March 2017 in a formal letter to Donald Tusk, the then President of the European Council.[149] However, in a portent of what was to come, this was rapidly challenged in the Courts by Gina Miller, a highly pro-Remain activist, who argued that Article 50 could only be triggered by a full Act of Parliament. This was rapidly escalated to the Supreme Court, where the Government's Attorney General, Jeremy Wright (with whom I had served in the Whips Office years ago) argued that legislation was not necessary to allow the Government to trigger Article 50, given the clear result of the Referendum. Conversely, Gina Miller argued that in fact an Act of Parliament was required and to the delight of Remainers, the Supreme Court found in her favour.[150]

This necessitated the Government producing a Bill, which given the majority that May had inherited from her predecessor David Cameron, managed to get through Parliament successfully, clearing the House of Commons by a margin of 384 votes. With the authority of an Act of Parliament now behind her, the Prime Minister then wrote again formally to the President of the European Council, Donald Tusk, on the 29th March 2017, thus triggering the "two-year clock", with the intention that the United Kingdom would formally Leave the European Union on 29th March 2019.

However, up to this point, other than the Lancaster House speech, the Government had given out little detail on its negotiating objectives and how exactly it intended the discussions to proceed. With two years to go, this in itself might not have been a major problem at this stage, had not Theresa May suddenly – and completely out of the blue called a General Election in May of that year, to be held on Thursday 8th June 2017.

Unusually in politics, this was an extremely well-kept secret. Theresa May had apparently taken the final decision whilst on a walking holiday on the continent with her husband, Philip. With hindsight, it is perhaps easy to see why she did so.[151] At that point, the Conservatives were enjoying a significant poll lead over Jeremy Corbyn's Labour Party, of something like 20 points. In a poll of 12th-13th April 2017, the Conservatives were on 44% and the Labour Party were on 23% and several other polls around that time produced similar results.[152] The opportunity of a snap General Election (for which MPs would have to actively vote, under the strictures of Cameron's Fixed Term Parliament Act) thus offered the prospect of a crushing victory over Labour, and a strengthened mandate for Theresa May to carry out the instructions of the British people in the Referendum and finally take us out of the EU.

Unfortunately, however, it didn't quite turn out like that.

The 2017 General Election – "Nothing has Changed!"

A previous Labour Prime Minister, Harold Wilson, once famously opined that: "A week is a long time in politics".[153] Perhaps this was never more true than in the case of the 2017 General Election campaign. From a seemingly unassailable position, with the Labour Party in a state of disarray under an untested and relatively elderly, left-wing Labour Leader in Jeremy Corbyn, the initial indications were that the Conservative Party was heading for a landslide. The campaign planners (who had put together the campaign in conditions of extreme secrecy in the bowels of Conservative Campaign Headquarters) decided to run a very Presidential Campaign, based around the personality and status of the Prime Minister, and encapsulated in the slogan: "Strong and Stable" – designed to emphasise her Leadership and the reliability that it would provide. However, the campaign itself turned out to be something of a disaster.

To begin with, Theresa May proved to be a rather wooden and uncharismatic campaigner, famously almost losing her temper at one press conference when she was challenged on an element of policy and sternly replied to the assembled journalists that: "Nothing has changed!".[154] Conversely, Jeremy Corbyn, for many years a left-wing firebrand on the Backbenches, who had won the Labour Leadership to the surprise of many, turned out to be an extremely energetic, even passionate campaigner, for the causes in which he believed and who came across on the evening news bulletins as more committed and passionate than his rather stilted Conservative opponent. Theresa May's unfortunate nickname of "the Maybot" was to haunt her throughout the latter stages of the campaign.[155]

In addition, the Conservative Manifesto, which numbered some 84 pages, contained a great deal of technocratic detail, involving minor tweaks to Government policy in this area and that, but singularly lacking in any popular or exciting "big idea" along the lines of Margaret Thatcher's famous pledge in 1979 to allow council tenants to buy their own homes. Conversely, however, it did include proposals (allegedly inserted at the last moment by one of her senior aides, Nick Timothy) to solve the knotty problem of how to pay for Adult Social Care by asking people if necessary, to sell their own properties – but with a cap guaranteeing that they would be able to retain £125,000 in residual capital. For many voters, including those who regarded their primary home as a family asset to be passed down the generations, this policy was an anathema and Conservative poll ratings immediately began to nosedive as soon as it was revealed.[156]

I remember that up to this point, canvassing on the doorsteps had been going relatively well, even in the marginal seat of Thurrock, where, yet again, our Association campaign team were helping Jackie Doyle-Price with her defence.

However, once the Manifesto appeared and was slated in the national media, it became a much more uphill struggle and I remember a number of very difficult conversations on the doorstep with my own constituents, who, were damned if they were going to allow anyone to take their family home away from them. The policy was badly constructed and apparently the Cabinet were not even made aware of this before the manifesto was published, a classic example of the kind of control freakery for which Theresa May was by now famous. Normally, me and my Association go out canvassing, even if it's raining (at least moderately) but the evening after the Manifesto came out, there was absolutely torrential rain and so, having agreed that we would abandon canvassing for that night, I sat in and read the Manifesto from start to finish. I recall thinking at the time, there is nothing remotely exciting in here to get Conservative voters or even floating voters juices going and simply repeating the mantra of 'Strong and Stable' isn't really going to be enough. If we're not careful, this could now go horribly wrong, and so it turned out to be.

In the midst of the campaign, I remember receiving a phone call from the Whips Office telling me that the canvass returns showed that Jackie Doyle-Price was home and dry in Thurrock and therefore we should switch our campaigning efforts to Dagenham and Rainham in East London, in order to try and unseat the long-standing Labour MP, John Cruddas. I protested vehemently that, having already been to Thurrock several times, whatever Central Office were saying was incorrect. Our own canvassing had shown that this still remained a knife edge, three-way marginal between ourselves, the Labour Party and UKIP (who were essentially arguing that the Conservatives could not be trusted to deliver Brexit). When I was basically ordered to abandon Thurrock and take our troops to Dagenham and Rainham instead, I reported that, unfortunately, this was an extremely poor connection, and I would have to ring the Whips Office back. I never did. Having discussed this in detail with my Chairman, Hilton Brown, and mindful of the promise that I made to Jackie, that after what had happened between Thurrock and Castle Point in 2015, (when we had helped both seats rather than abandon Thurrock), there was no way that we were going to abandon Thurrock this time either, and so instead we exercised "Nelson's eye" and stuck with campaigning in Thurrock instead. In the end, we failed to win Dagenham and Rainham by 4,652 votes but we did help Jackie to survive in Thurrock by a majority of 345.[157]

There were a whole series of other problems with the 2017 General Election campaign, including that Central Office had decided to adopt a sophisticated version of highly targeted canvassing (where rather than going down a street and knocking on every door, we were encouraged to only knock on very selective doors instead, guided by a highly complex computer algorithm). This was all well and good - except for the fact that it basically didn't work. Perhaps, having been knocking on doors for over 30 years by this stage and perhaps being a creature of habit, we again disobeyed these instructions and carried on knocking on every door, pretty much as we always had done. It was a combination of a very poor "air war" in the media, combined with an overly complicated "ground war" (in terms of doorstep campaigning) compounded by a highly unpopular Manifesto commitment on Adult Social Care, that saw Theresa May's 20 point poll lead rapidly evaporate and the Conservatives lose their overall majority in the House of Commons. When all the votes were finally counted, the results for the major parties were as follows:

General Election Results for the UK, 2017

Party	Seats
Conservatives	317
Labour	262
SNP	35
Lib Dems	12
DUP	10
Sinn Fein	7
Plaid Cymru	4
Green	1
Government 9 short of a majority	

Unsurprisingly, this was reflected in the result in my patch which was as follows:

General Election Result for the Rayleigh and Wickford Constituency, 2017

Mark Francois	Conservative Candidate	36,914
Mark Daniels	Labour Candidate	13,464
Peter Smith	UKIP Candidate	2,326
Ron Tindall	Liberal Democrat	1,557
Paul Hill	Green Candidate	1,062
Conservative Majority		23,450
Turnout		70.4%

This was still a pretty healthy majority in my constituency. By now, the United Kingdom Independence Party were much diminished as an electoral force (after all, we had won the Referendum so what was the point of them?) and so Labour were now in second place in Rayleigh and Wickford.

I remember watching Theresa May appear at her count in Maidenhead that night, where she looked almost shell-shocked by the result, her aides from CCHQ having obviously briefed her beforehand, that her majority was effectively likely to disappear. In the end, in order to continue to govern with a workable majority in the House of Commons, Theresa May was forced to agree a "Confidence and Supply" arrangement with the Democratic Unionist Party from Northern Ireland, whose 10 MPs now became crucial in ensuring that she could win critical votes in the House of Commons.

Whilst Theresa May still remained in No 10 Downing Street, hers had been something of a pyric victory, as she was now damaged in the eyes not just of the public, but of her own MPs. Napoleon, when choosing Generals, would traditionally have their military CVs read out before he famously asked the question: "That's all very well, but are they lucky?". In contrast, Theresa May had turned out to be an unlucky General – but at a post-election meeting of the 1922 Committee of Conservative backbenchers, Theresa May famously told them: "I'm the one who got you into this mess but I'm also the best person to get you out of it!" As it transpired, that was not exactly true.

May's new Government

Deprived of a working majority in the House of Commons, Theresa May now had to carry out another reshuffle and reform her Government. However, her Cabinet, which contained a considerable number of Remainers, were by no means united on European policy and were increasingly hesitant about their ability to drive through her vision, as previously outlined at Lancaster House. Theresa May's Department for Exiting the European Union (DEXEU) Secretary, David Davis, had for many months been working on a White Paper, which would outline the Government's negotiating objectives in the forthcoming EU negotiations and thus spell out the type of future relationship that the UK wished to achieve. This was based around a comprehensive Free Trade Agreement, of the type that the European Union had signed with Canada in 2016. In essence the concept was to take this existing template – which by definition the EU had already agreed to with another country – and add to it a number of additional sub agreements or "protocols", for instance on areas such as Defence and Security (because the UK would still have important military responsibilities in Europe, not least via NATO, after Leaving the EU), the transfer and management of data and a few other areas besides. Because it was based on the EU/Canadian deal, this concept was known within Government as "Super Canada" or "Canada +++".

Jacob takes the Chair

In the June 2017 reshuffle, following the General Election, the ERG Chairman, Steve Baker, was appointed as a Parliamentary Under Secretary of State at DEXEU, to assist David Davis in fleshing out the preparations for the negotiations. As has often been the way in the history of the ERG, he was replaced by his Deputy, Jacob Rees-Mogg MP.

Jacob, an old Etonian, famous for his classic-cut suits and charming manners, had risen to prominence in the previous few years as a highly articulate exponent of the Eurosceptic cause. Having famously campaigned with his Nanny whilst fighting a seat in Glasgow during an earlier General Election, he had been elected as the Member of Parliament for North West Somerset in 2010 and had immediately established a strong rapport with his constituents. Perhaps because of a combination of his strong intellect and eloquent speaking style, Jacob increasingly achieved a higher media profile, up to and including playing an important part in the EU Referendum in 2016.

Jacob

I remember a little while after Jacob had been elected in 2010, when I was then serving as the Ops Officer in the Whips Office, keeping an eye on a debate one evening on Food Security. For reasons I can no longer recall, the Government were keen to run this business long and so I was trying to find additional Backbenchers who might chip into the debate, albeit at very short notice.

When I asked Jacob if he could possibly contribute, he replied that he didn't know a great deal about the subject, but he would be delighted to chip in, if it helped the Government. He accordingly approached the Deputy Speaker (who at that time was Dawn Primarolo, my old adversary from Shadow Treasury days) and was called to speak about half an hour later. He had said to me: "Would half an hour be alright?" and I replied that if he could extemporise on this subject for 30 minutes, with virtually no preparation, then even I, as a slightly cynical Whip, might be impressed.

In the end, he did 43 minutes at the drop of a hat, based mainly on the contents of a Fortnum and Mason Christmas Hamper and how its produce could be relied on to be "delicious, nutritious and above all, safe".[158]

From that point on, I remember thinking that this chap was out of the ordinary to say the least although I had no idea at that stage that he would go on to become something of a national treasure, as he is today. Nevertheless, it was following Steve's promotion that Jacob became the highly capable, charismatic Chairman who would lead the ERG through what became the bitter debates on Brexit that were to follow.

Negotiations with the EU

Crucially, Theresa May's poor showing in the 2017 General Election put her and the UK negotiating team firmly on the back foot in their negotiations with the EU on how "Brexit Means Brexit" would be translated into practical reality. The Prime Minister had lost her majority in the House of Commons, which the EU exploited ruthlessly.

The EU's Chief Negotiator, Michel Barnier, was a French former EU Commissioner, with very polite manners but a steely resolve. From the very outset, he worked closely with the other key EU institutions, the European Council (representatives from the remaining 27 EU Member States), the European Commission (the EU's civil service) and the European Parliament, led on this subject by a former Belgian Prime Minister and avowedly Federalist MEP, Guy Verhofstadt, to make sure that they all remained clearly aligned throughout the negotiations, so that any UK attempts to gain ground would prove unsuccessful.

Barnier's diligent approach soon began to bear fruit, particularly when the UK agreed to the EU's insistence on "sequencing" in the negotiations including that they would effectively have to be divided into two halves, the first being the "Divorce Deal", including issues such as rights for EU citizens remaining in the UK, future UK financial contribution to the EU (in light of previous commitments) and the position of the EU/UK border in Northern Ireland – which would have to be secured before the negotiation could move onto the second half, the so-called "Future Relationship" on how the UK would relate to the EU, post-divorce after March 2019. In June 2017 the UK agreed to adhere to the EU's prolonged timetable – and to determine a "divorce settlement", (ultimately totalling some £39 Billion) first – the EU negotiating team thus having secured a major diplomatic victory over their UK counterparts.

The December 2017 Joint Report

Having successfully dictated the sequence in which the negotiations would be conducted, Barnier and his team did not rest on their laurels. Fully aware throughout that Theresa May, now leading a minority administration, would be under domestic pressure to continually demonstrate progress in the talks, the EU negotiators made increasing demands, with the ever-present threat, that if they were not acceded to, the EU would not agree that "sufficient progress" had been made, to allow the talks to transition to the Future Relationship phase.

This highly effective "stonewalling" tactic produced further British concessions, including over the vexed question of how to deal with goods crossing what would become a land border between the UK and the EU on the island of Ireland, between Northern Ireland (UK) and the Republic of Ireland (EU).

With both sides keen to avoid a "hard border" (a return to checkpoints and border posts, reminiscent of "The Troubles", prior to the 1998 Good Friday Agreement) the EU negotiating team persistently raised the question of how goods entering the EU Single Market from Northern Ireland to the Republic would be effectively monitored. In this, Barnier also worked hand-in-glove with the Irish Government.

These intensive discussions, in which the EU didn't budge an inch (or even a centimetre) eventually led to the December 2017 "Joint Report", in which both sides agreed that: if these issues could not be resolved in the subsequent negotiations about the Future Relationship, then it would be necessary for Northern Ireland to remain part of the EU Customs Union – and thus was born what was to become known as "The Backstop" – although at this stage relating primarily only to Northern Ireland. It was this fateful decision which was to lead to so much subsequent misery and argument over the next two years.

The Chequers Summit – A fait accompli

In July 2018, in order to bind her Government into her evolving negotiating approach with the EU, Theresa May called a special Summit of Cabinet Members at the Prime Minister's country retreat at Chequers. However, unbeknown to them (including even David Davis) the White Paper which his Department had been working on in good faith for months, had been quietly abandoned and was replaced by an alternative White Paper, which had been drafted by Civil Servants under the auspices of No 10 and the Cabinet Office. Chief amongst these was Oliver (Ollie) Robbins, a Civil Servant who had previously won May's confidence whilst working for her at the Home Office but who had a track record of being instinctively pro the EU.

This alternative White Paper, which had been drafted under conditions of great secrecy, was then given to Cabinet Members only just prior to the Chequers Summit itself, so that by the time the Cabinet assembled at the Prime Minister's private residence in Buckinghamshire, they had had very little time to digest its contents. This new White Paper presaged a fundamentally different approach from Super Canada. Instead, the Government would be committed to a much closer relationship to the EU, including a policy of "high alignment" or effectively following EU rules in multiple areas for many years even after we had left the European Union.

Worst of all, the White Paper had envisaged the United Kingdom effectively remaining part of a "Customs Union" with the EU, which meant that the UK would be unable to set its own independent trade policy in the future but would remain wholly reliant on International Trade Agreements that were negotiated collectively, via the European Union. This facility was described as a "Backstop", into which the UK would only enter if it could not reach alternative agreements with the EU, i.e. as a form of fallback position. However, partly at Treasury insistence, the Backstop had now been increased in scope and would now apply to the UK as a whole, rather than just Northern Ireland, as envisaged several months earlier.[159]

It was this White Paper with which the Prime Minister effectively bounced the entire Cabinet at Chequers, with all Cabinet Members present told very clearly, that they could either accept it or resign. To drum home the point, the media were briefed that a number of "taxi cards" would be left prominently in the lobby at Chequers, so that any Minister who refused to go along with the new deal, could call a taxi to take them home – as their Ministerial car would immediately be withdrawn as they had effectively resigned from the Government.[160] This extremely aggressive way to deal with a highly controversial topic, displayed chronic mismanagement of the Cabinet, who were effectively now being asked to materially alter the destiny of the United Kingdom, despite a clear result in the 2016 Referendum.

It is perhaps difficult to discern exactly why the White Papers were switched at such short notice. Nevertheless, it would appear that somewhere along the way, in the first half of 2018, perhaps encouraged by the fact that she had lost her working majority in Parliament after the disastrous General Election, Theresa May was effectively persuaded by the pro-EU upper echelons of the Civil Service, to dramatically change course and to advocate a new negotiating stance, (which actually meant that, in effect, the United Kingdom would barely Leave the European Union at all).

The switch of the White Papers was carried out ruthlessly and in conditions of great secrecy, such that many Cabinet Ministers who arrived at Chequers were caught off guard by what the Prime Minister and the coterie around her had actually done. On the day, everyone in the Cabinet appeared to go along with the new strategy – although a number of them privately had serious doubts.[161]

The complete *volte-face* by the Prime Minister was particularly embarrassing for David Davis, her DEXEU Secretary, who had spent the best part of a year working on a completely alternative White Paper, along the lines of Super Canada. He had been kept in the dark for weeks or even months, about this change of heart by the Prime Minister, as indeed had Steve Baker, his junior Minister.

Worse still, while the EU had placed strong faith in their own Chief Negotiator, Michel Barnier, Theresa May had effectively undermined David Davis, by increasingly relying on Olly Robbins as her interlocutor with Barnier – a point certainly not lost on the EU. During this period, Davis increasingly complained in private that he was being side-lined by No 10 and thus undermined as a result.

In fact, David Davis did receive at least some prior warning of what was afoot, when the Prime Minister telephoned him just a few days before the Chequers meeting, to inform him that there was going to be a change of plan. Initially, Davis tried to talk the PM out of it, arguing that the Super Canada option was still viable. However, when he realised that the PM had effectively already made her mind up to radically alter course, he instinctively realised that he would have no honourable option, other than to resign.

Having made this decision, David Davis then summoned his two junior DEXEU Ministers, Steve Baker (a staunch Eurosceptic) and Robin Walker (son of the late Tory Cabinet Minister, Peter Walker) to a private meeting and explained to them what had just happened. David Davis insisted that for reasons of continuity as much as anything else, they should not all resign and leave the Department without any Ministers at all. So, it was agreed that David Davis would resign shortly after the Chequers summit and that Steve Baker would follow him shortly thereafter, while Robin Walker would remain at his post and await the arrival of a new Secretary of State, to take over the Department.[162]

The resignations begin– Davis and Baker quit

As per the private arrangement with his junior Ministers, David Davis then resigned, shortly after Chequers, and Steve Baker, his junior Minister, who had been enraged by what the Prime Minister and her coterie at No 10 had done, followed him out of the door very shortly thereafter.[163]   Thus, began an unprecedented series of some thirty Ministerial resignations which were, over time, to debilitate Theresa May's Government, to the effect that, by the end, she became what some referred to as a Prime Minister in Name Only. (PRINO).

Steve rapidly returned to the ERG fold, and was soon appointed as Jacob's Deputy Chairman, whilst I remained one of several Vice Chairmen within the group. By now we had got into a pattern whereby the upper echelons of the ERG would meet in Iain Duncan Smith's office, in the Palace of Westminster on Monday afternoons, followed by a full or "plenary" meeting of the entire ERG in one of the House of Commons Committee Rooms the following evening.

For the ERG, who had had no more prior warning of the switch at Chequers than anybody else, the Prime Minister's about-turn came as a bombshell. Having been originally encouraged by the Lancaster House speech and its direction of travel, it now became apparent that the Prime Minister, egged on by senior Civil Servants in No 10 and a number of pro Remain elements within her Cabinet, was now moving in a fundamentally different direction.   In fact, this actually represented a complete *volte face*, which meant that the UK would remain very closely aligned with the European Union, and, if we entered the Backstop, we would effectively not have left the EU at all.

In truth, it took a while for us to fully absorb the enormity of what had happened. Despite the Referendum, in which 17.4 million UK citizens had voted to Leave the European Union, suddenly a Conservative Government, led by a Conservative Prime Minister, appeared set on betraying that decision and effectively keeping us in the EU after all. Moreover, there were many pro-Remain elements in the media who welcomed this "wise decision" as a way of maintaining economic continuity, rather than actually obeying the wishes of the people.[164]

The "British Establishment" – which had always been overwhelmingly opposed to Britain Leaving the EU – many of whom regarded the ordinary voters of this county as stupid or uninformed or both – had seized their opportunity and persuaded a now weakened Prime Minister to change tack and effectively override the result of the Referendum. Careful reading of the artfully drafted subsequent White Paper only confirmed this, for instance in one section it said the following:

"The arrangements would include robust and appropriate means for the resolution of disputes, including through a Joint Committee and in many areas through binding independent arbitration – accommodating through a joint reference procedure the role of the Court of Justice of the European Union as the interpreter of EU rules, but founded on the principle that the court of one party cannot resolve disputes between the two. And they would make sure both the UK and the EU interpreted rules consistently – with rights enforced in the UK by UK courts and in the EU by EU courts, with a commitment that UK courts would pay due regard to EU case law in only those areas where the UK continued to apply a common rulebook".[165]

This stance, a "common rulebook" i.e. continuing to follow EU laws even after "Leaving" the organisation and with the European Court of Justice still, in reality, overseeing the process, was now the official policy of HM's Government – and one with which most members of the ERG could not possibly agree. To all intents and purposes and despite the Referendum, it meant remaining in the EU after all.

Boris resigns

Some days later, on the 9th July, the Foreign Secretary, Boris Johnson, followed David Davis out of the door and also tendered his resignation over the Chequers deal. As he told the media at the time, the UK was headed "for the status of a colony".[166] This was a serious blow to the Prime Minister, who had now lost two senior Cabinet Ministers, her DEXEU Secretary and her Foreign Secretary, in close succession. It would appear that the threat of the taxi cards in the lobby at Chequers was no longer quite as effective as a deterrent, once people had gotten safely home.

As one of the champions of the Vote Leave campaign, Boris quite rightly decided that he could not continue to sit with any honour in a Cabinet which had adopted a policy fundamentally at odds with the results of the Referendum. Theresa May now faced the prospect of having a significant "Big Beast" from her Cabinet on the Back Benches, ready to help campaign against the Chequers Deal. However, Boris Johnson never was and never has been a member of the European Research Group. I don't believe this is because he held any dislike or distain for the group or what it stood for but in a sense the ERG was never really Boris' "thing". As someone who had no trouble in generating media attention (indeed had sometimes generated a lot more than he wanted), Boris did not need a group such as the ERG in order to put forward his viewpoint. Indeed, Boris had written a book about Winston Churchill. *'The Churchill Factor'* (Hodder & Stoughton, 2014) and, rather like his hero, he too has always been something of a maverick.[167] Nonetheless, after he resigned, Boris' interests were to some degree aligned with those of the ERG, at least at the very basic level that we were strongly opposed to the Chequers Deal – and so now too was he.

A "Chuck Chequers" campaign soon began to ferment on the Conservative Back Benches and indeed among the wider Voluntary Party around the country, many of whom were deeply uneasy about the fact that two senior Cabinet Ministers had resigned and that prominent Eurosceptic MPs, such as Steve Baker and Jacob Rees-Mogg, were beginning to explain to the public why the Chequers proposals were so awful in practice.

"Jaw Jaw" rather than "War War"

Despite this (and with hindsight perhaps naively) the ERG attempted to open discussions with the Prime Minister and her team at No 10 with the objective of attempting to persuade her to change her mind and to revert to a policy more akin to Super Canada and the original Lancaster House speech. As a result of this, numerous meetings were organised between ERG leaders and staffers at No 10 and indeed with the Prime Minister herself. As a Vice Chairman of the organisation, I only attended some of these meetings, but the ones that I was present at were memorable – including for the fact that the Prime Minister barely said a word throughout.

Perhaps because of her personality, Theresa May only ever seemed to trust an extremely small circle of people. Prior to the 2017 General Election, her inner circle had been dominated by her two Special Advisers, Nick Timothy and Fiona Hill (or "Nick and Fi" as they were known throughout Whitehall). Following the debacle of the 2017 General Election, both of them were forced to resign and Theresa May appointed a new Chief of Staff in the form of Gavin Barwell, the former MP for Croydon Central, who famously wrote a book about how to win a marginal seat – prior to then proceeding to lose his in the 2017 General Election.[168]

Barwell was an instinctive Remainer, who on the morning after the Referendum result, in reference to both Croydon and London voting strongly in favour of Remain famously tweeted: "Proud that my home town and the great city of which it is part rejected the politics of hate and division yesterday".[169]

Gavin Barwell ✓
@GavinBarwell

Proud that my home town and the
great city of which it is part rejected
the politics of hate and division
yesterday

07:10 · 24/06/2016 from Croydon, London · Twitter
for Android

45 Retweets **49** Quote Tweets **66** Likes

Most of the other senior Civil Servants in No 10 – led by the Prime Minister's new Chief Negotiator – Olly Robbins – were broadly sympathetic to Remain and had little intention of pursuing a policy in line also with Super Canada or Lancaster House. However much the ERG tried to argue the case for a genuine break from the EU, we were frustrated at every turn by a combination of Barwell and senior Civil Servants who, enjoying the confidence of the Prime Minister in a way which we quite patently did not, sought to undermine our every effort to get her to reconsider.

In one meeting that I attended with the Prime Minister at No 10, she made a few opening remarks and then invited those present to comment. In a meeting that lasted nearly two hours (I timed it), after her opening remarks, she barely said a single word. Rather she sat there, akin to the Sphinx alongside the pyramids at Giza, perhaps absorbing what was said, but not offering anything whatsoever in return. After a while, we realised that we were, in effect, talking to a brick wall. No matter how hard we tried to put forward an alternative case, she clearly was not listening. Nevertheless, it is important to establish for the record, that in the autumn of 2018, the ERG tried again and again to persuade the Prime Minister and her senior advisors to change course. Having made quite plain up front that if they did not, we would fight ardently against such proposals in the House of Commons.

Article 50 envisaged a negotiated agreement by which a Member State Leaving the EU could establish future relations with the remaining Members of the European Union. Because this would be a matter of international law, it would need to take the form of an international Treaty, which would mean, in turn, it would need a Bill in the House of Commons to Ratify it – in much the same way that a Bill had been required to Ratify Maastricht, Lisbon and so on. By convention, such a Bill would be debated "on the floor of the House" i.e. in the main Chamber, rather than upstairs in a Committee Room because, as a constitutional measure, every MP would then be allowed to be involved in the debates and to table amendments.

Both sides were therefore aware that, if push came to shove, this would come down to a series of crunch votes in the House of Commons, which the Government would have to win if they were to Ratify any agreement they had come to with the EU. The ERG made plain that if the Government would not change course, then we would be forced to oppose any such legislation and would do so with all the Parliamentary experience at our disposal but, nevertheless, our absolute preference was to try and negotiate with the Government, some form of compromise that both we and they could accept. In other words, our desire was still for what Churchill famously characterised as: "Jaw Jaw rather than War War".

The Withdrawal Agreement is published

On the 14th November 2018, the Government finally published the Withdrawal Agreement (WA) by which they planned to "Leave" the European Union.[170] This agreement, over an inch thick, numbered 585 A4 pages (as opposed to the 300 A4 pages in the Lisbon Treaty) and was extremely detailed. It was written in the bureaucratic language at which the EU excels, assisted by some very artful drafting by the British Civil Service. The Withdrawal Agreement was effectively a draft International Treaty, which, if it were Ratified by Parliament via a specific Bill for that purpose, would then have full force in International Law.

As I had done with the Lisbon Treaty, I took the Withdrawal Agreement home and spent an entire day reading through it in detail. Although as I have said before, I am not a lawyer by training, the experience I had gained regarding EU Treaties from having studied Lisbon for months and then debated it in Parliament, certainly stood me in good stead this time around. I remember sitting down with a cup of coffee, armed with a variety of pencils, post it notes and colouring pens, to begin reading the Treaty at about 10:00am on Saturday morning. By the time that I got to the end, at around 8:00pm that night, I had graduated to some decent malt scotch with just a splash of ice. When I got to the finish and looked back over my notes, I was absolutely appalled.

In effect, the Treaty was a brilliant piece of drafting, which meant that we would not actually Leave the European Union at all. Calling it "the Withdrawal Agreement" was a fantastic example of what the Russian's call "*Maskirovka*" or strategic deception. Because unless you read the Treaty very carefully, in great detail, it was difficult to discern how in fact the trick was achieved. But nevertheless, it was.

Blair gives the game away at The Strand Group

By sheer coincidence, on the day that the Withdrawal Agreement was published, former Labour Prime Minister and Arch-Remainer, Tony Blair, gave a speech at the Thinktank, The Strand Group (which is based at my old Alma Mata at King's College London, in The Strand). On its website, The Strand Group states that it explains "HOW GOVERNMENT REALLY WORKS: Examining the institutions of British Government". Their website goes on "The Strand Group brings together figures from Government, business, journalism and academia to shed light on contemporary challenges facing the economy, defence and intelligence, foreign affairs, the public sector and the machinery of Government".[171]

As a guest, Tony Blair then proceeded not so much to shed light on the Withdrawal Agreement as to illuminate it with a search light. In his speech to the Group (subsequently published on The Strand Group website) he described the Withdrawal Agreement in the following terms:

"It isn't a compromise but a capitulation. The withdrawal agreement will keep us tied to EU trade policy until there is an end established by "joint consent" – that means the EU has a veto. It is coated in heavy fudge but that is the inedible biscuit beneath the coating.

As for future arrangements, that is essentially the Chequers proposal which leaves us accepting existing EU rules and agreeing to abide by future ones.

This is Brexit in theory but still tied to Europe in reality, thus making a mockery of the reason for leaving. Whatever people voted for, it wasn't this."

It should be appreciated, that Tony Blair was criticising the Withdrawal Agreement from the standpoint of someone who very much wanted a second Referendum (having been rather disappointed in the result of the first one). Nevertheless, Blair was sufficiently candid to admit, even in his text, that both he and Boris Johnson would now be opposed to the Withdrawal Agreement:

"Remainers like me and Leavers like Boris Johnson are now in unholy alliance: we agree this is a pointless Brexit in name only which is not the best of a bad job but the worst of both worlds. In the cause of 'taking back control' we lose the control we had."[172]

But he didn't stop there. The journalist Harry Cole, writing for *The Sun Online* that evening, penned an article entitled "BLAIR BOAST: Tony Blair claims Eurocrats gloated to him about defeating Britain during Brexit talks". The article was then subtitled "The ex-PM also claimed Theresa May's Brexit guru deliberately tricked the Cabinet about the terms of the deal".

According to Harry Cole's account, during his address, "Mr Blair highlighted the PowerPoint presentation used to promote Mrs May's Chequers plan, claiming that the Prime Minister's Europe adviser Olly Robbins and the civil service had used 'elaborate camouflage' to disguise elements of the proposals". According to Cole, Tony Blair then paid Olly Robbins perhaps the mother of all backhanded compliments when he said:

"I take my hat off to Olly Robbins, Olly is a very skilled guy, the elaborate camouflage of all the different points is a tribute to the skills of the British civil service, I say that sincerely".[173]

Blair's potentially explosive remarks were also picked up by *UK News* ("Blair condemns PM's Brexit deal as 'capitulation' to EU")[174] and also by the popular commentator on Parliamentary affairs, Guido Fawkes (aka Paul Staines) who published an article on his website *order-order.com*, under the headline "Blair: Robbins' Chequers camouflage a 'tribute' to civil service". Guido Fawkes repeated the Blair quote about Olly Robbins and as part of his analysis then said:

"The familiar tactic of details being withheld from Cabinet Ministers until the last minute has led to Ministers being bounced bit by bit into a soft Brexit by stealth. Blair's claim that EU officials privately say that Britain has 'basically caved in' will not leave anyone too impressed either. Cock-up or conspiracy?"[175]

Of course, Blair was attacking the Withdrawal Agreement from a Remain rather than a Leave perspective. Nevertheless, as a former Prime Minister who understands full well the inner machinations of Government, his remarks were absolutely damning. The Withdrawal Agreement was indeed very elaborately camouflaged – which was entirely deliberate.

The Government (and the EU) obviously relied on the fact that few Members of Parliament, let alone busy commentators in the media, would actually take the time and trouble to read the document in detail and therefore truly understand what it meant.

At this point, the genius of Michael Spicer came into play. With incredible foresight, he had created a group, the European Research Group, whose *raison d'etre* was to plough through complex European documents, to ascertain exactly what they really meant. Thus informed, those MPs could then, in turn, warn their Parliamentary colleagues and, via the media, the wider British public, about what any new EU treaty actually contained – which is pretty much what then happened in this instance. The European Research Group really did exactly what it said on the tin.

I was by no means the only member of the ERG to read through this document in detail that weekend. By the end of the process, we had come to the shocking collective realisation that it was a total con, the purpose of which was to keep us effectively locked into the European Union for ever – directly opposed to the wishes of the British people, as democratically expressed in the Referendum of 2016.

As I said to one of the other ERG Officers at the time: "What these people have done is actually extremely clever. It's basically a version of Orwellian 'doublespeak'. They have created a highly complex International Treaty, the net effect of which is to keep us in the EU – and then labelled it the 'Withdrawal Agreement' so that they can accuse anyone who opposes it of trying to keep us in, whilst claiming that they really want to Leave – when they don't! This is going to be bloody difficult to fight, but we have to try, nevertheless. They have obviously gambled that very few MPs will actually bother to read this turgid 585-page tome – but then they reckoned without us!"

What the Withdrawal Agreement <u>really</u> meant

In order to amplify this point, it is necessary to examine at least a few key extracts from the original Withdrawal Agreement – which remember was a draft International Treaty – to see what it <u>really</u> contained. For instance, Article 4, stated the following:

ARTICLE 4

"1. The provisions of this Agreement and the provisions of Union law made applicable by this Agreement shall produce in respect of and in the United Kingdom the same legal effects as those which they produce within the Union and its Member States. Accordingly, legal or natural persons shall in particular be able to rely directly on the provisions contained or referred to in this Agreement which meet the conditions for direct effect under Union law".

"2. **The United Kingdom shall ensure compliance with paragraph 1**, including as regards the required powers of its judicial and administrative authorities to disapply inconsistent or incompatible domestic provisions, through domestic primary legislation". (Emphasis added) [176]

The European Union frequently relies on the fact that ordinary members of the public will not take the trouble to decipher all of this legal gobbledegook but what this basically means is that the agreement, once Ratified, would represent "higher law". In other words, this would have the full status of an International Treaty, akin to the United Nations Charter for instance, which could not simply be overridden or amended, even by an Act of Parliament. Once signed, at least some parts of this agreement would remain on the international Statute book forever, forming part of International Law, unless superseded by a subsequent agreement.

In many ways the most controversial part of the Withdrawal Agreement was the so called "Backstop", formally known as the Northern Ireland Protocol, contained between pages 302 to 475 of the Treaty. This part of the Treaty, crucially, contained the fallback provision by which the United Kingdom could be forced to enter a "Customs Union", if other negotiations with the EU on the Future Relationship did not succeed.

Once you are in a Customs Union, you could not have an independent trade policy of your own but could only do trade deals with other countries such as the United States, India or Brazil, via the auspices of the European Union. They could, therefore, effectively still control your terms of trade and economic interface with the rest of the world and thus, by any normal measure, you would not be a sovereign country and thus not really have left the European Union at all.

But it gets worse, as once inside the Customs Union the United Kingdom would not be permitted to leave, unless with the consent of the other Members of the EU. There was no "Article 50" by which the UK could unilaterally opt to leave the Customs Union at some point in the future. Once in, there was no unilateral way out. This was well summarised during the subsequent debates in Parliament as the "Hotel California dilemma", i.e. "You can check out, but you can never leave".[177]

As Article 20 of the original Northern Ireland Protocol (the 'Backstop') clearly states:

ARTICLE 20
(Protocol on Ireland and Northern Ireland)

Review

"If at any time after the end of the transition period the Union or the United Kingdom considers that this Protocol is, in whole or in part, no longer necessary to achieve the objectives set out in Article 1(3) and should cease to apply, in whole or in part, it may notify the other party, setting out its reasons. Within 6 months of such a notification, the Joint Committee shall meet at ministerial level to consider the notification, having regard to all of the objectives specified in Article 1. The Joint Committee may seek an opinion from institutions created by the 1998 Agreement.

If, following the consideration referred to above, and acting in full respect of Article 5 of the Withdrawal Agreement, the Union and the United Kingdom decide **jointly** within the Joint Committee that the Protocol, in whole or in part, is no longer necessary to achieve its objectives, the Protocol shall cease to apply, in whole or in part. In such a case the Joint Committee shall address recommendations to the Union and to the United Kingdom on the necessary measures, taking into account the obligations of the parties to the 1998 Agreement".[178] (Emphasis added).

This was in many ways the most objectionable part of the whole Treaty, and time and again, was at the heart of the debates in Parliament. The ERG focused on this point in particular, as it meant that if Parliament were to Ratify it, we would never really Leave the EU at all – exactly as many of the European bureaucrats and British senior Civil Servants who had negotiated the Withdrawal Agreement, between them, had no doubt wanted all along.

In fairness, someone at *The Daily Telegraph* did clearly take the trouble to read through the document in detail, as indeed did their counterparts at *The Sun*.[179] At Prime Ministers Questions on 26th November 2018, I told the Prime Minister in the House that both of them had described the document as a "surrender", in the following terms:

"Prime Minister, there is one thing on which we can all agree. It is that when we come to vote on this in two weeks' time, it will be about the most important thing that we in this House will ever vote on in our entire lives. *The Sun* and *The Daily Telegraph* have described the deal this morning as a "surrender", and I am afraid it is. As soon as the ink is dry, the Spanish will be after Gibraltar and the French will be after our fish. The Prime Minister and the whole House know the mathematics. This will never get through. Even if it did—which it will not—the Democratic Unionist party Members on whom we rely for a majority have said that they would then review the confidence and supply agreement. So, it is as dead as a dodo. Prime Minister, I plead with you: the House of Commons has never, ever surrendered to anybody, and it will not start now". [180]

This was one of many exchanges which I and my ERG colleagues were to have with Theresa May over subsequent months but, time and again, she insisted that her deal was a good one – and that the House of Commons should therefore support it.

The Joint Committee

But it gets worse still. It is a common trait of EU Treaties to try and disguise some of their most pernicious elements, deep within the text. One of the worst elements of the Withdrawal Agreement was the so-called "Joint Committee". This was a Committee of representatives from the UK and EU, designed to oversee the operation of the Withdrawal Agreement, under the Auspices of Article 164-166 of the Treaty, which make its decisions binding in International Law, as follows:

ARTICLE 164

4. The Joint Committee shall:
   a) supervise and facilitate the implementation and application of this Agreement;
   b) decide on the tasks of the specialised committees and supervise their work;
   c) seek appropriate ways and methods of preventing problems that might arise in areas covered by this Agreement or of resolving disputes that may arise regarding the interpretation and application of this Agreement;
   d) consider any matter of interest relating to an area covered by this Agreement;
   e) adopt decisions and make recommendations as set out in Article 166; and
   f) adopt amendments to this Agreement in the cases provided for in this Agreement.[181]

ARTICLE 166

1. The Joint Committee shall, for the purposes of this Agreement, have the power to adopt decisions in respect of all matters for which this Agreement so provides and to make appropriate recommendations to the Union and the United Kingdom.
2. The decisions adopted by the Joint Committee shall be binding on the Union and the United Kingdom, and the Union and the United Kingdom shall implement those decisions. **They shall have the same legal effect as this Agreement**. (Emphasis added) [182]

The powers of the Joint Committee were to be further supplemented by anodyne sounding "Rules of Procedure" for the Joint Committee, contained within Annex 8 of the Treaty, almost literally at the back of the 585-page document (for completeness, there was also a brief Annex 9). Annex 8 even covered how the

Committee could fund their expenses, but it also contained some more worrying elements.

ANNEX 8
(Rules of Procedure for the Joint Committee)

Rule 1: Chair

1. The Joint Committee shall be co-chaired by a Member of the European Commission and a representative of the Government of the United Kingdom at ministerial level, **or by high-level officials designated to act as their alternates**. The European Union and the United Kingdom shall notify each other in writing of the designated co-chairs and their alternates.
2. The decision of the co-chairs, provided for by these Rules of Procedure shall be taken by mutual consent.
3. A co-chair who is unable to attend a meeting may be replaced for that meeting by a designee. (Emphasis added)

Rule 7: Agenda for the meetings

3. No later than 10 days before the date of the meeting, the Co-chairs shall decide on the provisional agenda for a meeting. They **may** decide to make that provisional agenda, or any part thereof, public before the beginning of the meeting. (Emphasis added).

Rule 8: Minutes

5. The Secretariat [of the Joint Committee] shall also prepare a **summary** of the minutes. After having approved the summary, the co-chairs **may** decide to make it public. (Emphasis added)

Rule 9: Decisions and Recommendations:

1. In the period between meetings, the Joint Committee may adopt decisions or recommendations by written procedure, if the co-chairs decide to use this procedure. **The written procedure shall consist of an exchange of notes between the co-chairs**". (Emphasis added) [183]

Incredibly, this part of the Treaty not only meant that decisions of the Joint Committee, would have the same force in international law as the Treaty itself – but that, under Annex 8, the Committee could meet effectively in secret, without ever having to publish either its Agenda or its Minutes. (Unlike, for instance the Bank of England which has to publish the Minutes of its Monetary Policy Committee meetings, which sets UK interest rates, a few weeks after they have taken place).

Even more incredibly, via use of the "Out of Committee Procedure", contained in Annex 8 (Rule 9), the two co-Chairman of the Joint Committee who could be one EU and one UK official, could effectively take decisions "by an exchange of notes" without the Committee even having to meet, to discuss their content.

In sum, if the British Minister Chairing the Committee were replaced by a Civil Servant – as the Rules of Procedure clearly allowed – then that British Civil Servant and their EU counterpart in the European Commission could effectively take decisions, binding in European and International Law, merely by exchanging notes.

In other words, the Withdrawal Agreement was not only designed to keep us within the European Union but represented a potential power grab by the Civil Service, who would, if poorly overseen by weak or inattentive Ministers, effectively have the power to make law in relation to its future operation without the specific consent of Parliament. On 20th March 2019, I managed to provoke an Urgent Question, (akin to a mini emergency debate) in the House of Commons specifically on the Joint Committee and its extensive powers in which around a dozen members of the ERG fired detailed questions about its proposed operation at an ill-prepared junior Minister, who was clearly reading from a prepared script and barely understood what we were talking about.

Unsurprisingly, despite the important constitutional issues at stake, to the best of my knowledge, other than broadcasting it on BBC Parliament in the normal manner, the BBC did not report a single word of that debate.[184]

The Supremacy of the ECJ

To compound the problems inherent in the Withdrawal Agreement, the draft Treaty also contained a dispute resolution provision, known as the "Ukrainian Clause", (because it was lifted almost word for word from the EU-Ukraine agreement from 2014, which Ukraine had signed in a hurry, following the Russian incursion into the Crimea and Eastern Ukraine). This provision meant that, in the event of a dispute between the EU and the UK, regarding "a question of interpretation of Union Law" (i.e. just about all of it!) the European Court of Justice, would have the final decision, over and above an "arbitration panel", which would be convened, theoretically at least, to attempt to resolve the dispute. This was laid out clearly in Article 174, in the following terms:

ARTICLE 174

Disputes raising questions of Union law

1.　　　Where a dispute submitted to arbitration in accordance with this Title raises a question of interpretation of a concept of Union law, a question of interpretation of a provision of Union law referred to in this Agreement or a question of whether the United Kingdom has complied with its obligations under Article 89(2), the arbitration panel shall not decide on any such question. In such case, it shall request the Court of Justice of the European Union to give a ruling on the question. **The Court of Justice of the European Union shall have jurisdiction to give such a ruling which shall be binding on the arbitration panel.** (Emphasis added) [185]

So, taken as a whole, the Government proposed to sign us up to a Treaty which to all intents and purposes would keep us so closely aligned to the European Union, including especially our inclusion in the EU's Customs Union, such that we would never have really left the European Union at all.

Highlighting the dangers of the Withdrawal Agreement

Nevertheless, over the next several months, the ERG played an important role in beginning to explain to other MPs, the media and through them the wider British public, what the Withdrawal Agreement really meant. For instance, only four days after the publication of the Withdrawal Agreement, on the 18th November, the ERG published a simple seven-page guide, entitled "Your Right to Know: The case against Chequers and the Draft Withdrawal Agreement in plain English", which achieved a certain degree of pick up in the media and which was quite widely read when it was published shortly thereafter on the internet.

Frequent media appearances by senior members of the ERG, led from the front by Jacob Rees-Mogg as our Chairman, gradually began to shift public opinion against Chequers, the associated Withdrawal Agreement and what it all represented. For my part, as I was now very familiar with the contents of the Withdrawal Agreement, I also began to undertake some of these media appearances as well, although assistant producers would normally only ring me to request an interview once they had already established that both Jacob and Steve were unavailable. In addition to us, however, other prominent members of the group such as Iain Duncan Smith, Bill Cash, Bernard Jenkin, John Redwood, Owen Paterson and Theresa Villiers, also did quite a lot of media in attempting to get across our message to the British public that the Withdrawal Agreement was not at all what it purported to be.

Why did the Conservative Party put up with it?

I would like to be able to say that every MP in the House of Commons took the Withdrawal Agreement home and diligently worked through it in the way that I and my colleagues in the ERG had done. However, that would not be true. The House of Commons Authorities, anticipating that MPs would want to read the Treaty in detail produced over 800 copies, most of which were never collected from the Vote Office, even by MPs' researchers. Even allowing for the fact that a number of Members may have preferred to read the detailed Treaty online, speaking to numerous colleagues privately, it became increasingly apparent that relatively few of them had barely read a word of it at all.

Instead, exactly as those in the Establishment had foreseen, most Tory MPs had been prepared to rely on reassurances from the Government and the blandishments of the Whips, that in effect there was really nothing here to worry about so "move along please" and it was only those wonks and obviously swivel-eyed nerds in the ERG that were "banging on about Europe" yet again and obsessing over minor and irrelevant points of detail, in an otherwise perfectly agreeable deal.

Almost six months of attempting to negotiate with No 10 since Chequers had clearly been to absolutely no avail. Persistent attempts at "jaw jaw" had obviously failed, so now this left only one option to try and honour the result of the Referendum: "war war". Not physical combat of course, but rather procedural battle in the Chamber and ultimately the division lobbies – of the House of Commons.

With the Government and the Whips Office arguing the Withdrawal Agreement could finally take us out of the EU once and for all – and the ERG, having examined it in detail, now vociferously arguing precisely the opposite – and with a Bill still required to ratify the Withdrawal Agreement, there was clearly going to be a monumental struggle for the Hearts and Minds (and ultimately votes) of Conservative MPs.

That, in turn, would require the ERG to create its own Whipping Team to fight this trenchant and yet absolutely vital Parliamentary battle – which is precisely what we then did.

Steve

Steve Baker, the MP for Wycombe in Buckinghamshire, succeeded my old friend Paul Goodman as the representative of that constituency. A staunch Christian, before entering politics, Steve served as an Engineering Officer in the Royal Air Force, including on both the Jaguar and later Tornado fighter-bombers. In the later role, at one time Steve programmed Tornado aircraft to carry nuclear weapons as part of our Nuclear Deterrent during the Cold War.

Steve's technical skills, honed in the RAF, made him a great asset to the ERG, as an organiser as well as a politician in his own right – whether designing the voting database for the Buddies or forming the WhatsApp group by which MPs tend to communicate during the modern era.

A strong libertarian by instinct, he once described himself as "the Hard Man of Brexit", which in many ways was true, even despite his "wobble" on the eve of Meaningful Vote Three.

Throughout the whole Battle for Brexit, Steve was my closest confidante and staunchest ally and the success of the Buddies in helping to defeat the original Withdrawal Agreement is in no small measure down to him.

He has Chaired the ERG twice (the only MP to do so, as far as I know) firstly from 2016–17 and then again from 2019–20, having been David Davis' Junior Minister at DEXEU during part of the negotiating period and then resigning alongside his boss immediately post-Chequers in mid-2018.

There are a handful of people, without any one of whom Brexit might never have been achieved – but Steve Baker is undoubtedly one of them.

Chapter 10: Fighting the Withdrawal Agreement That Did the Opposite

It rapidly became obvious that what we were going to need in this situation was our own dedicated Whipping operation, in order to persuade colleagues to try and vote against the Withdrawal Agreement and to organise ourselves to maximise the number of colleagues who would do so. As a former "Operations Officer" for the Whips Office, I discussed this with Jacob and Steve and we collectively agreed that I would form a team of "ERG Whips", hand-picked for the process, in order to carry out this function. Steve and I discussed a series of names between us and then, over the next few days, we proceeded to confidentially invite a number of colleagues on whom we felt we could rely, to form the team. From memory, of the several people we approached very confidentially, only one refused.

Enter "The Buddies"

In the end we put together a team of around a dozen trusted colleagues and held our inaugural meeting in Westminster. One of the first items of business was how we were going to describe ourselves (even in private). Perhaps for old fashioned reasons, I took the view that there was only one Whips Office – even if we were going to be up against them – and therefore we shouldn't really call ourselves Whips. Steve took the point and then suggested, as a way through, that we should call ourselves "the Buddies" instead. This immediately caught on and I therefore became the "Chief Buddy", with Steve Baker as my Deputy. The other Buddies in the group were: David Jones MP, Laurence Robertson MP, Theresa Villiers MP, Anne-Marie Trevelyan MP, Adam Holloway MP, Charlie Elphicke MP, Simon Clarke MP, Michael Tomlinson MP, Ross Thomson MP and one other Member of Parliament who still wishes to remain anonymous.[186] We divided the Parliamentary Party into groups with a Buddy each assigned a number of Members of Parliament who they would attempt to Whip in order to vote against the Agreement. We were materially aided in this exercise by Steve, who came up with "the mother of all spreadsheets" which he had specifically designed, in order to record the likely voting intention of every Member of the Conservative Parliamentary Party.

Steve, with advice from the rest of the team, graded every Conservative MP from +5 to -5 on their likelihood to vote against the Treaty. As a simple example of this, Bill Cash was +5, whereas Ken Clark was -5 and so on. The spreadsheet also had a wonderful system of colour coding and various other bells and whistles, all created by Steve, which made it something of a work of art.

That said, I explained to the Buddies from the outset that if we were to do this in as disciplined a manner as the real Whips Office, then while all intelligence they gathered would be collated and fed into the system, only Steve and I would know the overall results and thus the overall likely figures in any given vote. This was not in any way meant to be disrespectful to any of the other Buddies but was a necessary security measure. To their credit, all of the Buddies accepted this discipline without demure. We now effectively had a team with which we could fight what we knew would be an extremely difficult and challenging battle, up against not just "the professionals" of the Government's own Whips Office, but the rest of the weight of the Government and the Prime Minister, and indeed much of the media as well.

We were also very careful to keep the identity of the Buddies secret, so that even the other senior members of the ERG didn't know who was in the team and which Buddies were responsible for lobbying which MPs. Again, the other senior members of the group assented to this procedure (only one of them reluctantly) as I stressed that only by maintaining strict internal security, were we likely to be able to win the votes. Thus, I began my brief career as the "Chief Buddy", about to take on my opposite numbers in the Government Whips Office, where I had learnt my trade in the first place.

The 'Nuclear Weapon' – A Vote of No Confidence

Within any organisation, when great matters are at stake, there will always be those who argue for decisive action and those who argue for caution. In this respect, the ERG was no different but in the period between Chequers in July 2018 and the publication of the Withdrawal Agreement in November, the balance of opinion within the ERG had begun to harden, fortified by an increasing realisation that despite months of attempting to negotiate with the Government, it was apparent that Theresa May had no intention, whatsoever, of changing course and was determined to drive her deal through Parliament, whatever the cost.

In seeking to resist this outcome, the group potentially had access to a "nuclear weapon" – which was to try and call a Vote of No Confidence in Theresa May as the Leader of the Conservative Party. The Party's rules stated that in order to trigger a Vote of Confidence, 15% of the Conservative Parliamentary Party (at that time representing 48 MPs) would have to write letters to the Chairman of the

1922 Committee, Sir Graham Brady, requesting such a ballot. If triggered, the vote would take the form of a secret ballot of all Tory MPs, with the Chairman of the 1922 Committee effectively acting as the Returning Officer.[187] As the autumn wore on, debate raged within the upper echelons of the ERG about whether or not to attempt to trigger such a ballot, but as time elapsed it became increasingly evident that the Prime Minister (no doubt egged on by her small coterie of senior Advisors) was effectively implacable. It was already clear that we would have to resist her subsequent legislation in the Voting Lobbies of the House of Commons – but should we try to challenge her as Prime Minister herself?

In arguing this back and forth, we were all well aware that we would be very unlikely to actually win such a contest – which would be decided by a simple majority of Conservative MPs. Rather, a Vote of No Confidence would provide, in effect, a mini referendum within the Conservative Parliamentary Party on her European Policy in general and the Chequers deal in particular.

It may come as a surprise to some, but I was actually more at the dovish end of this debate, at least initially. From my point of view, as a former senior Whip, seeking to gather 48 names as quietly as possible and then triggering a ballot, was never going to be easy, not least as the Prime Minister's allies would have their eyes out on stalks for any such manoeuvre. At one ERG meeting, I cautioned that if we attempted to trigger a Vote of No Confidence in Theresa May, this effectively amounted to a declaration of all-out war between us and her and perhaps I still hoped, that somehow, we could come up with a negotiated solution.[188]

Nevertheless, the publication of the Withdrawal Agreement, and the full horrors it contained, on the 14th November, was very much the straw that broke the camel's back. By this stage it had become obvious that the Government had simply been stringing us along for months, to buy time while the Withdrawal Agreement was being finalised and the necessary ratifying legislation was no doubt being drafted as well. The Prime Minister showed no sign of being willing to compromise, despite months of negotiations with her and her lieutenants, led by Gavin Barwell.

On the morning following the publication of the Withdrawal Agreement, 15th November, Dominic Raab (who had replaced David Davis as DEXEU Secretary after Chequers) also resigned because he could no longer go along with the Chequers Deal either, particularly as represented by the Withdrawal Agreement. At this point, the clamour within the ERG leadership to attempt to trigger a Vote of Confidence became almost irresistible. There was a certain sense that Dominic Raab's resignation presented a "now or never" moment and if we were to prevent the Withdrawal Agreement from ever getting through the House of Commons, the best way to do this would be to invoke the procedure to change the Leader of the Conservative Party, by activating the Party's own internal mechanisms to trigger a secret ballot.

At a crunch meeting at lunchtime on the 15th November, the ERG decided that they would call publicly on Conservative MPs to submit letters of No Confidence to Sir Graham Brady, with the aim of triggering a ballot. I agreed to go along with this but, with the important caveat that if we were going to do this, we had to do it wholeheartedly and without reservation – in other words, as I put it at the time, once we came out of the trenches, we could not afford to get caught in no-mans-land. Ironically, the military analogy proved apposite, but in a way in which I did not anticipate at the time.

The Brexit "Buddies"

The Brexit "Buddies" was the name we ascribed to the highly secret whipping team which we created to combat Theresa May's ill-fated original withdrawal agreement. Comprising a dozen MPs its members were as follows:

Mark Francois MP (Chief Buddy):
As a former Senior Whip, when it became obvious that Theresa May was utterly determined to drive her flawed Withdrawal Agreement through the House of Commons, the Officers of the ERG tasked me with forming a secret whipping team to defeat the agreement. What we achieved was, arguably, one of the most successful whipping operations in Parliamentary history. In any event, we helped inflict the largest Commons defeat on any Government since records began. Had it not been for "the Buddies" then Theresa May's so-called Withdrawal Agreement might actually have been passed by Parliament after all.

Steve Baker MP (Deputy Chief Buddy):
Steve Baker was my absolute right-hand man in both forming and organising the Buddies during the Battle for Brexit. His bespoke database helped to record the likely voting intentions of any Conservative MPs during Meaningful Votes One, Two and Three and, for instance, during MV1 his original "upper estimate" of how many MPs would vote against the Withdrawal Agreement was correct, almost to the last single MP. We could not have done this without him.

Theresa Villiers MP:
A former Northern Ireland Secretary under David Cameron and an MEP before entering the House of Commons in 2005, Theresa Villiers did not share her namesake's affection for the original Withdrawal Agreement and, despite holding a narrow majority in her North London constituency, helped organise the resistance to the Withdrawal Agreement amongst Conservative MPs. Theresa is a shrewd judge of people, a skill which proved very valuable to the Buddies in early 2019. She was, of course, also a fellow member of the fateful CFI trip to Israel, with Boris, George and me back in 2002.

David Jones MP:
David Jones is a canny Welsh lawyer, with a very dry sense of humour, which enlivened several meetings of the Buddies in the early part of 2019. A former Welsh Secretary and like Theresa Villiers, a former member of the Cabinet, he brought considerable senior experience to the operations of the Buddies when it really mattered. Moreover, David was (and still is) a good judge of character, which is a vital skill when you are attempting to judge how colleagues are likely to vote, especially when under pressure. David's intuition on those matters was often very valuable in helping to defeat Theresa May's Withdrawal Agreement.

Laurence Robertson MP:
Laurence Robertson has been the Member of Parliament for Tewkesbury since 1997. We have been friends for years and as such, I attended his 40th birthday party, in a local community centre in his constituency back in 1998. When asked to address his birthday guests he memorably said: "As a Member of Parliament, I cannot tell you how rare it is to be in a room with 50 other people, and genuinely not hate any of them!" A former Whip (we served in the Whips Office together) and also a past Chairman of the Northern Ireland Select Committee, Laurence has always enjoyed close links with the DUP – as well as being a staunch Eurosceptic and a great member of the Buddies.

Adam Holloway MP:
Adam Holloway, the MP for Gravesham in North Kent, entered Parliament in 2005 after military service in among others, the Brigade of Guards, where he served as an officer in the Grenadier Guards, including during the first Gulf War in 1991. After leaving the Army, Adam served as a journalist with, among others, ITN, BBC *Panorama* and the *Sunday Times*. Perhaps unsurprisingly given this background, Adam was one of the most dynamic members of the Buddies, frequently coming up with sparky suggestions on how best to fight the campaign.

Anne-Marie Trevelyan MP:
Anne-Marie Trevelyan (or 'AMT' as she is widely known in Parliament) was elected as the Member of Parliament for Berwick-upon-Tweed on the Anglo-Scottish border, in 2015. A former accountant with Price Waterhouse Cooper (PWC), AMT first made an impact in Parliament as an active member of the Public Accounts Committee. A strong Eurosceptic, she resigned as a Parliamentary Private Secretary (PPS) in November 2018, in opposition to Theresa May's Withdrawal Agreement. She was therefore another natural candidate to join the Buddies and was one of its most active team members. AMT now sits in Cabinet, as the Trade Secretary.

Charlie Elphicke MP:
Charlie Elphicke was elected as the Member of Parliament for Dover in 2010. A lawyer by training, he served as a Government Whip under David Cameron in 2015–16 and thus had practical experience of what dealing with colleagues in this way was actually like. Charlie Elphicke stood down as the MP for Dover prior to the 2019 General Election and was succeeded as the local MP by his wife, Natalie, at the subsequent contest.

Simon Clarke MP:
Simon Clarke was first elected as the Member of Parliament for Middlesbrough South and East Cleveland, in the traditionally pro-Labour North-East of England, in 2017. Born in North Tees Hospital and having grown-up in the village of Marton, prior to studying history at Oxford, he trained as a solicitor and also worked, among others, for Dominic Raab as a staffer, prior to being elected to Parliament. Simon was one of Steve's wise nominations to join the Buddies, not least as he was well connected among the new 2017 intake. Simon is presently the Chief Secretary to the Treasury and also a member of the Cabinet.

Michael Tomlinson MP:
Michael Tomlinson, the MP for Mid Dorset and North Poole, was another relatively new MP, who Steve recommended to become one of the Buddies. Already an active member of the ERG, Michael had been made Deputy Chairman in 2016 and was thus a natural choice to join the team. Particularly good on the likely voting intentions of MPs, he had been appointed as Parliamentary Private Secretary (PPS) to Dominic Raab at DEXEU, barely 48 hours before the latter resigned from the Cabinet once the original Withdrawal Agreement was published. Perhaps ironically, Michael now serves as a (no doubt very effective) Whip in the official Government Whips Office.

Ross Thomson MP:
Ross was elected the MP for Aberdeen South at the 2017 General Election, in which the Conservative Party made a number of notable gains in Scotland. We therefore asked Ross to be responsible for dealing with Scottish Conservative MPs regarding the Withdrawal Agreement. Unfortunately, on several occasions at meetings of the Buddies I got his name confused with Douglas Ross, another of the newly elected Scottish Conservatives, which meant that he was assigned the internal nickname of "Ross Douglas" within the group. Ross stood down at the 2019 General Election but not before he had made an important contribution to the work of the Buddies. Ross now works for the Royal British Legion.

"X" MP:
The final member of the Buddies, a recently elected member of the 2017 intake and one of the most committed members of the group has asked to remain anonymous – a wish that I have respected.

Jacob's Press Conference

Accordingly, our Chairman, Jacob Rees-Mogg, went downstairs to an impromptu press conference which Steve had rapidly organised with the national media. Standing outside St Stephen's Entrance, with Steve chairing questions from the press, Jacob effectively called on fellow Conservative MPs to submit letters to Sir Graham Brady to trigger a Vote of No Confidence in the Prime Minister. Unsurprisingly, this created a media frenzy, and the Whips went into overdrive in order to try and persuade colleagues not to comply.[189]

In modern politics, an initiative like this generally either develops momentum quite quickly or withers and dies. In this case, it was the latter. The media rapidly became obsessed with how many letters Graham Brady had received but he played an absolutely inscrutable straight bat and delighted in telling one journalist from the BBC, that not even his wife knew how many letters he had and if he wasn't going to tell her, he certainly wasn't going to tell them. At a subsequent media appearance several days after the press conference, Jacob was taunted by the fact that the ERG had failed to assemble the required 48 letters and we were compared to "Dad's Army" the wonderful comedy series about a fictional platoon of the Home Guard during World War II. On the 20th November, the *Evening Standard*, edited by David Cameron's old friend and arch Remainer, George Osborne, delighted in publishing a front-page headline, "Stupid Boy", jumping on a light-hearted remark that Jacob had made about always being a fan of Captain Mannering (who commanded the fictional Warminster-on-Sea Home Guard Platoon in question).

Members of the ERG were immediately mocked up as members of Captain Mannering's Home Guard unit, including David Davis as Sergeant Wilson and Steve Baker as Private Pike.[190] A whole series of other memes followed and essentially, the media set out to make the ERG a laughingstock. Some months later (according to a pretty reliable source) I was told that we had actually got very close to the 48 letters required but had not quite crossed the threshold.[191] Nevertheless, we didn't know this at the time and, unsurprisingly we came in for a degree of media ignominy, as a result.

By now, it was clear that if we were going to fight at senior level as it were, we needed to be a lot better organised than this. This applied both if we were to mount a subsequent attempt at gathering the 48 letters (the rules didn't say you couldn't have more than one try) but also if there were subsequently to be hotly contested Divisions in the House of Commons on the Withdrawal Agreement itself.

No half measures

Despite our failure – and it was a failure – to persuade 48 of our colleagues to submit letters to Sir Graham Brady calling for a Vote of Confidence in the Prime Minister, as November turned into December there was growing dissent on the Conservative Backbenches about what the Withdrawal Agreement really meant. The ERG did have some success in explaining to the wider world what this draft international Treaty really comprised and, once the Buddies started to engage with their assigned target groups of MPs, to explain to them privately and in detail, one-to-one, what the Withdrawal Agreement *really* entailed, the disquiet on the back benches began to grow.

By early December there were increasing worries on the Backbenches about the direction in which the Prime Minister was leading the Party and indeed the country and within the inner councils of the ERG, it was suggested that we might have another crack at garnering the 48 letters. As previously explained, at that time, we did not know precisely how many letters Sir Graham Brady had locked in the safe in his office, but under the rules of the Conservative Party, the letters remained "live" unless withdrawn by their author. In other words, you didn't have to start from square one all over again; if you had got close (although again we never realised quite how close) if you could then persuade a few more colleagues to put in additional letters, then that might carry you over the line.

Against this background we debated whether or not to have a second go. My input into this was that we had clearly been embarrassed first time around, because the attempt had gone off somewhat at half-cock and if we were to do this again, there should be "no half measures". If we really meant it, then we should pull out all the stops and anybody who had been hesitating to put in a letter – including one or two people then in the room – would now have to overcome their reservations and finally do this, all or nothing. Based on our understanding by this stage that despite months of negotiations, there was no question whatsoever of the Prime Minister changing course, it was therefore resolved to have "one more heave" at trying to get over the 48 letter try line and finally force a Vote of No Confidence, to test Backbench opinion.

To be absolutely clear, the Buddies were not actually constituted for this purpose. People had joined the team on the understanding that they would be asked to Whip colleagues to vote against any attempt by the Government to pass a Bill to turn the Withdrawal Agreement into law. Nevertheless, some of the Buddies, who also believed by this stage that the Prime Minister had lost her way, individually volunteered to speak to colleagues to encourage those who we knew privately to be wavering, to summon up the courage to send in letters to Sir Graham Brady.

In early to mid-December, we thus began a second attempt (this time without a press conference) to persuade additional colleagues to submit their letters. Again, Sir Graham quite rightly remained inscrutable about the number of letters he had in his safe, although we began to receive intelligence that a number of colleagues who previously had been indecisive had finally decided that "enough was enough" and that they were going to write to Sir Graham after all. The media again got wind of this (Westminster is, after all, a very leaky place) and a second wave of speculation rippled through Parliament that we were going to finally get to the magic number of 48 letters. We began to realise that a number of colleagues who had previously been unwilling to do so, had now become exasperated at the supine direction of the Government's policy and were indeed prepared to contemplate submitting letters to Sir Graham Brady.

The Prime Minister's challenge was compounded by the fact that some months previously, a number of pro-European Conservative Backbenchers, acting with others, had managed to pass an Amendment to the earlier EU Withdrawal Act, meaning, in effect that before the Government were able to bring in a Bill to Ratify any agreement with the European Union, they would first have to win a vote in principle in the House of Commons. The wording in the Amendment specified that this would be a so-called, "Meaningful Vote" – and that is indeed what it turned out to be (in fact, thrice over).

By this stage, the Government had earmarked a date of Tuesday 11th December for the much anticipated "Meaningful Vote" to take place. However, the Whips Office, having taken detailed soundings among Conservative MPs, were already well aware that the Withdrawal Agreement, at least in its original form, was likely to be heavily defeated. The Buddies, who had by now been running a parallel exercise of our own, had reached a similar conclusion (although only Steve and I knew the actual numbers, which from the Government's perspective were truly awful).

The Government's confusion about whether or not the Meaningful Vote was actually going to go ahead or not only intensified during the several days of debate leading up to it when, one after another, Conservative backbenchers made plain that they had no intention of voting for the Agreement – each of them carefully noted by the Whips and the Buddies in turn.

The Government's position eventually descended into farce, when on the eve of the vote, Michael Gove was sent on to the *Today* programme to reassure listeners that the Meaningful Vote was still going to go ahead as scheduled. When asked if the vote was definitely, 100 percent going to happen, he replied very clearly: "Yes", and re-emphasised the point again later during the same interview.[192] This was then widely reported across a variety of media outlets throughout the morning, as a senior Cabinet Minister reaffirming that the vote was going to go ahead after all.

Nevertheless, most likely on advice from the Whips Office and in order to stave off a certain heavy defeat, the Government then announced several hours later, in the early afternoon, that they would be deferring the vote, probably until after Christmas. This led to derision in the media, plus criticism from a number of backbenchers that the Government had effectively "bottled it". The Buddies had done a great deal of work preparing for the vote, and I too was pretty angry. As I said in the House:

"What the Government have done today is shameful. It is a complete abuse of this House. Having been found in contempt recently for the first time in living memory, they have now gone for a "buy one, get one free". The whole House wanted to debate this. We wanted to vote on it. The people expected us to vote on it, and the Government have gone and run away and hidden in the toilets. People watching this on television will be confused and bemused, and very, very angry at the way their own Parliament has let them down. The Government Front Benchers should literally be ashamed of themselves".[193]

With the long-anticipated Meaningful Vote having been pulled on the very eve of it happening and the Government's approach now clearly in disarray, more

Conservative backbenchers began expressing doubts, at least in private, about the PM's strategy and the desire for a Vote of No Confidence began to escalate accordingly.

By the 11th December, speculation had reached fever pitch that we were very close to meeting the required total. I had spoken to several MPs myself and, assisted by a number of the Buddies, I knew that five further Conservative MPs were due to submit their letters on the morning of the 12th December. On the evening of the 11th, a little after 9:00pm, I received a telephone call out of the blue from Laura Kuenssberg, the Political Editor of the BBC. She suggested (and Laura is undoubtedly one of the most clued-in correspondents in Westminster) that she was picking up whispers that we were now very close to getting 48 and she wanted to know whether or not I could confirm this, before she put together her final package for the 10:00pm news. In response, I said that I honestly didn't know and the only person who did know the true total was Sir Graham Brady. When she pressed me on the point, I told her: "Look Laura, I cannot tell you, hand on heart, that we've got 48 letters – because the honest truth is I don't know. What I do know, strictly privately, is that I think we're pretty close and I've got five more going in in the morning, so if we aren't at 48 tonight, I believe there's a fighting chance we will be at 48 tomorrow. So, if you really want a steer, I would say something at 10:00pm to the effect that you thought that the ERG was close to the required number but that you couldn't confirm that they'd achieved it. Further than that, I honestly can't say".

To be fair to Laura Kuenssberg, she's a fiercely independent minded journalist (despite what some may think) and she was not going to blithely follow any line from me or from anybody else. That said, she did report in her 10:00pm bulletin that rumours were circulating at Westminster that Theresa May's opponents were now growing increasingly close to achieving the required target. This seemed to me to be a very fair summary of the situation. At about 10:45pm, I received a phone call from my old friend, Paul Goodman, now the Editor of the authoritative Conservative Party "fanzine" website, Conservative Home, who said down the phone slightly breathlessly: "You've done it! You've got 48 letters!". When I asked him how he knew, he retorted: "I'm the Editor of Con Home, it's my job to know! Just take it from me Mark, you've done it and there's going to be a ballot, I just don't know when".[194]

I rapidly exchanged phone calls with Jacob and Steve and a few others, and we agreed that we would need to be on our metal, as we thought that Sir Graham Brady, as the Returning Officer, would not want to drag this out but would be likely to call the ballot within the next few days. I therefore went to bed quite late that night, feeling tired but nonetheless encouraged, that we had finally managed to provoke a Vote of Confidence in the Prime Minister and what we genuinely believed was her highly misguided policy.

Now we could test whether the Prime Minister's policy of Chequers and the Withdrawal Agreement, of "high alignment" and a probable Customs Union, rather than a clean break from the EU, really did have the support of the Conservative Parliamentary Party after all.

The Vote of No Confidence

In the end, Sir Graham Brady acted very swiftly.[195] When I woke up to the early morning news bulletins, they announced that the 48 letters had indeed been received and that Sir Graham Brady had decided to call a Vote of No Confidence in Theresa May as Prime Minister and Leader of the Conservative Party *for that afternoon*. The ballot boxes would be open for several hours in Committee Room 14 (which is where Tory MPs traditionally vote upon these things) and the result would be announced later that evening. Within about five minutes, my phone started to ring, and we rapidly convened a meeting of the ERG leadership in Iain Duncan Smith's office at 10:00am that morning.

The rest of the day was a blizzard of activity, in trying to persuade colleagues that they would have to vote against the Prime Minister, in order to prevent us betraying the Referendum. Arguments raged back and forth among colleagues throughout the day, as Steve and I received updated reports on how we thought the vote was going to go. By the time the polls had closed my best guess, as the ERG Chief Whip, was that around 120 colleagues had voted against the Prime Minister. The rules of the Parliamentary Party said that she only needed 50% of the MPs plus one in order to win and moreover that if challenged unsuccessfully, she would effectively be immune from another such vote for at least a period of 12 months – by which time the battles in Parliament would probably effectively be over. It was thus most certainly a high stakes game. However, as previous Conservative Leadership contests have proved in the past, even if a sitting Prime Minister were to win, what was vitally important was the margin of victory.[196] Whilst we always knew it was highly unlikely that we would actually win the vote, the realistic objective was to score a significantly high dissenting vote, to effectively challenge the Prime Minister's authority, to a point where she could probably continue in office, but would no longer be able to force the wretched Withdrawal Agreement through Parliament.

Sir Graham Brady had announced that the result would be read out in Committee Room 14 at 9:00pm that evening, once he and the officers of the 1922 Committee had completed and verified the count. The media would not be admitted but would be allowed one pool camera (so called because it then "pools" its feed with all the other media organisations) which would record the result live, for transmission across the country and indeed internationally. It would probably be fair to say that there were many people in the upper echelons of the European Union, from Brussels to Berlin, who were anxiously awaiting the outcome of this ballot as well.

In theory, the Prime Minister could rely, from the outset, on at least around 140 votes from "the Government payroll". This term refers to Government Ministers (including Whips) and Parliamentary Private Secretaries, who effectively form part of the Government (although, perhaps confusingly, PPS' are not paid). By tradition, all these MPs were obliged to support the Prime Minister, or if they felt they could not, to resign on a point of honour. Even allowing for a limited degree of mendacity in the privacy of the ballot box – and I do know at least one Government Minister who definitely voted against Theresa May that evening – it did seem likely that the vast majority of the payroll would vote for the Prime Minister. As she only needed 158 votes to win, that meant that she was virtually over the line even before the contest began.

Nevertheless, what really mattered was whether or not she still enjoyed support on the Backbenches too. If a vast number of backbenchers voted alongside the payroll and she won emphatically, then we would have suffered a clear defeat and her authority to drive the Withdrawal Agreement through the Commons would have been greatly enhanced. Conversely, if a majority of her Backbenchers voted against her, then even though the payroll were with her, this would represent something of a pyrrhic victory and her authority would be badly dented in the battles that were to come. As we went into Committee Room 14 at 8:30pm, I had a scrap of paper in my pocket with my and Steve's best guess – which was that around 120 Tory MPs would actually have voted against Theresa May.

At about 8:45pm, Christopher Hope, the senior Political Correspondent of *The Daily Telegraph* (known universally across Westminster by his nickname, "Chopper"), texted me and said: "What do you reckon? 120?". I was mildly impressed by the fact that he had, completely independently of me, as far as I know, come up with the same number, but nonetheless, I simply texted back non-committally: "Dunno Chopper, but either way we haven't got long to wait to find out!". At about 8:50pm, Nick Robinson, from the *Today* programme – whom I still remembered from my FCS days – approached me and whispered to me: "Good evening General. Whatever the outcome of this vote, there's going to be massive interest in this, and I know you've whipped it. So, after it's been announced would you mind coming and doing an interview for me that we can record for tomorrow's *Today* programme?" When I remonstrated that the corridor outside Committee Room 14 was already packed to the gunnels with journalists, and I thought an interview would be difficult, he replied that he had already thought about that and he would be waiting at the far end of the Committee Corridor (which is actually pretty long), so we could have a quiet interview there. I accordingly agreed, whatever the result might be.

When John Redwood stood against John Major for the Leadership of the Conservative Party in 1995, Major's team had planned ahead and made sure that all the major media outlets were covered with Major supporters, so that they could comment within moments of the result being declared. Redwood's team, for whatever reason, did not plan as thoroughly and therefore when Major was announced to have defeated Redwood (by 218 votes to 89), his supporters immediately declared this as a massive victory on the airwaves and effectively put the issue to bed by nightfall.[197] We had learned from this example and therefore we made sure that we had most of the major media outlets covered too. For instance, Jacob was waiting in the makeshift media village on College Green to give a comment on the announcement as soon as it came through. The ERG has agreed certain lines to take depending on whatever the outcome was, the key one of which was that even if the Prime Minister, as expected, won the vote, if she had lost the support of a majority of her Backbenchers, she no longer really had a mandate from the Parliamentary Party to push through the Withdrawal Agreement.

The minutes seemed to pass agonisingly until, a few minutes before 9:00pm, Sir Graham Brady, surrounded by the Executive Committee of the 1922, entered the room and called for order. The chatter rapidly fell away until the room was absolutely silent and as the old saying has it, you could have heard a pin drop. Sir Graham Brady then rose to his feet and declared that as the Returning Officer, there had been 100% turnout in the ballot (which drew a certain degree of ironic laughter from the audience). He then announced that those who do have confidence in the Prime Minister were 200 votes. At this point, a massive cheer went up in the room and Alan Duncan, a Government loyalist, obviously in accordance with some pre-arranged plan, led a North Korean-style standing ovation in response to the result. One of our supporters sitting next to me turned around and exclaimed: "Oh no, we're fucked!". To which I retorted: "Hang on, it's binary, just wait for the other number". When Sir Graham Brady then read out that those who do not have confidence in the Prime Minister were 117 votes, there was an audible intake of breath around the room. Suddenly it began to sink in to all present that the Prime Minister had indeed won, but by no means convincingly and in fact a large majority of her Backbenchers had voted against her, rather than in favour. In percentage terms, the Prime Minister had secured 63% of the overall vote but, given that she had virtually all of the payroll from the outset, she had lost out on the non-payroll backbenches by a ratio of almost 2:1.

A pyrrhic victory for May

In the end, Steve and I had been three votes out and I remember looking across the room to Chopper, who raised his hands with three fingers, as if to drive home the point. As agreed, I then walked out from Committee Room 14, did my best to avoid the media scrum and walked down to the end of the corridor in order to be interviewed by Nick Robinson, as I had promised. However, Nick was fiddling around slightly with his recording equipment and by the time that he finally turned the microphone on, I found myself surrounded by a gaggle of at least a dozen journalists, all with mics or tape recorders in their hands. Up to this point in my career, I had never really been on the receiving end of a media gaggle of this type and so, when Nick asked me how I felt at the Prime Minister having won the result so convincingly, I replied that the reverse was true. I told him that: "This is a devastating result for the Prime Minister who has clearly lost the support of the majority of her own backbenchers and so, based on this outcome, we would seriously urge the Prime Minister to think again".[198]

I then had one journalist after another throw questions at me in a rapid-fire session, to which, as I say, I was pretty unfamiliar. I did my best to stick to my line, arguing that actually this had not been a good result at all for the Prime Minister and vastly more Backbenchers had voted against her than for her – and that she would be very wise to take note of this result and not to simply plough on regardless.

Meanwhile, on College Green, Jacob went slightly further than me and called on Theresa May to resign! This led to an absolute media fire storm, but Jacob was arguing very much from a constitutional position because, as he felt she had clearly lost the support of her own Backbenchers, he believed she would have to stand down.

The morning after

When the dust had settled, on the morning of the 13th December, the view in the media was, unsurprisingly, affected by the viewpoint of the commentators concerned. Pro-Remain outlets made much of the fact that the Prime Minister had won and had defeated "the rebels" and that as a result her authority was enhanced. Conversely, more Eurosceptic outlets picked up on the fact that she had actually lost the support of the vast majority of her Backbenchers and was clearly now in trouble as a result. My own view was that whilst she had won, it had been very much a pyrrhic victory. Her policy of supporting the Withdrawal Agreement had by no means received a ringing endorsement from her own rank and file MPs and, had it not been for the loyal support of the payroll, she would almost certainly have been defeated and would indeed have had to resign. [199]

What this meant in practice was that she was now effectively a wounded Commander, leading a minority administration, trying to force an increasingly unpopular policy through the House of Commons, whilst opposed by all the other Parties (for a variety of different reasons) plus a growing compliment of her own Backbenchers – with the ERG at its heart. Moreover, her precious Withdrawal Agreement was also staunchly opposed by the DUP, on whom she now relied to win other crucial Commons votes, via the Confidence and Supply arrangement with them.

As the House of Commons rose for the Christmas recess and the protagonists paused to draw breath, all sides in this struggle knew that, at some point early in the New Year, they would still face a Meaningful Vote, on whether or not in principle, the House of Commons wished to sign up to this new International Treaty.

Whilst others settled down to a quiet Christmas, the Buddies, every one of whom instinctively understood what was at stake, really set to work.

Chapter 11: Meaningful Vote One –
The Government are Crushed

Over the Christmas break, as well as doing their Christmas shopping and wrapping their presents, many MPs were frantically telephoning each other to try and decide what to do when the House of Commons returned on the 7th January. The Government had pulled the Meaningful Vote on the Withdrawal Agreement prior to Christmas but had not yet confirmed when it would be rescheduled – although most people expected it to be sometime in January 2019.

The Whips were actively hitting the phones over Christmas, doing their best to lobby wavering Tory MPs to support the Prime Minister's Agreement. Conversely and perhaps more subtly, the Buddies were doing the same – although I had made plain that contacting colleagues by telephone was often less effective than speaking to them face to face (and being able to look them in the eye) and therefore we didn't want to be too pushy when speaking to people by phone. Conversations would be best if kept relatively light and gentle rather than "full on".[200]

The Five Families conference call

In addition, by this stage the senior members of the ERG had evolved into a regular pattern of holding a conference call at 6:30pm, every Sunday evening, to compare notes and discuss our strategy. These calls were Chaired by Iain Duncan Smith, as a former Party Leader (and because Iain also has a very good knack for Chairing a telephone conference call – which is not an easy thing to do, when you have a number of passionate Brexiteers all trying to speak at the same time!). These telephone calls were nicknamed the "Five Families" conference call, by David Canzini, one of our supporters, in a reference to the discussions by the five leading gangster families in New York, led by Marlon Brando in *The Godfather*.

On these calls, I would report back (but only in general terms and always avoiding giving specific numbers) on our progress in speaking to colleagues and the sort of reactions that we were receiving regarding the Withdrawal Agreement. Other colleagues did the same and therefore we were able to pool our knowledge during the discussions, which usually lasted around an hour or so, before people broke off for their Sunday evening supper.

As far as I know, none of the contents of these calls *ever* leaked (although we did joke amongst ourselves from time to time about needing to speak slowly, so that the stenographers at GCHQ could write down accurately what we were saying!).

More seriously, one of the reasons we were ultimately successful was because all the participants well understood what was at stake and therefore the need to keep such information strictly confidential, if it were not to leak back to the Government and ultimately be used against us.

The Buddies reassemble

Shortly after Parliament returned on the 7th January, I called a meeting of the Buddies, in order to take stock of how we had been doing with regard to lobbying our colleagues. Each Buddy went through their assigned group of MPs in turn, reporting back any intelligence that they had been able to glean in conversations with them over Christmas. All of this information was systematically entered into Steve's spreadsheet. Once we were back in the House of Commons, we were able to supplement this telephone information with face-to-face conversations with Tory MPs.

As I explained to the team, Whipping is rather like bespoke tailoring. Your approach to each colleague has to be specifically designed for them as an individual and is based on knowing them as a person and understanding their hopes and fears, as well as their beliefs on the European issue. Unlike the real Whips Office, we had no inducements to offer – we were not in a position to hint at eventual promotion, or significant, multi-million-pound investments in their constituencies, for those who might be helpful. If anything, we were only offering quite the reverse(!) as many colleagues well knew that to vote against the Prime Minister over the Withdrawal Agreement would not exactly be career enhancing, at least as long as she remained in office.

Perhaps ironically, our greatest weapon was the Withdrawal Agreement itself. When we were able to explain to colleagues privately, in detail, exactly what it comprised, they were often disconcerted to discover that what was after all a draft International Treaty, was not in fact quite the same as had been explained to them by Government Ministers or Members of the Whips Office. However, that is not to say that we were always successful. On one occasion, I remember sitting down with a senior colleague in my office and taking him through the key aspects of the Withdrawal Agreement, to which he replied: "Mark, I know its shit, but I fear I'm still going to have to vote for it nevertheless". When I asked him why, he said that he felt he needed to do it out of loyalty to the Prime Minister. So, it would be a mistake to say that our collective powers of persuasion were such that we managed to convince every MP that we spoke to – however, it is fair to say that we convinced quite a few. When I relayed this unsuccessful conversation back to our next meeting of The Buddies, one of them replied: "What's he on about? We are asked to vote for shit a lot of the time in this place – but that doesn't mean we always have to, does it?!"[201]

Of course, the Government Whips Office would have been carrying out an operation to mirror our own (although as far as we knew, whilst they realised we had some kind of Whipping Team, they never knew what it was called or, crucially, who was in it). As an additional security measure, I never told the rest of the ERG who the Buddies were either – a point which the other senior members of the group accepted as a necessary precaution. Because only a few of them had ever served in the Whips Office themselves, they were basically prepared to take my word for it.[202]

The Government woos Labour

Given the difficulties that the Government were experiencing in persuading Tory MPs to back the Withdrawal Agreement, especially given that after the 2017 General Election disaster the Party no longer had a majority in the House of Commons, they sought out support from other elements in the House, to try and get the Withdrawal Agreement over the line. As part of this, they opened discussions with a group of Labour Backbenchers, led by several MPs including John Mann, Caroline Flint (a former Labour Europe Minister, who I had Shadowed some years ago) and also Ian Austin, to see if they could generate a sizeable number of Labour MPs, who might be prepared to break their Party's own strict Three Line Whip and vote with the Government. In some ways this was reminiscent of the Lisbon Treaty scenario 11 years earlier, when we had tried to persuade a band of Labour rebels to break ranks and vote for a referendum.

As part of this gambit, the Government stressed their willingness to increase the protection for workers' rights in subsequent negotiations with the EU and also hinted at the possibility of substantial investment in a number of Labour constituencies, if those MPs could be persuaded to see their point of view. As a result of these discussions, the optimists in No 10 managed to convince themselves that a substantial number of Labour MPs would effectively come riding over the hill at the last moment, in order to rescue them (but, in practice, such a posse of horse riders never existed, as was brutally exposed only a few days later).[203]

The Government courts the DUP

As well as trying to woo Labour MPs the Government made overtures to the ten MPs of the Democratic Unionist Party (the DUP). Although they had not joined a formal Coalition after the 2017 General Election, the DUP, led by Arlene Foster back in Belfast, but with their Parliamentary delegation at Westminster led by Nigel Dodds MP, had agreed to a so-called "Confidence and Supply" agreement, in which they would help keep Theresa May's Government in office, by voting with them on key votes, for instance on the Queen's Speech and on the Budget. In return for this, the Government had agreed to help address some of the long standing economic and infrastructure issues in Northern Ireland – to the tune of over £1 billion![204]

I happened to know a number of the Leaders of the DUP at Westminster reasonably well, including Nigel Dodds, their Leader, Jeffrey Donaldson (who had served as a Major in the Ulster Defence Regiment during the Troubles) and Sammy Wilson, who had been their Europe spokesman with whom I had worked to some extent during the Lisbon Treaty debates, over a decade previously. One thing about the DUP, was that they were very tough negotiators but once they gave you their word and shook hands, they invariably kept it. The Government knew this too and were therefore desperate to secure their ten votes, in order to try and achieve a majority for the Withdrawal Agreement. Moreover, they also hoped that if they could bring the DUP on board, this would have a powerful knock-on effect on the ERG.

However, the DUP have historically been quite a Eurosceptic Party and they too were very anxious about the Withdrawal Agreement – and in particular the original version of the Northern Ireland Protocol and the associated Backstop, which they rightly perceived as a threat to the integrity of the United Kingdom. Therefore, despite considerable blandishments from the Government (financial and otherwise) the DUP proved very difficult for the Government to "capture" and made very plain that they would not be supporting the Withdrawal Agreement, at least not initially anyway.

The Cabinet – A House divided

Within Theresa May's Cabinet, there was also considerable disagreement about how best to proceed. Most of the pro-Europeans in the Cabinet, led by the

Chancellor, Philip Hammond, the Deputy Prime Minister, David Lidington and the Work and Pensions Secretary, Amber Rudd (supported by others such as David Gauke) were firmly in favour of the Withdrawal Agreement. Added to these were a group of Theresa May loyalists, such as the ever popular James Brokenshire and also Karen Bradley, who had both served under her in the Home Office and were determined to give her their personal support.

At the other end of the Cabinet table (metaphorically if not physically) were those Brexiteers, who had severe doubts about the Withdrawal Agreement but who, unlike David Davis, Boris Johnson and Dominic Raab, had not been persuaded to resign. This group began meeting for takeaway pizza in the office of the Leader of the House of Commons, Andrea Leadsom, and were therefore nicknamed by the media as "the pizza club". As well as Andrea Leadsom (who had briefly stood against Theresa May for the Leadership), this group included the new Defence Secretary (Penny Mordaunt), the Trade Secretary (Liam Fox), the Transport Secretary (Chris Grayling) and the Environment Secretary (Michael Gove).[205]

The bulk of the rest of the Cabinet was somewhere in the middle and the Prime Minister faced a constant challenge in trying to keep her Cabinet together, especially as events wore on. Although she had won the Vote of No Confidence a month previously by 200 votes to 117, the fact that so many of her Backbenchers had voted against her was not lost on all those around the Cabinet table and her authority going into January had clearly been severely damaged. These divisions within the Cabinet only became far worse as the whole Brexit experience dragged on, perhaps enhanced by an element of personal ambition in some cases, as individual Cabinet Ministers began to contemplate "life after May".

The Grieve Amendment

On the 9th January 2019, the Government recommenced the debates on the Withdrawal Agreement and shortly afterwards announced that the Meaningful Vote would be rescheduled for week commencing the 14th January i.e. the following week. This announcement clearly "upped the ante" on all sides and so the Whips Office intensified their lobbying efforts – as indeed did the Buddies in return. The temperature was further raised when Dominic Grieve, the MP for Beaconsfield in Buckinghamshire (and a former Attorney General), tabled an important Amendment to the Business Motion (or timetable) which would determine how the debate on the Withdrawal Agreement, which was eventually fixed for Tuesday 15th January, would take place. In essence, the Grieve

Amendment committed the Government to announcing their "plan B" within 3 days, if they were to lose the Meaningful Vote on 15th January.

However, this amendment provoked a massive Parliamentary row, as the previous Business Motion (dating from before Christmas) stated very clearly that it could only be changed by "a Minister of the Crown", which as a Backbencher, Dominic Grieve, clearly was not. Sometimes to outsiders, the procedures of the House of Commons and particularly the wrangling over Motions and Amendments, no doubt seems arcane. However, what was really at stake here was an attempt by Backbenchers, who were hostile to ever Leaving the European Union, to take control of the business in Parliament away from the Government, or to use a Parliamentary term, "to seize control of the Order Paper" (the document that lays out the business to be conducted each day in Parliament). In other words, the Remainers (including diehard Conservative Remainers) in the House of Commons, were now trying to hijack the entire Brexit debate.

The Speaker wields considerable power, in that he can decide which Amendments to select i.e. what the House of Commons can and cannot vote upon. So, when Speaker Bercow allowed the Amendment to be selected for a vote, this effectively overruled an existing Motion of the House of Commons – which was virtually unprecedented in modern Parliamentary history. As a result, when the Grieve Amendment came up for debate on the 9th January and Speaker Bercow announced that the Amendment had been selected and therefore could now be voted upon – a massive Parliamentary argument erupted.

For one hour, John Bercow in the Chair was bombarded with Points of Order from Conservative Backbenchers asking him to justify why he had broken with all recent precedent in allowing such an Amendment to be selected. Sebastian Whale, in his unauthorised biography, "*John Bercow: Call to Order*" (Biteback Publishing 2020) reveals that Dominic Grieve had already discussed this Amendment with Speaker Bercow in private; he then also gives some insight into the arguments which had apparently gone on in private prior to the day, between Speaker Bercow and the House of Commons Clerks. As Sebastian Whale explains:

"There was this massive row where the Deputy Speaker's and the Clerks in the Speaker's conference said: 'You can't allow this'. Bercow said, basically 'I don't give a fuck, I'm going to do what I want', and stormed out. That's why there was a lot of pressure from Tory MPs to ask: 'What did the Clerks say?'"[206]

Like everybody else, I could see full well what was going on i.e. the Remainers on the Backbenches were seeking to take control of the whole Brexit process and the Speaker was seemingly allowing it. Although I had not exactly been flavour of the month on the Backbenches for some time, because I had been asking increasingly awkward questions of the Prime Minster and the Government about their Brexit policy, on this one occasion, when I stood up to challenge the Speaker, the Tory Backbenches were roaring me on, as I raised with him what he had done, in the following terms:

"Now, I have not been in this House as long as you have, Mr Speaker, but I have been here for 18 years and I have never known any Speaker to overrule a motion of the House of Commons. You have said again and again that you are a servant of this House, and we take you at your word. When people have challenged you in points of order, I have heard you say many times, "I cannot do x or y because I am bound by a motion of the House." You have done that multiple times in my experience, so why are you overriding a motion of the House today?"

When Speaker Bercow replied that what we were dealing with was only an *Amendment* and not a *Motion*, there was immediate uproar on the Tory benches, and I accused him of "utter sophistry". The row carried on for about another hour during which Crispin Blunt, a former Army Officer and previous Chairman of the Foreign Affairs Committee effectively accused John Bercow of deliberate bias in favour of the Remainers.[207]

The Speaker having allowed the Amendment, when the procedural row finally died down, and the vote was taken, the Grieve Amendment was passed by 308 votes to 297 (a majority of just 11 votes). However, this had two important effects. Firstly, it had proved that the narrow pro-Remain majority in the House of Commons (including a number of very pro-European Tory Backbenchers) had sufficient votes to outvote the Government, in situations where the Speaker would permit it. The other effect was that, rightly or wrongly, this led to increasing suspicions on the Conservative benches that John Bercow (whose views on Europe by now were no longer a secret) was effectively abandoning the traditional position of strict neutrality from the Speaker of the House of Commons and aiding the Remainers in their cause.[208]

The day of the vote, 15th January 2019

The first Meaningful Vote (now known as Meaningful Vote One or MV1 for short), finally took place on the following Tuesday, 15th January 2019. The Whips had been trying frantically to win over sceptical Conservative Backbenchers but by the day of the vote itself, the Whips Office were already estimating that the Government would lose by around 200 votes.[209]

Within the Buddies, we too knew that the Government was heading for a crushing defeat. In preparing for the vote, we established a "war room", where Steve and I based ourselves throughout the day. The Buddies spent the whole day checking on the MPs in their individual groups, to see if any had changed their mind and to also try and persuade any last-minute waverers to vote against the Withdrawal Agreement. They reported back to the war room at pre-arranged regular intervals and fed in their intelligence, which Steve faithfully entered into the sacred database on his laptop.

Within just a few hours, a clear pattern set in, in that individual Buddies were coming back to report that X or Y MP, who we had down as being undecided, were now finally making their mind up and would vote against the Government. As the day wore on, the vote was clearly slipping away from the Government, rather than moving in their favour. The vote itself was due at 7:00pm.

By chance, the ERG plenary meeting is traditionally at 6:00pm on a Tuesday evening, which meant that the whole group would be assembling in Committee Room 9, about an hour or so before the crucial division. This was very convenient, as it allowed an opportunity for a few rousing speeches and reinforcing the idea of what was at stake. Given this, I had asked the Buddies to bring in their final intelligence by 5:30pm, shortly before the plenary was due to start and at about 5:45pm, Steve and I were alone in the war room as he double-checked the final calculations on the spreadsheet. When I turned to him and said: "How is it looking?", he grinned at me and replied: "Well, if these numbers are accurate, and I have no reason to believe they are not, the Government are about to be massacred". We had produced both a "best case" and "worst case" scenario – with our "best estimate" falling somewhere between the two. In the end, our best estimate, with an hour to go, was that the Government would lose by 217 votes (with a best case of 230 and a worst case at around 200). Armed with this knowledge, we set off for the plenary meeting at 6:00pm and having arrived just a few minutes early, I whispered into Jacob's ear, that our best estimate was that the Government would lose by 217 votes. Jacob smiled briefly and then called the meeting to order, as Chairman of the ERG.

As might be expected, an hour before such a historic vote, there was quite a charged atmosphere at the plenary meeting, which Jacob opened with a rousing address as to what was wrong with the Withdrawal Agreement and how it would lead to us becoming a "vassal state".

One after another, members of the ERG rose to their feet to announce their determination to vote against the Government when the bells rang at 7:00pm. In such situations, when colleagues are contemplating rebelling against their own Government *en masse*, such speeches are important, as this gives colleagues confidence that they are one of a larger number, rather than being isolated. As the *de-facto* Chief Whip, I was one of the last to speak and reminded colleagues to remain polite and not to get into any arguments – or worse – with any of the Government Whips who might be standing on the doors of the division lobbies, in a last-minute attempt to persuade them to support the Prime Minister.[210]

The largest defeat in Parliamentary history

With a few minutes to go, the meeting broke up in good heart and colleagues traipsed down in large numbers to await the Division Bells at 7:00pm. When the Division was called, we all headed into the No Lobby, and soon found ourselves accompanied by MPs from all other Parties across the House – including the DUP. As MPs only have eight minutes to get into the Division Lobbies, with a couple of minutes left to go, the Division Lobby looked reminiscent of a Central Line train on the underground, in the middle of [a pre-pandemic] rush hour. I had never seen the No Lobby as packed as this in 18 years as an MP and indeed there were cries for MPs to "move down" (just like on a busy tube train) in order to allow the remaining MPs outside the Lobby to get in. Eventually the eight-minute limit expired, and the doors were locked behind us, and there was actually something approaching a physical crush – so many Members of Parliament were there, all in the same lobby, all at the same time.

At this moment, my phone rang, and it was Laura Kuenssberg of the BBC. "Are you in the No Lobby?", she asked. "Yes", I replied. "Well," she enquired, "How is it looking?". I said, "Laura, I've never seen the No Lobby this packed in all the time I have been in the House of Commons, so I think the Government are almost certainly going to lose – and they're going to lose big". When she asked me to put a number on it, I double checked that she wasn't about to tweet anything before the result was going to be read out, to which she replied: "Of course not Mark – I JUST WANT TO KNOW!". I certainly wasn't going to give her our "best estimate" so I contented myself by saying that it was difficult to judge, but I wouldn't be surprised if the Government lost by around 200 or even a few more, which drew a sharp whistle from the other end of the phone. We agreed that in any event there wouldn't be long to wait but in return Laura did offer that all of her intelligence was also that the Government were likely to suffer a very heavy defeat.

A few minutes later (once the Tellers had been put in place), the exit doors at the other end of the Lobby were opened and MPs, to their relief, began to file through, one by one in the traditional manner, with a Government Whip and an Opposition Whip counting them through as they went. Given the very large numbers in the No Lobby, the Division took slightly longer than the normal 15 minutes but when the result was finally read out, to the House, there was, very briefly mind you, absolute silence as everyone keenly anticipated the outcome.

The result of the Division was: Ayes (for the Government) 202 and Noes (against the Government) 432. When this was read out, there were literally gasps in the Chamber. The Government had been defeated by 230 votes (including as it turned out, 118 Tory MPs – just one more in total that had voted against Theresa May's Leadership a month earlier).[211]

It is difficult to overstate the significance of this result. This represented the greatest defeat of any Government in the entire history of the House of Commons, stretching back to 1265. The previous heaviest defeat had been against Ramsay MacDonald's brief Labour Government back in 1924, when the Government had been defeated by 166 votes, relating to the response to the Government's decision to drop criminal proceedings against John Ross Campbell, editor of the Communist newspaper Workers' Weekly.[212] Nothing in living memory had even come remotely near to this defeat. In the end, our calculations were 13 votes out (although thanks to the diligent work of The Buddies, our "best-case" upper estimate had been exactly bang on). This must have come as a body blow to the Government as it showed that there was tremendous opposition to their so-called Withdrawal Agreement in the House of Commons and, in its current form at least, it was very unlikely *ever* to get through.

Drinks at Jacobs

Following the defeat – with the Government Front Bench looking understandably dejected – the Leader of the Opposition, Jeremy Corbyn, leapt to his feet and announced that he would be tabling a Vote of No Confidence in Theresa May's Government the following day. There had been much speculation in the media that if the Government were defeated, that he would do this and the historic scale of the defeat no doubt helped egg him on. However, there had also been much speculation about what the ERG would do in such an eventuality – although we had already decided that in the event of a Confidence Vote, we would back the Prime Minister – not least because none of us were keen on yet another General Election either. Secure in the knowledge that the Withdrawal Agreement had been overwhelmingly trounced but that the Government were likely to win a Vote of Confidence the following day – we went off to celebrate – with a number of us enjoying Champagne at Jacob's London home nearby.

Jeremy Corbyn's Vote of No Confidence, 16th January 2019

As promised, Jeremy Corbyn tabled his Motion of No Confidence – which traditionally takes precedence over virtually any other Motion on the Order Paper – and which the Government accordingly agreed would be debated and voted upon the following day. Perhaps unsurprisingly for a Leader of HM Opposition, Jeremy Corbyn sought to capitalise on the situation and to paint a picture of a Government in chaos. As he said during the debate:

"Last night, the Government were defeated by 230 votes —the largest defeat in the history of our democracy. They are the first Government to be defeated by more than 200 votes. Indeed, the Government themselves could barely muster more than 200 votes. Last week, they lost a vote on the Finance Bill—that is what is called supply. Yesterday, they lost a vote by the biggest margin ever—that is what is regarded as confidence. By any convention of this House—by any precedent—loss of confidence and supply should mean that they do the right thing and resign".[213]

However, much to his disappointment, the Conservatives rallied against this clearly opportunistic attempt to unseat the Government. During the debate, I intervened on the Prime Minister, in order to make clear that the ERG would be supporting her. As I said: "It is not exactly a secret that in the last few months on matters of European policy, the Prime Minister and I have not exactly seen eye to eye" – Simon Hoare, one of the wettest Europhile Members of the new intake (but also one of the most quick-witted) cat called from the backbenches "Well, she's taller than you!" which drew large laughs around the Chamber. All I could say in reply was, "Simon, everyone in this place is taller than me!", which drew merriment of its own. I then proceeded to tell the Prime Minister that when the bells rang that night, the ERG would be supporting her in the Lobbies. The look of utter dejection on Jeremy Corbyn's face at this development was a sight to behold.[214]

At this point, it was obvious to Labour that their gambit had failed and most of the heat went out of the debate shortly thereafter. Indeed during the debate, the DUP also declared their support for the Government – in line with the principle of their commitment under the Confidence and Supply agreement – and so eventually that night, Labour's No Confidence Motion was defeated by 325 votes to 306 (a Government majority of 19).

Following this episode, all protagonists returned to their tents in order to take stock and to plan their respective next moves. Nevertheless, it was very apparent to the Government that the Withdrawal Agreement had been overwhelmingly rejected by the House of Commons and they were going to have great difficulty indeed in getting it through in the future, unless the ERG could, somehow, be brow-beaten into submission.

In addition, the significant grouping of Labour MPs on whom those in No 10 had been optimistically relying to support the Withdrawal Agreement, completely failed to turn up. In the end, only a handful of Labour MPs voted with the Government on MV1. Nevertheless, those in what was rapidly becoming the No 10 "bunker", continued to believe, throughout the crunch vote in the House of Commons that a sizable number of Labour MPs would eventually come to their rescue – despite a very forceful whipping operation by the highly experienced Labour Chief Whip, Nick Brown. Buoyed up by this continuing act of faith, the Prime Minister's advisers placed their hopes in making the House of Commons vote again just a few weeks later.[215]

Chapter 12: Meaningful Vote Two – Holding the Line

As the Government attempted to take stock of the scale of their defeat, the Prime Minister announced that she would be seeking discussions with other Party Leaders across the House of Commons (including Jeremy Corbyn for Labour) to seek to find a way forward. In addition, in order to try and soften ERG opposition to the Withdrawal Agreement, that weekend, a number of prominent members of the group were invited to lunch at Chequers; these included Jacob as the Chairman, Steve Baker as the Deputy Chairman and also several others. I was not invited to Chequers, perhaps because I was not considered sufficiently important or, alternatively, they may already have written me off as irreconcilable. Either way, I never got the call.[216]

Nevertheless, over what was subsequently described to me as "an agreeable lunch", a number of members of the ERG took the opportunity to try and explain to the Prime Minister their ongoing concerns about the Withdrawal Agreement, just as we had been doing since it was published in November and had also been attempting to do, ever since its precursor at Chequers had been unveiled, the previous July.

Enter the Brexit Party

These discussions were given added impetus by the announcement that weekend by the former UKIP Leader, Nigel Farage MEP, that he had registered a new political Party called "The Brexit Party", with the Electoral Commission, the aim of which would be to campaign strongly for the UK to Leave the European Union, if necessary with no deal.[217] Nigel Farage also gave notice that the Brexit Party would vociferously contest the European Elections in May – if the Prime Minister did not keep her word and take us out of the European Union on 29th March 2019 (as envisaged under Article 50). At the launch, Farage made his intentions perfectly clear: "I said that if I did come back into the political fray it would be no more Mr Nice Guy, and I mean it".[218]

There was therefore a new factor in the Brexit equation. UKIP itself had largely fallen away following the victory for Leave in the 2016 EU Referendum – essentially on the basis that many voters felt that it had served its purpose, in securing a Referendum, where the people had voted democratically to Leave the EU. UKIP's *raison d'etre* was included in its name – and now that the people had voted for independence – and Parliament had promised to deliver it – there was in the eyes of most voters, effectively no need for UKIP to continue.

Although the Party limped on nevertheless, it had been steadily draining members and support ever since the Referendum (and particularly after Farage stood down as its leader) and UKIP did very poorly in the 2017 General Election, when it failed to secure a single MP. However, what Farage was now planning to do was effectively to create a brand-new Eurosceptic Party (but without some of UKIP's "baggage") that would put additional pressure on the Government to Leave the European Union. Unsurprisingly, the Brexit Party proved to be vociferously opposed to Theresa May's deeply flawed Withdrawal Agreement – with Nigel Farage making no secret of his preference for the United Kingdom to Leave with "No Deal".[219]

The Malthouse Compromise

When Parliament returned, in early January, a group of prominent Backbenchers, including Jacob Rees-Mogg and Steve Baker as the Chairman and the Deputy Chairman of the ERG, but also traditional pro-Europeans such as Damian Green (a former Deputy Prime Minister) and Robert Buckland, began meeting privately under the Chairmanship of the Policing Minister, Kit Malthouse MP, to try and see if they could agree some compromise way forward. Indeed, these discussions, which were conducted very quickly and which Steve in particular threw his heart into, resulted in something which became known at the time as the "Malthouse Compromise", after the Chairman of the talks.

In essence, the Malthouse Compromise proposed a two-stage plan for Leaving the European Union, known, for simplicity, as "Malthouse A" and "Malthouse B".

Malthouse A basically meant persuading the European Union to abandon the dreaded Backstop (i.e. the Customs Union) – but leaving the bulk of the remaining Withdrawal Agreement in place. If it was not possible to achieve this, then the concept was to fall back on Malthouse B, which would have involved a so-called "Managed No Deal", by which, the transition period during which the UK would negotiate a future economic relationship with the EU would be extended, to allow further negotiations to take place.

In parallel with this initiative, on the 15th January the ERG produced a paper entitled: "A Better Deal and a Better Future" which had largely been written by Steve, although with input from others including Sir Bill Cash, Sir Bernard Jenkin, Lord Lilley, Marcus Fysh and the Economic expert Shankar Singham which laid out, a plan very similar to what became the Malthouse Compromise.[220]

On the 24th January a delegation of those MPs who had been involved in the Malthouse Compromise discussions, including Steve, went to see the Prime Minister at 10 Downing Street, in order to explain what they had achieved and to argue that this might perhaps be a way of getting a revised Withdrawal Agreement through the House of Commons. However, Theresa May's initial reaction (supported by her Advisors in No 10) was somewhat sceptical, not least because she felt it would be very difficult to persuade the European Union to reopen the Withdrawal Agreement, which they had painstakingly negotiated over a period of months, following Chequers.

Nevertheless, this was an important initiative, in which Jacob and Steve as Chairman and Deputy Chairman of the ERG respectively, had been intimately involved, in order to try and broker some way through and still achieve Brexit. It would have involved removing the Customs Union – which for Brexiteers was always the most toxic element of the Withdrawal Agreement – but still risked accepting other elements of it, if these could not subsequently be successfully negotiated away. Steve in particular, threw himself into this effort heart and soul and had devoted literally hundreds of hours since Christmas in helping to come up with and then flesh out the idea, and he was very much the driving force within the ERG to persuade the rest of us to accept it.[221]

From my own point of view, I was wary of the concept, because I doubted whether or not, No 10 would ever actually buy the idea and I rather feared that they were simply stringing us along, to buy time as they attempted to regroup and have another go at pushing the Withdrawal Agreement through the House of Commons.

Nevertheless, Steve was so passionate about this, I and a number of others agreed to give No 10 the benefit of the doubt and to see how this played out. Besides, at this stage, I had something else on my mind (regarding Airbus).

Airbus and the Tom Enders letter

Airbus, the European Aerospace manufacturer, is one of the largest manufacturing companies in the United Kingdom, with around 14,000 employees, the bulk of whom work at their very large manufacturing plant at Broughton in North Wales, just on the Welsh side of the Anglo Welsh border.

As, by then a Member of the Defence Select Committee, I had attended the Aerospace and Defence Society (ADS) Dinner at the Grosvenor House Hotel a year previously, where the Airbus Chairman, the rather combative Tom Enders, had been the keynote speaker.[222]

However, when he addressed the ADS Dinner in 2018, Tom Enders basically attacked the UK's decision to vote to Leave the European Union, in uncompromising terms. You could hardly accuse the man of not making his opinions clear – although I do remember a certain amount of grinding of teeth on the table I was sitting at, at him basically berating the British for having, in his opinion, done the wrong thing.

Despite this, I had tried to remain on good terms with Airbus as a company, and indeed in the autumn of 2018, at the company's invitation, I had attended a dinner which they were holding at the House of Commons for MPs, partly to discuss the implications of Brexit for the European Aviation Industry. The guest of honour that night, was Mr Dirk Hoke, who ran Airbus' military business – which made products from the A400M Atlas Transport Aircraft (a slightly larger version of the American C-130, Hercules) through to Puma Helicopters, which have given many years of loyal service to the RAF. Although Dirk was also a German like Enders, he was a very different personality, and over dinner proved a very engaging conversationalist. At the end of a convivial evening, he and I ended up sharing several pints on the House of Commons Terrace, and swapping stories of when we had both served in uniform, he while doing his National Service as an infantryman in the Bundeswehr, which in some ways mirrored my service as an infantryman in the Territorial Army during the Cold War. We parted on good terms and I offered to go out to Airbus' UK's offices, near White City in West London, at some future date, in order to try and give him my best guess of what was likely to happen regarding the Brexit issue in the House of Commons.

I subsequently kept my word and went to visit Dirk at White City, shortly after Meaningful Vote One, where, along with one of his UK colleagues, we spent the best part of an hour going through what I thought might happen, before he got into his limousine and caught a flight home, from Heathrow. He said that he was grateful for my private advice, which I didn't mind giving, given the fact that we had got on so well at the House of Commons dinner.

Imagine my anger, therefore, when shortly thereafter, on the 24th January, Tom Enders published an open letter, again highly critical of the Brexit process and effectively hinting at withdrawing Airbus' 14,000 jobs from the United Kingdom, unless MPs in the House of Commons voted for the Withdrawal Agreement, in the following terms:

"Please don't listen to the Brexiteers' madness which asserts that, because we have huge plants here, we will not move, and we will always be here. They are wrong. Make no mistake, there are plenty of countries out there who would love to build the wings for Airbus aircraft".[223]

Because there was so much going on, I didn't actually see the letter until the following morning, January 25th and when I read it, I was furious. It seemed to me that here was a foreign industrialist effectively attempting to bully Members of the House of Commons into voting a particular way over the Brexit issue – with the implied threat of making people in Britain redundant if they did not. In my book, this was bullying, pure and simple – something that my father had always taught me to stand up to. I remember saying to my then Researcher, that I thought what he had done was wrong and someone ought to call him out for it.

As sometimes happens in life, chance then intervened. About half an hour after I had read the letter a call came in from *BBC News 24* down at Millbank, asking if I could possibly come down to do a live interview at midday about the latest situation regarding Brexit. At this point Tom Enders' letter was sitting in front of me on my desk. I asked again if this was a live or a pre-rec and when they reassured me that it was a live interview (but apologised for the short notice as it was only 20 minutes hence), I readily accepted. With the letter in my hand, I trotted down to Millbank to do the interview.

The BBC took me up on to a small rooftop terrace at Millbank (which has the House of Commons and Parliament Square in the background and which they therefore often use as a backdrop for interviews from Westminster). The presenter was Jonathan Blake, who was new on the BBC Westminster team and who I hadn't previously met. When he asked me what I had in my hand, I said they were just a few notes and we settled down for the interview. Once we got going, I waited for my moment and then took my opportunity. Looking directly at the presenter, I highlighted Tom Enders' letter and then said the following: "My father, Reginald Francois was a D-Day Veteran, he never submitted to bullying by any German, neither will his son. So, if Tom Enders is watching, that's what he can do with his letter" which I then proceeded to rip up, live on air.

The presenter was, to use a colloquialism, "gobsmacked" but, to be fair, recovered his composure enough to continue the interview. Nevertheless, the point was made and the reaction on Twitter was almost instantaneous. My PA Adele, who was also watching it, apparently let out a deep sigh as she saw the interview – because she knew what would happen and indeed the first emails began pinging into my inbox within five minutes of the interview concluding.[224]

The mixture of emails that subsequently arrived were fascinating. On the one hand, because I had pointed out that Tom Enders had served in the German military as a paratrooper (because I was trying to point out that he had a rather assertive mentality) a number of people accused me of blatant xenophobia. Conversely, quite a few emails were very supportive and agreed with the simple principle that a foreign industrialist shouldn't attempt to tell British MPs how to vote, in the House of Commons. Indeed, one email I received from a group of factory workers (who admitted they were Labour supporters) said that they had been watching the interview live in the staff canteen at lunchtime and "a tremendous cheer went up from everyone" as I tore up the letter.

Of course, what all the people watching didn't know – indeed how could they? – was that I had actually been trying to help the company over a period of months and indeed had gone out of my way to brief Tom Enders' colleague and fellow countryman privately, less than a fortnight previously, on what I thought might actually happen over Brexit. Having done all of that, being human, I was perhaps understandably upset to see Enders' subsequent intervention. Either way, the interview rapidly went viral and led to a great deal of debate in the Twittersphere about the rights and wrongs of the Withdrawal Agreement. With hindsight, while I never pre-planned it (indeed, I only received the media bid with literally 20 minutes notice) it was probably this interview which really brought me to some degree of national prominence, for the first time in the Brexit debate.[225]

The Brady Amendment

Having been crushed in Meaningful Vote One, the Government subsequently announced that on Tuesday 29th January, they would be holding a number of so-called "Indicative Votes" – which would allow the House of Commons to vote on a variety of different options, to see if it was possible to build a consensus around any alternative way forward. There was a relatively recent precedent for this when, during debates on House of Lords reform, the House of Commons had been asked to undertake a number of "Indicative Votes" on different options for reforming the Upper House. However, in the end, none of the options ever received majority support and, partly as a result, the momentum behind House of Lords reform began to fall away. (As it turned out, this topic was another of those issues which led to growing acrimony between the Conservatives and the Lib Dems during the Coalition Government under David Cameron).[226] Nevertheless, the point was that such a device, of giving the Commons a number of different options from which to choose on a controversial subject, in order to try and find a way forward, had been used before.

In the run up to the Indicative Votes, The idea evolved of putting down an Amendment to encapsulate the spirit of the Malthouse Compromise, so that the House of Commons would be given an opportunity to vote for it – alongside other options, ranging from "No Deal", through to a "Norway style" deal (a European Free Trade Area concept) through to a full up Customs Union.[227] In the end, the influential Chairman of the 1922 Committee of Conservative Backbenchers, Sir Graham Brady, became the lead name on the Malthouse Compromise Amendment, which was then rapidly christened "the Brady Amendment" as a result. The operative part of the Brady Amendment itself read as follows:

"…Requires the Northern Ireland Backstop to be replaced with alternative arrangements to avoid a hard border; supports leaving the European Union with a deal and would therefore support the Withdrawal Agreement subject to this change".[228]

The Whips Office, who had witnessed the absolute drubbing the Government had suffered on Meaningful Vote One, rapidly seized on this initiative as an opportunity to try and provide a unifying option – even though some in No 10 remained deeply sceptical, not least as they were still firmly wedded to the Backstop. Nevertheless, the whole Conservative Parliamentary Party was very strongly Whipped to vote for the Brady Amendment, with the Whips enthusiastically seeking to persuade colleagues to support it in the Division Lobbies.

This presented the ERG with something of a dilemma. On the one hand, the Brady Amendment would have meant seeking to remove the Backstop (and thus the Customs Union) from the Withdrawal Agreement and, in so doing, deleting the bit to which the ERG had been most fundamentally opposed. However, it would mean potentially accepting other unwelcome elements of the Withdrawal Agreement, including the Joint Committee, which might subsequently be negotiated away – but which also might not. This led to some considerable debate within the ERG. Again, as the vote was scheduled for Tuesday 29th January, this meant that there was a lively debate in the ERG plenary meeting at 6:00pm, on whether or not to support the Brady Amendment, as the Whips were proposing, at 7:00pm.

The ERG Steering Committee and the Officers had already debated this in advance and had eventually taken the decision – after no small amount of discussion it should be said – to back the Brady Amendment, as a way of trying to find a compromise and on the private understanding that the Government would also try to get rid of some of the other worst elements of the Withdrawal Agreement in any subsequent negotiations. As the ERG Chief Whip, I then had the unenviable task of trying to persuade some of the most ardent Eurosceptics in the United Kingdom to vote for the Brady Amendment. When the Plenary met at 6:00pm, Jacob gave a very skilful speech, supported by both Steve and I, arguing that, despite our reservations, it would be best to support Brady when the bells rang at 7:00pm. In the end, only one or two members of the ERG actively spoke against this (including John Redwood, who it must be said made a very articulate speech) but as the *de facto* Chief Whip, I urged the group to stick together and that, as far as possible, we should all vote as one.

When the Division came, the Amendment was passed by 317 votes to 301 (a Government majority of 16). In the end, the entire ERG voted for it, with only two abstentions (who were John Redwood and Christopher Chope). The Conservative Parliamentary Party had therefore managed to unify behind a compromise option and the Whips were notably delighted to have won the vote which, by this stage, was a relatively high victory margin in Parliamentary terms. The argument was strongly advanced on the night by a number of Tory MPs, (with the enthusiastic support of the Whips) that by voting for the Brady Amendment, the House of Commons would be giving the Prime Minister a powerful mandate to go back to Brussels and negotiate away the most undesirable parts of the Withdrawal Agreement, in particular, the dreaded Backstop itself.[229]

It has since often been put about that the House of Commons was never able to agree on *anything* for three years regarding Brexit. This is patently untrue. The Brady Amendment on the 29th January was the one time that the House of Commons actually voted for a positive course of action, which, if the Government had followed through on it, could actually have got them out of trouble (assuming that they had been able to persuade the EU to drop the Backstop). The ERG had played an active part in supporting the Brady Amendment – to the considerable relief of the Whips – and basically, we had swallowed our doubts in order to try and find a way through. It is therefore simply untrue to say, as some have claimed, that throughout the entire process, the ERG never attempted to compromise, as on the 29th January 2019 that is precisely what we did.[230]

The Brady Amendment (based essentially on Malthouse A) was in effect the grand compromise that so many in the Conservative Party had been seeking. There was just one problem – despite actively whipping the entire Parliamentary Party to vote for it and then successfully getting it through by a majority of 16 votes – Theresa May and her Europhile Advisors in No 10 were then, maddeningly unwilling to actually adopt it in practice.

The Irish backlash

The decision of the House of Commons to vote for the Brady Amendment was met with fury within the Irish Government, who regarded the Backstop as fundamentally important to their economic security. Karen Bradley, the Northern Ireland Secretary (and a strong Theresa May supporter) was effectively summoned to the Irish Ministry of Foreign Affairs to be given an extremely lively dressing down for what the Irish Government regarded as an act of bad faith.[231] Moreover, the Irish Taoiseach (Prime Minister), Leo Varadkar, remarked on the decision: "We have been down that track before and I do not believe that such alternative arrangements exist and that is why we have the agreement that we have now. The only way we can avoid a hard border, physical infrastructure and checks and controls in the way foreseen in the original December agreement is through full regulatory alignment, to use the language of that December agreement".[232]

In reaction to this, Karen Bradley persuaded the Prime Minister to make a short-term trip to Belfast in order to appreciate for herself the degree of anger which had been created by this decision. Theresa May flew out on the 5th February and spent a day in Northern Ireland engaging with both the Unionist and Nationalist community over the issue of the Withdrawal Agreement and in particular the Backstop. It was not by accident, that she was introduced to a large number of members of the Nationalist community who were adamant that dropping the Backstop and the Customs Union would be a disaster for Anglo-Irish relations. It was also put to the Prime Minister that to do so would be against the spirt of the 1998 Good Friday Agreement. The Prime Minister's anxieties were amplified by the suggestion by a number of "Securocrats" in No 10, that to abandon the Backstop could even lead to a renewal of paramilitary unrest in Northern Ireland.[233]

As a result of this, by the time that she flew back to the British mainland, the Prime Minister had effectively been convinced (in what some would argue was a very carefully choreographed visit) that to seek to abandon the Backstop would be politically unacceptable in Northern Ireland. All this, despite the fact that at Chequers barely a fortnight earlier she had asked senior members of the ERG and others to seek to come up with some kind of compromise way forward and indeed had then witnessed the Conservative Party being heavily whipped to vote for it. In so doing and effectively rejecting the Brady Amendment, which almost the entire Conservative Parliamentary Party had just voted for, she threw away the one great chance of a compromise in Parliament.

Needless to say, the ERG, which had swallowed its reservations and voted almost unanimously for the Brady Amendment and in particular its Deputy Chairman, Steve Baker, who had invested such an immense amount of personal time and energy into the Malthouse compromise process, were furious.

Looking back on it, for many in the ERG, this really was the final straw. After having promised that "Brexit meant Brexit" and all the good intentions of the Lancaster House speech in 2017, the Prime Minister had then effectively abandoned that course in favour of a much closer relationship with the EU, as devised by her Civil Servants and then effectively bounced the Cabinet into it at Chequers. When her Withdrawal Agreement was slaughtered in the House of Commons she had asked for a compromise, whipped her MPs to vote for it, and then rejected it barely a week later. It was flaws like this in her Leadership that only led to even greater problems later on.

For some in the ERG, this was the point at which it became starkly apparent that further attempts to compromise with May's Government, were completely fruitless and that all we could now do was either a) surrender or b) fight this thing through to the bitter end. We resolved not to surrender.

"You're inept Mark"

The day after Theresa May's rapid dash to Belfast, the Conservative Party held a major fundraising social event at the "Battersea Evolution" venue in South West London. This is the sort of Black Tie event, at which major Tory donors rub shoulders with politicians. This is not a uniquely Tory idea, other political Party's do much the same – but this event was well attended, and the Prime Minister was the keynote speaker.

By chance, I was placed on the same table as the Attorney General, Geoffrey Cox, a key member of Theresa May's Cabinet (whose legal advice was subsequently to become extremely important during critical votes in Parliament). Cox was a Eurosceptic by inclination and had really exploded into the public consciousness when he gave an extremely entertaining, sub Churchillian warm up speech for the Prime Minister, just before she addressed the Party Conference (more successfully than the previous year) in October 2018.[234]

Geoffrey and I had tended to get on well on a personal level and as Attorney General (and the son of a regular Army NCO, who had spent part of his time growing up on one Army Barracks after another) he had been involved with a number of us in seeking to explore ways to solve the problem of repeated legal claims against Military Veterans – something which I and a number of other Conservative MPs felt very strongly about.

On the night, it is fair to say that the wine flowed freely and there was a certain degree of light-hearted banter between him and me, over the outcome of Meaningful Vote One. After dinner, we had a conversation during which he turned to me and said: "Mark, we do like you, you know". Oh, really, I thought, what's coming now? He went on: "No really, Mark we do like you and we all know that you feel passionately about this thing but at the end of the day, I have to say, that despite your strong feelings your tactics are *inept*". To which I responded, "Oh really Attorney General? Forgive me, but unless I am much mistaken the Government recently suffered the largest defeat in Parliamentary history and I helped to Whip against it, so, tell me please, what do I have to do to impress you?". In fairness to Geoffrey, he didn't take umbridge at this retort in the way that a more thin-skinned Cabinet Minister might have done, if anything he seemed to see the funny side of it; I was basically giving as good as I got.

I made a point of relaying this to the Buddies at our next meeting, when I told them that as part of a Whipping team which Geoffrey didn't know existed, we were presumably all "inept" – which the team proceeded to wear as a private badge of honour.

However, the other significant development that evening was that I got into a conversation with Steven Parkinson (or "Parky" as he is universally known in Westminster), an important member of the 2016 Vote Leave campaign and one of the Prime Minister's Political Secretaries at No 10. As part of this discussion, Steven Parkinson suggested that maybe it would be helpful if I were to go for a private drink at some point with Robbie Gibb, the Government's Communications Director and one of Theresa May's key aides at No 10. I said that I would, and so we made a provisional arrangement to stay in touch and try and set something up in the near future.

In vino veritas

Nevertheless, for No 10, things went from bad to worse. On the 12th February, the *Guardian* newspaper ran an article reporting that Olly Robbins, who was by now the Prime Minister's Lead Negotiator, had been overheard in a bar in Brussels, discussing the Government's negotiating position. The *Guardian's* piece, entitled "Theresa May's Brexit tactic: my way or a long delay" stated the following:

"Theresa May's high-stakes Brexit strategy may have been accidentally revealed after her chief negotiator Olly Robbins was overheard in a Brussels bar saying MPs will be given a last-minute choice between her deal and a lengthy delay."

Moreover, according to the *Guardian* at least, Robbins had apparently argued that eventually MPs would be presented with an acid choice between voting for the Withdrawal Agreement or having to ask for an extension of the 29th March leaving date, and that, when push came to shove, eventually we would give in.[235] As *the Guardian* expressed it:

"The tactic appears to be aimed squarely at members of the backbench Tory European Research Group (ERG), who may fear Brexit could ultimately be cancelled altogether, if MPs accept a delay."

Unsurprisingly, this led to a certain degree of additional comment in the media and indeed in the House of Commons. On 19th February, I stood up in the House and asked the following question:

"The Solicitor General has told the House clearly that the Government will not provide a running commentary on the negotiations—unless, of course, it is Olly Robbins, the Government's chief negotiator, who can get hammered in a bar in Brussels and give a detailed running commentary to anybody who happens to be in earshot. That is extremely unprofessional behaviour for a senior civil servant. A Minister who did that would be sacked. What disciplinary action has been taken against Mr Robbins? Or does he get away with it because he is teacher's pet?".[236]

Unsurprisingly, the Minister at the Despatch Box did not agree with my suggestion to sack the Government's Chief Negotiator. Nevertheless, Olly Robbins had never really endeared himself to the ERG and the incident in the bar – whatever precisely happened that evening – only served to make relations worse, rather than better.

The ERG backlash

On Valentine's Day 2019, after it had become apparent that the Prime Minister was not prepared to actively pursue the Brady Amendment, the House of Commons voted again on a second series of further so-called Indicative Votes. By this stage, trust in the Prime Minister within the ERG had sunk to something of an all-time low and I had personally commiserated with Steve that, despite all of his genuine and very energetic efforts, the Prime Minister was clearly never going to back the Malthouse Compromise and the Brady Amendment after all.

The ERG accordingly decided that they would now abstain rather than support the Government in the votes that evening, as a result of which the Government were defeated on a key division by 303 votes to 258. The following day Steve, as the Deputy Chairman, put out a message on the ERG WhatsApp group to the effect that we had been betrayed by the Prime Minister.[237]

In reply, on the 17th February, Theresa May wrote to all Conservative MPs, imploring us to back her original Withdrawal Agreement (including the Backstop) and warning us that "history will judge us all". By this stage many of us were actually very happy to be judged by history regarding Brexit, as we felt that it was the Prime Minister who had acted inconsistently and not us. Also, we had just demonstrated very clearly that she was unlikely to be able to get anything through the House of Commons unless it was with our support.

On a personal level, I really felt for Steve, because he had put his heart and soul into the Malthouse Compromise and clearly felt badly let down by the lack of support in No 10. Whilst many other members of the ERG also felt very disappointed, it was Steve, more than anyone else, who felt that No 10 had behaved appallingly – a point in which he had my sympathy.

Enter The Independent Group (TIG)

On the 18th February, a number of Labour MPs, partly disillusioned with Jeremy Corbyn's Leadership of the Labour Party and his failure to deal with persistent issues of anti-Semitism, announced that they were formally leaving the Labour Party and would now sit as "Independents" in the House of Commons. A few days later they were joined by three ardent pro-European Conservatives, Anna Soubry (who had served alongside me as a Minister in the Ministry of Defence), Heidi Allen (a Cambridgeshire MP) and Sarah Wollaston (the Chairman of the Health Select Committee and also of Parliament's powerful Liaison Committee – which holds hearings with the Prime Minister).

This combined group of around nine MPs (all of them committed pro-Europeans) subsequently became known as "The Independent Group" – or TIG for short. In the Parliamentary battles that followed, TIG consistently voted for pro-Remain options but also voted against the Prime Minister's Withdrawal Agreement as well. In numerical terms, this loss of more previously Conservative MPs further reduced Theresa May's majority in the House of Commons, and only served to increase her reliance on the Eurosceptic DUP.

Drinks with Robbie – at the Grenadier

Around this time, following on from Parky's suggestion, Robbie Gibb and I agreed to meet up very confidentially for a drink, to see whether it might be possible to find a way forward in the aftermath of the debacle over the Brady Amendment. Only a handful of members of the ERG even knew that I was doing this. Both Robbie and I had agreed that it would be advisable to meet up somewhere discretely, outside of the "Westminster Village" where hopefully we wouldn't be recognised by passing journalists. So, we eventually met up for pint in a lovely old pub called *The Grenadier* in Belgravia (which long ago had acted as the original Officer's Mess for the Grenadier Guards).

I still remembered Robbie from my days in FCS. He had subsequently gone on to have a successful career in the BBC, including as the Editor of *Newsnight* before being recruited by Theresa May to head up her communications operation in Downing Street. He was therefore her equivalent of Alastair Campbell during the critical Brexit debates in Parliament. As neither of us were shrinking violets, we both thought it might be a good idea to sit down and talk frankly about the difficulties that both sides faced. By repute, I knew that Robbie could be charming and very good company but, as a number of journalists I had spoken to over previous months had told me, he could rapidly turn a bit more aggressive, if he felt he wasn't getting his way. In the event, this is exactly what happened on the night. I got there first and Robbie arrived and explained that he only had time for a quick drink because he then had to move on to dinner afterwards (therefore effectively putting a narrow time limit on our meeting).

I didn't really think this was unreasonable and over a pint he began to lay out why he felt the ERG should back the Withdrawal Agreement after all. Robbie's gambit was to explain that he too was a Eurosceptic – and passionately wanted to Leave the European Union and was confident that we could do so if only the ERG were prepared to back the Withdrawal Agreement and thus help us take back control of "our money, borders and our laws" (exactly the mantra which the Government had been arguing for months). In fairness, at least the Government Communications Chief was able to keep to the Government line!

I listened politely as Robbie laid out why the Withdrawal Agreement meant that we would in fact Leave the European Union – but without assenting to anything he said. After about a quarter of an hour or so, when he could see that I clearly wasn't agreeing, he started to get a bit pushier, and I initially stood for that too. Eventually, I thought "I've had enough of this" and so I leant forward and said: "Robbie, I've listened very patiently to everything that you've said, do you mind if

I ask you just one question?". "Of course," he said, "Go ahead". "Robbie", I asked, "Have you actually *read* the Withdrawal Agreement yourself?". At this point he started to bluster and when I pressed him on the point, he said, "No, but I've read a summary". "Oh, and who wrote this summary that you read?". "Err, it was compiled for me by the Civil Servants", he replied. "Oh", I said, "Presumably the same Civil Servants who helped negotiate the Withdrawal Agreement in the first place?". At that point he went silent for a moment and I decided to press my advantage. So, I said: "Well, unlike you, I have read the thing and so I genuinely know what's in it and you don't. Don't you ever tell me again how to vote on a Treaty that I've read, and you clearly haven't. I'm perfectly willing to continue this conversation another time but all I ask is that you read the bloody thing for yourself, in private, so that you're not reliant on a Civil Service interpretation on what it really means. If you do that, I'll gladly have another conversation with you but until you do that, we are wasting each other's time!".

I think Robbie was rather taken aback by this, but he said he'd seriously consider my request and, in any event, was keen that we should meet up again in the very near future to continue our dialogue. He subsequently sent me a text the following morning, reiterating how useful he'd found our private conversation and saying that he very much wanted to follow up on it, within the next few days. I never heard from him again, until after the Battle for Brexit was over.

Yet again, here was an example of how the No 10 regime was prepared to engage in discussion – but only on the proviso that people would eventually give in and do as ordered. If Robbie had genuinely read the Agreement, I would certainly have kept my word and agreed to meet with him again – as at least we would have been on the same page, as it were. Nevertheless, for whatever reason, he never decided to take me up on my offer and we never spoke again, whilst Theresa May was still Prime Minister.

My own dash to Italy

In early February 2019, I received a message from my Italian relatives that my Aunt Renza, who by now was aged 94, was seriously ill. So, I had asked Adele to try and book me some flights as soon as practically possible to fly out to Italy to see her – just in case. I subsequently flew out on the 21st February from Stansted to Falconara (Ancona) on the Adriatic Riviera and caught a train down the coast to Pesaro and went round to see my Aunt that evening. Given that she was 94 and they didn't want to risk the shock of surprising her, they broke the news to her that I was coming that afternoon. But when I arrived in the evening, she was delighted to see me. By that stage Zia Renza had been housebound for nearly a year and she had a live in Romanian Carer, called Rica, who had escaped from the Ceaușescu regime and who had some extremely robust views about communists and communism in general. Leaving the politics of it aside, she was clearly devoted to my Auntie who it turned out, had been suffering from high blood pressure and poor circulation, but who was otherwise not seriously in danger at that time. My Zia Carla and her niece, Lena (Arda's daughter) also came round to join the gathering and invited me while I was still in Italy to go and visit my Zio Valentino, who by that stage was living in a Care Home in Ancona (ironically quite nearby to the Airport that I had just flown into).

Accordingly, we jumped into the car the following morning and drove down the coast road to go and see Valentino in what was a very well-appointed Care Home, with beautiful grounds. As a former Italian Army Colonel, Valentino enjoyed quite a reasonable pension and was therefore able to afford to live in quite a nice facility. I had known him for over 50 years since I had met him as a toddler on one of my parents' annual pilgrimages to Italy. In his younger years, he had matinee idol looks and had married an extremely attractive East German girl called Angelica. However, as they had married in the 60s, and she came from Communist East Germany, this had impeded his military career and he finally topped out as a Full Colonel (although perhaps if he had married someone else, he might have gone far higher).

In any event, when we went into the Care Home, I was shocked. This "matinee idol" was now a shadow of his former self, hunched in a chair in the home's common room and, even more concerning, he didn't recognise me when I walked in. As a constituency MP, I had dealt with a number of constituents down the years whose relatives had developed Alzheimer's and who had explained to me in my constituency surgeries how very difficult this could be to deal with. However, this was the first time that this had ever affected me personally and I was very moved by it. In the end, after about 20 minutes of prompting (and references to both my mother and my father), Valentino suddenly exclaimed "Reginaldo", my father's name and then seemed to remember me, as Reginaldo's son. What then followed was a rather awkward conversation but gradually his memory seemed to come back to him, and we ended up talking about happy memories during visits to Pesaro in years gone by.

On the Saturday evening, I went out to a bar in Pesaro with my cousin Michele (one year my senior) and talked about the whole family and how many of them had passed away, since we had both enjoyed those wonderful family feasts at the White House, in the hills above Pesaro, many years ago. He explained to me that Valentino had gone into a Care Home around about a year previously and that he was finding it increasingly difficult to remember even members of his own immediate family.

Because my PA, Adele, had had to book my flights at short notice, I had a very late flight flying back to the UK on the Sunday night, but I remember looking out of the aircraft into the star speckled night and thinking: "I'm in my early 50s now and in a few decades that could be me sitting in that chair. None of us knows in this world how long we've really got but I am in a position to genuinely make a difference over Brexit and if this is my one chance in life to do something that's really important, I'm determined not to duck it – even notwithstanding my promise to Dad".

I eventually got to bed in the small hours of Monday morning but by the time I travelled back to Westminster several hours later, I was completely resolved that whatever pressure we were put under by the Whips, or indeed anybody else regarding the Withdrawal Agreement, there was absolutely no way that I was going to give in.

"Cox's codpiece"

By mid-February, the Government were in an increasingly difficult position. The Prime Minister had effectively refused to accept the Malthouse Compromise and the Brady Amendment and instead decided to try and ram her ill-fated Withdrawal Agreement through the House of Commons at the second attempt. However, it was apparent that if nothing changed, the Government were still likely to suffer another heavy defeat. As she was clearly not prepared to abandon the Backstop, instead the Prime Minister sought to persuade the European Union to agree to some form of exit mechanism, whereby the UK could ultimately leave the Backstop unilaterally, *without* the EU's consent.

On the 18th February, the Attorney General, Geoffrey Cox (who the Prime Minister had charged with trying to achieve this objective) departed for Brussels accompanied by the new DEXEU Secretary, Steve Barclay, to attempt to enter into negotiations with the EU, with the aim of persuading them to modify the Withdrawal Agreement to allow the UK, if only in *extremis*, to leave the Backstop under its own steam.

For the next three weeks, Geoffrey Cox and Steve Barclay provided Eurostar with good business, in shuttling backwards and forwards between London and Brussels, in seeking to try and persuade the EU to give way. However, it became apparent early on that the European Union – having painstakingly negotiated the

Withdrawal Agreement – was in little mood to compromise and therefore Cox's overtures were systematically rebuffed.

This endeavour was light-heartedly nicknamed "Cox's codpiece" by Steve Baker during a media interview, and as is sometimes the way of these things, the name caught on and the term stuck. The media then began to speculate endlessly on what Cox would produce from his codpiece (the name coming from an Elizabethan device devised to improve the appearance of a man's personal physique in a delicate area). As Cox and Barclay shuffled back and forth, the speculation only grew more intense.

This also placed the Government and indeed its Attorney General in a difficult position. As the Attorney General, it was Cox's job to provide the Cabinet and thus the Government (and indeed Parliament) with legal advice on the interpretation of the Withdrawal Agreement. Geoffrey Cox had made plain in the run up to Meaningful Vote One that there was no way out of the Backstop unless the EU consented. He was very keen to achieve concessions from the EU, such that he could genuinely change his legal advice to the Cabinet and say, in all honesty, that some unilateral exit route now existed. However, others at No 10, including a number of the Civil Servants, were never keen on this idea anyway and were advising the Prime Minister that Cox's entreaties were unlikely to be successful. Geoffrey Cox who, following his barnstorming speech at the Party Conference had also developed something of a reputation as a showman in Parliament, nevertheless very well understood that unless he was able to sincerely alter his legal advice, the Government was heading for another heavy defeat, as Theresa May prepared to put the Withdrawal Agreement to a second Meaningful Vote – MV2 – sometime in the middle of March.

The "Stare Off" with Will Self

It was in the midst of all this speculation that I accepted a last-minute invitation to appear on the BBC *Politics Live* programme, filmed live on air, as the name suggested, from Millbank on Friday 8th March. As I was to discover only months later, I had been rung up at the last minute because Nigel Farage, the Leader of the Brexit Party, had originally been asked to appear as a guest but had decided late in the day, when he heard that the so called Marxist intellectual, Will Self, would also be appearing on the programme, not to go ahead and sit on the panel after all. (Nigel subsequently explained that when he heard Will Self was involved, he feared that it would become some kind of stunt, which turned out to be absolutely true, except the target turned out to be me instead).[238]

Having accepted the invitation, I dashed down to Millbank and got into the studio with only a couple of minutes to spare before the programme was due to go on air. In the studio was the BBC Presenter Jo Coburn; Jo Tanner, a former Spin Doctor who had worked at No 10 for Nick Clegg, Grace Campbell (Alastair Campbell's daughter) a feminist and comedian and representing "youth" and of course, Will Self, a Marxist Professor of Sociology and frequent guest on BBC programmes, including *Question Time*, on which he had previously clashed with Nigel Farage (hence Nigel's caution, second time around).

When I got into the studio itself, there was only one seat still empty, next to Will Self, so I scuttled into it and sat down as the make-up lady came on to dab some powder on my face (they do it mainly to avoid reflection under the studio lights) – and the technicians came over to start "miking" me up. I obviously knew who Will Self was, but I'd never actually met him before in person, so as anyone else might have done, I said "Good morning". To which he replied: "Good Morning Mark, so what's in your codpiece then?". Slightly taken aback, I responded, "I'm afraid that's rather personal, Will, so I'm afraid I can't tell you", he then shot back immediately, "Are you saying that because you've got an exceptionally small penis?". I was completely flabbergasted. I just couldn't believe that this guy, who I had never met before in my life, would say something so patently rude (and untrue) within 30 seconds of meeting me. I almost got out of my chair to walk out at which point the BBC crew realised that something had gone wrong and did everything they could to calm me down and make me retake my seat. By this stage, even I had managed to figure out that clearly Self seemed to want some kind of staged confrontation and I resolved that I wouldn't give him the pleasure.

Therefore, when we started to broadcast, even though he had a couple of digs at me, I did my best to answer as calmly as possible, until we got on to the subject of anti-Semitism in the Labour Party, which I remarked at least had nothing to do with Brexit. Self responded that it did in fact have something to do with Brexit:

"Well, I mean, it is Brexit in a point of fact, I mean, you know…Mark may decry this, well, it actually has, it's got a lot to do with Brexit…Well because, since 2016, your problem really Mark is not that…it's not that you have to be a racist or an anti-Semite to vote for Brexit, it's just that every racist and anti-Semite in the country did".

At this point, I thought, alright, that does it, as far as I'm concerned, you've just slurred everyone who voted leave as a racist and an anti-Semite and I'm not going to let you get away with that unchallenged. If you really want a row that much you Marxist idiot, you can have one! I retorted that what he had said was 'outrageous'. For the record, having replayed the interview several times, the following exchange took place:

Will Self: "Well, I mean, it is Brexit in a point of fact, I mean, you know, Mark may decry this …"

Mark Francois: "Anti-Semitism has got nothing to do with Brexit".

Will Self: "Mark may decry this, well, it actually has, it's got a lot to do with Brexit".

Mark Francois: "Well how?"

Will Self: "Well because, since 2016, your problem really Mark is not that..it's not that you have to be a racist or an anti-Semite to vote for Brexit, it's just that every racist and anti-Semite in the country did".

Mark Francois: "I think that's a slur on 17.4 million people…"

Will Self: "It's not".

Mark Francois: "…and I think you should apologise on national television. I think that's an outrageous thing to say".

Will Self: "Oh well, you seem to find a lot of things outrageous though, don't you?"

Jo Coburn (Presenter): "But Will, is it fair to say that?"

Mark Francois: "So are you saying that 17.4 million people….

Will Self: "No, I'm saying…No, I'm saying"

Mark Francois: "… are racist and bigots because they voted to Leave the European Union?"

Will Self: "No, that's not what I said"

Mark Francois: "That's pretty close to what you said!"

Jo Coburn: "What did you say?"

Will Self: "It's not remotely close to what I said"

Mark Francois: "So what exactly are you saying?"

Will Self: "You seem to be a little exercised, Sir".

Mark Francois: "Well because I'm offended!".

Will Self: "Oh well."

Mark Francois: "Well, say it again then so we can all understand".

Will Self: "The Politics of offense, eh Mark?

Jo Coburn: "Well look, alright, well look, let me move on".

Will Self: "What I said was that: 'Every racist and anti-Semite in the country, pretty much, probably voted for Brexit – that's all! And that doesn't mean…."

Mark Francois: "But, how do you know that in a secret ballot?

Will Self: "I don't know it"

Mark Francois: "How can you possibly know that?"

Will Self: "I suspect it".

Mark Francois: "I think you should apologise!"

Will Self: "To who?"

Mark Francois: "To 17.4 million people".

Will Self: "To racists and anti-Semites?"

Mark Francois: "Because you've basically tried to slur anybody who voted to Leave as a bigot, and I think you should apologise".

Will Self: "No, I haven't. I said that's the problem…

Jo Coburn: "Listen, listen, Mark, Mark, what he said is, everyone who is a racist voted Leave".

Will Self: "That's the problem with Brexiteers"

Mark Francois: "How could he know that, how could he possibly know that! It's a secret ballot!"

Jo Coburn: "Well that of course is up for discussion".

Mark Francois: "It's a secret ballot, how could he know?"

Will Self: "He knows that for all the reasons I have used already, which is that the problem for Nationalists generally, is that they fall into the hands of what we call 'Ethnic-Nationalists'".

Mark Francois: "Utterly ridiculous".[239]

Clearly, Will Self, who tended to try and intimidate other people on panels with his "intellect" was not used to people talking back to him in the way that I just had and when I turned to look at him again, he was giving me what the *Evening Standard* subsequently described as the "death stare".[240] To which I thought: "Look mate, I grew up in Basildon and where I come from that tactic just doesn't work", so I simply stared straight back at him and sipped slowly from my cup of coffee, for effect, whilst I was doing it.

Although I wasn't actually timing it, what subsequently became known as "the stare off", apparently lasted for about 15 seconds – and then temporarily broke the internet.

Afterwards the programme continued for a few minutes but by now Twitter was going berserk with what had just happened. At the end of it, I got up and left and when Will Self tried to say something after me, I just said: "Good luck with your life" and walked out. However, the story didn't end there. When I did an interview in defence of the ERG the following Monday on *BBC Breakfast* live from College Green (at about 8:15am) the *BBC Breakfast Time* Presenter, Dan Walker, raised the issue of what had happened on *Politics Live* the previous day and asked, in essence, if as an elected Member of Parliament, I thought it was appropriate to have got into such a stare off with another guest live on television.

I replied that as this was a breakfast programme and there would be a number of children watching who hadn't yet departed for school, I couldn't say live on air exactly the words that Mr Self had used but, suffice to say, he had asked me a question about my genitalia. At this point, Dan was clearly rather taken aback and decided it was probably better to change the subject.

However, I had also accepted a bid that morning to be interviewed on *BBC Essex*, my own local radio station (with whom any MP worth their salt always tries to remain on good terms if they can help it). No sooner was I a few minutes into that interview than the subject of the Will Self stare-off cropped up again. By now, it was coming on for 10:00am and clearly children would now be in school, so I then went on to explain in detail exactly what had happened, including, importantly, what Will Self had said to me at the time.

He subsequently denied saying this to me[241] but I was exonerated by, of all people, Alastair Campbell's daughter, who had said very little throughout the programme but who had nevertheless been in the studio throughout and who Tweeted on 8th March:

"If you thought there was tension between Will Self and Mark Francoise on #BBCPoliticsLive today, you should have heard them before the show where Self told Francoise he had a little penis making Francoise blush and threaten to leave the studio. Happy international womens day xx"

The irony of being borne out by the daughter of arch Remainer Alastair Campbell is not lost on me to this day. Nevertheless, I undoubtedly owe his daughter a debt of gratitude, as she did have the moral courage to go onto Twitter and tell the truth about what had happened. Of course, I had no idea when I accepted this bid at short notice (not being as canny as Nigel) what would happen but nevertheless, I have seen the clip repeated very many times ever since and it even made an appearance on Channel 4's "*Gogglebox*" programme.[242] Following on from the "Tom Enders letter" interview on 25th January and the "stare-off" on 8th March, suddenly people started to recognise me when I walked into pubs or boarding the Tube.

Inadvertently, Will Self had provided me, as a leading Brexiteer, with massive national publicity which, rightly or wrongly, helped to raise my profile in a way that I could not possibly have envisaged. So, in the very unlikely event that you buy this book Will, I would like to say a sincere thank you, for doing more to raise my profile in 20 minutes, than in 18 years as a hard-working Member of Parliament, I had ever got anywhere near.

It has sometimes been put to me by cheeky Assistant Producers that they would love to arrange a "rematch", which I wouldn't shun, but only if I am allowed to ask Will Self some fairly personal questions of my own, next time we meet.

The Star Chamber

Whilst I was engaging with Comrade Self at Millbank, Geoffrey Cox and Steve Barclay were still embroiled in the more serious matter of attempting to persuade the EU to give them at least some kind of concession on the Backstop, that would allow Geoffrey Cox to legitimately alter his legal advice. Cox honourably warned No 10 on several occasions that he would not, and indeed could not, change his legal opinion, unless the EU genuinely altered their position. By around this time, the Government had fixed Meaningful Vote Two for Tuesday 12th March, so the imperative on trying to win a concession became ever stronger. However, this put Cox himself in something of a difficult position.

As he was now effectively leading the negotiations, but then would have to provide legal advice to the Government and ultimately Parliament on their outcome, he would end up effectively "marking his own homework" a point which I, and several others, had made to him in the House of Commons.

Pointing this out, was in no way to impugn Cox's integrity (as subsequent events proved, he had plenty of that) but it is to say that because it was apparent from early on that the legal advice regarding any potential changes to the Backstop would undoubtedly be material in affecting any vote in the House of Commons, the ERG decided to set up a legal team of its own, in order to analyse the advice, independent of Government and regardless of the personalities involved.

Once it became public knowledge that the ERG were doing this, the media rapidly nicknamed this team "The Star Chamber" (after the Tudor Court of Inquisition, which met in a Chamber in the old Whitehall Palace, decorated with star motifs on the ceiling).

As this was essentially a legal matter, the natural choice to Chair the Star Chamber was Sir Bill Cash, a constitutional lawyer by training. He was supported by Suella Braverman MP, Robert Courts MP, David Jones MP, Dominic Raab MP (who had resigned as Foreign Secretary over Chequers), Michael Tomlinson MP, Dr T D Grant, Martin Howe QC, (the Chairman of Lawyers for Britain and an eminent legal adviser to the ERG throughout) and also Barnabus Reynolds, a Partner in the law firm, Sheerman and Co LLP, and also a notable City lawyer in his own right. In addition, the ERG achieved something of a minor coup in also persuading Nigel Dodds MP, also a lawyer by training, to serve on the Star Chamber (as well as being Parliamentary Leader of the DUP). Moreover, what virtually nobody else knew was that both David Jones and Michael Tomlinson, as well as serving on the Star Chamber, were also members of our Whipping team in the Buddies, for good measure.

The Star Chamber, under Bill's leadership, had resolved to analyse any proposed changes in detail with a view to providing expert legal advice not just to the ERG but to the whole of Parliament and indeed via the media, to the wider public as well. It is fair to say that as Meaningful Vote Two approached, the primary journalistic interest was obviously in what Geoffrey Cox would advise but there was also a strong degree of interest among the media about what the ERG's Star Chamber would make of this too.

Meaningful Vote Two – 12th March 2019

In the end, Cox and Barclay, despite persistent efforts, were unable to secure any meaningful concessions from the European Union, that would have allowed the United Kingdom unilaterally to exit from the Backstop.

Having warned No 10 in advance that he would find it very difficult to change his legal advice as a result, Geoffrey Cox sat down on the evening of Monday 11th March to write his legal opinion which he would deliver to Cabinet the following morning. There have been previous occasions in Parliamentary history when the advice of an Attorney General to the Government has been extremely important, for instance, in the run-up to the votes on the Iraq war in 2003.[243] Geoffrey Cox was well aware of how fundamentally important to the Government's chances of winning MV2, his legal advice would be, and he came under considerable pressure from some in Government to write something which would help the Government's case.

Nevertheless, on the morning of the vote, Cox delivered what was, in effect, his verdict to the Cabinet at an early morning meeting. His advice was devastating and concluded that he could not change his legal opinion from that which he had previously provided in advance of Meaningful Vote One. In other words, there was still no way that the United Kingdom, if it were to enter the Backstop, would be able to subsequently exit it, without the EU's consent. At 11:30am that morning the Conservative Parliamentary Party had a meeting in the Atlee Suite, in Portcullis House, at which a copy of the letter containing Cox's advice was distributed. The killer sentence at the end, paragraph 19, stated the following:

"However, the legal risk remains unchanged that if through no such demonstrable failure of either party, but simply because of intractable differences, that situation does arise, the United Kingdom would have, at least while the fundamental circumstances remained the same, no internationally lawful means of exiting the Protocol's arrangements, save by agreement".[244]

As the meeting broke up, to the evident consternation of the Whips, Many Tory MPs could be heard emerging from the Atlee Suite telling each other that they still couldn't vote for the deal as we would still be trapped in the Backstop and couldn't get out of it, of our own volition. I had slipped out of the meeting a few minutes early and was immediately leapt upon by a clutch of reporters all asking me for my verdict. So, I simply explained that Cox's legal advice had clearly not changed and therefore there was no reason for any MP to change their vote from MV1.

The Buddies had already met prior to the Parliamentary Party meeting, by which time rumours that Cox had not changed his advice were already starting to emerge and we again went through the process of "man to man marking" individual MPs, who we thought might be wavering, so that we were able to communicate with them. We refreshed this process throughout the day.

Ironically, I had to break off from this briefly at lunchtime, to attend a meeting in the Ministry of Defence, with my new Parliamentary Researcher, Rory Boden, in order to commence a second study for the PM and the MoD on Military Retention (following on from the first one that I had undertaken on Recruiting). Parliamentary life is often full of these sorts of coincidences and this was a good example of it.

When the Buddies reassembled again early in the afternoon, it was apparent that some Conservative MPs, including among them some notable names like David Davis, who had resigned over Chequers, had now decided to support the Government second time around. Nevertheless, there was still a hard core, comprising mainly members of the ERG, who were clearly still resolved to vote against. It thus still seemed highly likely that the Government would lose again, although not as disastrously as at MV1.

As it was a Tuesday, the ERG Officers, met at 5:00pm, under Jacob's Chairmanship and the plenary meeting of the whole group then commenced an hour later. On these occasions Jacob would normally sit in the Chair, with Steve as the Deputy Chairman on his right and myself as, in effect, the Senior Vice Chairman on his left, which meant that I was in a good position to survey the room and to watch like a hawk to see if anybody had changed their mind. When

Jacob explained that as with MV1, the unanimous decision of the Officers was to recommend to the group that we should still vote against what was, in effect, the unaltered Withdrawal Agreement on MV2, the vast bulk of the room was still in agreement.

When the bells rang at 7:00pm, we again traipsed into the No Lobby which was still very busy (but not quite as packed as last time) and when the result was read out this time, the Government lost by 391 votes to 242, a majority of 149, including 75 Conservative MPs.[245] This still represented one of the largest defeats in Parliamentary history (indeed still more than Ramsay MacDonald had suffered in 1924) but was obviously not quite as crushing as the 230 that the Government had been massacred by some two months earlier.

Although the Government had made some progress, in peeling away a number of Conservative MPs, the fabled 20-30 Labour MPs on whom No 10 were forever relying, again failed to materialise and only around five Labour MPs defied their respective Three Line Whip and voted with the Government. Thus, the Government had still been heavily defeated, not least because they had made only very tentative inroads into the voting base of the ERG.

In response, Jeremy Corbyn did not repeat his failed strategy of calling for a Vote of No Confidence (which had only served to unify the Conservative benches last time around) but in return, the Government announced that on the following day there would be a debate on what to do next, including a vote on ruling out Leaving with No Deal.

The Star Chamber

The "Star Chamber" was the nickname rapidly described by the media to the team of Eurosceptic lawyers rapidly assembled by Sir Bill Cash to scrutinise the legal aspects of the Withdrawal Agreement and – in particular – the ability or otherwise of the UK to leave the Backstop unilaterally if the EU did not give its consent.

Samantha King, writing on the Talk Radio website on 12th of March 2019, described the group in the following terms: "The 'Star Chamber' is a group of Eurosceptic lawyers that have been assembled in an Avengers-esque Fashion by the Eurosceptic European Research Group (ERG) and the Democratic Unionist Party (DUP)". The membership of the Star Chamber (which took name from the Tudor Court of Inquisition in the old Palace of Westminster, which met in a chamber with star motifs on the ceiling) was as follows:

Sir William Cash MP (Chairman):

As a senior MP with many years' service and the ERGs pre-eminent "legal eagle", Sir Bill Cash was the obvious choice to Chair the Star Chamber. In fact, Bill succeeded in assembling a very strong team of MP lawyers, supported by other eminent legal brains, in a very short period of time. Similarly, they were collectively very industrious and produced their verdict on the Government's legal advice against a very tight timescale.

Dominic Raab MP:

Dominic ("Dom") Raab's career before entering Parliament was as a forensic lawyer, specifically, among other things, in human rights issues. He joined the Foreign Office Diplomatic Service in 2000 where he worked in the Hague, helping to bring war criminals to justice. He served as David Davis' Chief of Staff from 2006-2010, prior to being elected as the MP for Esher and Walton in Surrey in 2010.

He then served in a number of junior Ministerial posts prior to succeeding his old boss, David Davis as DEXEU Secretary in July, after the former had resigned over Chequers, only to resign from that post in November, the day after Theresa May's so-called Withdrawal Agreement was published (and the legal implications of which Dom would have well understood). He was thus a natural choice to serve in the Star Chamber.

A one-time rival to Boris Johnson for the leadership of the Conservative Party, subsequent to the 2019 General Election, he was appointed Foreign Secretary and deputised effectively when the PM was briefly incapacitated due to Covid-19. Dominic Raab has now returned to his well-established legal roots as Lord Chancellor and Justice Secretary and is also now officially Boris Johnson's Deputy Prime Minister as well.

Suella Braverman QC MP:

Suella Braverman (née Fernandez) succeeded my old friend, Mark Hoban, as the MP for Fareham in 2015. In another sign that it is indeed a small world, her mother was an activist in Brent Conservatives during the time I was fighting Ken Livingstone in the mid-1990s. Already a QC before she was elected, Suella succeeded Steve Baker as Chairman of the ERG in July 2017, a post which she held until January 2018 when she was appointed a Parliamentary Under Secretary at DEXEU. She resigned on the same day as Dominic Raab in November 2018, for much the same reason. (After the Battle for Brexit, she was appointed Attorney General by Prime Minister Boris Johnson in February 2020).

David Jones MP:
David Jones was elected the Member of Parliament for Clwyd West in 2005 and held a variety of posts in Government, including as Secretary of State for Wales from September 2012 to July 2014. David, a fluent Welsh speaker energetically headed up the Welsh element of the Vote Leave campaign, after which he was made a Minister of State at DEXEU. After leaving the Government in July 2017, he became the third ex-DEXEU minister to serve in the Star Chamber in early 2019. David who is renowned among his colleagues for his dry wit, now serves as the Deputy Chairman of the European Research Group.

Nigel Dodds MP (Lord Dodds of Duncairn):
Nigel Dodds was first elected as the MP for North Belfast in 2001. Having graduated from Queens University Belfast, he was called to the Bar in Northern Ireland and enjoy a distinguished legal career in his own right, before entering Parliament also serving as an MLA (Member of the Northern Ireland Legislative Assembly). As Deputy Leader of the Democratic Unionist Party (the DUP) and their Parliamentary Leader in the Commons throughout the Battle for Brexit, Nigel Dodds was a key figure in opposing Theresa May's original Withdrawal Agreement. It was therefore a bit of a coup for Bill to recruit him to the Star Chamber, where he provided important advice, including on the Northern Ireland related aspects of the Withdrawal Agreement. Nigel was subsequently elevated to the House of Lords, as Lord Dodds of Duncairn.

Robert Courts MP:
Robert Courts took up the challenge of succeeding David Cameron as the Member of Parliament for Witney in Oxfordshire when the latter resigned from the House of Commons shortly after losing the 2016 EU Referendum. A bright young lawyer, he was called to the Bar at Lincoln's Inn in 2003. Eurosceptically minded, although not a fully-fledged member of the ERG, Courts thus added additional legal weight to the Star Chamber, as well as providing some representation from among the newly elected tranche of MPs. Robert was subsequently made a junior Minister by Prime Minister Boris Johnson.

Michael Tomlinson MP:
Michael Tomlinson was elected as the Member of Parliament for Mid Dorset and North Poole in 2015. Prior to entering Parliament, he was called to the Bar at the Middle Temple, who he represented at international debating competitions around the globe. A keen member of the ERG, including having served as its Deputy Chairman from 2016-18, Michael also served as one of the Buddies and on Bill Cash's Star Chamber, as well. Michael was made a Government Whip by Prime Minister Boris Johnson in February 2020.

Martin Howe QC:
Martin Howe QC, the Chairman of Lawyers for Britain is one of the pre-eminent legal brains in the UK on matters of European law and has been a key legal advisor to the ERG for many years (all *pro-bono* – we could never afford him!). Martin's great expertise is to be able to plough through highly dense legal text and then explain it all in concise English to an audience without any formal legal training – including me. Martin was an indispensable legal advisor throughout the entire Battle for Brexit, particularly in offering up the true implications of Theresa May's original Withdrawal Agreement to the whole ERG. As such, although he was one of the only non-politicians to serve on Bill's Star Chamber, he made a vital contribution, nonetheless.

Barnabus Reynolds:
Barnabus (Barney) Reynolds is one of the leading lawyers in the City of London and a partner in the firm of Sheerman and Co LLP. Specialising in Corporate Law and the potential benefits of the English legal system (especially regarding international trade). Barney also added considerable legal firepower to Bill's Star Chamber team. He also generously worked pro-bono too (as we couldn't afford him either!).

Dr Thomas D Grant:
Dr Thomas D Grant is an international lawyer and Fellow of the Lauterpacht Centre for International Law in Cambridge and Senior Research Fellow at Wolfson College in the same city. Another eminent legal brain on Sir Bill's team, he subsequently authored a paper for the Think Tank *Politeia*, entitled: 'Avoiding the Trap – How to move on from the Withdrawal Agreement'.

When they published their detailed "verdict" on 13th March 2019 (Verdict of the "Star Chamber" under Sir William Cash MP on the UK-EU Political Agreement), the Star Chamber effectively concurred with the legal advice of Geoffrey Cox QC, that once it entered the Backstop (i.e. the UK-wide Customs Union), the UK could not subsequently Leave it without the consent of the European Union. This powerful combination of legal advice had helped to seal the Government's fate on MV2 (and indeed on MV3 as well).

"I was a soldier – I wasn't trained to lose!"

When the debate took place the following evening, there were again multiple votes on several options. The first was on an Amendment in the name of Yvette Cooper, the wife of Ed Balls but also an arch-Remainer, to rule out leaving the EU with 'No Deal'. The Government were Whipping against this Amendment, because at least at this stage, the Prime Minister did not want to take Leaving with No Deal off the table as a negotiating tactic (although, in private, she had already made it very clear to her officials that she did not favour the option).

Nevertheless, when the vote was called, the Amendment was only defeated by four votes, 312 vs 308, meaning that when the amended Motion was voted on again in a few minutes, there was a possibility that this time the Government could win, thus effectively "keeping No Deal on the table". At this point, and not by accident, a number of pro-European Ministers, including several Ministers in the Cabinet, collectively abstained in what seemed a coordinated action, probably organised via some WhatsApp group.[246] In the end, 13 Government Ministers abstained, and the Motion was defeated by 321 votes to 278 – again despite the Conservative Party opposing it on a Three Line Whip.

In Westminster, it is very difficult to keep these things secret for very long. Indeed, one of the junior Ministers who abstained was down to do the Adjournment Debate at the end of the day's business but, the Whips, now pretty angry, effectively intervened to stop him taking the Adjournment Debate, because he had just failed to support the Government in the Division Lobbies, and another Minister was rushed in, at virtually no notice, to take the debate instead. This is but one example of how exasperated the Whips Office were now becoming with the behaviour of Ministers in their own Government – let alone Backbenchers in the ERG.[247]

When word went round like wildfire that around a dozen pro-European Ministers had obviously deliberately abstained, members of the ERG were furious. I received this news just as I was about to do an interview with Beth Rigby of *Sky News* in Central Lobby. Quite rightly, Beth pushed me on the fact that No Deal had been defeated and basically said that given this, the ERG would surely be better to vote for Theresa May's deal after all? When I remonstrated that we couldn't do that, she pressed the point several times and said: "But that would be a win, why don't you just take it as a win?"[248]

By this stage I was pretty exasperated, and I snapped back: "It's not a win, it's a lose. I was in the Army and I wasn't trained to lose!". Beth was to subsequently tell me some months later that apparently that remark went viral too but not in the way that I had intended. Whilst I had served in the Army, it had only been as a Reservist Officer during the Cold War and I had never seen active service (nor had I ever pretended that I had). Nevertheless, I was rapidly lampooned on Twitter by ardent Remainers as some kind of "Walter Mitty" who had somehow implied that I had served in the SAS.

For the absolute avoidance of doubt, I have nothing but admiration for those who have served on active service, be it those such as my father who did so in World War II or those who fought in Korea, or Iraq or Afghanistan or indeed on Operation Banner in fighting terrorism in Northern Ireland. Nevertheless, for ardent Remainers (for whom, by now, I was becoming something of a hate figure), this was a bit of a gift and they proceeded to make fun of my remark for months thereafter.

Looking back on it, it would probably have been better to have chosen my words more carefully but, suffice to say, I have been taking stick for it ever since.

The death of collective responsibility

The British constitution relies heavily on the concept of "Collective Responsibility". In essence this means that Ministers who serve in the Government, in whichever Department, are bound to abide by the policies of the Government as a whole, i.e. they take responsibility *collectively* for the Government's actions. By convention, if a Minister cannot in all conscience support some aspect of Government policy, particularly if it is put to the vote, then they are expected to tender their resignation to the Prime Minister.

Nevertheless, by this stage in the Battle for Brexit in Parliament, collective responsibility had already begun to disintegrate, to the point where 13 Ministers deliberately abstained on a critical division. It is just possible that one or two may have even made a mistake but the idea that all 13 of them did so simultaneously, is highly unlikely.

When I appeared on the *Victoria Derbyshire* programme the following morning, to discuss the morning after the night before, I said that: "Collective Responsibility fell off its horse last night and died". When I was pressed by Victoria on what this meant, I elaborated by saying that discipline in the Government had clearly broken down. When she asked me if the Ministers concerned should be sacked (which would normally be their punishment in such circumstances if they hadn't had the honour to resign) I immediately replied that they should – as that was the long-standing Parliamentary convention in these situations.[249]

That afternoon (in no way connected with my remarks) the Prime Minister, who was furious, effectively held an inquest at Cabinet about what had happened. The Chief Whip, Julian Smith, was also clearly angry that so many Ministers had defied a Three Line Whip and abstained in what was clearly a coordinated action. When one member of the Cabinet attempted to suggest that there had been some ambiguity in the voting instructions from the Whips Office, an exasperated Julian Smith reportedly exploded: "Don't tell lies, check your phone!", and apparently promptly got up and stormed out.[250]

Despite this, no Ministers volunteered to resign, and none were sacked, proving to the outside world (and indeed to backbenchers in Parliament who watch these matters very closely) that the Prime Minister's authority, even over her own Ministers, was now very seriously weakened.

Geoffrey Cox QC MP

Charles Geoffrey Cox QC MP was first elected to Parliament as the Member for Torridge and West Devon in 2005. He is the proud son of a senior NCO in the British Army and spent much of his childhood during the Cold War growing up on various army bases, including those forming part of the then British Army of the Rhine (BAOR).

Geoffrey Cox was reported to be one of the highest earning MPs in the House of Commons due to his successful legal practice, having been appointed a Queens Counsel (QC) in 2003, prior to being elected to Parliament. However, he undoubtedly took a substantial pay cut to become Theresa May's Attorney General – the senior Government law officer – in July 2018. He really came to political prominence at the 2018 Conservative Party Conference, when he quoted Milton as part of a barnstorming sub-Churchillian speech as, in effect, the warm up act for Theresa May.

Eurosceptic by instinct (though never a member of the ERG) in February 2019 he was given the task by Theresa May of heading up negotiations with the EU to try and provide some form of unilateral exit from the Backstop – which Steve Baker nicknamed "Cox's Codpiece". He was then placed in the awkward position of having to advise the Cabinet and subsequently Parliament itself, of the legal implications of the outcome of his own negotiating efforts.

As Meaningful Vote Two drew nearer, the ERG established its own eminent panel of lawyers, the Star Chamber, Chaired by Sir Bill Cash, to provide its own legal analysis of the outcome of negotiations. Nevertheless, Geoffrey Cox, who must've been under immense pressure to compile a legal opinion which was helpful to the Government, proved his integrity by ultimately concluding that his legal advice on the Backstop had not changed since MV1 – i.e. the UK still could not Leave the Backstop unilaterally if the EU did not consent.

As a result of his refusal to alter his advice, despite significant pressure, the Government was still substantially defeated over Meaningful Vote Two on the 12th of March 2019. So, there was something morally very substantial in Cox's Codpiece after all.

Extending Article 50 – the Whips Revolt

The following night, incredibly, it got even worse. In light of the failure to win Meaningful Vote Two, but with the UK still due to leave the European Union within a fortnight, the Government put forward a Motion seeking Parliament's consent to extend the deadline when the UK would Leave the European Union to the 30th June. The Prime Minister had already begun trying to negotiate an extension with the EU to this date, designed to buy her some more time in order to try and finally get the Withdrawal Agreement through the House of Commons.[251]

Such were the divisions in the Government, including by this stage in the Cabinet itself, that the Prime Minister had been forced to declare that this would be a "free vote" rather than a traditional three-line whip. Nevertheless, it was clearly the Governments recommendation that Article 50 should be extended and that we would therefore not leave on the 29th March, as envisaged all along.

Unfortunately for her, Dr Julian Lewis, the Chairman of the House of Commons Defence Committee (HCDC) and a member of the ERG, aided by a bright researcher, had calculated that by this stage, Theresa May had told the House of Commons that we would be Leaving the European Union on the 29th March on no fewer than 109 occasions.[252] This number was rapidly picked up by the media and repeated in the Commons and on the air waves multiple times thereafter. And then a truly extraordinary thing happened.

The DEXEU Secretary, Steve Barclay, who had worked tirelessly alongside Geoffrey Cox to try and win a unilateral exit from the Backstop, summed up the debate for the Government and urged Members of the House of Commons to support the Government's motion to extend Article 50. As part of his peroration, he told the House:

"This is a time for responsibility, yet we have a motion from the Leader of the Opposition that ducks the choice, ducks the time, ducks the clarity and ducks any sense of national responsibility. It is time for this House to act in the national interest. It is time to put forward an extension that is realistic. I commend the Government motion to the House".[253]

A few moments later, when the bells rang for the Division, Steve Barclay then marched briskly into the No Lobby and voted against his own Government and indeed his own recommendation to the House to support the Prime Minster. In my 18 years up to this point as a Member of Parliament, I had never seen anything remotely like this – and indeed neither had most of the rest of the House of Commons either. Barclay was probably so exasperated by what had happened the previous day that he had obviously decided to vote against the Government to make a protest of his own.

But it was even more incredible than this. The ERG were obviously opposed to any further delay in Leaving the European Union and therefore when the Division came, most of us instinctively went into the No Lobby as well. When I walked in, one of the first people I saw was a senior Member of the Whips Office – voting against his own Government. Slightly stunned, I muttered "Good evening", to which I received, a smiling "Good evening to you too, Mark". As I walked further into the No Lobby, I saw another Whip doing the same thing and then another.

This was completely unheard of. Members of the Whips Office, the Prime Minister's Praetorian Guard, blatantly voting against their own Government on a Government Motion! I went up to another of the senior Whips and enquired, "Are you boys trying to make some kind of point?", to which he smiled at me and said simply: "We might be, we might not". I then proceeded through the No Lobby, slightly dazed by it all, to record my vote against delaying our departure from the European Union. Having voted and heard the result which was: 403 to 202, this time the Government had overwhelmingly won, only because they had Labour support, as the majority of Labour MPs objected to Leaving the EU, under almost any circumstances.

I remember sitting in the Chamber and thinking to myself, she just can't go on like this. I recalled having served in the Whips Office in the dying days of Iain Duncan Smiths' Leadership and the real signal that it was effectively all over was when his Whips Office fractured and now it appeared that the Government's own Whips Office was doing the same thing.

It later transpired that the Chief Whip himself, who could not bring himself to vote against the Government, had abstained! So even the head of the Government Whips Office – the body specifically designated to help the Government win votes in Parliament – had failed to support them in a key Division. I remember saying to Steve shortly after all this: "She can't possibly continue on like this much longer Steve, when you lose your own Whips Office, it's the beginning of the end".

As it turned out, I was about right.

Julian Smith

Julian Smith, who was born in Stirling and grew up in Scotland was elected as the Member of Parliament for Skipton and Ripon in North Yorkshire in 2010.

A Remainer in 2016, Julian Smith was a strong supporter of Theresa May's candidacy for the Leadership of the Conservative Party and, partly in reward, she appointed him as a senior Whip and then subsequently her Chief Whip a while after she became Prime Minister.

As the Battle for Brexit drew on in Parliament, as Chief Whip, Julian Smith became increasingly angry with the breakdown in collective responsibility among Ministers – and Cabinet Ministers in particular – to the point where he apparently stormed out of a Cabinet meeting in disgust at numerous Cabinet Ministers abstaining on a Three Line Whip to effectively "keep No Deal on the Table", as the Prime Minister had asked.

In addition, as I privately understand it from some of those who worked with him at the time, he never lacked the moral courage to "speak truth to power" in No 10 and the Cabinet Office; the problem was that power wasn't listening, because the Chief Whip was delivering an inconvenient truth, that the Prime Minister's much vaunted deal was deeply unpopular in Parliament.

As this process wore on, Smith faced internal criticism from some in No 10 for basically "not trying hard enough" when, in fact, he was trying quite hard to explain the realities of what was really going on in Parliament to an increasingly unreceptive audience. Despite this, the Government Whips continued to loyally collect information and transmit it "across the road" to No 10 but even many of them became more and more frustrated at the refusal of some key aides in the Prime Minister's inner circle to listen to their experienced advice, about what was really happening within the Parliamentary Party. By the end, even her own Whips Office were privately telling Theresa May to her face that it was time to go.

While we were obviously on different sides of the argument regarding Theresa May's Withdrawal Agreement – indeed we led directly opposing Whipping operations – Julian Smith and I only really had strong words on one occasion and even then, only very briefly. In my opinion, despite repeatedly trying to Whip the ill-fated original Withdrawal Agreement through a highly reluctant House of Commons, which was after all his job, Julian Smith still deserves considerable credit for helping to hold the Conservative Parliamentary Party at least broadly together, during an extremely stressful period in its history.

Piggy in the Middle

In fact, the rot had set in, in effect, some weeks earlier when in the aftermath of Meaningful Vote One, some in No 10 felt that the Chief Whip and his fellow Whips were not trying hard enough to persuade Tory MPs – including the ERG – to support the Government. Some of the civil servants clearly thought they knew more about the House of Commons than the people who actually work in it and, as a result, a room was made available in the Cabinet Office, manned by "more reliable" senior civil servants and from which further Whipping operations in Parliament would ultimately be run.

Part of the lot in life of Whips is to act as "piggy in the middle" between the Government on one hand and the Parliamentary Party on the other. This doesn't just mean transmitting the Government's instructions to Backbenchers and attempting one way or another to persuade MPs to vote as the Government would wish, it's actually a two-way process whereby the Whips are also there to feed back the concerns of Backbenchers, which they collect together and give to the Chief Whip, so that he can, in turn, give the Prime Minister and the Cabinet a frank read out on what Backbenchers are thinking. There is a long-established process for this (which I won't go into in detail) but nevertheless, when it works properly it does provide the Chief Whip with a very accurate assessment of the state of Parliamentary opinion, at least within their own Party.

For weeks the Whips had been talking to Backbenchers and conveying back to the Chief Whip, Julian Smith, the strong sense of opposition to the Withdrawal Agreement, which Smith then loyally relayed back to the Prime Minister and Cabinet. However, while I obviously was not serving in the Whips Office at this time, from what I have been able to discern subsequently, Julian Smith did not lack moral courage and did indeed "speak truth to power" but the difficulty was power didn't really want to hear what he had to say. It was partly as a result of this that this alternative Civil Service manned operation, known colloquially to some as the "Vote Office" was established effectively to oversee the efforts of the Whips Office based in the House of Commons.[254]

From the Government's point of view, this was a fundamental mistake. Firstly, because Civil Servants, however bright or intuitive, cannot be expected to know Members of Parliament anything like as well as their own colleagues, many of whom have been elected at the same time as them and have shared Parliamentary careers with them. Secondly, such a move only served to demoralise the Government Whips in Parliament – whose only crime was to tell the centre something that it plainly didn't want to hear. Tactically, by mid-March

2019, the Government was starting to resemble the dying days of the German Army on the Eastern Front, as staff in No 10 and the Cabinet Office redeployed phantom voting armies which never existed in the first place and constantly held out for the 20 or 30 Labour MPs who were forever about to ride over the hill to rescue the situation but who never turned up when it actually came to the crunch.

The Buddies never had any such constraints, and we had the added advantage that whilst everybody knew who served in the Whips Office (Whips are after all Ministers and their appointments are made public) nobody outside of the team itself really knew who the Buddies were. Whilst the Government suspected that we had a Whipping operation and that Steve and I were running it, as far as we knew, they never got far beyond that and never actually knew who our colleagues were. To their credit, none of the Buddies ever leaked or, perhaps with a couple of drinks inside them, started bragging in a bar; they were all more disciplined than that, not least because they all knew what was ultimately at stake.

So, by mid-March 2019, Theresa May was relying on an increasingly frustrated Whips Office, which had offered her a way out by Whipping the Parliamentary Party so effectively in favour of the Brady Amendment, only to have it effectively thrown back in their faces by the Prime Minister and her advisers barely a week later. Many of the Whips had just about had enough of this, which explains what was, in effect, a rebellion by the Whips Office itself on the 14th March.

Nevertheless, despite these obvious warning signs for anyone who knows anything about the workings of Parliament, the Government ploughed on regardless and resolved to have "one more heave" in the hope of finally getting the Withdrawal Agreement over the line, by the end of the month.

In the end, despite their tactical (dare I say it) ineptitude, they still very nearly succeeded.

Sir Keir Starmer

Keir (now Sir Keir) Starmer, in his role as Shadow DEXEU Secretary throughout most of the key Brexit debates in Parliament, aided and abetted the Remainer cause at just about any possible opportunity.

A former Director of Public Prosecutions (DPP) Starmer is, in many ways, the living embodiment of the smooth lawyer, but he is also an arch Remainer, who said on one occasion Leaving the European Union would be "a risk to the safety" of people on British streets.[255]

Although our relations in the Chamber were sometimes convivial – on one occasion I lost a £50 bet with him for Help for Heroes on the most likely date of Meaningful Vote Three – he provided consistent support for the Remainer cause in Parliament, despite Labour's clear manifesto pledge in the 2017 General Election to respect the result of the EU Referendum.

It was a combination of Labour MPs, aided and abetted on this issue day-to-day by Starmer rather than Jeremy Corbyn, who alongside the SNP, Euro-fanatical Lib Dems, The Independent Group (TIG) and Europhile Tories, constantly ganged up, time and again, to frustrate any attempts to genuinely Leave the European Union. Starmer, who understood full well what he was doing, night after night, to frustrate Brexit, now likes to play this down – for obvious reasons.

Although he may now be the Leader of the Labour Party (and a Knight of the Realm), I have no doubt that he "remains a Remainer" at heart and would gladly take the UK back into the European Union, if the opportunity ever presented itself. While Jeremy Corbyn was always something of a Eurosceptic by instinct – his successor remains quite the opposite.

La Nostra Casa. With mum and dad, Anna and Reginald Francois, pictured with our pet Dachshund "Tiger", and my Aunt Renza and Uncle Ciccio outside our new home in Basildon, Essex in the early 1970s.

Who knew? With mum and dad, my Uncle Walter and my cousin Michele (Michael) during a visit to Westminster during the 1970s.

Bog Standard Comprehensive. St Nicholas Comprehensive School in Basildon,
(which is now the much more successful James Hornsby Academy, recently rated GOOD by OFSTED).

On parade in Berlin. 2Lt Francois (bottom right of centre) commanding a detachment of officer cadets from
Bristol Uni Officers Training Corps during a week-long detachment to Berlin with 1 GLOUCESTERS in 1986.

Elected! A victory party in Basildon (with some bleary-eyed celebrants) following election to Basildon District (now Borough) Council in 1991.

Maiden Speech. Delivering the first speech following election to Basildon District Council (note the ballot boxes still piled up at the back of the Council Chamber).

Amess holds Basildon! David Amess with his wife, Julia, pictured at his iconic General Election victory in Basildon in 1992, which heralded John Major's defeat of Neil Kinnock.

Out on the stump. With the Brent East Conservatives campaign team during the 1997 General Election. (Note my tireless Chairman, Tony Eastman on the right and one David Gauke standing at the back).

"A General Election is a chance to commune with your 68,000 employers."
At a hustings with Ken Livingstone at Willesden Green Library in 1997.

Keep the Pound! Campaigning in South Woodham Ferrers with
County Councillor Norman Hume, during the 2001 General Election.

Elected – and at Prime Minister's Questions.
(Flanked by two other 2001 newbies).

"Who touched the bloody fence?!" With Boris Johnson MP, George Osborne MP, Theresa Villiers MEP
(now an MP) and Stuart (now Lord) Polak on a CFI trip to Israel in 2002.

Let the people decide! Supporting the Daily Mail's campaign calling for a referendum in 2004 on the new EU Constitution (subsequently brought back as the Lisbon Treaty).

Fighting the Lisbon Treaty. Debating the Lisbon Treaty in Parliament as Shadow Europe Minister in 2008, with William Hague, the Shadow Foreign Secretary and Keith Simpson, looking on

Help for Heroes. At a Help for Heroes concert at the Cliffs Pavilion in Southend with James Duddridge MP (Rochford and Southend East), David Amess MP (Southend West) and Stephen Metcalfe MP (South Basildon and East Thurrock). (Note the matching Help for Heroes ties!).

Defence of the Realm. My friend David Amess MP visiting me in my Ministry of Defence office as Minister of State for the Armed Forces.

Why the Government believes that voting to remain in the European Union is the best decision for the UK.

The EU referendum, Thursday, 23rd June 2016.

A once in a generation decision

The referendum on Thursday, 23rd June is your chance to decide if we should remain in or leave the European Union

The Government believes it is in the best interests of the UK to remain in the EU.

This is the way to protect jobs, provide security, and strengthen the UK's economy for every family in this country – a clear path into the future, in contrast to the uncertainty of leaving

This is your decision. The Government will implement what you decide.

If you're aged 18 or over by 23rd June and are entitled to vote, this is your chance to decide

Registration ends on 7th June. Find out how to register at *Aboutmyvote.co.uk* and register online at *Gov.uk/register-to-vote*

If you would like to know more about any of the information in this leaflet go to: *EUReferendum.gov.uk*

"The Government will implement what you decide." Crucial extract from the Government Leaflet put through every door in the UK prior to the 2016 EU Referendum. (Emphasis added).

An event in a Brewery!
The Posh Boys Brewery and Tap Room, just off Wickford High Street.

"A Special Place in Hell". A bottle of the special, limited edition Brexiteer ale brewed by
The Posh Boys Brewery for their local MP during the Battle for Brexit.

With my well-thumbed copy of Theresa May's so-called "Withdrawal Agreement", first published on 14th November 2018 and which, in fact, did quite the opposite.

Boris Johnson meeting with the ERG Leadership, following his resignation as Foreign Secretary. (Courtesy of Steve Baker MP)

No surrender! Challenging PM Theresa May over the contents of the recently published "Withdrawal Agreement" in the House of Commons in November 2018.

Dads Army. Jacob Rees-Mogg MP, then Chairman of the ERG, at an impromptu press conference at Westminster in November 2018, urging colleagues to call for a vote of confidence in the PM.

The stare off! Locking eyes On the BBC *Politics Live* show at Millbank with Marxist commentator Will Self in March 2019.

The Ayes to the Right 286. The Noes to the left 344. So the Noes have it! The result of Meaningful Vote Three (MV3) being read out in the Commons on the 29th of March 2019.

Look, do you want to address 11,000 people or not?
Addressing the Leave.eu rally in Parliament Square, a few hours after Meaningful Vote Three.

Thumbs Up! The ERG negotiating team arriving for a meeting at No 10 to discuss
Boris Johnson's plans for a Revised Withdrawal Agreement, in late 2019.

Get Brexit Done! With my energetic Rayleigh and Wickford campaign team at the victorious 2019 General Election count in Hawkwell.

Sunrise in a free country! With my partner Olivia and friend Julian Brazier, watching the sunrise from Parliament Hill on the morning of 1st February 2020, having just left the European Union!

Spartan Victory! Commemorative photo taken at The Spartans Reunion Dinner at the Carlton Club, in September 2021.

Chapter 13: Meaningful Vote Three – Spartan Victory

Following the Government's second heavy defeat in Meaningful Vote Two, the Cabinet met again on 19th March to attempt to agree a way forward. By this stage, the Cabinet was effectively beginning to disintegrate as one collective entity at the apex of Government, as it found it increasingly difficult to agree on any common European policy at all.

At one end of the ideological spectrum, the Europhiles in Cabinet, still led by David Lidington and Philip Hammond, pushed increasingly for the Government to publicly rule out No Deal and to move more formally towards a Customs Union and possibly even a second Referendum. Conversely, the "pizza club" of Leadsom, Mordaunt et al, were becoming increasingly alarmed at the pro-European drift in Government policy and the willingness of Theresa May to contemplate working with the Labour Party, in order to try and get the Withdrawal Agreement through the House of Commons (something which her Chief of Staff, Gavin Barwell was particularly keen on).[256] In the middle of this debate as it were, remained a number of May loyalists, such as Karen Bradley, who continued to remind people about the importance of the Northern Ireland protocol for security in the province and other traditional May adherents, such as James Brokenshire. Despite his prominent role in the Vote Leave campaign, Michael Gove also continued to back the Withdrawal Agreement, including in the Division Lobbies, night after night.

On the 19th March, it was agreed that the Prime Minister would again travel to Brussels and ask the EU to agree an extension, as provided for under Article 50, in this case until the 30th June 2019. May wrote to the President of the European Council, Donald Tusk, to this effect the same day. The Prime Minster and several of her advisers hoped that this would provide sufficient breathing space for the Government to regroup and recruit sufficient supporters on the Labour benches (and ideally the DUP as well) in order to overcome the resistance of the ERG and, finally, force the Withdrawal Agreement through Parliament on a third attempt.

This task had been complicated, however, when Speaker Bercow suddenly intervened, without warning, on 18th March and announced that as the Government had already held two Meaningful Votes on the principle of accepting the Withdrawal Agreement, he was not minded to allow them to hold a third vote on the same thing all over again. This threw the Government into a state of panic, as it now provided an extra front, on which it also had to fight. As Speaker Bercow told the Commons:

"If the Government work to bring forward a new proposition that is neither the same nor substantially the same as that disposed by the House on 12th March, that would be entirely in order. What the Government cannot legitimately do is to resubmit to the House the same proposition or substantially the same proposition that of last week, which was rejected by 149 votes".257

The Urgent Question on the Joint Committee

By this stage, there were strong rumours circulating that Dominic Grieve, had been to see the Speaker privately before John Bercow had decided to select the Grieve Amendment for a Division on the 9th January. By now, I was arguing within the ERG that whilst our primary concern was always the Backstop and the Customs Union that it would entail, we also needed to be mindful of the risk of the Joint Committee and its ability to effectively make legally binding decisions governing the Withdrawal Agreement, by one UK and one EU official simply by exchanging letters.

On the basis that "what is sauce for the goose is sauce for the gander", I asked for a private meeting with the Speaker, so that I could explain to him personally the potential role of the Joint Committee and the threat that it posed to the Sovereignty of Parliament. In fairness to Speaker Bercow, he granted me such a meeting to which I took along my by now, well-thumbed copy of the Withdrawal Agreement and walked him through the relevant sections (Articles 164-166 and Annex 8) that related to the Joint Committee. By the time I had finished explaining to Speaker Bercow the power over Parliament that this Joint Committee could potentially wield, he had become quite concerned and when I hinted to him that I might well put in for an Urgent Question (in effect a mini emergency debate in Parliament) the following day he in turn led me to understand that such a request was quite likely to be granted – so that I could raise the whole matter on the floor of the House of Commons.

I accordingly put in for the UQ early on the morning of Wednesday 20th March, which was granted to take place following Prime Minister's Questions that lunchtime. I had tipped off other senior members of the ERG about what I was up to and around a dozen or more of them were present in order to back me up. The Government effectively had no warning of what I, and the ERG were about to do and therefore Kwasi Kwarteng, the Parliamentary Under Secretary of State at DEXEU, was rapidly thrown the Parliamentary equivalent of a "hospital pass" and summoned to the Chamber, with barely an hour's warning, in order to reply for HM Government.

Kwasi (who ironically fought Brent East as the Conservative candidate in 2005, eight years after I fought exactly the same seat) is a bright bloke and indeed has written several books, including on the history of the British Empire.[258] Nevertheless, experienced Parliamentarians can tell when a Minister is really on top of his brief or merely when they are reading out the text that the Civil Servants have prepared and, without wishing to be uncharitable, on that day, Kwasi was very definitely slap bang in the middle of category B.

In introducing the Urgent Question, I had only a few minutes to lay out the case for why Parliament should be so concerned about the Joint Committee and I summed up my case as follows:

"In summary, the Joint Committee contained in the Draft Withdrawal Agreement has hardly ever been discussed in the House of Commons or the media, despite the fact that it potentially gives two unelected Civil Servants, the power to make decisions that are binding in international law by an exchange of notes, without the knowledge, let alone consent, of this House. If we are to approve the Withdrawal Agreement, we will approve this procedure too, which is why it is so important that we should know about it. I believe that these facts must be open for debate in the House before the Prime Minister departs for the European Council tomorrow. I thank you, Mr Speaker, for granting the Urgent Question and I look forward – I will be intrigued to hear – the Minister's reply".[259]

In response, Kwasi faithfully read out his Civil Service briefing but you could tell from his body language that he was reading out words which he didn't fully understand. In fairness, he had only recently been appointed to DEXEU and he would have been given very little time to prepare for this outing at the Despatch Box. Nevertheless, the ERG well and truly put him through his paces.

There were subsequent questions from Iain Duncan Smith, John Redwood, Theresa Villiers, Owen Paterson, Steve Baker, Bernard Jenkin, Jacob Rees-Mogg, David Jones, Andrew Bridgen, Desmond Swayne, Laurence Robertson, Marcus Fysh and Henry Smith, with only in effect one Conservative Backbencher, Luke Graham (the MP for Ochil and South Perthshire) attempting to come to the Government's defence. In total, the Urgent Question lasted for slightly over half an hour, during which the Minister gave a number of faltering answers that never really attempted to address the central question of the powers that would be invested in the Joint Committee if the Withdrawal Agreement were passed. This was, in effect, an emergency debate, on the floor of the House of Commons, about an extremely important element of the Government's proposed

Withdrawal Agreement – and other than showing it on *BBC Parliament* (as indeed they do with most other Parliamentary proceedings) the BBC didn't report a single word of it.

The late Enoch Powell allegedly once commented that a good way to keep a secret was to make a speech about it in the House of Commons and at the end of that exercise, I knew exactly how he felt. I had really tried to raise the importance of this aspect of the Withdrawal Agreement in the House of Commons, but the Minister clearly didn't have his head round it and the Europhile Opposition effectively failed to latch on to it as well. Nevertheless, I received several compliments from my ERG colleagues for mounting a "good operation" in the Chamber and, if nothing else, it had shown the Government that we couldn't be taken for granted.

In fairness to John Bercow, whilst he did admittedly allow the Grieve Amendment, he also allowed this UQ, when it was easily within his power to dismiss my request. This is not to say that Bercow was somehow a Brexiteer (he publicly admitted that he had voted Remain and had clearly been on quite a "journey" since first being elected as a very Eurosceptic Tory back in 1997). Nevertheless, it is important to record for posterity, that on this occasion John Bercow gave the Brexiteers a very fair crack of the whip and therefore to say he was purely aiding the Remainers throughout the Battle for Brexit is to oversimplify what was, in fact, a very complex situation.

May goes to Brussels

The following day, 21st March, Theresa May again set out for Brussels to meet with other EU leaders and to request a formal extension of Article 50 to the 30th June (along the lines of the Motion which the House of Commons had approved – despite a number of the Whips voting against it – on the 14th March).

In the end, despite her pleading for 90 minutes for what was, in effect, a three-month extension, the EU leaders, after some eight hours of debate, only agreed an extension of barely a fortnight until the 12th April (or till the end of May if the House of Commons were to pass the Withdrawal Agreement). Again, Theresa May's inability to persuade European leaders to do what she asked was laid bare by this rather brutal selection of a different date by the European Council.

By now, the Prime Minister's frustration with her inability to get her Withdrawal Agreement through Parliament was becoming extremely evident and indeed only a few days previously on the 19th March (reportedly at the behest of Julian Smith and Gavin Barwell) she had decided to effectively go above the heads of Parliament and to broadcast directly to the nation. However, in fairness to the Chief Whip, he was not shown the speech until virtually the last minute and was apparently horrified by what he saw. The speech laid the failure to Leave the European Union on the 29th March squarely in the laps of MPs – rather than the Government. In her address, which lasted only around four minutes, the Prime Minister said:

"Two years on, MPs have been unable to agree on a way to implement the UK's withdrawal. As a result, we will now not Leave with a deal on the 29th March. This delay is a matter of great personal regret for me. And of this I am absolutely sure: You, the public, have had enough. You are tired of the infighting. You are tired of the political games and the arcane political rows. Tired of MPs talking about nothing else but Brexit when you have real concerns about our children's schools, our National Health Service and knife crime. You want this stage of the Brexit process to be over and done with. I agree. I am on your side. It is now time for MPs to decide".[260]

To say that this 'cri de coeur' from the Prime Minister went down badly with Members of Parliament, would be a herculean understatement. Many MPs, on all sides of the House, were outraged by the fact that the Prime Minister had dumped the blame for not getting her Withdrawal Agreement through the House firmly in their laps, but without seeming to accept any responsibility for her shortcomings herself. Indeed Greg Clarke, one of her allies in Cabinet, privately recorded the following comment:

"It was a disastrous intervention. We had been not far off getting a majority and Labour MPs were willing to come onside, but as a result of the speech, we lost them. We'd been getting the Trade Unions on side. I immediately sent a text to Gavin Barwell to say, 'What on earth did you think that achieved?'".[261]

MPs anger was not assuaged when the Prime Minister subsequently returned from the European Council and it was revealed that she had only been granted an extension to the 12th April. Reaction in the media was equally unforgiving with The Times reporting that the Prime Minister had a "Three-week lifeline" and The Telegraph writing that the "EU takes control of the Brexit timetable as May is side-lined".[262]

Nevertheless, egged on by some of her inner circle, Theresa May resolved to have one further attempt to force the Withdrawal Agreement through the House of Commons and deliberately decided to hold the vote on the 29th March, the day on which the United Kingdom had been due to Leave the European Union all along. Part of the thinking in Downing Street was that by deliberately upping the ante in this way, they would increase the pressure on Conservative MPs – and in particular the ERG – who might well be worried that if they were not to vote for the Withdrawal Agreement on the day that we were due to Leave the European Union, Brexit could be lost all together.

In the event, this strategy, brutal though it was, very nearly succeeded.

The Spartan Legend

For those who are not students of ancient Greek history, Sparta was a city-state in ancient Greece whose citizens, the Spartans, had a fearsome reputation in the ancient world as warriors on the battlefield. Part of the Spartan code was that under no circumstances could any Spartan ever be allowed to surrender. By tradition, Spartan women, seeing their males depart for battle, would tell them to: "Come back with your shield – or on it".

When the Persian Emperor, Xerxes invaded Greece in 480BC, the Spartan King, Leonidas, in defiance in effect of his own Parliament, took 300 Spartan warriors to defend a narrow pass at Thermopylae, through which the invading Persians would be forced to progress, in order to invade the rest of mainland Greece. According to the legend, the Spartans were overwhelmingly outnumbered with a Persian Army numbering in the tens of thousands, but nevertheless, they refused to surrender under any circumstances. When they were challenged by Xerxes' messenger to lay down their weapons, the defiant response from the Spartan's phalanx was: "Come and take them".

The Spartans built a wall in order to block the pass and fought off repeated Persian attacks to storm it before they were finally betrayed by one of their own, Ephialtes, who led a large Persian force through a mountain pass to emerge behind them, effectively cutting them off (this is where the expression "the pass is sold" originally comes from). Despite having no chance of escape, the Spartans, under Leonidas, refused all entreaties to surrender and were eventually massacred to the last man, rather than submit.

To this day, a statue to Leonidas the Spartan King exists at the site on which is written the inscription: "Spartan, go tell the passer-by that here, by Spartan law, we lie". The whole episode was captured in a wonderful film called "300" starring Gerald Butler as Leonidas and which came out in 2006. The legend is based on fact and the Battle of Thermopylae definitely took place.

Significantly, although they were massacred, the 300 Spartans were able to delay the Persian Army for sufficient time for the rest of the Greek states to rally and ultimately beat off the Persian invasion.

The Spartans have thus gone down in history as perhaps the ultimate example of fighting on till the end and refusing to surrender, whatever the odds. It was this analogy that the UK media drew on in 2019, when nicknaming these members of the ERG who held out until the last against Theresa May's deeply flawed version of the Withdrawal Agreement.

Enter The Spartans

The diehard ERG members who held out to the end on MV3 were christened the "Spartans" by the media, but the nickname came about entirely by accident. What in fact happened was that shortly after MV2, I was having dinner with my old friend, and former colleague, Paul Goodman, who was by now the Editor of the Conservative fanzine website, *Conservative Home*, which is closely followed by many Conservative Party Members, including MPs and Ministers. Over the meal, Paul suggested that it must have been quite a stressful thing to have been holding out so doggedly against the Withdrawal Agreement, despite unremitting pressure from the media and the Whips to give in. In a light-hearted reply, I told Paul he was right and that, at times, "we have felt like the 300 Spartans guarding the pass at Thermopylae!". At that point Paul's eyes lit up and he said that he liked the analogy and might even be minded to write something about it on *ConHome*. I didn't really give the matter a second thought and simply said something like, "Well please go-ahead Paul" before completely changing the subject and asking Paul about the welfare of his family.

I was therefore somewhat surprised when on the 18th March (after MV2 but before MV3), Paul wrote a very good article on *Conservative Home* entitled: "Enter – or rather exit – the Spartans". As part of his piece, Paul wrote:

"*Conservative Home* is told that a hard core of those determined to hold out now refer to themselves as "the Spartans". These include a significant chunk of the ERG – though calculations are complicated by the fact that not all those who oppose the Deal are ERG members. If the Prime Minister's Deal gets through, among the corpses of MPs slain in the pass, should be those of: Peter Bone, Bill Cash, Christopher Chope, Mark Francois, Andrea Jenkyns, John Redwood and we believe, Steve Baker".[263]

Paul then went on to discuss the likelihood of our holding out. He then posited the question:

"Among those well placed to pronounce on the question (of what might happen) is Boris Johnson. What will he do when the vote comes? Will he stand with the Spartans and return 'With my shield or on it' as he sometimes likes to write, or will he swap sides and join the Persians?".

Paul then concluded, prophetically;

"In this case the city wouldn't be saved if the Spartans are massacred, since a consequence of their defeat would be the Deal passing. And in any case, this time round, the Spartans may actually win".[264]

Somehow, Paul's analogy caught on and the media began referring to the ERG members still determined to resist the Withdrawal Agreement as Spartans – with some other commentators predicting a similar fate to the original 300, in political terms at least. (The full copy of Paul's article is at Appendix 2).

The ERG splits

It is difficult to convey, some two years after the event, the kind of pressure cooker that Parliament had become by this stage. When it became apparent that Meaningful Vote Three would take place on March 29th, all Members of Parliament – and the ERG in particular – came under remorseless pressure to finally give in and to vote for the Government's Deal, for all its faults.

The ERG, for all its success to date had not been impervious to this pressure and in the various meetings at Westminster (and on the five families conference calls on Sunday nights), I had noticed a number of senior members of the group beginning to waiver. Leading among these, was our own Chairman, Jacob Rees-Mogg, who came to be supported by Iain Duncan Smith. As the weeks wore on, I began to say to Steve confidentially that I could envisage a situation where, if push really did come to shove, the ERG might actually split and that some of our members would reluctantly vote with the Government for fear that this was the best Brexit that they were likely to get. We therefore began to discuss, very privately between us, how many in the ERG might hold out if such a scenario were to come to pass (no pun intended).

In the end, this is broadly what happened – although it has to be said, it was an honourable disagreement among Brexiteers about how best to achieve Brexit. Iain Duncan Smith, as a former Party leader, and indeed one who had effectively been removed in brutal circumstances, perhaps understandably had considerable sympathy for Theresa May's position as a beleaguered Prime

Minister. He wanted to offer her an honourable way out and had been lobbying her for some time in private to agree to publicly announce that she would subsequently stand down, if that was the price that it took to get the Withdrawal Agreement through the House of Commons. For his part, Jacob was also very concerned that if the ERG did not "take the bird in the hand" and vote for the Withdrawal Agreement, even as an imperfect Brexit, there might be a long extension under Article 50 and in the end, we would be worn down by the Remainer media and entrenched opponents in the Civil Service and perhaps never Leave the European Union at all.

Conversely, in what might be called the Baker/Cash/Francois camp, we believed that if we were to vote for the Withdrawal Agreement, Theresa May would not stand down anyway and moreover, we would almost certainly enter the Backstop from which, as we well knew from our own reading of the Draft Treaty and both the legal advice of Geoffrey Cox and indeed our own Star Chamber, we could never escape. Once the Government had won in principle, opposition was likely to collapse and they would almost certainly get the necessary legislation through the Commons to Ratify the Withdrawal Agreement, the key parts of which (including the Backstop) would then become permanent in international law. We felt that we would be kidding ourselves as a group if we thought we could subsequently negotiate our way out of this. So, for us, this really was all or nothing.

As the days slowly ticked by towards the vote on the 29th March, the split became more apparent to the point that when the ERG met in its usual Tuesday night plenary meeting on Tuesday 26th March, Jacob stunned some of the members of the group, by announcing that he would reluctantly be prepared to vote for the Withdrawal Agreement, providing the DUP did so as well.[265]

At the same time Iain Duncan Smith was in almost constant contact with the Prime Minister, trying to persuade her to find an honourable way out by announcing at the meeting of the 1922 Committee, due the following evening, that she would indeed stand down as Tory Leader and Prime Minister, if in return the Parliamentary Party agreed to vote for the Withdrawal Agreement.

Iain's hand had been strengthened in this regard by the fact that May had recently held an emotional private meeting with the Government Whips Office, at which one whip after another apparently told her that she would soon have to stand down.[266] This could not have been easy news for any Prime Minister to accept but, had she treated her Whips Office with greater sympathy, perhaps she would not have received quite the same reaction.

The ERG goes to Chequers

With only a few days to go before MV3, some of the key members of the ERG, including Iain Duncan Smith, Jacob Rees-Mogg and Steve Baker, were invited to visit the Prime Minister at Chequers on Sunday 24th March in an attempt by the Government to win them over and thus, as they hoped, to deliver at least the bulk of the ERG to vote for the Withdrawal Agreement. Whilst there, Jacob apparently indicated that he might in the end vote for it, whilst Steve continued to hold out. In the margins of this gathering, Iain Duncan Smith apparently told the Prime Minister to her face that the only possible way of getting the Withdrawal Agreement through in a few days' time would be if she were publicly to promise to stand down in return.[267]

The Letwin Amendment

In this increasingly charged atmosphere, on the 25th March, with only four days to go to MV3, Oliver Letwin, David Cameron's former Cabinet Office Minister, tabled "the Letwin Amendment" which again sought to take control of the Order Paper and to facilitate a further series of Indicative Votes on Wednesday 27th March. Again, this Motion was carried by 329 votes to 302, with the aid of a number of pro-European Conservative MPs, some of whom were, by this stage, keen to prevent us Leaving the European Union, at almost any price.

By now, the Cabinet was so split on which position to take on these Indicative Votes, that it was announced that they would collectively abstain, when the respective questions were put to the House of Commons. This effectively showed that Cabinet Government had completely collapsed, as the Prime Minister was unable to get them to agree on anything. In fact, she was reduced to only being able to get them to agree collectively to keep out of it.

I remember Steve saying to me at the time that this showed that Theresa May's Government was in a state of near collapse, to which I replied: "Government? What sodding Government? There isn't a Government anymore, Steve, there's only a group of Ministers driven around in Jaguars at public expense, but a Government implies some kind of collective direction. If they can't even decide to oppose a vote in favour of revoking Article 50 – which would mean that we officially would never Leave the European Union at all – then we haven't got a Government, at all. I have never seen anything like this in my life. It's a complete and utter bloody shambles!".

The 1922 Committee on 27th March 2019

On the Wednesday evening, prior to the indicative votes and two days short of Meaningful Vote Three, the 1922 Committee of Conservative Backbenchers, met as usual in Committee Room 14 at 5:00pm, with Sir Graham Brady in the Chair. However, this was to be no ordinary meeting and arguably will go down in history as one of the most significant meetings ever of the 1922 Committee.

When Theresa May entered the room, there was an obviously pre-arranged demonstration of desk banging, although it seemed to me less vocal than perhaps on some previous occasions. The Prime Minister made a rather faltering plea to Members of the 1922 Committee to swallow their doubts and finally back her Withdrawal Agreement in two days' time. In order to try and win the Committee round, she then dropped the bombshell (previously agreed with IDS) that she would eventually stand down as Conservative Leader and Prime Minister if the Withdrawal Agreement was passed on Friday – although as a number of Members of the Committee immediately picked up, she was very vague about the precise timings for doing so. A number of MPs pressed her on when exactly she would stand down, if they were to vote for the Deal, including Adam Holloway (one of the Buddies, though she didn't know it), who pushed her twice on *exactly* what she was offering us all. Again, May obfuscated, saying that she didn't want to get into "hypothetical situations".

This hesitant performance led to a considerable amount of murmuring in the Committee. Nevertheless, by now there were a number of Tory MPs who had simply had enough of the whole process and when other Brexiteer Backbenchers attempted to raise doubts, they were howled down with shouts of "Vote for the Deal!", "Just support the Deal!". By now, the mood was beginning to turn ugly and many MPs (the bulk of whom had never even read the Withdrawal Agreement in the first place) simply started yelling at their colleagues to "support the Deal", no matter what. From what I could see, some of the Whips were egging them on – although interestingly by this stage, not all of them.

Amidst everything else, I was now very concerned that during the Letwin inspired Indicative Votes that evening, the option for a "confirmatory" Second Referendum, which was one of those tabled by ardent Remainers, might actually pass, if the Cabinet were to still abstain. So, I asked the Prime Minister in front of the whole Committee (some 300 Tory MPs) if she could make an exception, at least for that one vote, so that the Cabinet would be allowed to resist that particular option. When I stood to ask my question there was a certain amount of cat calling before I had even opened my mouth and so I had to raise my voice in order to be heard.

Nevertheless, when I put the point, there was a general murmur of agreement around the Committee and yet the Prime Minister effectively said that the Cabinet had agreed to abstain, and she couldn't make an exception on that one question. So, despite "Brexit means Brexit" and the 109 previous promises to leave the EU on 29th March 2019 (which the Withdrawal Agreement didn't do anyway) the PM and her Cabinet was now prepared to stand by and watch the Commons potentially vote for another Referendum, all over again. The baying then began again to "Vote for the Deal". It is I think the most unpleasant meeting I have ever been to in 20 years in the House of Commons and by the time that it broke up, some colleagues were openly shouting at each other, whilst others were almost in tears.[268] In short, the 1922 Committee of Conservative backbenchers had just descended into something akin to a Roman mob.

Because of the impending votes, we had already arranged for the ERG to hold an emergency plenary meeting, just a few yards along the Committee Corridor in Committee Room 9, which commenced at 6:00pm, immediately after the 1922 Committee meeting concluded. As usual, Jacob was in the Chair, I was on his left and when Steve came in to sit on his right, he was almost physically shaking with rage.

When Steve was called to address the plenary, he then delivered, straight from the heart, one of the most powerful speeches I have ever seen in the House of Commons – albeit that it was made in a Committee Room rather than in the main Chamber. Literally pulsating with anger and with his eyes starting to moisten, Steve began his speech:

"I am consumed by a ferocious rage ... after that pantomime of sycophancy and bullying next door".

As Steve went on to express his utter disgust at what had happened, I looked round the room and saw that a number of MPs, some of whom had served in the House of Commons for longer than I, had tears rolling down their cheeks. Steve then continued:

"Like all of you, I have wrestled with my conscience, with the evidence before me, with the text of the Treaty, and I resolved that I would vote against this deal however often it was presented, come what may, if it meant the fall of the Government and the destruction of the Conservative Party.

By God, right now, if I think of the worthless, ignorant cowards and knaves in the House today, voting for things they do not understand, which would surrender our right to govern ourselves, I would tear this building down and bulldoze the rubble into the river. God help me, I would".

And he summarised as follows:

"Jacob's case is persuasive. Catherine makes a good point, and I am grateful. But by God this will cost me dear if in the end I go back on what I said to Mark and others, if in the end, because of the consequences of a communist governing this country I have to vote for this deal".

It will cost me dear. I may yet resign the Whip in fury rather than be part of this.

So, I've been honest with you. I have been proud to be your Deputy Chairman, to be your Chairman before, when we made this thing, when we – when I – designed this ERG to be what it is today. I'm proud to have been the Bill Minister for the EU Withdrawal Act.

But I fear today we may be beaten. We shall find out later".[269]

When he sat down, the room erupted into thunderous applause and Jacob spontaneously got out of his chair and hugged him. I sat there transfixed for a moment but then had to stand up and as usual give my de facto Chief Whips briefing on the order of the forthcoming votes, pretty much all of which (other than John Baron's motion, saying we should be prepared to Leave with No Deal, if necessary) the ERG officers were clearly recommending the group should vote against.

Steve Baker's speech that night was absolutely electric; one of the most emotive moments I can remember as a Member of Parliament, but the strain of the whole ordeal was by now clearly showing in his face as well. As we walked out of Committee Room 9, I went over to Steve just to check that he was alright. He was still shaking and by now there were tears in his eyes and so I made sure that I stayed with him, as we walked down to the Division Lobbies just off the House of Commons Chamber on the floor below.

In the end, despite the collective abstention of the entire Conservative Cabinet on the future destiny of the United Kingdom (I still have trouble believing it, even writing these words today) all of the options, including revoking Article 50, a Customs Union, and indeed a "confirmatory" Second Referendum, were mercifully defeated. Although by this stage it was apparent how utterly divided the Government was from top to bottom and that, in effect, Theresa May had now lost all control over her own Cabinet, her Ministers and much of her Parliamentary Party as well.

Steve's wobble

On the morning of the eve of the vote on Thursday 28th March, I did interviews for *BBC Breakfast* and the *Victoria Derbyshire Show* on College Green, where I made very plain that many of the ERG were still fully intending to vote against the Withdrawal Agreement (although I did my best to paper over the fact that the group were almost certainly going to split). By this stage my great friend and self-confessed "Brexit hard man", Steve, was in agony. He was truly riven about what was best to do, as he had indicated in his speech at the plenary, the night before.   Unbeknownst to me, he then met up with Jacob at lunchtime on Thursday, who finally persuaded him to vote for the Withdrawal Agreement and to help try and persuade the DUP to do so as well.

However, their joint expedition to the DUP offices proved unsuccessful, as the DUP weren't there and entirely by chance after Steve and Jacob had separated, Steve bumped into two members of the ERG, Suella Braverman (herself a former Chairman of the Group and one of Bill Cash's Star Chamber), and Julia Lopez, the recently elected new Member of Parliament for Upminster and also a pretty ardent Eurosceptic. When Steve explained what he was now contemplating, both of them basically berated him for considering giving in.[270]   To my discredit, despite having been present for Steve's highly emotive speech the night before, I hadn't really fully taken on board quite the agony that my friend was in. Had I done so I would have attempted to find him and talk to him about it.

However, in the event, Steve went out for a long two hour walk that evening with Christopher Montgomery, one of the former Directors of the Vote Leave campaign who he had known for years and who, from time to time, had also acted as an adviser to the ERG. During this perambulation, Steve basically bounced his thoughts off "Monty" (as he is universally known) and tried to work out the implications of both courses of action. He also spoke on the phone to Dr Julian Lewis, the Chairman of the Defence Select Committee, the essence of whose advice was, as he couldn't be certain of any given outcome, he should stick with his Eurosceptic instincts and still vote against. Steve went to bed that night still in agony about what to do and which Division Lobby to walk through the next day.

Steve has been honest about this in subsequent interviews and the matter has been covered in several publications, including Anthony Seldon's "*May at 10*"

(Biteback Publishing 2019). However, as far as I know, what is not in the public domain is what then happened the following morning.

The day of the vote – Steve's Rally

Mid-morning, Steve came round to my office looking like he had been up half the night. He explained to me that he had been seriously contemplating voting for the Withdrawal Agreement, as perhaps the best Deal that we could get but, having had a long chat with Monty the day before and having had the opportunity to sleep on it, he was now resolved to hold out and vote against the Government later that day, whatever the consequences. As the House was sitting on a Friday (as the Government had deliberately opted for 29th March), the crucial vote would come at 2:30pm in the afternoon.

The two of us then had a long conversation about what was best to do, which was only interrupted when my Whip came to my office to make one last plaintive plea for me to back the Prime Minister and vote for the Withdrawal Agreement. Given everything that Steve had been going through, the absolutely last thing I wanted to do was now go through all the arguments, all over again, in the presence of a Government Whip.

So, I tried to politely explain that there was absolutely no way I was going to change my mind, yet she still persisted. I explained calmly but very firmly that I was "damned" if I was going to vote for this "rancid" thing and would she therefore mind getting out of my office before I really said something I would regret. At which point, she finally took the hint, decided discretion was the better part of valour and withdrew. With hindsight, I probably should have done better to be gracious, but, in my defence, I can only offer that by now it was an extremely charged situation and one of my best friends in Parliament was standing in my office, still feeling the pressure as much as I was.

In the end, Steve explained that having come this far, he felt we still needed to hold out, because if we gave in, it would be the end of everything that we had fought so hard for and he simply couldn't bring himself to do it. For my part, I told him that I too had thought about it, but that giving in had never seriously crossed my mind and that, for family reasons which would take too long to explain, I felt honour bound to fight on. We then shook hands and privately resolved that whatever happened later that day, we would fight it through to the bitter end and "die in the pass" if we had to – but we would do it together whatever.

Every Man Has His Price – Well Almost

Steve and I had now decided what to do on MV3, but it is difficult to exaggerate the degree of pressure that members of the European Research Group were subjected to in the run up to that fateful vote. Some buckled in return for promises of career advancement, others in return for guarantees of Government investment in their constituencies. One colleague publicly resigned from the group (reportedly in return for a £32m bypass) whilst another told me, some days later, that he had held out for and subsequently secured in writing, a promise of £7 million for a major investment project in his constituency. When I challenged this colleague on his actions, he was unrepentant; in the following terms: "Look Mark, my constituency is less affluent than yours and they really needed that £7 million quid. And besides, I was double-banked, as I knew that you and Steve were always going to kill the bastard thing off anyway. So, I couldn't lose." Such are some of my illustrious co-workers in the House of Commons.

One senior member of the ERG was even offered a Minister of State's job, in a department he had always wanted to serve in, on the day of the vote itself – in reply to which he very honourably told the Whip proffering the position that he would have to regretfully decline! Of course, Whips and Government supporters traditionally tried to cajole recalcitrant backbenchers in the run up to key votes in Parliament for decades, or even centuries, but what was happening in the last few days prior to MV3 was simply completely off the scale.

The ERG Plenary at lunchtime

Perhaps by now the Government had finally worked out that having votes on a Tuesday evening was a bad idea, because the ERG normally held its plenary meeting that night at 6:00pm. Moreover, they had switched the vote deliberately to Friday 29th March, in order to generate the maximum pressure cooker effect. However, we had previously agreed that just as with MV1 and MV2, the ERG would hold a plenary meeting immediately prior to the vote, so that, as before, the Officers could make recommendations to the wider group on how they should vote. However, the difference on this occasion, was that we already knew that the Officers would be split.

By the day of the vote itself, the overwhelming opinion of the media (both broadcast and print) was that the time had come for the ERG to finally give in and allow the Withdrawal Agreement to pass. The editorial that day in *The Sun* said:

"MPs of all stripes must set aside their politics today — and vote, in the national interest, for the Withdrawal Agreement".[271]

Whereas the *Daily Mail*, which had supported Theresa May's Withdrawal Agreement pretty much from the outset offered the following advice:

"11pm tonight was meant to be the moment Britain became a proud sovereign nation once more. Instead, Parliament's in paralysis. To every MP, the Mail says this: Put your country first. Uphold democracy. Back the Brexit deal today. You've got one last chance".[272]

Even the *Daily Express*, a normally very Eurosceptic newspaper, perhaps by now exasperated by the whole process, had advocated in its editorial that we should finally acquiesce:

"Quite rightly a fed-up nation is telling MPs "a plague on all your houses". As things stand this morning our exit date is April 12th. It may end up being May 22nd later today, but we can have no confidence that this Remainer Parliament and its self-indulgent Speaker John Bercow will allow Brexit to happen. Most likely Britain is heading to a long extension. A true betrayal of the vote 1,009 days ago. This has to end. The will of the British people needs to be enacted and we must leave Deal or No Deal or trust in democracy will be destroyed for a generation".[273]

The Times, the newspaper of the British Establishment had long been in favour of Theresa May's Deal anyway. Only the *Daily Telegraph*, held out and still urged the ERG to resist, in the following terms:

"The Tories cannot legislate by chicanery, manipulating convention or repackaging motions in order to avoid a proper meaningful vote. If the Agreement does not have the support necessary to pass now, then logic dictates that it is finished. Only when it has been given a decent burial can the country move on".[274]

When the ERG plenary meeting commenced, at 1:30pm in the Grand Committee Room (just off the ancient Westminster Hall next door), there were about 50 members of the group present, including several peers who could not vote in the Commons. As usual, Jacob was in the Chair, with Steve on his right and me on his left. Because of the physical dimensions of the large room, the officers were sitting on a raised dais, which gave me an excellent view of all the members of the group sitting immediately below.

I think we all sensed that we were participating in something truly historic, and this was our last chance, as a group of colleagues who had been through so much together, to decide, privately amongst ourselves, what we should do.

Given the unique circumstances, Jacob, Steve and I had agreed in advance that we would all have a fair opportunity to put our points of view and that in no way would we attempt to heckle or interrupt each other. As the Chairman, Jacob was also determined to give every member of the group an opportunity in principle to speak, although admittedly time would be limited to only around an hour, as the vote itself was due to take place at 2:30pm.[275]

Whilst in the Commons Chamber nearby, the debate was still raging, in reality, it was how this group of MPs were going to vote, within the hour, that would effectively decide the outcome. Unbeknownst to us (although we suspected it) the Government had been making desperate last-minute efforts to persuade Labour MPs to come across at the final moment (and indeed, as we were later to discover, around a dozen or so were meeting Theresa May in her House of Commons office, whilst the ERG plenary was still underway).[276]

Jacob opened the meeting by stressing that the ERG had come a long way and that whatever happened in the forthcoming vote, it was important that ERG colleagues should respect each other thereafter and the group should not fracture as a result. He then laid out his case as to why, reluctantly, he had decided to vote for the Withdrawal Agreement (even though his friends in the DUP had by now made plain that they would not). As you would expect, Jacob was both articulate and engaging and argued, that the deal was certainly imperfect but that, in essence, we should 'take the bird in hand' – or risk a long extension of Article 50 – and thus losing everything instead.

He was then followed by Steve, who admitted that he had thought long and hard about what best to do but that, on balance, he had decided that we would still be right to hold out and to not give in at the 11th hour, having come this far. He also made a personal plea that we should "all honour one another" – whatever the final outcome.

With the Chairman and Deputy Chairman having now given conflicting advice to an ERG plenary meeting – for perhaps the first time in the Group's history, at least on a crucial subject –- Jacob then opened the meeting to contributions from the floor. Up to this point, the ERG had achieved something of a fearsome reputation in Parliament (and indeed, in the European Parliament and the European Commission) for its voting discipline. Providing the Group's Officers were unanimous, the rest of the Group almost always followed their collective recommendations on how to vote. But this was different; it was unique. The Officers were clearly split, so what would the ERG do now?

As other members of the Group made their own contributions, it was soon evident that, precisely as the Government had hoped all along, the Group was now deeply divided. Dr Julian Lewis, the Chairman of the Defence Select Committee and an academic, drew historical parallels with June 1940 and Churchill's 'No Surrender' speech shortly after Dunkirk. Conversely, Mark Harper, a respected former Chief Whip, heralded the prospect of a long extension of Article 50 if the Withdrawal Agreement did not pass, of Brexit being effectively lost forever and of Jeremy Corbyn then becoming Prime Minister for good measure. I didn't agree with what Mark Harper was saying but I could tell that he really believed it.

Other MPs then chipped in, some arguing that the PM's deal, imperfect though it was, was the best we were going to get and that we should back it or risk losing everything, while others, like Bernard Jenkin, one of the original Maastricht Rebels, from almost three decades ago, drew on his previous experience to argue that "we must hold the line" and not submit.

At this point, Jacob turned to me and indicated that he was going to call me to speak. Given what was at stake, I should probably have been very nervous but – for some reason – that was not the case. I had written a speech, but I decided that, given the occasion, the really important point was to directly address the dilemma the ERG now faced and, crucially, to speak from the heart.

Although I had perhaps not been in the same agony as Steve, I too had thought long and hard the night before about what was best to do, not just for my Party but more importantly for my country. I would have given almost anything to have been able to speak to my father that evening and seek his advice but, as that was not possible, I remembered what he had told me to do back when I was thirteen if ever I faced a dilemma and he was not around to help. I therefore dug out a copy of "If". By the time I had finished reading it the night before, I was absolutely settled in my mind about what to do and so, I then decided to incorporate part of it into my speech. (See Appendix 5 for the full text of my speech that day).

As I stood up, I endorsed everything that Jacob had said about the need to handle this very difficult decision in an atmosphere of mutual respect. I then went on to explain that I had been given a copy of "If" by my father when I was a boy and said that even though it had been written over 100 years ago, it could almost have been crafted for this moment.

I then read out the opening stanza of the poem:

"If you can keep your head when all about you
Are losing theirs and blaming it on you,
If you can trust yourself when all men doubt you,
But make allowance for their doubting too"

I said that this was a very good summary of the situation in which we now found ourselves and we now had to trust ourselves too. I added for emphasis that when the bells rang, around 30 minutes hence, the destiny of our entire country and indeed what Churchill called our "island story", would effectively be decided by the people that were present at this meeting. I remember that there was now absolute silence elsewhere in the room.

I went on to argue in essence, that the Withdrawal Agreement was still the same as it had always been and if we had voted against it twice, we should be consistent and vote against it a third time as well. I reiterated that by now most of us were familiar with the Treaty and that we all knew in our heart of hearts that once we entered the Backstop – as thanks to our Europhile Civil Servants, we undoubtedly would do – there would be no escape and we would be trapped in a Customs Union and therefore effectively in the EU, forever after.

I said that this was something that I could not possibly contemplate, and I suspected many others in the room could not bring themselves to vote for it as well. As I argued to the Plenary:

"Remember, the Backstop has no Article 50, no unilateral escape cause – because it was quite deliberately drafted that way, including by some of our own senior officials, who have never accepted the result of the Referendum and probably never will. It falls on us, as elected MPs, sent here by our constituents, who we serve, to prevent this. There is no-one else who can intercede. We are now, just the few of us here today, absolutely our country's last line of defence.

As effectively your Chief Whip throughout this whole process I know full well this has been difficult, sometimes very difficult, for many of us. But we have not come this far, marched all this way, fought so hard and for so long, only to buckle at the last moment. If we do, if we give in now, history will never forgive us for it. But if we hold out, Article 50 cannot be extended forever and eventually we will obtain our liberty, perhaps even as early as next month".

I concluded my speech by asking members of the group to look into their hearts and decide what was best for their country and urged them not to give in. as follows:

"In summary, all I have ever really wanted is to live in a free country, which elects its own Government, makes its own laws – and then lives under them in peace. If that is also what you want, not just in your head but in your heart, then I earnestly appeal to you: walk through the lobbies with me and Steve this afternoon - and don't just save your country but set it free!"

After the three senior officers of the group had spoken, Jacob then took further contributions from the floor and one after another, members of the group rose to explain to their fellow ERG comrades how they were going to vote and why. At this stage, Steve and I had a very private list of at least 20 or so members of the ERG who we thought were likely to hold out no matter what and we knew that if we could maintain at least that number then, barring a massive defection of Labour MPs (about which we could do little anyway) we were still likely to defeat the Government, albeit narrowly.

Chris Heaton-Harris, a long-standing member of the ERG (and indeed a previous Chairman of it) had already asked for permission to address the meeting, even though he was now a Government Minister and Steve and I had previously agreed with Jacob that we thought that that was fair. Chris then made an impassioned plea for the group to vote with the Government in the hope that we could subsequently negotiate away some of the worst parts of the Withdrawal Agreement later on. Shortly afterwards Lee Rowley, one of the new Members of the 2017 intake, representing the marginal seat of North East Derbyshire, which he captured from the Labour Party for the first time since the 1930s and narrowly held with a majority of only 2,860 votes, rose to his feet and gave an equally passionate speech arguing exactly the other way.

I remember one passage of it very clearly when he said:

"I've been told that as I represent a marginal constituency, I should now vote for this Deal even though I've always thought it was shit. Well, I don't care how narrow my majority is, and if I lose my seat, then so be it – but I still think it's shit and I damned if I'm going to vote for it!".

To this day, I can still recall the look of utter defiance on Lee's face when he uttered those words.

By now a number of members of the group had spoken and we were within ten minutes or so of the Division bells ringing, at which point the oldest member of the ERG present asked in a whisper if he might be allowed to speak. It was Sir Micheal Spicer, by now Lord Spicer of Cropthorne, who, as everyone in the room already knew, was dying from Parkinson's disease (although perhaps they did not know that he had come from his hospital bed, in order to speak). He had formed the ERG for almost exactly this type of eventuality, some 26 years previously and he had specifically asked Jacob if he might be allowed to attend the meeting and contribute. By now, Michael Spicer was aged 76 and was speaking very softly, not for any dramatic effect but simply because of his advancing illness. Around the room, people strained forward to hear what advice the founder of the ERG would offer them, in their hour of need. It's a cliché to say that you could have heard a pin drop – but you really could have, nonetheless. Sir Michael Spicer looked slowly around the room and addressed the group, urging us to fight on. As part of his speech, he said the following:

"I know this is extremely difficult for you, we went through agonies like this when we were fighting Maastricht, but in some ways for you, this is even more difficult. You have held out for months and have been vilified by many of your colleagues and in sections of the media as a result, but you were right all along. If you do vote for this Withdrawal Agreement, the Referendum notwithstanding, we will effectively be trapped in the European Union forever and everything that everyone in this room has fought for, some of you for many years, some of you for most of your adult lives, will come to nought. I realise I am asking a great thing of all of you, but please, please, do not give in".[277]

If I had Jacob's vocabulary, I would be able to give you a more eloquent account of what it felt like at that moment, however, I don't, and so I can only say that this was perhaps the most emotional moment of my life since Uncle Tom had told me from the bottom of the stairs all those years ago that my father was dead. There was a stunned silence in the room, and nobody quite knew how to follow what Michael Spicer had said. In the end, one or two members made a final, very brief contribution but by this stage, it was probably true to say that even for those who had been wavering, their minds were now made up, either one way or another.

If you had spent years of your life calling yourself a Eurosceptic – this was Judgement Day.

MV3 – Judgement Day

As we filed out of the Grand Committee Room, with just a few minutes to go before the bells rang, I turned to Steve and whispered: "If everybody does in the Lobbies what they just said in there, then unless the Government have got a large number of Labour MPs up their sleeve, I think there are still enough". He looked at me and simply said: "After all of this Mark, I bloody well hope so". We got to the Chamber just as Michael Gove was concluding his summing up for the Government and then the bells rang.

There were some Whips still pleading with members of the ERG to go into the Government Lobby and indeed quite a number of them did but, in the end, a smaller and yet still significant number did not. Again, the No Lobby was quite busy but noticeably less so than it had been on the past two Meaningful Votes. As we went through the Lobby, I was mentally ticking off members of the ERG as I saw them go by and quietly totting up in my head how many of us had still, despite everything, voted against.

Then suddenly, the doors had been locked behind us and there was no going back. Take whatever analogy you want, the die was cast, the Rubicon was crossed, and it simply remained for us all to walk out of the exit of the No Lobby and for the tellers to count the numbers and then announce them to the House. In normal circumstances, I would want to see the Government Tellers line up on the right, which means that they have won the Division but, on this occasion, I was praying that it would be the Opposition Tellers instead, which meant that the Government had lost, and the Treaty was defeated.

After a certain degree of faffing around with the sheets on which the results were written, the Speaker called the Tellers to Order, and the Opposition Tellers fell in on the right – which meant the Government and the Withdrawal Agreement had indeed been defeated! In the end, the Government lost Meaningful Vote Three by 344 votes to 286 votes, a majority against of 58 MPs. The fabled Labour MPs who would ride to the Prime Minister's rescue yet again failed to turn up and 28 members of the ERG had voted against the Government for the third time (plus six "pro-European" Tories, led by Dominic Grieve).[278]

By my maths 28 x 2 = 56, so had we all voted the other way and if only a handful of Labour MPs, sensing this, had broken their own Whip and voted with the Government, they would have narrowly won Meaningful Vote Three - and our national destiny would have taken an entirely different path, on that fateful day.

As it was, "The Spartans" held out to the bitter end and the Treaty, which would have effectively locked us into the European Union forever, exactly as the Establishment had wanted all along, was defeated for the third and final time. I remember filing out of the Chamber, not screaming or shouting but with an overwhelming sense of relief that we had managed to defeat this awful beast yet again, despite the incredible pressure put upon us and the overwhelming advice of the media to do the opposite. I parted company with Steve and went back to my office to find my loyal researcher, Rory, grinning broadly from ear to ear at the result.

"Look, ...do you want to address 11,000 people or not?"

I rapidly decided there was no point in trying to get any further work done that day and simply told Rory that I wanted to go and get a pint to wind down, an endeavour in which he was happy to join me. By now, the Leave.eu rally, outside in Parliament Square, had swelled to over 10,000 people, who apparently had cheered when the result from the Commons was broadcast over loudspeakers to the assembled throng. I said to Rory we would face a challenge because given all the Leave supporters outside, most of the pubs in the Westminster area would be heaving and we might have to queue for a long time to get a drink – which by now I was really in no mood to queue up for. However, having worked in the Westminster area for years, I said I knew of a small pub called the Two Chairman, in Queen Anne's Gate and therefore we agreed that we would go out into the rally, cut across Parliament Square and try and get down there for a swift pint.

When we went out onto the Square blinking into the sunlight, to my genuine surprise, we were mobbed. I was recognised (thank you again Will Self) and one after another, people I had never met in my life came up to me and started avidly shaking my hand and thanking me and my colleagues for not giving in. Suddenly, everybody seemed to want a selfie and there was a great mood of celebration among the crowd that Theresa May's Deal had been defeated.

Sensing the atmosphere, I suggested to Rory that before we went off for a drink, we might want to sneak backstage, as I was curious to know what time Nigel Farage was going to be appearing and thought that maybe we could grab a quick pint or two and come back to hear what the Leader of the Brexit Party now had to say. When we appeared backstage, I was recognised by one of the Assistant Producers standing there with a clipboard and an earpiece round his head. He seemed delighted to see me and asked me if I would like to come on to the stage and speak to the crowd. I mumbled in reply that it was very kind of him, but I hadn't actually been invited to speak and therefore I didn't think it was my place. He was having none of it and told me that Nigel was due on around 5:15pm and that my colleague (and fellow Spartan) Peter Bone would be speaking a little after 5:00pm, and would I like to have a slot after Peter and a little before Nigel? When I hesitated again, he fixed me firmly with a stare and said: "Look, you just won this bloody historic vote, now do you want to address 11,000 people or not?"

At this point, Rory (who had now been working for me for all of one week) looked at me as if to say: "Well, why not boss?" and so I said: "OK, but that only gives me 45 minutes and I haven't prepared a speech". To which the Assistant Producer replied, "Well then, I humbly suggest you go and get on with it". At this point, I well and truly took the hint and promised to be back at 5:00pm, dragged Rory through the crowd to the Two Chairman (by this stage politely turning down selfies on the way), and got to the pub only to be met by Tracey Chapman, a Member of my own Rayleigh and Wickford Association and an ardent Eurosceptic, who, unbeknownst to me, had come up to London to be part of the rally. She was overjoyed at the result and when we got into the pub, we were unable to buy a drink. People recognised us and pints of beer were rapidly thrust into our hands by well-wishers, (but it is quite difficult to drink a pint, no matter how thirsty you are, when people keep slapping you enthusiastically on the back).

We chatted to Tracey for a while until, with my trusty copy of the Order Paper still in my hand with the result of the Division scrawled on it, Rory and I managed to find a little peace and quiet across the road whereupon we sat down and jotted a few bullet points which were to comprise my impromptu oration. After saying goodbye to Tracey, we hurried back to arrive at the back of the stage just to hear Peter Bone in full cry, at fractionally after 5:00pm. We were then ushered immediately backstage where I was miked up and then Richard Tice, the Chairman of the Brexit Party, who was acting as Master of Ceremonies for the event, announced me to the waiting crowd.

If you've never done it before, it is quite a thing to step out on to a large sound stage and have 10,000 or so people cheering you. This is somewhat different from me giving my quarterly speech to the Association Executive at the Women's Institute Hall in Bellingham Lane, Rayleigh.

Nevertheless, sensing that this was very much a "once in a lifetime moment" I decided to enjoy the atmosphere and I must confess that my allocated three minutes then turned into six and a half! I began by reading out the result of the Division which had taken place in the House of Commons some two and a half hours ago. As I said: "For the rancid Withdrawal Agreement, 286 votes, against the abandonment of British self-governance 344 votes", whereupon a massive cheer went up right around Parliament Square and people began waving Union flags with some gusto. I then went on to read the same extract from "If" that I had used at the ERG plenary barely three hours before. (I subsequently received an email from a lady who lived in the Midlands, who had apparently been standing at the back of the Square, who kindly told me that when I quoted the poem, "I felt a shiver go down my spine").

My peroration was when I told the crowd that less than a mile from here could be found the Bomber Command Memorial in Green Park, on which were inscribed the words of Pericles, namely: "Freedom is the sure possession of those alone who have the courage to defend it". I complemented all those who had come to the rally as being willing to defend our freedom too and seemed to go out on a high note, with a generous cheer from the audience. As I walked off the main stage, I'm not sure whether Richard Tice wanted to belt me for going over time or pat me on the back, but, either way, I then stood off to one side to watch Nigel Farage walk on, realising that I had, in effect, just become Nigel's warm up man. Farage's take on the matter was slightly different and rather than praising the brave MPs of the ERG who had held out, he turned towards the House of Commons and basically berated us, collectively as an institution, for not Leaving as originally scheduled on 29th March in the first place!

I subsequently took that up with Nigel, light-heartedly, when I was given an impromptu invitation to the Leave.eu party in the Altitude Bar at Millbank later that night. Whilst I never quite matched William Hague's fabled "14 pints" I certainly had quite a few that night, as my hangover the next morning readily informed me.

MV3 was undoubtedly the most eventful day of my life up to that point and certain aspects of it will live with me forever, not least the spectacle of the softly spoken but incredibly well-respected Sir Michael Spicer, issuing that final plea to the ERG "not to give in". Well, in the end, enough of us held out to ensure that the "rancid Withdrawal Agreement" was defeated.

Chapter 14: The Fall of the House of May

Despite the high drama of Meaningful Vote Three on 29th March, it was not long before further important (if perhaps not quite so critical) votes took place in the House of Commons. On the 1st April (no, really) given the failure of the Government to pass the Withdrawal Agreement at the third attempt, MPs yet again held another series of Indicative Votes, to see if the House of Commons could agree on a way forward. The closest of these was on a vote in principle in favour of a Customs Union, on an Amendment proposed by arch Europhile and Father of the House, Ken Clarke. This was only narrowly defeated by 276 votes to 273, with the bulk of Conservatives voting against it, minus the usual Tory Europhile minority, who voted for.

On this occasion, the position was really saved by Greg Hands, the Conservative MP for Chelsea and Fulham. Although a Remainer, Greg is also a great trade expert and he well understood that a Customs Union in principle (as envisaged in the dreaded Backstop) would have meant the inability of the United Kingdom to agree its own trade deals around the world, something which as an ex-Trade Minister to boot, he was very opposed to. With Her Majesty's Government (or what little was left of it) now in absolute turmoil, after the defeat on the previous Friday, Greg did a great job in rallying the troops, including producing a detailed and articulate briefing note to explain to all Conservative MPs why the Customs Union was such a bad idea in principle.

Of course, the ERG to a man and woman opposed the motion as well, although Greg never was (and probably never will be) a member of the ERG. Nevertheless, had it not been for his determined and single-minded intervention, it is possible that Ken Clarke's Amendment would have passed and then the Remainers would have claimed a Parliamentary majority for a Customs Union. So, it has to be said, that despite the irony of the vote taking place on April Fool's Day, it was Greg Hands who undoubtedly saved the day.

Laura Kuenssberg's documentary

That evening, the BBC aired a documentary on Brexit, which their Political Editor, Laura Kuenssberg had spent around a year in filming, and which had been originally intended to be broadcast immediately after the UK had left the European Union on the 29th March. Nevertheless, despite the delay, the BBC still went ahead and aired the programme. After the drama of the Indicative Votes and the narrow defeat of the Customs Union only a couple of hours earlier, I was happy to sit down with Steve Baker in his office, alongside fellow ERG member, Owen Paterson, to see what Laura had made of the whole drama.

Fortunately, Steve has a successful local brewery in his constituency, and he had a small fridge in his office containing some of their finest fare, so we were able to sit there, pints in hand, as Laura Kuenssberg appeared on the screen and began explaining the story of Brexit. Steve Baker in particular had spent a lot of time being interviewed by Laura and her team for this documentary and it had become something of a running joke at ERG meetings that Steve often had to leave early "for an interview with the BBC". True to form, Steve featured prominently in the documentary, including a rather poignant scene, where he was interviewed in his office, clearly quite emotional, in the run up to Meaningful Vote Two in mid-March.

I had texted Laura Kuenssberg earlier in the day just to check what time the programme was due to air and she had told me that she would be keen to know my opinion of it. Owen and I sat there and Steve appeared on screen again and again, which we met with calls of "Oh look Steve, it's you" or "Oh crumbs, it's you again Steve" and by the end of the one-hour programme, he was starting to look slightly embarrassed. When it had finished, I immediately texted Laura and said that: "I thought you did a very good job of this, but Steve is furious!", she instantly came back with, "OMG why?". I then replied, "He thought he ought to be in it a bit more!".[279]

In fairness, I did indeed think that Laura Kuenssberg, who had interviewed everybody from Boris and David Davis through to Dominic Grieve had actually put forward a very balanced summary of the extraordinary events that had been taking place in the House of Commons over the past year or so. Given the delay to Brexit, Laura and her team then set about filming a second programme on this topic (which we were to watch in the Smoking Room at the House of Commons months later). To this day, we still tease Steve about his multiple media appearances, but he (generally) takes it all in good heart.

The Cabinet sanctions talks with Corbyn

On 2nd April, Theresa May reassembled her bitterly divided Cabinet, in order to try and agree a way forward following the defeat on MV3. After a long and at times acrimonious Cabinet meeting, it was agreed that the Prime Minister would open direct talks with the Leader of the Opposition, Jeremy Corbyn, to seek to find some way of persuading the Labour Party to support a version of the Withdrawal Agreement in the House of Commons.

For a number of Eurosceptics in the Cabinet, this was a bitter pill indeed to swallow and moreover it went down pretty badly on the Backbenches as well. The reasons why are not difficult to calculate. Almost from the day that he had assumed the Leadership of the Labour Party, the Conservatives had consistently criticised Jeremy Corbyn for his neo-Marxist economics, his previous sympathy for terrorist groups such as Hamas and the IRA and also his very slothful approach to dealing with the cancer of Anti-Semitism, which was unfortunately growing among the hard left, who had come to dominate Corbyn's Labour Party.[280] In short, after calling this man just about everything under the sun and highlighting that he posed a genuine threat to the British way of life, here was the Prime Minister of the United Kingdom inviting him for talks in Downing Street!

Many of us in the ERG were disgusted by what May had done and were not afraid to say so; Jacob Rees-Mogg was quoted as saying: "You do find that Leaders who decide to go with the opposition rather than their own Party find their own Party doesn't plainly follow, I'm not sure this is the way to conciliate people to persuade them if they haven't moved already, to move at this stage. I think getting the support of a known Marxist is not likely to instil confidence in Conservatives".[281]

Nevertheless, Theresa May ploughed on with this course of action, in the hope that she could somehow secure Labour Party support, to allow her to "overmatch" the ERG and thus win what would then become 'Meaningful Vote Four'.

A tie in the House of Commons

Back in the Commons, despite their narrow failure to obtain a majority for a Customs Union, the Remainers then redoubled their efforts to prevent any possibility of Leaving the European Union in a timely manner. Oliver Letwin tabled another Motion to take control of the Order Paper, in order to facilitate the rapid introduction of legislation, via which the Remainers intended to use their voting power (including support from Tory Europhiles) to ram a Bill through the House of Commons the following day, extending the deadline for when we would be allowed to Leave the European Union. The issue was further complicated when another arch-Europhile, Hilary Benn (son of the famous Labour firebrand and, ironically, arch-Eurosceptic – Tony Benn) tabled an amendment to Letwin's motion, calling for yet another series of indicative votes. When this was put to a Division, it led to yet more extraordinary scenes in the Commons.

It normally takes around 15 minutes for a Division to take place. The MPs have eight minutes to file into the respective Division Lobbies before the doors are locked, after which they then file out one by one at the other end and are counted by the Tellers, who then confirm the number between them, hand it to the Clerks at the table in the Commons and then line up. At the Speaker's invitation, they then march forward and read out the result.

However, on this occasion, after about 25 minutes, the result of the Division had still not been declared and increasingly senior Whips, from both Government and Opposition, were called forward to consult with the Speaker. A rumour began to rush round the House that the result had been a tie (in which case, the Speaker is traditionally meant to vote with the status quo). In my 18 years up to that point in the House of Commons I had never seen a tied vote and, moreover, many people began wondering whether, if this turned out to be true, Bercow would uphold the convention and vote against change or whether he would do something different – as he had appeared to do by allowing the Grieve Amendment back in January.[282] The situation became even more dramatic when it emerged that one of the Government Whips had for some reason left the voting Lobby and then been locked out when she was too slow in returning. Had she done so, the Government would have won, and a tie would have been averted. It became even more bizarre when it turned out that the Whip in question was holding a proxy vote for another Tory MP, who was absent on maternity leave and so the Government side were in fact two votes down, rather than just one.

After almost half an hour and amid growing incredulity around the House, the Speaker finally announced that the result had indeed been a tie, 310 votes for each side, but that in accordance with convention he was casting his vote with the status quo, so that the Motion was effectively defeated by one.

The Cooper/Boles/Letwin Bill

Nevertheless, following this rather unique event and in accordance with the Letwin Motion passed previously, the following day the Remainers then proceeded to ram the European Union (Withdrawal) (No.5) Bill (known as the Cooper/Boles/Letwin Bill, after the three MPs who primarily sponsored it) through all its stages in the House of Commons, in barely over three hours. Normally such a thing would only happen if the Government were passing emergency legislation, for instance to respond to some terrorist threat and, even then, it would normally take a full day for such a Bill to pass the House. To add further to the incredible sense of drama that day, the Bill, actively aided and abetted by Keir Starmer, as Labour's Shadow spokesman, eventually passed its Third Reading by literally one vote. Their utterly brazen tactics drew fierce criticism from Eurosceptics on the Tory benches, myself included, who described it as: "A constitutional outrage" (which indeed, in these circumstances, it was).[283]

The Remainers, whom by now had effectively abandoned all pretence that they intended to use their small majority in the Commons anything other than as ruthlessly as possible, had rammed through the Bill knowing that it was unlikely to be given a difficult reception in the overwhelmingly pro-European House of Lords.

Thus, the Commons had experienced another two days of high drama, including a tie; followed by a very controversial piece of legislation being steamrollered though the House of Commons in under four hours, by a majority of one. This was high drama in Parliament indeed but showed very clearly how absolutely desperate some of the diehard Remainers were becoming, to keep Britain in the European Union, regardless of the Referendum.

May returns to Brussels

On 10th April the beleaguered Prime Minister went back to Brussels yet again, this time to ask for a further extension beyond the 12th April date that had been previously agreed. In the end, she had to deal with considerable scepticism among Members of the European Council that she would *ever* be able to get *anything* through the House of Commons, so it was finally agreed that under Article 50, the UK's date for Leaving the European Union would be formally put back to the 31st October 2019, with a potential review of the position in June.[284]

For many Brexiteers, who had originally set their hearts on Leaving by 29th March (but who knew that the Withdrawal Agreement didn't constitute Leaving at all), this was a deeply depressing moment, as it now seemed it would take another six months, at the earliest, before we were finally able to Leave the European Union, marking more than three years since the June 2016 Referendum. The mood on the Tory Backbenches was grim with Government loyalists attempting to blame all of this on the ERG and us in turn, blaming it squarely on the Government. Meanwhile, the Con/Lab negotiations, with Deputy Prime Minster, David Lidington and Steve Barclay leading for the Government and Sir Keir Starmer and Rebecca Long Bailey for the Opposition, dragged on, but without any signs of an early breakthrough.

Nevertheless, the ardent Remainers in the House of Commons were delighted when it was announced that we would not be Leaving the European Union for at least six months and saw this as a significant tactical victory, along the path to what they hoped would be a complete abandonment of Brexit in due course, regardless of the result of the 2016 Referendum. When the House of Commons rose for the Easter recess on the 11th April, it still seemed to be a pretty bleak time, from a Brexiteer point of view.

The bust up with Speaker Pelosi

With the House having risen for Easter and having had several run-ins with one Speaker, I somehow contrived to have one with another. I was surprised to receive a telephone call out of the blue over the weekend from Jacob when he explained that the Speaker of the US House of Representatives, the Democratic Congresswoman Nancy Pelosi, was on a visit to the United Kingdom, accompanied by a number of other Congressman and had asked if she could have lunch with the officers of the ERG on Monday 15th. Speaker Pelosi is a powerful figure in American politics and so I was both happy and intrigued to accept.

The lunch took place on Monday 15th at Roux, a nice restaurant just off Parliament Square. Present from our side were Jacob, Chairman of the ERG, Steve Baker, his Deputy, myself as Vice Chairman and also David Campbell Bannerman, a former Deputy Leader of UKIP and now a Eurosceptic British Conservative MEP, and long-time Brexiteer. Speaker Pelosi was accompanied by several Congressmen, including prominent representatives of the Irish American community representing Congressional Districts on the Eastern seaboard of the United States. Also present was Woody Johnson, the popular US Ambassador, who was helping to host the lunch.

Things began well enough when Speaker Pelosi said that she had heard a great deal about the ERG and had been keen to meet us during her trip to London. She explained that she had just come from a meeting with the Chancellor of the Exchequer, Philip Hammond and was eager to know whether there was any possibility at all that the ERG might somehow be persuaded to finally back the Government's Withdrawal Agreement.

She explained that it was important to her and many of her colleagues because they saw the Agreement, including the Backstop, as very important in helping to uphold the Good Friday Agreement of 1998 and preventing a return to a hard border in Northern Ireland. For our part, we did our best to explain that all of that was 20 years ago and that no one, in either the UK or the Irish Governments, or indeed anyone in Northern Ireland or moreover anyone in the European Commission was seeking a return to a hard border and that the kind of infrastructure that they were talking about dated from The Troubles, which mercifully the Province had now moved on from. At this point, the American delegation became more agitated, and the conversation became somewhat more pointed. When I sought to amplify this point to Speaker Pelosi, she turned round and said: "Don't patronise us, we didn't come all this way just to be patronised". Somewhat taken aback, I explained that that was never my intention but that, nevertheless, things had moved on and that perhaps the Speaker and her delegation had not been brought fully up to speed with the evolution of events in Northern Ireland in the last few years. (However, what I was really thinking – but didn't say – was: "Who the hell do you think you are? How dare you fly all the way across the Atlantic to tell us how to run our own country? How would you like it if we flew the other way and told you how to run yours in return?").

Jacob, with his charming manners, expertly smoothed the whole thing over but on the way out, I apologised privately to the US Ambassador in case I had caused "a diplomatic incident". So as not to embarrass the former Ambassador, I will not reveal his reply, save to say, he was not made Ambassador to the Court of St James by President Trump for being a lifelong Democrat – Quite the reverse!

The three Officers then retreated upstairs for a cup of coffee and a debrief, during which, we agreed that the whole thing had clearly been staged and that Speaker Pelosi's message had obviously been delivered as a diplomatic "demarche", almost certainly with tacit encouragement from the Government. It is important to remember that Philip Hammond had previously labelled the ERG "extremists"[285] so it's difficult to believe that he was issuing peons of praise for our group at the meeting Speaker Pelosi had just come from. You would think by this stage that people had realised that the ERG couldn't be bullied but Speaker Pelosi, for all of her undoubted authority in the United States, clearly never got the memo. Despite this, our lunch was rapidly leaked to *The Times* and whilst out canvassing for the local elections shortly thereafter, I had Frances Elliot, their Political Editor on the phone, enquiring about how I had been "put in my place" by the Speaker of the House of Representatives. In fairness to Francis, he did report my version of events as well, but it was a classic dig at the ERG, under the headline: "How 'condescending' Brexiteer Mark Francois met his match in US Speaker Nancy Pelosi".[286]

Dinner with Professor John Vincent

The following weekend, I travelled down to Bristol to spend part of the Easter break with my old Bristol friend Alan, his wife Monika and their two children, Alexander and Abigail, the former of whom is my Godson. It was a real pleasure to have a break some distance away from the hotbed of Westminster and to be able to unwind, whilst telling my old University and OTC friend about some of the experiences of the last few months, including the dramatic lead up to MV3.

As a bonus, I had contacted my old history professor, and mentor John Vincent, in advance of my trip and he and his wife, Nicolette, had very kindly invited me over for dinner on the Sunday evening. I spent an extremely pleasant night talking things through with John, himself a committed Brexiteer, and we mapped out between us a number of different scenarios. John Vincent agreed with me that we would never fully Leave the European Union while No 10 was largely dominated by instinctive Remainers.

With that thought ringing in my ears, I travelled back up to London on Easter Monday, against a background of increasing concerns on the Backbenches about the direction in which Theresa May was now taking the Conservative Party.

Michael Gove

Michael Gove is one of the most enigmatic and fascinating characters in modern British politics. The adopted son of Scottish parents, who worked in the Scottish fishing industry, he grew up in Aberdeen before going onto Oxford University, where he was a contemporary of both David Cameron and Boris Johnson and became president of the Oxford Union (the student debating society).

Highly intelligent, charismatic, quick-witted and with exquisite manners, he is also a strong administrator and one of the most accomplished debaters/speakers in the present-day House of Commons. Whilst Education Secretary, Gove, supported by his Special Adviser, one Dominic Cummings, courageously took on the educational establishment, which he then famously christened "the Blob". Although pretty much despised by the Teaching Unions, he refused to accept mediocrity in education, particularly in the inner-cities and was instrumental in accelerating the program of Academies, to help boost educational standards, especially in tough, urban areas. In addition, he was also a leading light for Vote Leave.

However, despite all of these powerful attributes, perhaps Michael's greatest challenge today remains the "T-word" – Trust. Unlike David Davis, Boris Johnson and Dominic Raab, he refused to resign over Chequers or the Withdrawal Agreement and remained in Theresa May's Cabinet throughout the three Meaningful Votes thereafter.

As a result, unsurprisingly, he achieved very few votes from the ERG during the 2019 Tory Leadership contest. Similarly, the "stab in the back" of Boris during the previous 2016 Leadership campaign, (as many in the media had characterised it at the time) having been his campaign manager up to that point, left a lingering bad taste in the mouth of many Conservative MPs, as it did the wider British public. In fairness, I believe there is no-one who now understands this better than Michael himself.

It is effectively an open secret at Westminster that Michael Gove's burning desire is to become Prime Minister, but it still remains to be seen whether, after the tumultuous events surrounding Brexit, he will yet achieve his lifetime ambition.

The men in grey suits

The Executive of the 1922 Committee of Conservative Backbenchers, which is made up mainly of long serving Tory MPs, are sometimes referred to colloquially as the "Men in grey suits", who by tradition are supposed to go in and tell a Conservative Prime Minister when their time is up. By late April, these men (and indeed several women, including one of the Vice Chairman, the popular Dame Cheryl Gillan and also Sheryl Murray, the feisty MP for South East Cornwall) were very aware of the growing disquiet on the Conservative Backbenches about Theresa May's faltering Leadership.

The Conservative Party's rules stated clearly that if a Leader survived a Confidence Vote (as Theresa May had done on 12th December) they could not be challenged again for a year. Nevertheless, such was the growing pressure on the Tory Backbenches for May to go, that on the 24th April, the 1922 Committee Executive held an extended discussion on whether or not to change the rules. In the end, a vote was apparently taken, and a proposition to amend the rules to allow for an early additional Vote of Confidence was narrowly defeated.[287]

Nevertheless, Westminster was now rife with rumours. The Cabinet were riven, collective responsibility had effectively collapsed, rival contenders were already making their campaign preparations and the Prime Minister's position was becoming increasingly untenable. Within the ERG, many of us had come to the conclusion that it was only a matter of time before May would have to go and so thoughts began to turn to who might be best placed to succeed her and finally take us out of the European Union, once and for all.

The "Posh Boys Brewery" and "A Special Place in Hell"

As some light relief from all this Westminster drama, on Sunday 28th April, I was invited to open a new micro-brewery in Wickford in my constituency. The background was that two likely Essex lads, called Ian and Andy, had been brewing ale in their back garden for some years and selling it at events such as Town Fayres and Country Shows. Having met them at one such event, I subsequently agreed to go and visit their "Brewery" a few months later. In planning my diary, my PA Adele ensured that I had a dinner to go on to that evening so that I couldn't "overstay my welcome" and strictly rationed me to two pints. In the end, I had three, and turned up at the dinner with a distinct smile on my face, because the ale these guys brewed was actually excellent.

They explained to me at the time of my visit, that their real life's ambition was to try and take over a disused shop unit or some such, effectively put the brewing kit into the back and turn the front into a tap room, so that they could sell their beer directly to the paying public. For my part, I had one of my regular meetings coming up shortly with the Chief Executive of Basildon Borough Council, Scott Logan (himself a Wickford lad) and promised that I would mention it to him and seek his advice.

To cut a long story short, following that meeting and at my instigation, the Council were extremely helpful at finding the "Posh Boys" (as they styled themselves) a disused clothes shop just off Wickford High Street which they subsequently converted into a tap room and in return for my help, they allowed me to perform the official opening one Sunday afternoon. In order to try and get them some publicity for their launch I had mentioned this in passing to several journalists, one of whom was Sophie Jarvis, who had recently obtained a job working on the diary column of the *Evening Standard* in London, now edited by one George Osborne. Sophie was good as her word and came down to cover the event on the day, only to discover that, completely unbeknownst to me, the Posh Boys had taken it upon themselves to brew a special ale for me to mark the occasion, which they christened, "A Special Place in Hell", in memory of Donald Tusk's famous insult to British Eurosceptics.[288] I had invited my neighbours in Rayleigh to the launch (having assured the Posh Boys that they knew a thing or two about appreciating good ale) and the whole event was something of a success.

To make matters even better, the Posh Boys presented me with around 20 or so bottles of "A Special Place in Hell", all of them with a specifically designed label of a pint glass with red horns and a devil's trident, which I subsequently used as a calling card with journalists. After I had given one to the BBC and Sky, and also the *Financial Times* and a few other newspapers, we received a call from the *Daily Mail's* lobby team, wanting to know where there one was as well. Perhaps best of all, at my suggestion, Sophie subsequently presented a bottle of "A Special Place in Hell" to George Osborne, who to his credit apparently got the joke. From the point of view of the Posh Boys, they got some return on their investment when *The Sun* website subsequently gave the whole thing an amusing write up and when I explained to the Posh Boys that this was viewed by several million people, their eyes lit up accordingly.

Dinner with Jacob

On Wednesday 1st May, on the eve of the 2019 local elections, I had invited Jacob to dinner at the Carlton Club to try and patch up any differences that might have arisen given our different approach during Meaningful Vote Three. All the Officers had stressed that fateful day that whatever happened it was important that everyone in the group should respect each other afterwards and Jacob proved to be absolutely as good as his word.

We had a convivial supper without any acrimony, made easier by the fact that Jacob is of course charming company and has a dry but extremely amusing sense of humour. Over our meal we discussed our mutual fears that the Party was going to do very badly in the local elections the following day. Not only were many Conservative Members very angry with Theresa May's direct negotiations with Jeremy Corbyn, the Government's whole approach was becoming increasingly unpopular around the country and to make matters worse, Nigel Farage and the Brexit Party were now waiting in the wings, although not standing local Council candidates at this stage.

The local elections of 2019

In the event, our fears were realised when the local election results began to come in later the following night. When we returned from campaigning and all the votes were counted, the Conservative Party lost 1,330 Councillors across the country, with the Lib Dems in particular making gains of over 700 seats. This was one of the Party's worst results in the local elections since the dark days under John Major in the mid-1990s, when a blue rosette was effectively a political death warrant for our local Government candidates.[289]

Having seen the Party do so badly, only increased the level of alarm at Westminster at the direction that Theresa May was taking the Conservative Party. In addition, the Voluntary Party of Conservative Members up and down the country (many of them Councillors or in some cases now ex-Councillors) were also rapidly losing faith in Theresa May's ability to lead the Party. For many of these staunch Conservative supporters, the sight of May in negotiations with Jeremy Corbyn, a man who represented a neo-Marxist ideology which they despised, was simply too much to bear. A survey of Conservative Party Members undertaken by *Conservative Home*, had recently found that 75% of Conservative Party Members now wanted to Leave the European Union as soon as possible, even if necessary, with No Deal.[290]

Eventually, Members of the Voluntary Party around the country invoked an obscure rule in the Party's constitution to summon a meeting of the National Conservative Convention (if you like, the Parliament of the Voluntary Party) to pass a Motion of No Confidence in Theresa May as Tory Leader. This procedure required 65 or more Conservative Association Chairmen to write to CCHQ requesting such a meeting and a leading Tory activist in East London, Dinah Glover, took up the challenge and began to organise Members to send in their letters (in something of a mirror of the 48 letters from MPs, that had been required to trigger a Parliamentary Confidence Vote in Theresa May, the previous Autumn).

The rules stipulated that once the requisite number of letters were received from Association Chairmen, CCHQ would have to organise a meeting of the National Conservative Convention (NCC) within 28 days. Such was the mood among Conservative members across the country that Dinah and her friends managed to rapidly amass the requisite number of requests, meaning that a meeting of the NCC was provisionally scheduled for the 15th June. Theresa May now effectively had this hanging over her as a Sword of Damocles, whilst her position in Westminster continued to deteriorate as well. Pictures in the media of Party Members cutting up their plastic membership cards, in protest at the negotiations with Jeremy Corbyn, hardly improved morale at No 10, or in the Commons Tea Room either.

BBC Four Documentary – "Behind Closed Doors"

On the 8th and 9th May, the BBC screened a quite remarkable documentary called "Behind Closed Doors". The essence of this was that a Belgian television journalist called Lode Desmet had been allowed to film a "fly on the wall" documentary, following Guy Verhofstadt MEP, one of the leaders of the liberal (ALDE) faction within the European Parliament and also the European Parliament's Rapporteur on the Brexit negotiations with the United Kingdom, for two years. When the documentary was broadcast over those two nights, in early May, it led to widespread reaction from Brexiteers on the internet.[291]

Basically, the documentary showed Verhofstadt and his aides and indeed other European Politicians consistently mocking British Politicians, including the Prime Minister, on camera, over two years during the course of the Brexit negotiations.

On one occasion, Verhofstadt's Chief of Staff, an Irish woman, had reacted to a difficult meeting between Mr Verhofstadt and ERG member, Andrew Rosindell (the MP for Romford and a fellow Spartan) by saying: "You really told him to fuck off!".[292] The whole programme was peppered with expletives, many of which were aimed at the British side in the negotiations. Perhaps most tellingly of all, was a scene in which two of Verhofstadt's key aides were filmed in November 2018, discussing the Withdrawal Agreement, which had now been agreed between the EU and the UK but not yet publicly announced and published.

The scene was filmed in Verhofstadt's offices in the European Parliament building in Strasbourg, the Parliament's second home after its principal complex in Brussels. The *dramatis personae* were Bram Delem, Verhofstadt's personal speechwriter and Jeroen Reijnen, his head of Media and Communications. Whilst awaiting the announcement from London. Bram Delem says to his colleague:

"We got rid of them. We kicked them out. It took us two years. But we managed on our terms and conditions!"

In reply, Jeroen Reijnen states:

"We finally turned them into a colony, and that was our plan from the first moment!"[293]

More than any other scene in the whole two years of filming, this exchange, between two senior aides to the European Parliament's Brexit Coordinator, betrayed the attitude of the European Union throughout the negotiations and the UK's Brexit process.

Indeed, a year later, the documentary maker, Lode Desmet, published a book with co-author and former *Today Programme* presenter, Edward Stouton, entitled "Blind Man's Brexit – How the EU took control of Brexit". The book outlines, in excruciating detail, how the experienced EU negotiating team, led by former EU Commissioner, Michel Barnier, often ran rings round their UK counterparts aided by constant divisions in Government.[294] Barnier, a highly-intelligent French politician, always immaculately turned out, was meticulous in his preparation, and took great pains throughout to keep the representatives of the European Council and the European Parliament well informed and thus onside in dealing with his British opposite numbers. In their introduction to the book, the co-authors make the following absolutely damning statement:

"This story is often uncomfortable; before the vote to leave the EU, Euro-enthusiasts like Verhofstadt regarded the United Kingdom as an awkward but formidable player on the European scene. After the vote they feared Britain's negotiating power. By the end of the negotiations, all too often they laughed at the UK leaders and pitied the British people".[295]

When the documentary was finally broadcast it led to a rapid backlash from Brexiteers on the internet, quite rightfully complaining at the way that continental Politicians had been treating their UK counterparts with utter contempt. Indeed, in the latter stages of the second programme, Verhofstadt becomes notably nervous and starts to ask questions like: "Are you filming this?" or "Are the cameras still running?" It should be remembered that Guy Verhofstadt MEP is the man who went to the pre-election 2019 Lib Dem Party Conference and told an adoring audience that "Britain should remain part of an EU empire" – for which he received a standing ovation from the Lib Dem delegates present.[296]

Although it was the BBC – of all channels – that actually broadcast this programme, it was only put out on BBC Four. Despite requests to broadcast the programme again in prime time on BBC One or even BBC Two, the corporation steadfastly refused to do so. It didn't exactly get lead billing on the *Today Programme* either. Nevertheless, here, on camera, was clear evidence of the contemptuous attitude of the European elite towards their British counterparts and indeed the British people who had had the temerity to decide, democratically, that they no longer wished to be ruled by people like this. In short, it was very much a giveaway moment. For my part, I tried to highlight this in an online article on the Euro-sceptic website, *Brexit Central,* in which I argued that it: "was absolutely plain for all to see, the sheer derision with which the British were treated throughout the two hours of footage".[297]

Oh Jeremy Corbyn

In electoral terms, despite an admittedly strong showing in the snap 2017 General Election, Jeremy Corbyn ultimately proved to be one of the poorest leaders in the entire history of the Labour Party. In the 2019 General Election he led his Party to its largest defeat for a generation, recording one of Labour's poorest vote shares since the Party was created in the early 20th Century and their worst General Election outcome since 1935.

Perhaps ironically, in his earlier career, Corbyn was a committed Eurosceptic, with a neo-Marxist critique of the European Union as a capitalist ramp, designed to assist bankers but disadvantage working people.

Indeed, during the ratification of the Lisbon Treaty he was quoted as saying that people do "not want to live in a European empire of the 21st century". This is hardly the rhetoric of an ardent would-be-Remainer.

During the 2016 EU Referendum Campaign, to the constant consternation of organisers of the faltering Remain campaign, he repeatedly cancelled scheduled campaign appointments – as he obviously didn't really believe in what he was being asked to do.

A more competent Labour leader would have made mincemeat of Theresa May's hopelessly divided Government in Parliamentary debates but Corbyn's maladroit tactics (such as calling a Vote of Confidence immediately after Meaningful Vote One, which only served to reunify the Tory benches) materially contributed to the chaos in Parliament throughout much of 2019.

In the subsequent General Election, Labour's European policy was so confusing that even many of its spokespersons were unable to clearly articulate it, in contrast to Boris' very simple mantra of 'Get Brexit Done!' In the end, perhaps Jeremy Corbyn's greatest contribution to the cause of Euroscepticism was to fail to turn up in 2016 but to then turn up quite a lot in 2019 instead.

The 1922 Committee finally loses patience

With the entire Conservative Party, the Cabinet, Ministers, MPs and Voluntary Party Members now in turmoil at Theresa May's obstinate adherence to the Withdrawal Agreement, despite it having failed to pass the House of Commons on three separate occasions, the "men in grey suits" finally began to make their move.

After several meetings of the 1922 Committee Executive, which had now become effectively divided into 'Pro' and 'Anti' May factions, chaired by Sir Graham Brady as referee, the '22 Executive began to discuss the possibility of amending the rules, so as to permit a further vote of No Confidence in Theresa May, despite the 'One Year Rule'. This whole internal debate was given added impetus on 13th April, when an article appeared in the *Daily Telegraph,* authored by Lord Archie Hamilton and Lord Michael Spicer, two distinguished former Chairmen of the 1922 Committee, arguing that the Executive could indeed alter the rules, if they believed it were in the best interests of the Conservative Party, to do so.[298] This article, which provoked a lot of comment among the Parliamentary Party, also led to considerable consternation among the PM's inner circle in No 10, who had blithely assumed that she was safe from another immediate challenge, under the "one year rule".

Theresa May's announcement that she now intended to attempt another Meaningful Vote – MV4 – over the Withdrawal Agreement in June helped to swing the balance of opinion within the Executive, some of whom were also mindful that the PM now faced a Vote of No Confidence by the Voluntary Party on 15th June and wanted MPs to be seen to remain ahead of events.[299] On 16th May, the 1922 Executive met the Prime Minister in her House of Commons office, and despite her pleas to be given a little more time to try and get the Withdrawal Agreement through, they effectively told her "that the game was up".[300] Even despite this, however, the Prime Minister attempted to limp on.

Labour withdraws from the talks

On the 17th May, Jeremy Corbyn wrote to Theresa May, formally ending Labour's participation on the talks on the Withdrawal Agreement. While this was greeted with delight across many sections of the Conservative Party, for Theresa May it was a crushing blow. Forming a voting alliance with Labour in the Commons in order to overcome the opposition of the ERG, had been in many ways May's last hope of getting the Withdrawal Agreement, which she still remorselessly clung on to, through the House. She was now rapidly running out of options and members of her Cabinet were now beginning to openly question her ability to survive for very much longer.

On the 21st May, in a desperate attempt to maintain some forward momentum, the Prime Minister published a "10-point offer" in order to try and revive support for her beleaguered Withdrawal Agreement. However, in order to try and win Remainer votes and to prop up support from Europhiles from within her Cabinet, this plan also contained a suggestion of holding a formal vote in the Commons on whether or not to have a second Referendum on whether to approve the Withdrawal Agreement. For many Conservative's this was the absolute final straw and indeed Andrea Leadsom, the Leader of the House of Commons, resigned from the Cabinet the following day, which was in itself the eve of the European elections. By now it was apparent to all but the most avidly pro-May observers, that checkmate for Theresa May's Premiership was barely days away.

On the 23rd May, given that we had not left the European Union as originally scheduled on 29th March, in accordance with EU law (which we were still bound by) the United Kingdom then took part in the 2019 European Elections. However, whilst Britain traditionally votes on a Thursday, much of the continent votes at the weekend, including in some cases on Sunday and so the British results were, as usual, held over so that they could be announced alongside all of the other EU nations, on the Sunday night.

Unlike the Local Government elections several weeks earlier, Nigel Farage's Brexit Party had been very actively campaigning in these European elections. They were roundly condemning Theresa May for her Withdrawal Agreement and the failure to Leave the European Union on time and arguing that only by voting for the Brexit Party, could the people of the United Kingdom uphold the spirit of the 2016 Referendum and eventually Leave the EU. The official Conservative campaign was a shambles, including an appallingly organised press conference in Bristol in the run up to Polling Day.[301] By the evening of the 23rd May, Theresa May had finally realised that the game really was up, and she began preparing a resignation speech for the following day, Friday 24th May.

Theresa May resigns

Having spoken to some of her closest Cabinet confidents that morning, around lunchtime Theresa May emerged into the sunlight outside Downing Street to deliver her resignation speech. In front of a large bank of cameras, she told the waiting world:

"I negotiated the terms of our exit and a new relationship with our closest neighbours that protects jobs, our security and our Union. I have done everything I can to convince MPs to back that Deal. Sadly, I have not been able to do so. I tried three times…But, it is now clear to me that it is in the best interests of the country for a new Prime Minister to lead that effort. So, I am today announcing that I will resign as the Leader of the Conservative and Unionist Party on Friday 7th June, so that a successor can be chosen".

As her voice began to falter, she then went on to conclude as follows:

"I will shortly leave the job that it has been the honour of my life to hold – the second female Prime Minister but certainly not the last. I will do so with no ill will but with enormous and endearing gratitude to have had the opportunity to serve the country I love".[302]

And so, Theresa May's role as Premier effectively came to an end. Whilst watching the broadcast, I did feel some sympathy for her, it must in fairness have been an incredibly difficult thing to do. She delivered her speech with dignity and no one could fault her for becoming slightly emotional at the end. Nevertheless, she sometimes conveyed the impression, whether rightly or wrongly, that in seeking to deliver Brexit, her heart never really seemed to be in it. She had voted Remain rather than Leave and often appeared to regard the Brexit process as more of a damage limitation exercise, than an exciting opportunity.

As Prime Minister, Theresa May stuck doggedly to her version of the Withdrawal Agreement, even after it had suffered the largest defeat, by 230 votes, in Parliamentary history. It was following this defeat, that she missed the greatest opportunity to compromise with her own backbenchers, when she effectively rejected the Malthouse Compromise and the related Brady Amendment, of late January 2019.

Almost three years on, I cannot be a hypocrite and say that I believed she was a great Prime Minister (otherwise why did I support a Vote of No Confidence in her Leadership?). However, I do believe that she acted in good faith as she saw it and that she was personally sincere in what she was trying to achieve – even though I passionately disagreed with the deal that she was advocating, for all the reasons outlined above.

Rory

Rory Boden began working for me in early 2019, right in the midst of the Battle for Brexit. I had recruited him from the upmarket estate agents, Knight Frank, due to his knowledge of social media, as I wanted to improve my social media presence and communications with my constituents in the age of Facebook.

Rory went to Bradfield, a public school in Berkshire and, like me, he subsequently served in the Officers Training Corps (OTC) at university, although in his case at Exeter (who were always our great rivals when I was at Bristol). Despite this chequered history, I offered him the job and on his first morning at work, I greeted him with the words, "Hi Rory, good to have you on the team. I'm live on Sky down at Millbank in about twenty minutes, grab your notebook and follow me!"

As well as being media savvy, Rory is also a very competent researcher, for instance all the detailed work he undertook in assisting me to compile the "Stick or Twist" report for the Prime Minister regarding the challenges involved in retaining personnel, particularly skilled personnel, in HM Armed Forces. Moreover, Rory drafts a good briefing note, even under time pressure.

He also, incidentally, owns a family pet, a ram, named "Boris", which apparently has something of an amorous trait.

Before he came to work for me, I remember saying to Rory: "I promise you only one thing, you'll never be bored working on this team!" As we were being mobbed walking across Parliament Square on 29th March, a few hours after the Government had been defeated over Meaningful Vote Three, I turned to him and asked, "Are you bored yet?" – to which he kindly responded he was not.

Rory Boden is an excellent researcher and I suspect that he will eventually go on to much bigger and better things, in either Westminster or Whitehall.

Chapter 15: Boris to the Rescue?

Although Theresa May had announced her decision to resign on Friday 24th May, the day after the polls closed in the UK, on Sunday the 26th, the results of the European Elections were made public. Many pundits (and indeed in private, many Conservative MPs) had been expecting the Conservative Party to do rather badly but even so, the results were even more shocking than many of us had feared.

Results of the 2019 European Elections in Britain

	Seats Won	Vote Share
Brexit Party	29	31.6%
Liberal Democrats	16	20.3%
Labour Party	10	14.1%
Green Party	7	12.1%
Conservative Party	4	9.1%
SNP	3	3.6%
Plaid Cymru	1	1%
Change UK	0	3.4%
UKIP	0	3.3%
Turnout		67.3%

Basically, the Brexit Party had romped it and had won in every region in England outside London. Conversely, the Conservatives, still nominally under Theresa May's Leadership when the votes were cast on the Thursday, came fifth, winning only four seats in the European Parliament and achieving a vote share of 9.1%, the Party's worst result *ever* in a national election, since it had been created. Even in the disastrous 1997 General Election, the Conservatives had still won over 30% of the total vote.[303]

Unsurprisingly, Nigel Farage was jubilant and predicted further success for the Brexit Party, particularly if the United Kingdom were continually frustrated from Leaving the European Union.

On the Sunday evening I was invited to be a guest on the BBC's European Election Results programme at New Broadcasting House and so had an opportunity to comment on the disaster. I said that the results showed that the ordinary people of the United Kingdom, outside of the M25 at least, still clearly wanted to Leave the European Union and that determination was obviously reflected in the clear success of the Brexit Party. I also said that we would need to learn lessons from such a heavy defeat, not least that it meant we would have to redouble our efforts to Leave the EU and to honour the spirit of the 2016 Referendum.[304]

In addition, I also won a bet. My old friend, Joe, who like me is a great Monty Python fan, had recently been discussing with me a well-known Monty Python "Election Night" sketch, based on the results night in a mythical national election, which featured the "Slightly Silly Party", one of whose candidates, Kevin Philips Bong, famously secures no votes at all at the polls.[305] The point of the sketch is to take the mick out of the hapless Politician's attempt to put a positive gloss on an absolutely disastrous result, as indeed were some people from CCHQ that night. Joe had promised me an absolutely slap-up meal in any restaurant of my choice if I could somehow get the Slightly Silly Party and Kevin Philips Bong into one of my answers. I obliged him by describing Change UK as "the Slightly Silly Party in this election" and characterising their nominal Leader, as akin to "Kevin Philips Bong, the guy who secured no votes at all".

About 10 seconds after I said it, the phone on the desk in front of me started buzzing repeatedly as Joe sent me a set of texts, the gist of which was: "I cannot believe that you just said that!". I remember that Huw Edwards, who is of a similar age to me, was grinning broadly when I referred to the sketch (which he obviously recognised) whereas Laura Kuenssberg, sitting opposite me in the studio and clearly far too young to have been a Monty Python fan, looked at my quizzically, as if I had somehow gone mad. Anyhow, I won the bet!

To make matters more interesting, following my stint in the TV studio, I was invited to another part of the building to give a further interview on Radio 4, and I found myself in the lift with Jo Swinson, who at that time was running for the Leadership of the Liberal Democrats, against her rival, Ed Davey MP. I've known both of them for some years, but I confided to Jo in the privacy of the lift that if it were down to me, I would vote for her, to which she reacted in sheer horror: "For God's sake Mark, please don't tell anybody that prior to the election – it'll absolutely do for me among the Lib Dems if anybody thinks I've got support from the ERG!". Of course, Jo did go on to win the Leadership of the Liberal Democrats, although things unfortunately did not work out quite so well for her after that.

The Tory Leadership Contest

The Liberal Democrats were not the only Party now facing a Leadership election contest. Politics abhors a vacuum and even before Theresa May had resigned a number of prominent big beasts in the Conservative Party were making it known to the media that they intended to run. Contests like this have a momentum all of their own, and one of the reasons that Theresa May ultimately lost the support of so many members of her Cabinet, is that quite a number of them around the table fancied a crack at the top job themselves, such is the nature of politics.

The rules had remained essentially the same as they have been for many years, whereby Conservative MPs would use a series of eliminatory ballots, knocking out those candidates with the fewest votes, until they finally whittled it down to two contestants, who would then be voted upon by the Voluntary Members of the Conservative Party, in a postal ballot. Of course, Theresa May had never had to undergo this last stage of the ordeal because her rival, Andrea Leadsom, had effectively imploded in the early stages of the final part of the campaign, which had led to Theresa May effectively undergoing a "Coronation" to become the undisputed Leader of the Party.

Perhaps because of this and with one eye to our Party's disastrous showing in the European elections, many MPs were determined to think very carefully indeed before casting their votes in the Leadership election this time around. Moreover, there seemed to be a strong determination, right across the Party, that whatever happened, this time around we would end up with two candidates in the final who would then campaign against each other for several weeks before the Voluntary Party finally made their decision. With around 150,000 Members in the Conservative Party at that time, just over 300 Tory MPs therefore had the vitally important role of whittling it down to the final two contenders to become "first among equals".

A very wide field

To begin with the number of contenders for the crown was in double figures. Among the more well known, there was obviously going to be a battle on the right of the Party between former Foreign Secretary (Boris Johnson) and former DEXEU Secretary (Dominic Raab) to garner, in particular, Brexiteer support. Other prominent candidates who were running included Michael Gove (the DEFRA Secretary); Andrea Leadsom (the former Leader of the House); Jeremy Hunt (the Foreign Secretary), Sajid Javid (the Home Secretary), Matt Hancock (the Health Secretary) and Rory Stewart (the rather idiosyncratic Department for International Development Secretary) – the last three of whom had all voted Remain in the 2016 General Election. Behind these, were what might be termed a second tier of candidates, including Mark Harper (a well-respected former Chief Whip); Kit Malthouse (the Policing Minister and the man who had helped to broker the Malthouse compromise); James Cleverly (the Deputy Party Chairman, with particular responsibility for youth); Esther McVey (the former DWP Secretary and partner of prominent Eurosceptic, Philip Davies MP) and also Sam Gyimah (the former Universities Minister and arch-Remainer).[306]

The first ballot of Conservative MPs was fixed for around three weeks hence, on Thursday 13th June with subsequent ballots on Tuesday 18th and Wednesday 19th and further rounds on Thursday 30th June, if required.

This rather compressed timetable was specifically designed in order to allow the final two candidates to campaign around the country, prior to a postal ballot and the result being announced in advance of the Parliamentary summer recess in late July. Normally, the Chairman of the 1922 Committee, Sir Graham Brady, would have acted as the Returning Officer for the Leadership election but given that he had also decided he might want to run, he had "recused himself" from the role and so his two Vice Chairmen on the Executive, Dame Cheryl Gillan and Charles (now Sir Charles) Walker, had been appointed "Joint Returning Officers" for the duration of the election. (This is slightly ironic as, in the end, Sir Graham Brady decided not to run after all).

Boris' viva with the ERG

Amidst all the jockeying for position in the run up to the first ballot, a key contest was on the right of the Party between Boris Johnson and Dominic Raab. Both Brexiteers and both of whom had resigned over Theresa May's mishandling of Brexit, they were both vying for the public support of the European Research Group, not just because they wanted their votes to get them through to the final round but also because they knew that having the ERG's imprimatur would be very important with the wider membership of the Voluntary Party, the bulk of whom had voted Leave during the 2016 Referendum. This rivalry resulted in both Boris and Dominic coming for a meeting with the senior members of the ERG on the 4th June, a little over a week before the first ballot of MPs was due to take place.

The "job interview" took place in Westminster and the top table of the ERG were present to do the interviewing. Those in the room that day included Jacob as Chairman of the ERG, Steve as his Deputy, myself as in effect the senior Vice Chairman and de-facto Chief Whip, Iain Duncan Smith, Sir Bill Cash, Sir Bernard Jenkin, Priti Patel, John Redwood, David Jones and Owen Paterson, plus several others. We had agreed in advance a number of issues on which we wanted to press both candidates but the absolutely critical one was which of the two was most likely to honour the spirit of the European Referendum and take us out of the European Union, once and for all. It might have been expected prior to the meeting that Dom Raab, an accomplished lawyer, would be very much across the detail and that Boris, famed for his showmanship would perhaps be less so – but on the day at least, the reverse was true.

When Boris came in, he was all business right from the start and explained to the ERG Leadership that he regarded the European Election results and the rise of the Brexit Party as an existential threat to the Conservative Party. In his view, unless we were able to deal with this and provide a realistic plan for exiting the European Union, within a few months, or even sooner, the Conservative Party might effectively cease to exist. It would be fair to say that this powerful opening gambit certainly secured our attention, and this was followed by a lively question and answer session, concerning exactly what Boris had in mind.

It transpired that his plan was essentially to seek to renegotiate the Withdrawal Agreement, including to get rid of the Backstop, but if this were not possible, to Leave with No Deal on the 31st October. In saying this, Boris' plan was not a million miles different from the original Malthouse Compromise, save with a much tighter timescale than Malthouse B. He explained several times that under no circumstances could he contemplate any further extension of Article 50, given its implications for the future survival of the Party. After almost an hour of what he described as "my viva" (an Oxford term for a detailed oral examination) he made way for Dominic Raab.[307]

Dom also put in a confident performance but was not so definite about his determination to Leave the EU on the 31st October. Moreover, he made the serious tactical mistake of getting into a debate on a point of European law with Sir Bill Cash, which any of us who have worked alongside Bill for many years, would know was akin to suicide. If you are going to try and catch Bill Cash out on a point of EU law you would have to get up very early in the morning indeed, in fact, to continue the metaphor, there would be no point in going to bed the night before.

At the end of the exercise, most of us were leaning towards Boris but knowing full well that he had something of a reputation for telling people what they wanted to hear, we decided that rather than take a decision there and then, we would ask Boris to come back the following day, so that we could put further questions to him. At first, Boris' team were rather reluctant for him to undergo a "second viva" but nevertheless, when we made it known that we were not yet convinced, and some people were still considering voting for Dominic Raab instead, resistance weakened, and Boris found himself back in Westminster at around

3:00pm the following afternoon. A series of highly detailed questions then ensued on the specifics of Boris' plan for Leaving the EU.

Given the number of times we felt that we had been duped by Theresa May's team at No 10, there was perhaps understandably a determination within the ERG leadership to get as clear a commitment as possible from the man who might become our next Prime Minister. Towards the end of the meeting, I deliberately asked Boris the following question: "Boris, are you telling all of the good people in this room, that if you become Prime Minister, we will Leave the European Union on the 31st October, come hell or high water?". It suddenly fell silent for a moment and a number of people leant forward, anxious to hear Boris' answer. In fairness, he looked me right in the eye: "Mark, that's exactly what I'm saying, because if we don't, this Party will soon cease to exist!". With hindsight, I think that was probably the thing that clinched it and shortly after Boris departed, we had a collective discussion and decided that we would endorse him for the Leadership of the Conservative Party.

Even so, the ERG's decision was not taken entirely without reservations. Some of us were concerned about Boris' perceived lack of attention to detail (although, to be fair, he had done well on EU detail in the two interviews) whilst others were worried about his infamously colourful private life – at least up to that point.

I discovered sometime afterwards that Boris had been very effectively "coached" for his two interviews with the ERG by IDS, who had already decided to support him, as the best person to lead us out of the EU. After an initial rehearsal had not gone well, IDS apparently said to him: "You are going to need much better answers than that if you are going to get Baker and Francois to support you Boris, let alone Bill Cash!".[308]

In the end, the Leadership of the ERG came to a collective conclusion and took a clear-eyed and deliberate decision to "Back Boris", as the candidate best placed to ensure that we left the European Union at last. After three years of frustration and eventual chaos under Theresa May, the ERG's overwhelming motivation was to support a future Prime Minister who was truly committed to our Leaving the EU – and given the available options, that meant Boris Johnson.

We realised that Boris was obviously looking to maximise his votes from across the Conservative Backbenches and so we decided not to officially endorse him "as the ERG's Candidate" – as that might well frighten off other potential voters from the pro-European wing of the Party. Instead, we agreed that we would come out one by one in his support, relying on the fact that as senior members of the ERG, one after another, publicly endorsed his candidacy, others in Parliament and the media (and indeed in the Voluntary Party) would soon get the message. In the end, that is exactly what we did. Tactically this also had the added advantage of providing multiple, rolling media hits in support of Boris' campaign, rather than just one.

The first ballot – 13th June 2019

By now Boris' campaign team was being guided by a number of prominent MPs, including Gavin Williamson (the experienced former Chief Whip) as his Campaign Manager, aided by Connor Burns, who had served as his PPS at the Foreign Office and then continued to serve effectively in that role when Boris returned to the Backbenches.

Another key member of the campaign was Grant Shapps, who came up with the most incredible database of Conservative Backbenchers and how they were likely to vote – which was in some ways even more impressive than Steve's equivalent for the Buddies and the Meaningful Votes. Having seen it, I subsequently described it to Grant as "the mother of all spreadsheets", which he said he took as a compliment "coming from the ERG's Chief Whip".

In addition, the ERG having effectively decided to vote for Boris, Iain Duncan Smith was brought onboard as the campaign Chairman, wherein he brought his experience both as an Army Officer and as a former Leader of the Party, to help to bring some order and discipline, to what, up to that point, had been a slightly fractious campaign.

On the 13th June, the results of the first ballot were as follows:

Name	Votes
Boris Johnson	114
Jeremy Hunt	43
Michael Gove	37
Dominic Raab	27
Sajid Javid	23
Matt Hancock	20
Rory Stewart	19
Andrea Leadsom (Eliminated)	11
Mark Harper (Eliminated)	10
Esther McVey (Eliminated)	9

n.b. 17 votes were required to progress to the next round

Following this, as is the way in such contests, a number of the second rank contenders, realising that they effectively had no chance of winning the prize, rapidly withdrew (in some cases having made deals with the remaining candidates in return for their support).

When the second ballot took place on Tuesday 18th June, the field was reduced further. The results that day were as follows:

Name	Votes
Boris Johnson	126
Jeremy Hunt	46
Michael Gove	41
Rory Stewart	37
Sajid Javid	33
Dominic Raab (Eliminated)	30

n.b. fewer than 33 votes eliminated

The ERG reunites

Having to effectively pick sides in the Leadership campaign turned out to be quite a reunifying influence on the ERG, which had been deeply split in the hothouse atmosphere leading up to Meaningful Vote Three. Whilst everybody had remained on speaking terms throughout, there was, nevertheless, something of a distinction between those who had voted with the Government and the 28 "Spartans" who had held out.

In April some of the Spartans began meeting unilaterally in Westminster, but by May, I had had dinner with Jacob and the Five Families conference calls on Sunday nights had recommenced. The fact that nearly all of the upper echelons of the ERG were now backing Boris for the Leadership, meant that the divisions of late March were fairly quickly put aside, as the mission now became to make sure Boris was elected, in order to then honour his promise of taking us out of the European Union at Halloween.

The final: Boris Vs Jeremy

As the contest wore on and the various campaign teams vied for the affections of wavering MPs (including those prepared to publicly "switch sides", sometimes for perceived personal advantage, whether real or just imagined) ballots took place in Committee Room 14, with the Joint Returning Officers then announcing the results each time.

The results of the third ballot were:

Name	Votes
Boris Johnson	143
Jeremy Hunt	54
Michael Gove	51
Sajid Javid	38
Rory Stewart (Eliminated)	27

n.b. last place candidate eliminated henceforth

On the 20th June, there were two final ballots, in the fourth ballot, the Remaining four candidates scored as follows:

Name	Votes
Boris Johnson	157
Michael Gove	61
Jeremy Hunt	59
Sajid Javid (Eliminated)	34

Eventually, on the afternoon of the 20th June, the fifth and final Parliamentary ballot took place:

Name	Votes
Boris Johnson	160
Jeremy Hunt	77
Michael Gove (Eliminated)	75

Which meant that the third placed Michael Gove had been eliminated and Boris Johnson was now to take on Jeremy Hunt in the final. Gove, who was understandably disappointed, had lost out to Jeremy Hunt by just two votes (whereas, in 2001, IDS had reached the final two over Michael Portillo, by literally a single vote). Such is sometimes the very narrow margin in Parliamentary contests of this type. In many ways, however, this now gave Party members a clear choice. Boris had been a key member of the Vote Leave campaign and had resigned from the Cabinet on principle after Chequers, whereas Jeremy Hunt had been a member of the Remain campaign, whilst serving as Health Secretary in David Cameron's Cabinet and had replaced Boris as May's Foreign Secretary, after the former's post Chequers resignation. There was no deep animosity between the two men (although on one occasion Jeremy Hunt did say "Being Prime Minister is about telling people what they need to hear, not just what they want to hear", which apparently went down badly in Boris' camp.[309]

As a Boris supporter but not a member of his inner campaign team, I nevertheless found myself doing a number of media appearances, in support of his campaign. One such was when I appeared on the James Whale show, alongside Tory donor, Charlie Mullins, who had enjoyed a rags to riches story, starting out as a self-employed plumber and eventually founding the empire which today is known as "Pimlico Plumbers", and which has made him a highly-successful multi-millionaire.

Charlie had voted Remain in the 2016 European Referendum but was also inclined to be a Boris supporter and we both found ourselves in *Talk Radio's* brand-new studios at 1 New London Bridge Street (now co-located in the same building with the staff of *The Times* and *The Sun*) where we were able to debate the forthcoming Leadership campaign. Sam Gyimah MP, a Europhile and a Jeremy Hunt supporter was later invited to dial into the studio, in order to provide some balance from the Hunt camp.

These arrangements all seemed reasonable but there was a very funny moment when James Whale explained that Charlie was a Boris supporter but asked him nevertheless what he thought about Jeremy Hunt. Charlie who was sitting next to me, simply replied: "Who's he?", at which point, I burst out laughing and James called me: "A very naughty man". Nevertheless, Charlie genuinely wasn't aware at that stage that Jeremy Hunt was the other contender for the Leadership – such was the power of Boris' image.[310]

It then got even more interesting when Sam Gyimah joined the programme. There had been rumours circulating for some time at Westminster that Gyimah, who also had resigned from Theresa May's Government, was contemplating defecting to the Liberal Democrats. As the interview became more barbative, I challenged Sam, live on air, to deny the rumour that he was considering defecting to the Liberal Democrats. He was absolutely furious and accused me of all sorts, saying that, in terms, he had always been a Conservative and would never contemplate defecting to the Liberal Democrats – something which he subsequently did only several weeks later. He then attempted to switch seats as well at the General Election – and was slaughtered.[311]

So, what had originally looked like a relatively straight forward interview turned into quite an exciting evening, not least because of Gyimah's exploding on air (which was then replayed quite a lot on Twitter in the next 48 hours).

I attended both the Eastern Regional Hustings of Conservative Party Members near Maldon (where Priti Patel was among the guests) and also the final London

Regional Hustings at the Excel Centre in London, which was attended by several thousand Party Members, and which, at one point, looked as it if could have taken place at the Conservative Party Conference itself. In fairness, both candidates put in good appearances at each of these events and most Party Members I spoke to seemed satisfied that the MPs had presented them with two credible candidates – and thus a genuine contest.

The public meeting in Rayleigh

Whilst this was all going on, at the suggestion of my previous Constituency Association Chairman and now Deputy Chairman (Political), Hilton Brown, I had agreed to do a public meeting in Rayleigh, so that I could explain to my constituents face to face, why I had fought so hard against the Withdrawal Agreement. In order to facilitate this, we booked the Main Hall at FitzWimarc Secondary School on the Hockley Road and put round a number of flyers and something on Facebook, inviting constituents, whatever their political views, to come along and hear from their Member of Parliament why he had fought so hard against Theresa May's Deal.

On the evening, we laid out around 200 chairs but by the time the meeting began, they had virtually all been taken, plus there were a healthy number of people standing around the sides of the room and at the back as well. I proceeded to speak for about half an hour, quoting directly from sections of my now very well-thumbed copy of the Withdrawal Agreement in order to try and explain, in plain English, to my constituents what the Withdrawal Agreement really meant.

I remember at one point, when I started reading out the powers of the Joint Committee, there were literally gasps in the audience and people started to shout out things like, "How could they do this?", and "What the hell did they think they were playing at?". I then proceeded to take questions from the floor for around an hour, from Brexiteers and Remainers alike and did my best to answer all of them.

In summing up, I told my constituents that night that the Withdrawal Agreement was effectively a surrender document and, as their MP, I would never walk through the Lobby of the House of Commons, to surrender my country to anybody – which was greeted at the end of my speech with a partial standing ovation. It was Hilton who persuaded me to do this, because he felt on principle that it was important that constituents had a chance to come along and hear directly from their MP about all this and in the end the evening turned out to be a considerable success.[312]

Boris Wins! (with ERG support)

After several weeks of active campaigning for the votes of Tory Party Members, on 23rd July Conservative MPs were invited to cross Parliament Square to the Queen Elizabeth II Conference Centre, in order to hear the final results of the Conservative Leadership ballot. To a packed hall, the Joint Returning Officers, Dame Cheryl Gillan and Charlie Walker, announced that the results cast had been as follows:

Results of the Conservative Party Leadership Election, July 2019

Boris Johnson	92,153	66%
Jeremy Hunt	46,956	34%
Turnout		87.4%

This represented an emphatic victory for Boris, by a majority of 2-1, with an extremely high turnout among the 160,000 or so eligible Tory Party Members, of heading on for 90%.

In what *The Guardian* of all newspapers subsequently described as a "characteristically light-hearted acceptance speech",[313] Boris conceded that even some of his supporters might "wonder quite what they have done". Nevertheless, such was the margin of victory, that no one could complain that Boris had not been very clearly chosen by the Party Members to lead them and to become Prime Minister. Moreover, even among Brexiteers, many MPs were happy to admit that Jeremy Hunt had fought quite a good campaign, in a positive spirit and that the Party Members had thus been given a genuine choice as a result. Nevertheless, in the end, the Leaver beat the Remainer hands down.

With the drama of the election campaign over, the House of Commons then rose for the summer recess on the 25th July, allowing everyone a bit of a break before the House was due to return in early September. This also gave the newly elected Leader of the Conservative Party, who was rapidly invited by Her Majesty The Queen to become Prime Minister and form a new Government, albeit still a minority one, an opportunity to take stock and to appoint members to his new Cabinet.

Although Boris undoubtedly drew support from right across the Conservative Party, given the history of the previous three years, Europe and the future of Brexit was indisputably a defining issue during the campaign and the support of the ERG, in effectively helping to make Boris the "Leave candidate" rather than Dominic Raab, and then supporting him around the country was fundamental to his success. Despite this, when Boris formed his Cabinet, very few members of the ERG were in it.

There are probably a variety of reasons for this, but part of it was undoubtedly that some of the key staffers who Boris took with him into No 10, whilst Leavers, (rather than the Remainers that they by and large replaced), were nevertheless, not exactly long-term fans of the ERG. Indeed, some of his closest staff seemed to believe that the ERG were "too much of a heady brew" and that having safely won the Leadership, Boris needed to gently distance himself from us.

Whatever the reasoning, given that the Government was still in a minority and continued to rely on DUP support to achieve a majority in the House of Commons, it was clear that any solution that Boris came up with to the Brexit conundrum was going to require the support of the ERG if he was going to have any hope of finally getting it through the House of Commons.

Similarly, the Remainers (who still had sufficient votes to narrowly win Divisions in the Commons), wasted little time in seeking to prevent any attempt by the new Prime Minister to adhere to his 31st October deadline.

The Remainer die-hards in the Commons

When David Cameron called the 2016 EU Referendum, all sides agreed to respect the result, whatever it might be. If you're a cynic, this may be because both sides genuinely believed that they were going to win but, in any event, over 80% of MPs in the House of Commons (certainly including Conservative and Labour MPs) had been elected in 2017 on their Party Manifesto's which promised to respect the Referendum result. Nevertheless, despite this, many MPs were in their heart of hearts, die hard Remainers and voted again and again, at every practical opportunity to frustrate Brexit. Unfortunately, this included a relatively small number of Conservative MPs but who, when combined with the other Parties in the House, including Labour, Liberal, SNP, TIG, and a few others were often narrowly able to out vote the remainder of the Conservative Party and the DUP. (Remember, that the Cooper/Boles/Letwin Bill only got through in the end by one vote). In terms of Parliamentary arithmetic in mid-2019, this "Remain Coalition", if they turned out in full force, very narrowly had the edge.

We had already spent literally months, night after night, listening to one pro-Remain MP after the other professing their earnest desire to respect the result of the 2016 Referendum – and then voting precisely the opposite way. Indeed, many of them stuck to a mantra of "I will not allow us to crash out with No Deal".

This was merely code, which translated really meant: "I will vote any way I can to stop us Leaving the European Union, but because of the Referendum result, I cannot say so openly, so I will use preventing No Deal as cover for that instead".

We thus went through this seemingly endless rigmarole of Remainer MPs saying again and again that they intended to respect the Referendum but voting the other way; the hypocrisy of all of this was nauseating. By the Autumn of 2019, it is probably fair to say that the public had well and truly seen through this behaviour and there was growing public frustration at the failure to deliver Brexit (as had already been clearly evidenced by the runaway victory of the Brexit Party in the European Elections, on an unusually high turnout back in late May).

Steve Bray – "The Twat in the Hat"

Steve Bray, a former second-hand coin dealer, achieved national prominence during the Battle for Brexit, principally by standing behind the TV platforms on College Green, Westminster and bellowing at the top of his admittedly very loud voice, "Stop Brexit!" in the background of every Brexit-related interview he could discover in progress. For extra effect, Steve would often brandish a very large EU flag, accompanied by a blue top-hat, emblazoned with 12 EU Gold stars.

Steve argued that in doing so, he was exercising his democratic right to contribute to the public debate over Brexit. However, it could also be argued that he was seeking to do precisely the opposite, by attempting to interrupt and shout down or "cancel" any Brexiteer who dared to contradict his ultra-Remain viewpoint.

When he had attempted to do this to me just once too often, I responded by nicknaming him "the Twat in the Hat". Steve spent much of this period living in a spacious, multi-million-pound townhouse in Cowley Street, just off College Green, which he claimed was paid for by "crowdfunding" but which some suspect was subsidised, at least in part, by some very wealthy Remainers.

In any event, during the 2019 General Election, Steve Bray finally put his convictions and belief in democracy to the acid test and stood as a Parliamentary candidate for the Euro-Federalist Lib Dems in the Welsh Constituency of Cynon Valley – where he proceeded to come sixth and lost his deposit.

Nevertheless, despite his electoral humiliation he can still be seen in and around Westminster, for instance, carrying a large Red Flag and playing the old Soviet national anthem on loudspeaker – thus making him "Comrade Twat".

For the record, his result was as follows:

Result in the Cynon Valley Constituency – December 2019 General Election

Name	Party	Votes	%
Ann Clwyd	Labour	19,404	61
Pauline Church	Conservative	6,711	22.2
Rebecca Rees-Evan	Brexit Party	3045	10.1
Geraint Benney	Plaid Cymru	2,562	8.5
Andrew Chainey	Cynon Valley	1,322	4.4
Steve Bray	Liberal Democrats	949	3.1
Ian McLean	SDP	114	0.4

The Benn Act (AKA 'The Surrender Act')

In September, the Remainers again took control of the Order Paper in order to pass the European Union (Withdrawal) (No. 6) Bill, partly devised by Hilary Benn, the Labour Europhile Chairman of the DEXEU Select Committee which had the effect of trying to stop us Leaving the European Union at Halloween. The Benn Bill, as it became known, in essence compelled HM Government to write to the European Council to formally request a further extension to Article 50, if a Deal had not been agreed with the EU by the 19th October, i.e. just under a fortnight before we were now due to Leave. The Bill even laid out the exact text of the letter the PM would be forced to write, as a Schedule to the Bill itself.

In reply, and to the great anger of Remainers, the new Prime Minister rapidly christened this the "Surrender Bill", because he argued that it gave away much of the UK's negotiating leverage in seeking to achieve a revised deal with the European Union, that meant that we could genuinely Leave the EU.

Yet again, it was evident that Remainers in the House of Commons, who were now running out of excuses for their blatant behaviour, were nevertheless prepared brazenly to walk through the Division Lobbies to keep the UK in the European Union, night after night. Oliver Letwin put down the Business Motion to facilitate the ramming through of the Bill, which passed by 328 votes to 301, with the support of 21 Europhile Conservative MPs, in defiance of a strong three-line whip.

However, perhaps having learned lessons from the reactions of his predecessor, the new Prime Minister was not prepared to take this important rebellion lying down and to the amazement of many commentators he subsequently withdrew the Conservative Whip from the errant 21 MPs, including former Chancellor Phillip Hammond, former Cabinet Office Minister Oliver Letwin and 19 others.

Amongst other things, this meant that none of these MPs would be allowed to stand as official Conservative Candidates at the next General Election – which was now looking increasingly likely, due to the continuing impasse in the House of Commons.

On 4th September the Benn Bill was again rammed through the House of Commons, much as the Cooper/Boles/Letwin Bill had been before it, passing its Second Reading and Committee stages in a single day. In reply – and having warned in advance that he would do so – the PM then put down a motion calling for an early General Election. This motion was passed by 298 votes to 56 (with Labour courageously abstaining) but, under Cameron's ill-fated Fixed Term Parliament Act 2011, this fell well short of the 2/3 "Super-Majority" needed to bring about a plebiscite. Thus began a stand-off, with the Prime Minister, now with a Commons majority of around minus 30, trying to force Labour into conceding a General Election, with the European issue and the continuing failure to achieve Brexit at its centre.

The Benn Bill flew through its stages in the pro-Remain House of Lords in barely a few days and then achieved Royal Assent on 9th September 2019.

"In the name of God, go!"

Again, Prime Minister Boris Johnson fought back and prorogued Parliament on 9th September 2019, thus bringing to an end the longest Parliamentary session since the Civil War in the 17th Century, when Oliver Cromwell had forcibly dissolved the notorious "Rump Parliament" with the damning description:

"It is high time for me to put an end to your sitting in this place, which you have dishonoured by your contempt of all virtue, and defiled by your practice of every vice; ye are a factious crew, and enemies to all good government; ye are a pack of mercenary wretches, and would like Esau sell your country for a mess of pottage, and like Judas betray your God for a few pieces of money.

Is there a single virtue now remaining amongst you? Is there one vice you do not possess? Ye have no more religion than my horse; gold is your God; which of you have not barter'd your conscience for bribes? Is there a man amongst you that has the least care for the good of the Commonwealth?...

...Ye are grown intolerably odious to the whole nation; you who were deputed here by the people to get grievances redress'd, are yourselves gone! So! Take away that shining bauble there and lock up the doors. In the name of God, go!"[314]

While there may, by now, have been some people in No 10 with some private empathy for what Cromwell had been trying to say about Parliament, there was nevertheless a media firestorm in reaction to Boris' decision to opt for Prorogation. *The Guardian* declared it a "Constitutional Outrage" on its front page.[315]

Remainers across the country were up in arms about what they perceived to be an unconstitutional act, brought about by a Prime Minister apparently determined to get his way at all costs. Conversely, Brexiteers (including most of the ERG) saw this as designed to overcome the by now, blatant attempts by Remainers in Parliament to obstruct Brexit, by whatever procedural or legislative means they could come up with.

This was only exacerbated by rumours that some of the Remainers had, been in private discussions with the European Commission about how to use legislative means to obstruct the new PMs determination to deliver Brexit on 31st October.[316]

"This country will explode"

On the 17th September, I was invited to go back on the BBC's *Daily Politics* show (no Will Self this time) to debate what was likely to happen next. I argued that again and again MPs had voted deliberately to frustrate the will of the people to Leave the European Union, as clearly expressed in the Referendum. When I was challenged on this point, I said: "I think if we don't Leave on the 31st October, this country will explode". That got quite a reaction, not least on Twitter (and even featured in a subsequent Remainer internet meme), but what I was seeking to do was to throw into sharp relief, the actions of those MPs who professed in public to still wanting to Leave the European Union, whilst doing everything they practically could to prevent it.[317]

(Incidentally, after the deadline was subsequently extended, yet again – to 31st January 2020, on 31st October 2019, I received approximately 500 emails wishing me a "Happy No Brexit Day" and/or asking me whether I had personally exploded yet?)

The Gina Miller case

This bitter argument was brought to a head when a pro-Remain businesswoman, Gina Miller (who had originally gone to the Supreme Court back in 2017, to argue that an Act of Parliament was required to trigger Article 50), again filed a legal action, this time arguing that the decision to prorogue Parliament under the circumstances constituted "an unlawful abuse of power".[318]   Given the importance of the issue, the case rapidly fast-tracked to the UK Supreme Court for a decision, with the new Attorney General, Jeremy Wright MP, putting forward the case for the Government.

Despite his best efforts, on 24th September the UK Supreme Court unanimously delivered a verdict against the Government, ruling that: "The decision to advise Her Majesty to Prorogue Parliament was unlawful because it had the effect of frustrating or preventing the ability of Parliament to carry out its Constitutional functions without reasonable justification".

Remainers across the country were cock-a-hoop at this verdict, with Keir Starmer describing it as vindicating "everything we've done last week and I think what I can do and what others need to do is get back to Parliament, see if we can't open those doors and get back in and get Boris Johnson back in Parliament so we can hold him properly to account".[319]

Moreover, Gina Miller, who bought the case, said it: "confirms that we are a nation governed by the rule of law — laws that everyone, even the Prime Minister, are subject to.   This was a breach of the central constitutional principle of Parliamentary Sovereignty to gain political advantage".[320]

Speaker Bercow also welcomed the decision and announced that the Commons would now sit again the following day, which it duly did. When the House sat, John Bercow announced that, following the verdict, the House had been Adjourned since 9th September and not Prorogued.

Within the ERG we were disappointed – but not entirely surprised – by the verdict, although we had little choice but to accept it. Having campaigned for years for the jurisdiction of the UK Courts rather than the European Court of Justice (ECJ) we could hardly now complain about a UK Supreme Court decision we didn't like!

So, we concluded in essence that we would just have to "suck it up" and see what the Prime Minister and Dominic Cummings would do next. At his speech to the Conservative Party Conference in Manchester on 2nd October, the Prime Minister made clear that he was still committed to seeing the UK's exit from the European Union by Halloween, in the following terms:

"We are continuing to chew the super masticated subject of Brexit
When what people want
What Leavers want

What Remainers want

What the whole world wants – is to be calmly and sensibly done with the subject, and to move on

And that is why we are coming out of the EU on October 31st, come what may Conference".[321]

The Evening Standard Awards

It was against this background that on the 3rd October, I attended the *Evening Standard's* Annual Awards Ceremony, held at the Design Museum in Kensington. I had been invited by the Editor, George Osborne, as I was apparently "one of a thousand prominent Londoners" who were to be asked to attend that evening. When I got there, I bumped into George and we exchanged pleasantries before he warned me privately that I might not like what was about to happen. He was absolutely right.

When it came to the Standard's main award for 2019, a group of pro-Remain MPs, who George christened the "Rebel Alliance", traipsed onto the stage to the Star Wars theme before being feted for all that they had been doing to prevent us from "Leaving with No Deal" (i.e. to keep us in the EU). In fairness to George, his Editorial line on this had always been consistent but, nevertheless, I was pretty angry by what I saw going on in front of me.

For those unfamiliar with the layout of the Design Museum, it has a very large central Atrium, with a number of balconies above it and I was standing on the top floor, admittedly drinking a glass of George's champagne, looking down beneath me at what I perceived to be "Remain at play". Almost by definition, the vast majority of people in the museum that night were indeed the fabled London "metropolitan elite", and I remember thinking "what have any of you people down there got in common with someone who lives in Darlington or Barnsley or Kings Lynn?"

I thought this is basically a thousand people talking to themselves, in their own little Remain bubble, totally cut off from the world outside the M25. I sent George a text, thanking him for the drink but telling him that I had to go as I had another engagement – which was not strictly true – but I figured it was more diplomatic to say that, than what I was really thinking.

Boris

Alexander Boris de Pfeffel Johnson, is, in many ways, one of the most extraordinary politicians of our age. Like one of his great heroes, Winston Churchill (another being Pericles of Athens) he has been a journalist and author, as well as being in and out of Parliament and then back in again – in this case after two terms as the Mayor of London, for good measure.

A man with a colourful private life, he now has two ex-wives, as well as a string of six children, the last of whom, Wilfred, was only born in 2020 when Boris was already in his mid-fifties. In the same year – 2020 – he almost died of the Covid-19 virus, having finally achieved his burning ambition of one day becoming Prime Minister, only a few months previously. In 2021 he married his fiancé, Carrie Symonds, whilst leading the country through a completely unforeseen worldwide pandemic, in Covid-19, from which he almost died himself.

Our paths have crossed a number of times since I beat him to become the Conservative Candidate in Rayleigh in 2000. His naturally optimistic/glass half-full nature has carried him through a number of political scrapes and may well yet do so again. Love him or hate him, Boris is undoubtedly a political "Rockstar" and can barely go anywhere in this country without someone asking for a selfie with him. In truth, there are very few other Members of the House of Commons who could say that.

Despite his highly complex personality, it was his absolute determination to finally take Britain out of the EU that won him the almost unanimous backing of the ERG during the 2019 Tory Leadership contest, which in turn, was important in securing the support of the predominantly Eurosceptic Voluntary Party in the final Leadership postal ballot in July 2019.

His remarkable 2019 General Election victory was largely based on his very clear commitment to "Get Brexit Done" – which he has consistently stuck to since entering No 10 Downing Street. In that sense at least, the ERG undoubtedly backed the right horse in 2019.

What the future still holds for this virtually unique and extremely capable politician is of course impossible to say. Probably the only safe prediction to make is that, knowing Boris, it will not be boring.

Deputy Chairman of the ERG

Alongside Priti Patel as Home Secretary, another exception to the dearth of ERG appointments in Boris' new Cabinet, was Jacob Rees-Mogg, who Boris appointed as Leader of the House of Commons on the 24th July. Jacob has always had a deep love of the House of Commons and its traditions so as one of my colleagues said to me: "He'll be a very round peg in a round hole", or as another put it to me slightly more bluntly, "He'll be as happy as a pig in muck".[322]

Either way, Jacob's promotion to become Leader of the House, the member of the Cabinet responsible for organising Parliamentary business in the House of Commons, created a vacancy as Chairman of the ERG. At Jacob's invitation, in line with ERG tradition and with the approval of the group, Steve then stepped up from the post of Deputy to become Chairman once again (as he had been only a couple of years previously, before himself having been made a Government Minister in DEXEU in 2016). This left a vacancy for Deputy Chairman and I was delighted when the officers invited me to fill the gap.

Having served as an officer under Steve and then Jacob, and now Steve again, I was very comfortable to have the self-confessed "Hard man of Brexit" back in the Chair. Nevertheless, it is fair to say that Jacob led the ERG brilliantly throughout all the trials and tribulations of the latter part of the May era, even though he and I eventually went our separate ways when it came to Meaningful Vote Three.

Nevertheless, Jacob now had an opportunity to move into Cabinet, which many of us were very glad to see, and at his final plenary meeting as Chairman, he was given a great send off by the members of the group, at the end of which Steve formally took the Chair, as the new Chairman, with me as his new Deputy.

The meeting with Dominic Cummings

One of the key Advisers that Boris brought into No 10 was Dominic Cummings, who had played a fundamental role in running the Vote Leave campaign and thus helping to win the 2016 EU Referendum in the first place. Although I was effectively a foot soldier in that campaign and was not involved in its direction, Cummings had a number of run-ins with other senior members of the ERG at the time, including Bernard Jenkin and Steve Baker which undoubtedly coloured his view of the group thereafter. Indeed, in an article in 2016, he was highly critical of the group and even described us as a "metastasising tumour" and "useful idiots for Remain".[323]

Despite this, I had heard a great deal about this man but had never met him, so I put out some feelers through the new Chief Whip, Mark Spencer, to ask if it might be possible to meet with Cummings, in my new role as Deputy Chairman of the ERG. The Chief was accommodating, and it was agreed that we would meet in his office at Number 9 Downing Street in September. In the end, Cummings basically stood me up. To say that I was not best pleased would be an understatement and I made very plain to the powers that be, that if they wanted to secure the support of the ERG moving forward, this was an extraordinary way to go about it.

After a rapid exchange of phone calls and texts, the meeting was rearranged for my office in Westminster early the following week. On the intervening weekend, I went as a guest of Michael Ashcroft's wife Susie's 70th Birthday Party at the Grosvenor House Hotel on Park Lane, which was a very grand affair (as a billionaire, Michael Ashcroft undoubtedly knows how to throw a party). The evening even included Lionel Ritchie coming on stage at the end to do a set, to rapturous applause from the assembled audience. About half the Cabinet were there, plus previous Conservative Leaders, including Theresa May and William Hague. Whilst there, I spoke to someone who knew Cummings well and explained what had happened and asked what I could expect, assuming he would turn up to our rescheduled meeting early the following week. My interlocutor, a Conservative MEP, who had known Cummings for years, told me that I would be lucky to get 20 minutes which would probably be accompanied by an element of sighing and looking at his watch, before he would plead that the Prime Minister needed to see him urgently and make an early exit.

Suffice to say, by the time he came to my office, accompanied by a Minister to ensure "fair play", my expectations had been suitably lowered. In the end however, it didn't turn out like that at all. To begin with, it was rather like two dogs sniffing around each other until we got onto the meat of Brexit and what the Government were trying to achieve. Cummings explained to me repeatedly that "No one Parliament can bind another" and therefore it would not be the end of the world if we were to vote for some elements of the Withdrawal Agreement as Parliament could always change it again, assuming that the Conservatives won a decent majority at the next General Election.

Cummings is undoubtedly a highly intelligent man, but it struck me that his grasp of the Withdrawal Agreement was not exactly comprehensive, so I looked him in the eye and asked him directly: "Dominic, have you read the Withdrawal Agreement?". In my experience, asking this direct question, was a very good way of disconcerting your opponents (see Robbie Gibb at the Grenadier for instance) and at this point they usually waffled something about having "flicked through it" or read a summary or some such excuse to prevent them admitting that they hadn't. To his credit, Cummings did not adopt this tactic. He looked directly at me and said: "No, I haven't". To which I replied: "Well given that so much of the row for almost a year has been about this document, don't you think you ought to?".

I then proceeded to grab my well-thumbed copy of the Withdrawal Agreement from the shelf in my office and to read a few key extracts of it to Dominic, with the Minister looking on. During the meeting Dominic had been liberally using the F word – not in fairness directed at me in any way but more at the iniquities of the world, including Remainers, and when I got to Article 174 (which lays out the superiority of the European Court of Justice, in the dispute resolution mechanism within the Withdrawal Agreement), he exclaimed: "Who the fuck negotiated that?", to which I replied: "Metaphorically – you did! Or at least your predecessors in No 10 did". I then went on to explain that the key elements of the Withdrawal Agreement, once ratified lasted forever, could not be over-trumped, even by an Act of Parliament and therefore, while it was true that, "One Parliament cannot bind another", in this instance, that didn't really apply, because this was "higher law" and effectively outranked even Parliamentary legislation, unless superseded by another international treaty, of equitable legal value. I then looked him straight back in the eye and said: "That's the whole fucking point Dominic! Why do you think we've been fighting this bastard thing, tooth and nail for well over a year?".

At this point, it is fair to say that Mr Cummings took out his notebook and started to make copious notes. As an MP of nearly 20 years, I appreciate that this could well have been that he was just "playing" me and simply wanted to appear attentive, in order to be polite but nevertheless, I do think I genuinely told him something that he didn't know. We then spent nearly an hour going into the intricacies of all of this and how the Government might have to alter the Withdrawal Agreement, in order to ensure that we left without No Deal if possible but were not irreparably tied into the European Union in doing so. The fundamental point of this was that they would, somehow, need to persuade the European Union to abandon the Backstop.

At the end of the meeting, I asked the accompanying Minister (who had said very little up to this point), for his comments to which he replied rather pithily: "I've been listening very carefully to you two going at it for over an hour and it strikes me that, as someone once said, although in a very different context, you have 'more in common' than perhaps you both realise".[324]

Dominic had asked me to follow up on a few particular matters and, on a point of honour, I made sure that he had a memorandum covering those areas delivered to him at 10 Downing Street by close of play that night. Cheekily, I also included a fresh copy of the Withdrawal Agreement and a scribbled note inviting him to enjoy "some bedtime reading". So, in fairness, I got much more than the 20 minutes that I'd initially been led to expect. In return he probably got a discourse on international Treaty law that he was not expecting either, but I did generously offer that if he wanted any more detail on this, I could probably arrange for Sir Bill Cash to pop over to Downing Street and take him through it! I meant this as a light-hearted comment at the time, without actually realising that, within a few weeks, we would effectively be doing something very similar.

The negotiations with the EU

Despite the EU and their Chief Negotiator, Michel Barnier, having told Theresa May and the British media *ad nauseum*, that they would never reopen the Withdrawal Agreement, as Prime Minister, Boris was determined to do exactly that. To his credit, despite great scepticism amongst the media and the Parliamentary Party (and I have to admit the ERG too) he finally persuaded the EU to enter into detailed negotiations on a revised version of the Withdrawal Agreement, on the proviso that he would then be able to get that revised Agreement through Parliament. Given the history of all of this, it was evident from the outset that he would need the support of the ERG in order to do so.

After a great deal of shadow boxing by both sides, in early October 2019, the EU negotiating team agreed to enter into intense detailed negotiations with a view to trying to finalise a revised Agreement. In diplomatic circles, this is known as "entering the tunnel" with the aim of focusing very clearly on the specific points at issue and then seeking to emerge at the other end, with a final agreement in place.

The Government were obviously keen to know whether or not the ERG would eventually support them but we pointed out that after all the previous experiences under Theresa May, we were not minded to offer any blank cheques and indeed it would be very helpful to understand, in confidence, where the Government had got to in their negotiations, so that we would not be presented with a *fait accompli* at the end, over which we had had no input or influence and which we might still feel honour bound to oppose.

At the Party Conference, I had asked for a meeting with Danny Kruger, the Prime Minister's Political Secretary, with the aim of beginning to open some kind of channel via which the ERG could negotiate with the Government, in parallel with them negotiating with the EU. In the end, Steve and I met with Kruger in his hotel suite at the Party Conference in Manchester and had what turned out to be a very positive meeting. A few days later, I rather cheekily suggested to No 10 that what they needed was a "mini tunnel" of their own between the ERG and No 10, so that we could negotiate with them, in effect about what we could and couldn't live with, if they were going to require us to vote for whatever came out of their negotiations. Somewhat to my surprise, the suggestion was readily accepted and therefore the ERG had to put together, at short notice, a team to negotiate privately with No 10.

Into the Tunnel

In the end, the task fell to four of us, Iain Duncan Smith, as a former Leader of the Conservative Party and also importantly in this context as the previous Chairman of Boris' Leadership campaign; Sir Bill Cash, as our undisputed legal expert, Steve Baker as Chairman of the ERG and myself as his new Deputy. Over the weekend, having consulted with the rest of the negotiating team, I sent across an email with our "red lines", as a device to try and provide some substantive basis to the negotiations. On the following afternoon, Monday 14th October, the four of us publicly walked up Downing Street to commence negotiations with No 10. From their side, these were Chaired by Danny Krueger, but also included a number of No 10 officials, including Oliver Lewis (Deputy to David Frost, the Prime Ministers Sherpa and Chief Negotiator) and also James Wild, one of the PM's political advisers (and now the Conservative MP for North West Norfolk). On the Tuesday and Wednesday, we again went back to No 10 to continue negotiations, about what we felt we could and couldn't support. I made a point of explaining to Danny and his team that the way the ERG operated was that if there was going to be a crunch vote in Parliament (by which stage was rumoured to be taking place on Saturday), the ERG would hold a plenary meeting before the vote, at which the officers would make a recommendation to members of the group on how to vote and give their reasoning accordingly.

I further explained that in the past, when the officers had made a unanimous recommendation, it had been accepted by the group almost universally and that the ERG had then voted as a single body in the Lobbies, with only very few exceptions (for instance the couple of abstentions on the Brady Amendment). Conversely, I explained that when the officers had been split, as in the case of MV3, the ERG itself had split and therefore, if the Prime Minister wanted the unanimous support of the ERG, they were going to have to convince all four of us, on behalf of all the Officers, to support his renegotiated Deal.

As our negotiations progressed, it was gradually revealed to us, in conditions of strict secrecy, that it looked as if the Prime Minister had in fact persuaded the EU to drop the entire Backstop from the Withdrawal Agreement, which meant that we would no longer face the prospect of entering into a Customs Union. There would still be some surviving elements of a much shorter Northern Ireland Protocol to govern trade between Northern Ireland and the rest of the United Kingdom, but the threat of a UK wide Customs Union (which would effectively have kept us in the EU) and to which the ERG had been opposed for so long, had abated.

Moreover, we were told that the Prime Minister had also managed to persuade the EU to change the accompanying Political Declaration, which in effect were the "tramlines" within which any subsequent trade deal would be negotiated, away from a Chequers style high alignment deal in the original Political Declaration, in favour of a "comprehensive free trade agreement" (FTA). By this alternative method, we would seek to trade in future with the European Union with low or in some cases, no tariffs whatsoever – in many ways along the lines of the original EU/"Super Canada" Agreement which David Davis had long been working on at DEXEU, before the White Papers were switched at Chequers, leading him to resign. An FTA of this type had been something that Eurosceptics had been broadly advocating for many years and thus this was indeed music to our ears.

For good measure, the Government also agreed to put provisions in the Bill (which would be needed to Ratify the revised Withdrawal Agreement) to curb the powers of the Joint Committee and in particular to ensure that legally binding decisions would not be able to be taken "ex Committee" as indeed the ERG had been very wary of all along.[325] By Friday morning, our two teams had pretty much reached agreement but I, awkward bloke that I am, was still holding out on a couple of points of detail.

I saw the Prime Minister twice that day, once in the morning and again in the afternoon, on the basis that if they wanted a unanimous recommendation from the officers, they still had to swing me in the end game. What I was particularly concerned about was the "Transition Period" of up to a year, between leaving the EU and negotiating the subsequent FTA, during which we would, albeit voluntarily, still be subject to the EU's legal rulebook.

In the end, on the Friday evening I finally agreed that I would vote for the Prime Minister's Deal and therefore the recommendation to the plenary the following morning would be unanimous, (which indeed it was).

My "price" was that the PM promised me faithfully that he would honour his pledge, made in writing in *The Sun*, during the 2019 Leadership Contest to rapidly bring in legislation to prevent Northern Ireland Veterans from an endless cycle of investigations. We even shook hands on this. However, while this pledge was effectively repeated in the 2019 Conservative General Election Manifesto, as this book went to press, the requisite legislation had still not been presented to Parliament.

Nevertheless, one of the reasons that these negotiations were successful was because we were treated completely and utterly differently from the May regime which had previously ruled at No 10. We were invited to discuss serious points of detail with senior members of the No 10 staff, with the Prime Minister only being brought in at the end, to help effectively seal the deal. For our part, we felt that we were finally being treated as "grown-ups" who were listened to, as well as talked at.

The negotiations were conducted in the Cabinet Room, and whilst they could have been just as well conducted in any part of No 10, nevertheless, as all four of us have a sense of history, it was certainly a nice touch. I remember saying to Danny Kruger, "OK Danny, we know you are doing a job on us, but to be fair, you are doing it well".

There was, however, still one issue over which the ERG team made very clear that there was still "unfinished business". We agreed to vote for the revised and slimmed down Northern Ireland Protocol (NIP), to replace the infamous UK "Backstop". Nevertheless, we made it absolutely crystal clear to the No 10 Team (and to the PM personally thereafter) that the NIP itself would have to be revised, or even replaced in the subsequent FTA negotiations, which would take place during the "Transition Period", once we had formally exited the European Union itself.

The ERG backs Boris' Deal

Down the years, I have got into a habit with my Association of agreeing the date for our quarterly Executive Meetings some way in advance. It was thus completely by chance that some months previously I had agreed that the next meeting of my Association Executive would take place on Friday 18th October. By this stage, Boris had travelled to the European Council in Brussels and had shaken hands with European Leaders on his revised version of the Withdrawal Agreement, minus the UK wide Backstop, and with the revised Political

Declaration to accompany it, specifying an FTA outcome for subsequent trade talks, once we had formally departed from the European Union.

I left No 10 at around 6:00pm on Friday evening, having now promised the Prime Minister that I would support his Deal and hurried back to my constituency for my Executive Meeting which was due to start at 8:00pm. When I got there, of course they didn't know how I intended to vote although I had seen Beth Rigby of *Sky* when leaving 10 Downing Street and when she asked me what I was going to do, I told her that I would be explaining that to my Executive before I explained it to the press – which we both agreed that she could then Tweet!

When I got to the Executive, it's probably fair to say that there was a certain degree of anticipation and I spent 20 minutes going through the pluses and minuses of the whole situation before revealing at the end that: "When the House meets tomorrow morning, I will be supporting the Prime Minister". At this point, the Executive burst out into spontaneous applause. When I explained to them what the Prime Minister had actually managed to achieve and, as I put it, "He had played a blinder" in his negotiations with the EU, there was great relief all around. As promised, I then texted Beth to tell her my decision, which she then Tweeted out via *Sky* within minutes, slightly after 10pm. It was now pretty apparent to the wider world that the ERG would be supporting the Prime Minister the following day.

The House of Commons then met, to vote upon Boris' revised Deal at 11:30am on Saturday 19th October. The only two previous post-war occasions when the House had sat on Saturday were during the Suez crisis in 1956 and after the invasion of the Falkland Islands in 1982. The House only sits on a Saturday in the most exceptional circumstances – and after the whole tortuous Brexit journey, this certainly met that high bar.

As on previous critical votes, the ERG held a plenary prior to the House voting, sitting at which were Steve as the Chairman and myself, and indeed the other members of our negotiating team. IDS laid out the essence of what Boris had achieved to the wider group and the fact that on behalf of the group, just about all of our concerns had been met. One after another, members of the ERG team chipped in.

While there was still some disquiet about the remaining operation of the redrafted Northern Ireland Protocol, and some form of residual EU influence over Northern Ireland, the overwhelming view of the meeting was nevertheless that the Prime Minister had negotiated very well and that he deserved our support in the vote later that day. (However, it was not completely unanimous, as John Redwood has reminded me).

During the subsequent debate in the House of Commons, that afternoon, I told the House:

"The European Research Group met this morning. Normally, our meetings are private, but in the circumstances, there were three things that I thought I could share with the House. First, the officers overwhelmingly recommended backing the Prime Minister's deal. Secondly, the ERG overwhelmingly recommended the same and no member of the ERG spoke against it. Thirdly, and most importantly, we agreed that those who vote for the deal vote for the Bill. If the deal is passed today, we will faithfully vote the Bill through to the end, so that we can leave the European Union. You have our word".

When the bells finally rang at 14:30 virtually the entire European Research Group walked through the Aye Lobby and thus helped to deliver the Prime Minister a majority of 16 for his revised deal, by 322 votes to 306.[326]

Boris Johnson had therefore achieved what Theresa May had never managed to do, he had indeed negotiated (or rather renegotiated) a Deal with the European Union which had managed to enjoy majority support in the House of Commons. Ironically, the principal element of this revised Deal was to drop the Backstop – very much along the original lines of the Brady Amendment of the 29th January – the only positive option ever to have previously commanded majority support in the Commons. The Prime Minister had therefore managed to agree a Deal which meant that we could finally Leave the European Union, with our honour intact, once and for all. However, for the Remainers in Parliament, even this was not enough.

The Remainers last stand

Having won his vote in principle, in favour of the Revised Withdrawal Agreement (it was not strictly a "Meaningful Vote" under the terms of the previous legislation and therefore never really became known as MV4), the Prime Minister still needed to put a Bill through the House of Commons to Ratify the Treaty, so that we could Leave by the now further extended deadline, of 31st January 2020. Nevertheless, it rapidly became apparent, that the diehard Remainers in the House of Commons, still with support from some on our own benches, were, even now, still determined to frustrate the passage of the Bill.

As anger grew on the Conservative Backbenches (and indeed among the wider public) the Remainers continued with their Parliamentary shenanigans, in an absolute last-ditch attempt to disrupt the legislation which would legally have allowed us to Leave the EU.

In the end, in an attempt to finally break the deadlock, the Prime Minister put down further motions calling for a General Election, but which still required a "super majority" in order to pass, under the terms of David Cameron's ill-fated Fixed Term Parliament Act (FTPA). There therefore appeared to be yet another stalemate, during which the Prime Minister repeatedly goaded the Leader of the Opposition, Jeremy Corbyn, to vote for the General Election, which he claimed to have been yearning for, for well over a year.

In the end, with the Bill deadlocked but with support for Labour in the polls dropping markedly, as a result of their obstructive behaviour, Labour finally consented and voted for an FTPA compliant Motion, to permit a General Election. This led to Parliament being dissolved at midnight on 6th November 2019, and the United Kingdom being plunged into its first Winter General Election campaign since 1974.

Despite the dark nights and the often foul weather, the Conservative Party, went into the December 2019 General Election on a Manifesto to "Get Brexit Done", by passing the requisite legislation to accept Boris' revised Deal, so that we would, at last, finally, after three-and-a-half years(!), Leave the European Union on 31st January 2020.

There was now just the small matter of winning the General Election first.

Chapter 16: Getting Brexit Done

Boris Johnson is amongst other things, a formidable campaigner, and along with his advisors (including Dominic Cummings and Isaac Levida) he put together a General Election campaign which was upbeat in character and which had at its heart, the simple slogan of "Get Brexit Done!". The fundamental thrust of the 2019 General Election campaign was that the Conservatives, if victorious, would settle the Brexit issue once and for all, by passing the necessary legislation to enact Boris' revised Deal and then Leave the European Union within a matter of weeks, on the 31st January. As the Conservative's 2019 General Election Manifesto made abundantly clear:

"Our priority as Conservatives is to get Brexit done – so that we can unleash the potential of this great country. So that we can push past the obstacles that other parties have put in our country's way. So that we can deliver on the people's decision in 2016 and use our new post-Brexit freedoms to transform the UK for the better by focusing on your priorities".[327]

In addition to this, the campaign also included stark warnings about the danger of a Marxist Government, led by Jeremy Corbyn with his equally left-wing Shadow Chancellor, John McDonnell, and the very severe consequences that this would have for Britain, both economically and democratically.

Whereas in 2017, Jeremy Corbyn had emerged as an energetic and passionate campaigner, two and a half years later, aged nearly 70, he was not in such good health. Perhaps worn down by the struggles over Brexit and internal disputes within the Labour Party over their failure to address the cancer of Anti-Semitism, he was nowhere near as effective a campaigner as he had been some two and a half years ago. In direct contrast to the disastrous 2017 campaign, the Conservatives were now led by an enthusiastic proponent of Brexit, in the form of Boris Johnson.

For my part, I did a limited amount of media in support of the Brexit element of the campaign and as well as campaigning in my own constituency, our Association performed their traditional "war role" of travelling down the A13 to defend Jackie Doyle-Price in Thurrock. On this occasion she was defending a majority of 345, meaning Thurrock was still very much a marginal seat going into the General Election.

I also did some travelling around the country, to support some of our candidates in marginal seats, including my old friend, and senior ERG Researcher,

Christopher Howarth, who had been selected as the Conservative candidate to fight the normally hopeless seat (from our previous viewpoint) of Houghton and Sunderland South, in the North East. In fact, Chris had genuine family links to the area. Sunderland is well known for glass manufacture (Pyrex for instance originates from Sunderland) and Chris' Grandfather had at one time run a glass factory in the city. Indeed, when I went up for a long weekend to support him, he cleverly held a meeting with the local press from the *Sunderland Echo* in Sunderland's modern glass museum, and so was able to genuinely point out to their political editor a number of exhibits which had been manufactured by his Grandfather's firm.[328]

I was really there to attest to Christopher's strong Eurosceptic credentials, not least as on the fateful night of the 2016 EU Referendum, the result from the city of Sunderland was the first firm indicator, that the United Kingdom had actually voted to Leave the EU. As part of the trip, I had asked Chris to take me out on to one of the toughest Council Estates in the constituency to see how the Labour vote was holding up given Jeremy Corbyn's increasing unpopularity as Labour Leader. Chris duly obliged and took me on to a large Council Estate, which was a traditional Labour heartland.

To make matters more interesting, the press event prior to this had overrun (as they often do) and by the time we arrived on the ground with Chris and his Agent, Donald Wood, it was dark and, for good measure, the heavens had opened. We therefore stood next to his Agent's car with the rain beating down wondering whether or not to go through with this or simply retire to the pub and take stock. In the end, having come all this way, I figured that I wouldn't have a chance to do this again and I really wanted to know how "soft" the Labour vote was in traditional Labour territory and so I suggested that we plough on, which we duly did.

After about an hour of door knocking in the pouring rain, we came round the corner and spied a local pub, at which point we decided that honour had now been satisfied and we headed straight for the warmth of the lounge bar. Once safely ensconced, the *Northern Echo* (who had been due to come out canvassing with us but had clearly taken one look out of the window and thought better of it) phoned up to ask Chris how it had gone. When he told them that the results had been remarkably encouraging, he then passed the phone over to me for a comment. When I was asked of my first impressions from canvassing in Sunderland, I replied quite honestly and said: "I got absolutely soaked. For one night only, I can honestly call myself a Wet Tory" – and the buggers printed it! In fairness, it was a direct, on the record quote and so they were well within their rights.[329]

352

However, all humour aside, what we found on the rainswept doorsteps of Sunderland that evening was absolutely fascinating. Again and again on working class doorsteps in this very down to earth city, we found lifelong Labour voters who said they were not going to vote for them. Moreover, almost without exception they didn't say: "I'm not voting Labour", but rather they said: "I'm not voting for Corbyn/him/that bloke/that Marxist....", and some considerably fruitier descriptions to boot. I was subsequently to relay this story when I appeared on *The Peston Show* on the night of 4th December, a week prior to Polling Day, when I explained exactly what had happened and that, from what I was finding on the doorsteps, including back home in Essex: "Jeremy Corbyn is toxic".[330]

Indeed, everywhere you went you found the same. Traditional Labour voters, many of whom are hardworking and patriotic, were simply not going to vote for a man, who they believe didn't really support the Monarchy or indeed had historically been sympathetic to the IRA. Indeed, on one occasion, towards the end of the campaign, Labour's Health spokesman, Jonathan Ashworth, was secretly recorded when speaking to someone he thought was a friend, during which he admitted that: "Outside of the city seats, if you are in small-town Midlands and the North, it's abysmal out there. They don't like Johnson, but they can't stand Corbyn, and they think Labour's blocked Brexit".[331]

Canvassing back in Essex

I'd begun to suspect that something extraordinary was going to happen when, right at the beginning of the campaign, I had gone out with some of my local Association activists to assist Jackie Doyle-Price in a canvassing session in an area of her constituency called Belhaus. This was very much a white working-class area, rather down at heel and which had, unfortunately, even voted in two BNP Councillors on to Thurrock Council several years previously. This was not exactly what you might call classic Tory territory.

Nevertheless, in two hours of canvassing (again much of it in the rain), I did not find one *single* declared Labour voter. I remember driving back that evening thinking, either this is a total one off or Labour are going to be slaughtered but I kept that thought rather to myself, as the whole line from CCHQ was to avoid any sense or even hint of complacency. Anyone in a media interview who in any way suggested we were going to walk it, would, quite rightly, have been torn apart by our Campaign Managers for appearing to take the electorate for granted. Nevertheless, having by now been canvassing on Essex doorsteps for over three decades since my formative days in Basildon, I couldn't get the thought out of my mind that I had never, ever, seen Labour in trouble like this before.

Our campaign in Rayleigh and Wickford

In total I visited something like 15 marginal seats during the campaign, including Ben Bradley's in Mansfield, Lee Anderson's in Ashfield, Jack Lopresti in Filton and Bradley Stoke and even Dagenham and Rainham in East London for good measure. Everywhere I went, the reaction was basically the same – "I'm not voting for Corbyn".

Back in my own constituency of Rayleigh and Wickford, the trend was even more pronounced. Despite that, it would not be true to say that I had everything my own way. For instance, when I was out canvassing in Hawkwell, one of my campaign workers beckoned to me, to say that the middle-aged gentleman on the doorstep opposite wanted to ask me a question.

As you do when you're a candidate, I went bounding up the drive and asked the elector how I could help him. To which he replied: "Look son" (I was 54 for goodness sake) "I only want to ask you one question – where do you stand on Brexit?". To be honest, having now done goodness knows how many national media interviews on this topic over the last three years or so I was slightly taken aback, so to try and inject some humour into the conversation, I said: "Forgive me Sir, do you not own a television?". This only appeared to anger him, and he replied: "Don't give me all that politician's bullshit – just answer the bloody question! Do you want us to Leave the European Union or don't you?". By this time, I thought to myself, crumbs, he really doesn't know, does he? So, I looked him firmly in the eye and said, "Sir, I voted Leave in the Referendum and I have passionately wanted to Leave the European Union for a number of years".

To which he responded, "Well that's alright then, I'll vote for you. Why didn't you just say that in the bloody first place!". By the time I returned from the doorstep, it would be fair to say that most of my campaign team, who had been listening avidly, were in hysterics.

About a week later, I was canvassing in Rayleigh, when I knocked on the door of a lovely little old lady who looked at my rosette and faithfully assured me that she would be voting for "that Mr Mark Francois". She then leant forward and asked me, slightly conspiratorially: "Have you met him?". When I replied that I was forced to confess that I was indeed Mark Francois, she looked at me rather quizzically and said: "Oh, well you look a lot taller in the photographs!". Again, cue hysterical giggling among canvassing team.

Tackling Nigel Farage

A key determinant in this General Election, was what the Brexit Party were going to do. On 19th October, Nigel Farage published an advert in *The Daily Telegraph* where he effectively attempted to browbeat the Prime Minister and the Conservative Party to accept his terms, in return for which he would agree not to stand Brexit candidates against Conservatives at the General Election (by this time there was only a limited period left to go before the formal deadline for nomination of candidates was due to close).[332]

Steve and I had already agreed with No 10 that the best contribution we could make to the national General Election campaign would be in helping to neutralise the influence of the Brexit Party. Although many of their candidates and supporters passionately wanted to Leave the European Union, if, by standing candidates they had ended up denying us an overall Conservative majority, we would effectively have been back to square one in the House of Commons and gone round and round in circles *yet again* unable to pass the necessary legislation which meant that we could legally Leave the EU on the 31st January. It was therefore vitally important to make sure that the Brexit Party did not, even inadvertently, save the Labour Party from what appeared likely to be a heavy defeat, and thus, bring about exactly the outcome which most of them were desperately keen to avoid in the first place, i.e. that we Remained in the EU after all.

In his subsequent press conference, Farage effectively accused the Prime Minister of being disingenuous and said that his revised Deal still meant that we wouldn't Leave the European Union after all (ironically, I had predicted to No 10 during our negotiations in the tunnel that this was exactly the line that Farage would take when we subsequently arrived at a General Election). We therefore agreed that before allowing his argument to gain any traction, it was very important to tackle it head on.

Within 90 minutes of his press conference, I appeared on the BBC's radio *The World at One* (universally known in the trade as "WATO") to challenge Farage over what he had said. When asked to respond to his press conference, I said: "I voted for Boris's deal and I'm sticking with it because it takes us out of the EU".[333] Steve Baker then followed up with further media interviews that afternoon where he criticised Farage for potentially standing in the way of a Conservative victory and thus stopping Brexit after all.

In fairness to Farage, and the Chairman of the Brexit Party, Richard Tice, down the years the Conservative Party has treated these guys like dirt. A Party dominated for many years at the top by pro-Remain politicians, had always regarded Farage and his ilk as "rather below the salt" and indeed Cameron had famously described UKIP, under Farage, as "UKIP is sort of a bunch of... fruitcakes and loonies and closet racists mostly".[334] Although it's true that UKIP was very occasionally infiltrated by a handful of extremists, in my experience this was a completely unfair characterisation of the whole Party – and certainly of Farage himself – who has desperately wanted to Leave the European Union for much of his adult life.

Had the Conservative Party treated Farage better and recognised him for the passionate Brexiteer that he undoubtedly is, then it might have been easier to come to some accommodation with him earlier on. Similarly, when he was a Member of the Conservative Party, Richard Tice had sought to be considered as a Conservative candidate for the Mayor for London but was barely even given an interview.[335]

Indeed, one of the Brexit Party's star candidates in the 2019 European Elections was Annunziata Rees-Mogg, Jacob's sister, who had defected from the Conservative Party to the Brexit Party, in frustration at Theresa May's inability to deliver a real Brexit.

There then began something of a cat and mouse game between Farage and Tice on the one hand and Boris' team on the other, as to under what circumstances, if any, Farage might be prepared to stand his candidates down. As part of this, several prominent members of the ERG, Steve and myself included, continued to argue strongly that by seeking to oppose Conservative candidates, Farage was likely to bring about exactly the opposite of the outcome he desired.

In the end, common sense prevailed, and Farage agreed to stand down Brexit Party candidates where they would have been fighting any sitting Conservative MP.[336] This effectively then gave those Conservative candidates a clear run against their opponents, without having to worry about a pro Brexit opponent off to their right. However, despite repeated entreaties, Farage refused to stand down his candidates in other seats where there was not a Conservative incumbent (such as, for instance, Houghton and Sunderland South). However, in seats like Thurrock, Farage's decision not to oppose Tory incumbents was a god send – as it gave Jackie Doyle-Price and her Tory counterparts in many other marginals a straight fight against their Corbyn-led Labour opponents.

Polling Day – 12th December 2019

After a hard-fought campaign, including a great deal of getting wet (it may be a caricature, but there's a very good, practical reason why some Tory candidates often wear Barbour jackets) we finally came to Polling Day itself. As in previous elections, having briefly been round my constituency in the morning, just to check that nothing was amiss, I then travelled down the A13, with around a dozen of my Association activists, to help Jackie Doyle-Price defend the marginal constituency of Thurrock. This was the fourth time in a row that we had done this, since first going down there in numbers in 2010.[337]

Nigel Farage's decision not to stand Brexit Party candidates against sitting Conservative MPs seeking re-election, meant in Thurrock's case, that it went from a long standing three way marginal to a straight fight between us and Labour. Jackie, as ever, supported by her partner and Campaign Manager Councillor Mark Coxshall, had fought a very energetic campaign and it now remained for us to help her Association Members run round on the door to remind identified Conservative supporters to vote, what is known in the political trade as "Knocking up". We did one round of knocking up at lunchtime and then a second round in the mid to late afternoon, by which time it was now pitch black (the Winter Solstice was on 21st December) and it was raining pretty hard to boot.

We decided to use a local pub, the Sandmartin (which is conveniently located directly opposite the local polling station) as our base and by late evening we had done two complete rounds of knocking up and retired to the pub, to dry off and get something to eat. A number of my team had tickets to my own General Election count, at Clements Hall Leisure Centre in Hawkwell but I was not returning with them as I had been booked by the BBC to appear on the General Election national results programme at Broadcasting House. I had agreed to be there by 10:15pm and at the appointed time of about 9:30pm, a rather nice BMW pulled up in the car park and having rapidly changed into a suit, I got into the back and was driven up to London. Luckily for me, there was a television screen in the rear of the front seat and so the driver, who was a very jolly chap, didn't mind at all when I asked if I could turn the television on, in order to catch the BBC's exit poll, immediately after 10:00pm.

The BBC's poll, which is overseen by their Psephology Expert, Professor John Curtis of the University of Strathclyde, has by now developed a reputation for being extremely accurate. In the last few General Elections, it has predicted the result across the entire country, to within a few seats either way. Thus, as soon as the exit poll is published, less than a minute after the actual polling stations have closed, you can be almost certain that it will represent the eventual outcome of the General Election, give or take only a handful of seats.[338]

As we drove down the A13 into central London, I remember a whole range of thoughts racing through my mind. What if we haven't won? What if it's another hung Parliament? What if we have to go round and round in circles again, with Remainer MPs pulling every Parliamentary trick in the book in order to frustrate Brexit, just as they have been doing for most of the last three years?

I tried to calm my thoughts by telling myself that I have been knocking on doors, one way or another for over 35 years since University and *surely* it couldn't be that all those people I had spoken to, in 15 different constituencies (plus of course my own) had all been lying and that Labour were going to do much better than everybody had predicted? If people in London, the Home Counties, the Midlands and the North of England were all saying that having voted Labour all their life, they were not going to vote for Jeremy Corbyn, how could we possibly do anything other than win?

By 9:55pm we were driving up the Aldwych towards New Broadcasting House at Portland Place and my heart was racing.

Four minutes to go to the Exit Poll…

Surely, we must have done it? If we have done it, then we can pass the legislation and we can finally Leave on the 31st January and all those ardent Remainers, from Hilary Benn to *LBC* radio's James O'Brien, will be confounded.

Three minutes to go to the Exit Poll…

But what if we haven't? I can't bear the thought of going back into the House of Commons and having to look at that lot laughing at us if, after all this effort and striving, we are still going to be trapped in the European Union. The British people are a pretty common sensical lot and they've begun to see right through what's been going on in Parliament, particularly in the last six months, and *surely*, they won't vote for this nonsense to continue, will they?

Two minutes to go to the Exit Poll…

Now, come on Mark, pull yourself together. All those people on the doorsteps weren't lying. Corbyn is a complete disaster and we're going to hammer these people. You've known that ever since you came back from that canvass in

Thurrock five weeks ago and hadn't found a single Labour voter in two hours. We're going to beat these people and we're going to beat them well and then we're going to pass this bloody Bill and finally get out, once and for all.

One minute to go to the Exit Poll…

Hold your nerve Mark! Either way, there's only 60 seconds left to go and after all these months and years, you're finally about to find out one way or another. Anyway, it's not as if you can change it now, so just take a deep breath and savour the moment.

And then Hugh Edwards appeared on the screen and said that the Polls had now closed, and the findings of the BBC's National Exit Poll were…Conservatives 365, Labour 198 and that the BBC were therefore predicting an overall Conservative majority!

The very first thought that popped into my head was: "Right, that's it – we're finally Leaving!", followed by a further thought, about a second later, that "Thank goodness, we've kept the Marxists out and the country is safe".[339]

When we arrived at New Broadcasting House only a few minutes later, it was as if someone had kicked over an ant hill and there were BBC staff scurrying in all directions (some of them, it has to be said, looking none too happy). I was rapidly shown up to make up and then put into the Green Room, to await going into the studio. By now my phone was going crazy with incoming calls and texts from friends and colleagues around the country, absolutely euphoric at the fact that we had won an emphatic victory.

The one thing that was praying on my mind was that I had told the Assistant Producers who had originally booked me for the programme that I wouldn't be able to wait too long, because I had to get back to my own count in my constituency and therefore, I would want to be out of NBH by about 11:15pm at the very latest. A lot of people came and went, and the clock kept ticking and by now my euphoria that we had won was becoming impaired by a nagging feeling that I was going to miss the declaration of my own result.

Mercifully, at that point a female producer came into the Green Room, apologised for the slight delay and asked me if it would help if she laid out "the batting order in the studio?". I gratefully agreed that it would, indeed, be very helpful, at which point she said the following: "Nigel's in the studio now but he'll be done in about ten minutes and then we'll have you straight in. You're not going to be on the panel after all, but instead you're being interviewed one-to-one by Andrew Neil".

"Oh lovely", I said, (thinking he's the fiercest interviewer in the business but show no fear in the face of the enemy). "How long will that be for?", I enquired, "Oh about ten minutes I should think", she said. "Oh, thank you very much", I said, trying to look as enthusiastic as possible and then rapidly nipped round the corner to collect my thoughts.

I took out a small piece of card that I had in my pocket and wrote down five bullet points and comforted myself with the thought that it didn't matter what on earth he asked me, those were the answers he was going to get. I was then miked up and ushered into the studio to see the great man himself, hunched over his laptop with numerous documents and reports on either side of him.

One of the reasons why Andrew Neil is such a fearsome interviewer, is that whereas lots of other television journalists will have teams of researchers (often bright and ambitious graduates) to do a lot of the background work for them, Andrew Neil makes a point of reading most of the source documents himself. For instance, he would definitely have read the entire Withdrawal Agreement – unlike some others of his journalistic counterparts. As I sat down, he looked up from behind his laptop and grunted "Good Evening", and as I replied, I looked at the weight of paper around him and took out my small A6 sized piece of card from my pocket and laid it on the table and I remember thinking: "Paper wise, this is hardly a fair fight is it?".

When it came to the interview itself, I nevertheless managed to hold my own. He asked me some questions about what the new Conservative Government was going to do for people on low incomes and I managed to come up with something about matters of taxation being for the Chancellor of the Exchequer and not for me, but nevertheless, we would want to allow people from all backgrounds to make their way in the world. He then switched to asking questions on Europe where I was now "playing at home" and got through the rest of the interview, I thought, reasonably unscathed. Indeed, shortly after I came out of the studio, I received a few texts from friends, basically saying "Well done".[340]

I was then asked if I could quickly do an interview for Radio 4 on the promise that they would have me out of the building swiftly afterwards. Just after I had agreed, I received a call from someone I had never heard of, claiming to be from the Media Department at CCHQ, telling me that the Prime Minister had just seen my interview and would be grateful if I would do no more national media that night. I replied that the Prime Minister had my number and if he was really concerned about it, he could phone me himself. When the voice on the other end of the phone pressed the point and insisted that I had not received "Clearance" to do the show, I brusquely reminded him that as I was no longer a Minister, I didn't require "Ministerial Clearance" from anybody and besides I didn't have time to stand around and argue about whether or not to do anymore national media that night – as I had to go and do an interview for Radio 4.

Without further ado I got into the lift and went up to the Radio 4 studio and, as I was walking in, Michael Gove was in the Chair grinning from ear to ear at what turned out to be a Conservative majority of 80. I duly did the interview (and for some mysterious reason, the Prime Minister never did phone me) before dashing downstairs to hop into a car, driven by one of my activists (who used to be a Police pursuit driver) to whisk me back to my constituency as quickly as possible.

However, as fate would have it, the Blackwall Tunnel was closed and the roads getting out of East London were absolutely chock-a-block, following a local traffic accident, even after midnight. To add to my joy, the phone started going off from some of the team at the count saying that for the first time in the entire history of Rochford District Council, they had actually counted the votes quite quickly and wanted to move to a declaration rapidly and could I possibly get there in the next 15 minutes? At this stage I was in the heart of East London and explained I thought this was unlikely but that I promised to get there as fast as I could.

What then transpired, was a series of phone calls back and forth where I was being told that they were on the brink of declaring the result and they were being told that after all this I would be pretty upset if I missed my own count. In the end we compromised, and they kindly agreed that they would hold the declaration until 1:30am, but they simply couldn't wait any longer.

Fortunately, we managed to weave our way out of East London and despite heavy rain, Ian put his foot down and having roared back to the constituency at 69.7 miles an hour (seasonally adjusted), we came to a screeching halt outside Clements Hall Leisure Centre at 1:29am.

I then rushed into the count (stopping only for a very brief comfort break) before bursting into the Hall to be met by a number of knowing smiles from my campaign team.

When the result was announced, about ten minutes later, the result was as follows:

General Election Result for the Rayleigh and Wickford Constituency, 2019

Mark Francois	Conservative Candidate	39,864
David Flack	Labour Candidate	8,864
Ron Tindall	Liberal Democrat	4,171
Paul Thorogood	Green Candidate	2,002
Conservative Majority		31,000
Turnout		69.5%

In my acceptance speech I thanked my campaign team for all their extremely hard work, in often very difficult weather over the past five weeks or so but said that we had achieved a truly remarkable result, with a majority of exactly 31,000 votes.

In the cold light of morning, it turned out that this was the second largest Conservative majority in the whole of the United Kingdom (second only to Dr Caroline Johnson, in Sleaford and North Hykeham, in rural Lincolnshire, and whose majority was a bit over 32,000). Nationally, I said that we had won a truly historic victory, over Corbyn's Marxist Labour Party, dwelling on the word *Marxist* as my Labour opponent was a committed Corbynista. Nevertheless, I thanked all of the candidates for a fair fight, and as is traditional thanked the counting staff, the police and particularly the Returning Officer, Angela Hutchings, for her patience.

I then said that at last, finally, this meant that we would now be Leaving the European Union and "Getting Brexit Done". After the usual handshakes and photographs, I retired home at about 3:00am to watch the rest of the results come in, as one by one, seats which had been Labour for a generation (or in some cases even a century) went down like nine pins as the Conservatives tore into what was subsequently christened Labour's crumbling "Red Wall" in the Midlands and the North of England.

In the end, all those people hadn't been lying at all, and Labour's vote had completely imploded. Tories were getting elected in seats like Ashfield, Bishop Auckland, Bolsover and Darlington and even my friend Christopher Howarth had come within 6,000 votes of defeating Bridget Phillipson in Houghton and Sunderland South. Ironically, had the Brexit Party candidate in that seat not polled 6,165 votes, Chris might already be serving in the House of Commons today (although I suspect he will still get there one day).[341]

Rayleigh and Wickford Constituency Conservative Association

To achieve the second largest Conservative majority in the 2019 General Election was a very pleasing result and some of it may perhaps have been due to my relatively high-profile during the Battle for Brexit, as reflected in a constituency which voted to Leave the European Union by 67% to 33% back in 2016.

Nevertheless, much of the credit must go to my excellent campaign team from the Rayleigh and Wickford Constituency Conservative Association (R&WCCA). I have been lucky during my political career in that I have worked with Associations, such as those in both Basildon and Brent East who are doughty campaigners and the officers, Councillors and activists of R&WCCA are no exception.

During the 2019 General Election, despite the cold and dark of a winter campaign, they went out repeatedly onto the doorsteps of our constituency, as well as delivering a considerable amount of literature and manning street stalls and other campaign events to boot. In addition, just as in the three prior General Elections of 2010, 2015 and 2017 respectively, they also found time to campaign alongside me some weekends in the marginal seat of Thurrock, in successful support of the redoubtable Jackie Doyle-Price (including about a dozen of us getting absolutely drenched whilst knocking up for Jackie on Polling Day itself!).

Rayleigh itself is an old market town, which was mentioned in Domesday Book and which features the remains of a Norman castle, as well as a windmill, a Dutch cottage and a fourteenth century church, Holy Trinity, at the top of the High Street. It is complemented by the more modern town of Wickford, part of which was built in the Post-War era, to accompany the growth of Basildon New Town, just to the south. The rest of the constituency comprises a number of smaller villages and settlements, all of which combine to create a very popular part of Essex (as any of the local estate agents will readily tell you).

We are fortunate to have numerous dedicated Councillors, at a variety of tiers of local Government, from Town and Parish Councils, through District (Rochford), Borough (Wickford is part of Basildon Borough Council) and Essex County Council level, as well as many more hard working Members and activists besides.

Sir David Amess MP was a regular guest speaker at our popular Association Supper Club, where he could normally be relied upon to have the audience in fits, with a combination of outrageous jokes and punchy jibes at the dangers of socialism and European Federalism too.

As any MP will tell you (if they are being honest); you cannot really do this job effectively without a good Association to support you. In that regard I am extremely fortunate to have such a good and dynamic Association in my constituency – and long may that remain the case.

"Their contracts were not renewed"

As Ken Livingstone had taught me all those years ago, a General Election was an opportunity to commune with your employers and effectively to ask them to renew your contract of employment for another Parliamentary term. There was an extremely clear pattern in the 2019 General Election which is that very many of those backbench MPs, who had done so much to deliberately frustrate Brexit, lost their seats.

The Independent Group (TIG) some of whom by now were standing under the revised label of "Change UK", were annihilated. For instance, Anna Soubry in Broxtowe lost by 22,000 votes and Sarah Woolston in Totnes was wiped out by 12,000 votes. Among former Labour MPs, Gareth Snell lost his seat in Stoke on Trent more narrowly, by 600 votes. However, not a single TIG/Change UK MP was successfully re-elected to Parliament.

Among those Conservatives who had had the Whip withdrawn by Boris Johnson but who attempted to stand as independents, there was also a massacre. Dominic Grieve, architect of the famous Grieve Amendment (which had effectively paved the way for pro-Remain Backbenchers to initially take control of the Order Paper), lost his seat in Beaconsfield by over 15,000 votes. Similarly, Sam Gyimah, who had defected to the Liberal Democrats (despite swearing blindly to me on national radio that he would never do any such thing) switched seats to what he regarded as the much safer prospect of Kensington and was duly defeated by a majority of some 7,000. Even David Gauke, who had fought Brent East after me in 2005, been Treasurer of the ERG and then a successful Treasury Minister for a number of years (but who stood as an Independent) still lost by over 14,000 votes, despite pretty-much everyone agreeing that he had been a very popular constituency MP.

The great irony in all this, is that some of these MPs had repeatedly assured us in the House of Commons that what they were doing to "prevent us crashing out with No Deal" had the enthusiastic support of their constituents. When this contention was actually put to the test – in the ballot box – it turned out to be less than wholly accurate, in the eyes of some of "their employers" in their own constituencies, at least. In the end, hardly any of these people had their contracts renewed.

As the final icing on the cake, Steve Bray (the "Twat in the Hat") who had so often tried to shout down his opponents on television, stood as a Liberal Democrat candidate in the seat of Cynon Valley, came sixth and lost his deposit. In fairness, Mr Bray could actually be quite affable company on occasion, but he is not a Member of Parliament – and he didn't "Stop Brexit" either!

There was one other facet of the 2019 General Election, which was that in over 30 seats, the Brexit Party polled more votes that the surviving Labour MP's eventual majority. The suggestion being, that in at least a number of seats, if pro-Brexiteers had actually voted for the Conservative Party candidate rather than the Brexit Party, even more Labour MPs would have lost their seats. For instance, Yvette Cooper (one of the primary architects of Remain resistance for years in the Commons) survived by a majority of a bit over 1,000 votes when the Brexit Party scored over 8,000 in her Pontefract and Castleford constituency. Similarly, Ed Miliband, a former Leader of the Labour Party and another prominent Remainer, survived by only around 2,400 (when the Brexit Party polled over 8,000 votes).

I am not an expert Psephologist, and it is difficult to prove a precise correlation in every one of those seats (as not every Brexit Party supporter would necessarily have voted Conservative if they had not stood). Nevertheless, if Farage had stood down his candidates entirely in 2019, it is quite likely that more of those Brexit Party votes would have broken for the Tories instead of Labour – and thus even more Labour MPs would have lost, and the Conservatives would have enjoyed a majority in three figures.

Either way, Labour had been slaughtered and we had won, hands down.

Andrew Neil

Andrew Neil is arguably the most formidable interviewer on modern British television. Known by many in media circles by the nickname "Brillo" (because of his wiry hair) he has been a journalist for some 50 years, including as Editor of *The Sunday Times* and now also as Chairman of *The Spectator*, the Conservative journal previously edited by one Boris Johnson.

Part of the reason for Andrew Neil's success is his assiduous preparation before each interview. Unlike many other interviewers, who have access to a team of researchers (often but not exclusively Oxbridge graduates) to plough through complex documents for them, Neil often makes a point of reading through the source documents himself. During the Battle for Brexit a handful of national journalists had read through the entire 585-page Withdrawal Agreement itself but Neil knew the key facts as well as many leading Brexiteers did too.

Having been interviewed by Andrew Neil several times down the years relating to Brexit (including on General Election night 2019) I was always conscious that my "opponent" would be very well prepared and that it was always a good idea to brush up on your arguments before going into a studio with him.

In the autumn of 2020, he announced that he had been unable to agree satisfactory terms to continue working with the BBC and would instead be seeking to found a new news channel called "*GB News*". Whilst the new channel eventually launched in 2021, Andrew Neil has since moved on. However, I suspect that his broadcasting career is still far from over – we have not heard the last of "Brillo" just yet.

Passing the Withdrawal Bill

When the House of Commons reassembled on the 17th December, it rapidly passed the Second Reading of the Withdrawal Bill, which was required to Ratify the Revised Withdrawal Agreement, so that we could Leave the European Union, under the now thrice extended Article 50, at 11:00pm on the 31st January. A whole swathe of newly elected Tory MPs now swelled our numbers in the Lobbies, and every single Conservative Candidate had already pledged in writing, prior to the General Election that they would vote to "Get Brexit Done" if they were returned to the House of Commons. The legislation, which the Remainers had previously said would take weeks and weeks to debate, flew through the House of Commons in a matter of days, indeed on a number of the days allocated for debate, the business collapsed early because so few Remain

MPs had taken the trouble to scrutinise it. In short, the Remainers had been routed numerically, as well as completely morally defeated by the General Election result and finally their resistance crumbled.

As a result, the Withdrawal Bill achieved Royal Assent on 23rd January 2020, and in a nice touch, the new Speaker, Sir Lindsay Hoyle, allowed one of his Deputy Speaker's, Nigel Evans (a long time Eurosceptic, dating back to the days of Maastricht) to read out the announcement of Royal Assent in the Chamber. The House of Lords could perhaps have tried to at least delay the Bill but there is something called the "Salisbury Convention" which states that the Lords does not attempt to hold up legislation which was promised in the Manifesto of the winning Party at a General Election.

Moreover, on a much more basic level, even the most ardent Remainers in the House of Lords – of whom there are no shortage – were under no illusions about what the public backlash against the Upper House would be, no doubt egged on by the print media – if, after such an emphatic General Election result, they attempted to impede Brexit in any meaningful way. As a number of Labour Peers admitted privately at the time, to try and prevent the Withdrawal Bill passing could have led to the end of the House of Lords, at least in its current form. [342]

Trust the people

Finally, after three years of Parliamentary trench-warfare, during which the decision of the British people in a peaceful, democratic Referendum to Leave the European Union had been frustrated time and again – the people had effectively re-endorsed their decision, this time via the 2019 General Election and, this time round, Parliament was forced to obey.

For those who had argued time and again for a second Referendum – they eventually got their wish for a "People's Vote" – in the form of a General Election. Labour's policy on Brexit during that election was admittedly, hopelessly confused:

"Labour will give the people the final say on Brexit. Within three months of coming to power, a Labour Government will secure a sensible deal. And within six months, we will put that deal to a public vote alongside the option to remain. A Labour government will implement whatever the people decide". [343]

In the end, the British people decided, overwhelmingly, not to vote Labour. But, for those who ardently wanted to Remain, then there was a very clear option – the "Bollocks to Brexit" Liberal Democrats, who had remaining part of the EU as a centrepiece of their offer to the British Electorate. Indeed, during the campaign, Lib Dem spokesmen repeatedly argued that for those who wanted to Remain, they were the obvious choice. Indeed, as their Manifesto promised:

"The election of a Liberal Democrat majority Government on a clear stop Brexit platform will provide a democratic mandate to stop this mess, revoke Article 50 and stay in the EU".[344]

In the end, the strength of this overtly Remain appeal was such, that the Europhile Lib Dems were reduced to 12 seats in the House of Commons, including losing their Party Leader, Jo Swinson, whose assertion, early on in the campaign, that she might become Prime Minister never quite caught on.

Instead, when asked whether or not they still wanted to Leave, the British people voted even more emphatically to "Get Brexit Done" than they had done in 2016.

Finally, three-and-a-half years after the original EU Referendum the MPs' employers well and truly asserted their contractual rights.

Nigel

Nigel Farage is undoubtedly one of the most influential British politicians of the 21st Century – at least so far. From 2006 onwards, he led UKIP from a position of relative obscurity to win the 2014 European elections in the UK outright.

In my view, it was a combination of "external" pressure from UKIP and "internal" pressure from Eurosceptic Conservative backbenchers which eventually combined (supported by a considerable amount of media comment) to persuade an embattled David Cameron to announce his intention to hold an In/Out Referendum, in his fateful Bloomberg Speech in 2013.

Although Farage and his supporters, including millionaire businessman Aaron Banks, did not succeed in securing the official designation as the Leave campaign, (they lost to Vote Leave), they and their supporters also played an important part in the wider Eurosceptic coalition that eventually persuaded the British people to vote to Leave the European Union in June 2016.

Having almost died in a plane crash on the day of the 2017 General Election (when he stood as a candidate against Speaker John Bercow in Buckingham) his anger at what he portrayed as the betrayal of the Referendum result by the British Establishment – including within parts of the Conservative Party – led him to form the 'Brexit Party', which subsequently won the 2019 European Elections in Britain by a clear margin.

Unbound and frequently controversial, I have not always agreed with Nigel Farage and have crossed swords with him in a number of media studios down the years. Nevertheless, I believe it is absolutely true to say that, if Nigel had never been born, there would never have been an In/Out Referendum in 2016 and that we would still be in the European Union to this day. As he once famously told the European Parliament: "When I came here 17 years ago and told you all we would one day leave the EU, you all laughed at me – well, you're not laughing now are you?"

They are still not laughing, to this day.

Chapter 17: Sunrise on a Free Country

With the Withdrawal Bill safely through, as the European Union (Withdrawal) Act 2020, the country then settled down to prepare to celebrate what was officially called "Exit Day" in the legislation but which many in the media had already christened "Independence Day" on 31st January 2020. As a number of pubs across the nation began to apply for late licenses to help their customers celebrate, Brexiteers across the country began to make their dispositions accordingly.

"Big Ben should bong for Brexit!"

Nigel Farage sought and was eventually granted permission to hold a large "Exit Rally" in Parliament Square (with echoes of the Rally that he had held on the day of MV3 back in March of the previous year). In addition, a whole number of people began to arrange Brexit parties for that evening, of which I was kindly invited to several. However, there was a remaining issue (no pun intended) because under Article 50, we were due to legally Leave the European Union at the very specific time of 11:00pm, Greenwich Mean Time (GMT). That meant that the nation would naturally look to a clock to mark the occasion (just as one does on New Year's Eve).

However, Big Ben, the natural choice for this role, was unfortunately out of commission as it was undergoing a maintenance programme at the hands of the House of Commons authorities (which was already running massively late and way over budget).[345] It was perfectly possible technically for Big Ben to chime (as exceptions were already made on both New Year's Eve and, also quite rightly, on Remembrance Sunday) but some in the House of Commons authorities were clearly reluctant to allow Big Ben back into commission to celebrate our Leaving the European Union. The main reason they gave for this, was the cost of interrupting the maintenance works in order to make preparations for the clock to chime.

After everything we had been through, we were still going to Leave the European Union either way, but it just struck me that there would be something slightly missing if Big Ben, the most iconic time piece in the world, did not chime to mark the occasion. I accordingly tabled some named day Written Parliamentary Questions, i.e. they have to be answered in a very short time frame, to simply ask what had been the cost of Big Ben chiming for New Year's Eve and Remembrance, as the House of Commons authorities had quoted a cost of up to half a million pounds to allow Big Ben to chime on the night. Despite the answers coming back that the cost had actually been £14,500 (including VAT) on each occasion, the Commons authorities continued to argue that because on this occasion Big Ben chiming had been unanticipated, the cost would be vastly higher.[346]

Indeed, a temporary floor had been put in to allow the clock to chime for New Year's Eve but then removed thereafter – because even despite the overwhelming General Election result, no genius had the common sense to ask the question "But what happens if we Leave the EU a month later?"

I and some other MPs began to campaign for Big Ben to chime regardless. However, some in Government were nervous at whether or not they could justify the cost. In the midst of this minor squall, the Prime Minister was asked live on *BBC Breakfast* whether or not the Government would be prepared to pay for the clock to chime? The Prime Minister responded that they were investigating some form of crowdfunding appeal, whereby the public could donate in order to cover the cost, rather than the taxpayer. As he famously put it in that interview: "We are looking at ways that people can bung a bob so that Big Ben can bong". I remember seeing this interview live and thinking that that sounded a good idea but wondering who was actually going to organise it?[347]

I happened to know privately that following the Prime Minister's interview, No 10 contacted a number of national newspapers and pleaded with them to host the appeal but for whatever reason, all of them declined to do so.[348] With the initiative appearing to lose momentum, I contacted some people at Go Fund Me and asked if they could come to my office and take me through "Crowd Funding 101" because if no one else was going to set up an appeal, then I decided that I and some Eurosceptic friends would have a crack at it.

The people from Go Fund Me were incredibly quick off the mark and explained the mechanics of such a campaign, but I didn't want to be solely responsible for it, so began looking for another organisation to help co-ordinate it. After being turned down by two or three pro-Brexit groups, I finally managed to persuade "Stand Up 4 Brexit", who had ardently campaigned for Brexit, to help organise the campaign and we subsequently launched it on the 15th of January, with only a fortnight or so to go before Independence Day.[349] The two leading lights in Stand Up 4 Brexit were two very dynamic ladies, Rebecca Ryan and Helen Meyer, both of whom stepped up to the plate enthusiastically and seemed to relish the challenge.

To our surprise and delight, the money absolutely poured in, indeed at one point it was coming in at over £10,000 an hour, with the average donation totalling less than £20, as people from across the country (and indeed even some from abroad) merrily donated out of their own pocket towards the cost of the exercise. Several national newspapers, including *The Daily Telegraph*, and *The Daily Express* then also enthusiastically endorsed the campaign. Within just a few days, we were already past £100,000 – until, barely a few days later, No 10 effectively pulled the plug on us!

It would appear that a number of Boris' advisors, seemingly worried that Big Ben chiming would somehow appear divisive or jingoistic, had persuaded him to withdraw support from the campaign and indeed at the following day's lobby briefing, the Prime Minister's spokesman effectively plunged the knife into our efforts. When this got out, unsurprisingly, donations began to dry up. Fortunately, we had made plain from the outset, that if we didn't hit the £500,000 target (or indeed if we exceeded it) all the money left in the fund, if it could not go to the primary purpose, would instead be donated to *Help for Heroes*.

After everything I had done for so many years to fight for Brexit, I remember being absolutely furious when it became apparent what No 10 had done. Indeed, at the following meeting of the Parliamentary Lobby, the Prime Minister's spokesman, was apparently monstered for almost half an hour by relentless questioning from experienced lobby correspondents about why No 10 had effectively withdrawn support for the campaign, which the Prime Minister had clearly sought to encourage in the first place!

Despite our best efforts, the U-turn by No 10 meant that the money dried up and it was never possible to actually make Big Ben chime on the night. In the end, the broadcasters merely played a recording of it chiming 11:00pm, which Nigel Farage also played over loudspeakers at the Rally. Nevertheless, every cloud has a silver lining, and in the end, we succeeded in raising over £200,000, for the very worthwhile charity *Help for Heroes*, for which I subsequently received a charming thank you letter from their Chief Executive.[350]

Independence Day

Finally, the calendar ticked over to the 31st January, on which the United Kingdom, some 47 years after joining the European Economic Community, was now legally due to Leave the European Union at 11:00pm that night. This decision had been taken peacefully and democratically by the people of the United Kingdom, firstly when they voted for it in the 2016 Referendum, when they effectively re-endorsed the decision, by emphatically voting to "Get Brexit Done" in the December 2019 General Election.

This is important, because after all this time, the arguments had morphed, from simply being one of Leave vs Remain into one of the People vs the Establishment, with the latter having done just about everything in their power to thwart the democratic decision of the former, including in their bastions of the media, the chattering classes and the upper echelons of the British Civil Service.

The BBC

The British Broadcasting Corporation once a truly world-class British institution, has now, sadly, badly, lost its way. The Reithian imperative, to "inform, educate and entertain" has, alas, now been firmly abandoned in favour of a culture of political correctness, reinforced by a workforce, many of whom are from comfortable even privileged backgrounds.

The *Today* Programme, which once firmly set the news agenda for the rest of the day, is now a shadow of its former self and is now referred to among a number of Tory MPs as "Woke FM". Recently Michael (now Lord) Howard, a respected former leader of the Conservative Party, even revealed that he has abandoned listening to the *Today* Programme because of its evident bias. This has been a very long drop from the heyday of *Today*, when it well and truly set the news agenda each weekday in Britain.

During the Battle for Brexit, the BBC (with a few honourable exceptions, such as Laura K, Norman Smith and Andrew Neil) was culturally massively pro-Remain, with Remainers permitted often fawning interviews, whilst Brexiteers were frequently struggling to get a word in. The BBC's public refusal to accept any allegations of bias – akin to the old doctrine of Papal Infallibility – may even have helped the Brexiteer cause, as many members of the pubic came to perceive just how warped the BBC's general coverage of Brexit actually was (and still is). Add in the Corporation initially attempting to ban "Rule Britannia" at the Last Night of the Proms, the Martin Bashir fiasco and BBC Breakfast presenters having to apologise for mocking the size of the Union Flag in a Minister's Office, alongside a portrait of HM The Queen – and you have a national broadcaster in near terminal decline.

The new BBC Director General, Tim Davie, once a Deputy Chairman of Hammersmith and Fulham Conservatives, is rumoured to understand quite how much difficulty the corporation is now in.

Party Time

That evening, I participated in the *Daily Telegraph's* Chief Political Correspondent, Christopher Hope's "Chopper's Brexit Podcast" pre-recorded in the upstairs room of The Red Lion pub in Westminster (to be subsequently broadcast after 11:00pm). My fellow guests were Alison Pearson, a leading columnist on the *Daily Telegraph* and indeed the man himself, Nigel Farage. There was a rather amusing moment, when I was asked what I was going to do later that night, to which I replied that I had kindly been invited to several parties after which I intended to stay up and watch the sun rise on a free country. Farage rapidly shot back that so was he and if this young pup Francois thought he could outdrink him, he had another thing coming! In the end, I confess that I didn't try.

From the Red Lion, I went to a party at 5 Hertford Street, which had kindly been organised by some prominent Brexit supporters, including Lord Greville Howard and some of the relatives of the late Jimmy Goldsmith, who had famously founded the Referendum Party after the great arguments over Maastricht. The party that night was effectively a Who's Who of the Eurosceptic pantheon, with guests including Charles Moore, past Editor of the *Daily Telegraph*, Paul Dacre, the long-standing past Editor of the *Daily Mail*, Jimmy Goldsmith's son, Zac, other members of his family and a number of prominent Brexiteers, including Iain Duncan Smith, Sir Bill Cash, Sir Bernard Jenkin, Owen Paterson and more besides. After a sumptuous meal, the historian Andrew Roberts gave a rousing speech about what had been at stake and then Lord Forsyth summed up, before a television screen was wheeled into the large dining room so that we could all cheer at 11:00pm when Big Ben (or at least a recording of it!) finally chimed our freedom. The atmosphere at the party was not riotous but more one of quiet satisfaction, even relief that, finally, after all those years, we were finally free.

My partner, Olivia, and I then jumped into a taxi and dashed down to Chelsea in order to attend another Brexit party headed by the pro-Brexit businessman, Jon Moynihan. When we got there, as soon as we'd handed over our coats the first person I bumped into was Steve Baker and we instantly hugged each other in delight at what we and everyone else had been able to achieve. Steve had to dash off to another party and I then remember speaking for a while to Jonathan Isaby, my friend and Editor at *Brexit Central*, before then having an animated conversation with our host, Jon, who was basically ecstatic that after all of these years we had finally done it!

It was then back into a taxi and another journey to the Cavalry and Guards Club in Piccadilly for a Leave.EU/Brexit Party bash, being hosted by Nigel Farage and Richard Tice. This was a far more boisterous affair than either of the two previous parties that we had been to and went on long into the night. By sheer coincidence, as it was the Cavalry and Guards Club, Brigadier Simon Goldstein (who had materially assisted with my Military reports for the Prime Minister) was attending an Army event in the adjacent room and by the time I bumped into him, he looked like he was having a pretty convivial evening as well.

When it came to the speeches, Tim Martin the Chairman and Chief Executive of Wetherspoons, gave a very funny address to be followed immediately thereafter by the comedian Jim Davidson, who had the audience in stitches. He told us that Tim Martin, despite being an ardent Brexiteer for many years, was really here to recce the Cavalry and Guards Club – one of the most exclusive in London – as the site for a new pub and that, unwittingly, we were now standing in what would soon become the new "Wetherspoons Piccadilly". Davidson then went on to tell us that the Brexit issue had caused considerable division in his own household, as he put it "I'm Leave, and the wife was Remain. Every morning, I'd leave for work – whilst she remained in bed!".[351]

With the audience now suitably warmed up, he handed over to Nigel Farage, who as might be expected, gave a rousing ovation (by now at about 3:00am in the morning) at which he toasted the fact that we had now finally, after so many years, regained our independence. At around about 3:30am, Liv and I thanked our host and then slipped out quietly, to go back to the Carlton Club, where we grabbed a couple of hours sleep, before getting up slightly after 6:00am to hop into a pre booked Addison Lee car, to take us up to Parliament Hill.

Sunrise on a free country

The reason for our early morning trip up Parliament Hill was that the previous summer, after the Brexit exit day had been extended to the 31st October, I had bumped into my old friend and previous Member of Parliament for Canterbury, Julian Brazier, at a Think Tank reception in the West End. Like me, a former Army Reservist, he had unfortunately lost his seat in the 2017 General Election, by an agonizingly close margin of only 20 votes. When I asked Julian over a drink what his plans were for the night that we finally left the EU, he said he didn't intend to go to bed but rather intended to stay up and "watch the sun rise on a free country". This immediately struck me as a really good idea and indeed I used that phrase in a number of media interviews in the run up to Independence Day.

And so, it came to pass, that in the pre-dawn half-light, accompanied by Liv (who was on crutches as she had recently had an operation on her hip) we walked up to the viewing platform on Parliament Hill, to be met by a smiling Julian Brazier and his wife, with four glasses and a decent bottle of champagne.

We then proceeded to watch the sunrise (at approximately 7:30am) as we looked south over Central London in the morning air. I experienced a whole spectrum of emotions at that moment but the greatest one of all was a feeling of immense relief.

At last, after so many years, we had finally, finally done it and at the third time of asking, (2016, 2017 and 2019) had managed to genuinely Leave the European Union. By now, Liv was shivering, and Julian very generously offered to drive us back down to the Carlton Club, in return for which, we bought he and his wife a slap-up breakfast. Liv and I then travelled back to Essex and crashed out around lunchtime and slept soundly – in a free country.

Avoiding "No Deal"

Nevertheless, as part of Boris' renegotiated Withdrawal Agreement, and in accordance with the similarly renegotiated "Political Declaration" (the PD) the United Kingdom voluntarily agreed to a Transition Period, up to the 31st December 2020, during which we would voluntarily agree to continue to follow the EU's legal rule book, whilst we negotiated a Future Relationship, i.e. a future trade deal that would govern our mutual economic inter-relationships into the foreseeable future. Crucially, under the revised version of the Political Declaration, both sides had already agreed that the desired end state would be a comprehensive Free Trade Agreement (FTA), in effect a long-standing objective of Eurosceptics for many years.

It is therefore completely untrue to say that, after all the furore, the United Kingdom eventually left the European Union with "No Deal". Conversely, we did indeed Leave with a "Deal" which was the revised Withdrawal Agreement (minus the Backstop) and the renegotiated Political Declaration. (Incidentally, the UK

Withdrawal Act 2020 also constrained the powers of the Joint Committee as well).

While Theresa May was Prime Minister, the European Union and their Chief Negotiator, Michel Barnier, stated repeatedly that they would never reopen the Withdrawal Agreement and, even in the unlikely event that they did, there was no question whatsoever that they would abandon the Backstop. In the end, when Boris Johnson became Prime Minister, he persuaded them to do both of these, and all within three months. As I have said several times in subsequent media interviews and this book, the Prime Minister "played a blinder" in these negotiations, proving that the European Union, which had previously appeared implacable, actually caved in, when we finally stood up to them.

Historically, the one thing that was always terrified the EU (and I use the word deliberately) has been the prospect of an unfettered United Kingdom, becoming in effect the Singapore of Europe and using a different Anglo Saxon economic model, to trade aggressively on world markets and effectively out-compete the European Union and EU Member States at every turn. Indeed, this is one of the reasons why the EU was so desperate to prevent the United Kingdom from Leaving the European Union in the first place. Moreover, it also explains why so many Politicians on the continent were quite prepared, to encourage Remain elements in the House of Commons in an attempt to subvert Brexit.

I may well be wrong, but all previous experience with the European Union shows that appeasement doesn't work and that only by taking a robust attitude to the EU and its Member States can you really achieve your objectives – exactly as the Prime Minister did when he re-negotiated the Withdrawal Agreement in the Autumn of 2019.

On the back of this, in the face of continuing Remainer obstruction in Parliament, Boris Johnson instigated – and then convincingly won a General Election by a majority of 80 seats – the Conservatives best result since the late 1980s under Mrs Thatcher.

A Further Deal – The Trade and Co-operation Agreement

Having won that December 2019 General Election, Boris Johnson, as Prime Minister, took the UK out of the EU at the end of January 2020. However, under the revised Political Declaration, we were still committed to negotiating a Comprehensive Free Trade Agreement (FTA), before the end of the Transition Period (TP), on 31st December 2020.

Again, the siren voices of Remain, both in Parliament and the media, began to argue that this was practically impossible and that, in a rehash of their earlier tired refrain, we would probably Leave with "No Deal", with no doubt cataclysmic consequences, at the end of the TP. Yet again, Boris Johnson confounded his critics. However, his secret weapon on this occasion was the same man who had successfully renegotiated the Withdrawal Agreement – David Frost.

David (now Lord) Frost, was and is a very different man from his predecessor as the UK's Chief Negotiator. A clear-eyed proponent of UK Sovereignty, he repeatedly insisted on this principle through months of tortuous negotiations with his EU opposite number, the wily Michel Barnier. Nevertheless, after many months of effort, the negotiation produced a UK/EU Trade and Co-operation Agreement (TCA) to govern trade and economic relationships, such as fishing rights, between the UK and the EU into the foreseeable future.

The ERG reconvenes the Star Chamber

As Prime Minister, throughout the extended negotiations over what was to become the TCA, Boris Johnson had repeatedly given assurances (in public to Parliament and the media and in private to the ERG) that he would not abandon the UK's hard-fought and newly won sovereignty, in any eventual deal.

As such, when the Government announced that both sides had agreed a deal (which would again require Parliamentary ratification, as a further International Treaty) in December 2020, many in the media and indeed the wider public then looked to the ERG, as "arbiters" of whether or not the deal really was, in actual fact, "Sovereignty Compliant".

Having already anticipated this eventuality, the ERG rapidly reconvened the "Star Chamber", with an amended membership but again under the Chairmanship of Sir Bill Cash, to scrutinise this new Treaty, in detail. However, this one was not 300 pages of A4 (Lisbon) or even 585 (the Withdrawal Agreement) but 1,245!

Nevertheless, in under a week, the Star Chamber (having initially divided the voluminous document, which amply filled an A4 Lever Arch File, among its members) between them began working through the fine detail of the new Treaty. For what it's worth I did too – although, this time, it took me an entire weekend to do it!

In the end, after what the Prime Minister estimated would be "Talmudic Scrutiny", I Chaired a virtual Plenary meeting of the ERG on 29th December 2020, when Sir

Bill declared the "verdict" of the Star Chamber, that the TCA was, indeed, "Sovereignty Compliant".

As a result, having received the "imprimatur" of the Star Chamber, and then the wider ERG (which meant there was unlikely to be any Commons row), the TCA flew through its stages in Parliament in rapid time and resulted in the European Union (Future Relationship) Act 2020, by which the UK legally exited the Transition Period, with a further deal, by the 31st of December 2020. Thus, the Remainers (of whom there were, by now, far fewer in Parliament), were confounded, yet again.

Just as before, by sticking to our guns, we in the United Kingdom were able to face-down the EU and agree an equitable agreement with them, to govern our economic relations into the foreseeable future. In welcoming the Second Reading of the Ratification Bill on 30th December, I said in the Commons:

"My colleagues in the European Research Group have fought long and hard for this day and we have sometimes been lampooned or even vilified by the remain-dominated electronic media for our trouble, when all we have ever wanted is one thing: to live in a free country that elects its own Government and makes its own laws here in Parliament, and then lives under them in peace. Now, thanks to the Prime Minister, who kept his word to the country and got Brexit done, who did exactly what it said on the tin, as our star chamber has verified, we can do that. What I call the Battle for Brexit is now over. We won, but I suspect the battle for the Union is now about to begin."[352]

So, the doom-mongers were beaten a second time, and the UK exited the Transition Period, again avoiding "No Deal" but with a nearly 1,300-page Treaty, between the UK and the European Union. The robust negotiating style of Lord Frost had again been vindicated and had delivered results in the face of considerable media scepticism, much of it inspired by diehard Remainers, who still found it almost impossible to reconcile themselves to the possibility that Britain might actually flourish, outside of the embrace of the European Union.

The numbers on the side of the bus

Some Remainers continue to console themselves that Vote Leave had "cheated" in 2016 by putting the gross figure of £350 million per week paid to the EU on the side of that now infamous red bus, rather than the net figure and that the public had therefore been deceived about how much money could be reinvested in the NHS. However, when the Government subsequently announced in 2019 an extra £34 billion a year for the NHS, by the end of the Parliament, under the NHS Long Term Plan, that equated to around £663 million per week extra funding for the NHS, almost twice the gross weekly figure on the side of the bus – let alone the net amount. So, "despite Brexit" the Government were still able to commit to record increases in NHS funding way beyond that promise by Vote Leave back in 2016 (although of course the money we save in our "subscription" to the EU could most certainly contribute towards that total).

The Northern Ireland Protocol – Unfinished business

Despite the very considerable success of negotiating the Trade and Co-operation Agreement with the EU (with the entire ERG subsequently voting for it in the House of Commons, with only two abstentions) there are still likely to be ongoing negotiations within the EU in the future, for instance over fishing quotas, once the five-year adjustment period for fishing within the TCA expires.

Similarly, we have yet to agree a further deal with the EU regarding Financial Services and reciprocal access between the City of London and related financial markets on the continent, e.g. in Paris and Frankfurt.

Moreover, as this book was being finalised, the UK and EU were still in discussions about the future of the much-revised Northern Ireland Protocol (NIP), which replaced the dreaded "Backstop" when the original Withdrawal Agreement was re-negotiated. Although the ERG took a clear-eyed decision to vote for the revised Withdrawal Agreement in the autumn of 2019 – so that we could *finally* Leave the EU several months later – it was on the strict understanding, as conveyed very clearly in private to the PM and No 10, that the NIP was unsustainable in the longer-term and would one day have to be re-negotiated, or ideally replaced.

This was all made more pressing when on 29th January 2021, out of the blue, the European Commission suddenly attempted to invoke Article 16 of the NIP, an "emergency clause", which allowed either signatory to resile from elements of the Protocol, in exceptional circumstances. Reputedly, the European Commission, which took this unprecedented step as part of a wider argument about access to Covid-19 vaccines, did not even bother to forewarn the Irish Government in Dublin that they were going to do it!

Following on from these events, in February 2021, the ERG produced a 38-page report entitled: "Re-uniting the Kingdom: How and why to replace the Northern Ireland Protocol", which argued, in detail, why the Northern Ireland Protocol should be replaced, by a system of "Mutual Enforcement" regarding goods passing between Northern Ireland and the Republic and also back into mainland Great Britain.

Negotiations between the UK Government and the EU on the future of the Northern Ireland Protocol are continuing, with the EU insisting that it can never be replaced. However, in this context, it is just worth remembering that they said very much the same about the original Backstop as well – but then replaced it anyway!

"Project Fear" – and the Covid-19 Pandemic

The immediate aftermath of Brexit, to some extent at least, has been overshadowed, as indeed have most other major events worldwide, by the worldwide pandemic, caused by the Coronavirus, or Covid-19. This has, tragically, led to multi-million fatalities worldwide, including, as of May 2021, over 125,000 deaths in the UK alone. Scientists worldwide have been involved in a collective "race against time", to develop effective vaccines against Covid-19, before casualties climbed even higher.

Nevertheless, the subsequent roll-out of national vaccination programmes, has provided a concrete example of the benefits of Brexit and one which does not require a detailed knowledge of Treaty Law, or Parliamentary procedure, to appreciate.

In short, the UK's decision, taken during the Transition Period, to opt out of the EU's collective vaccination programme and to provide a unilateral programme of rapidly sourcing multiple vaccinations worldwide, as well as producing a UK/Swedish Oxford/AstraZeneca Vaccine, led to a far more rapid initial Vaccination Programme in the UK than in the other countries of the EU. As of June 2021, almost 40 million UK adults had received at least one jab, with almost 20 million having received two.

While each death from Covid-19 represents an individual tragedy in its own right, the stark difference between the post-Brexit, more flexible and "fleet of foot" UK approach and the more ponderous, bureaucratic EU solution, has been clear. Given this stark contrast, even some prior Remainers, such as the previous *Today Programme* presenter, John Humphry's, have begun to question whether they should really have voted Leave after all.[353] Even allowing that the EU Vaccination programme now appears to have caught up, the far quicker initial UK response was plain for all to see, whether Leaver or Remainer.

Moreover, the United Kingdom, free from the continuing shackles of the EU Customs Union, has begun to negotiate multiple trade deals across the globe. As of September 2021, the new Department for International Trade (DIT), egged on by its then highly energetic Secretary of State, Liz Truss MP, had successfully negotiated some 70 such Trade Deals, with many more already in the pipeline.

While there have been some short-term economic issues relating to Brexit, e.g. initial Customs bureaucracy, these have been as nothing when compared to the economic challenges presented by the pandemic. Planes did indeed stop flying for a while – but this was entirely due to Covid-19 – not Brexit. The doomsayers of "Project Fear", who, it should be remembered, predicted the economy would nosedive as soon as we voted to Leave the EU – five years ago – were proven to be false prophets. The economy did not crash in 2016 as predicted, neither did house prices fall by 18% and neither did unemployment rise by 500,000 following the 2016 Referendum results. It was the people behind "Project Fear" who were really fearful – of their own population, who mercifully saw right through them when it really mattered.

In short, the 17.4 million people who voted, peacefully and democratically to Leave the EU, were right all along.

Chapter 18: Epilogue – The Case for the Spartans

The United Kingdom officially left the European Union, under both UK law (the UK Withdrawal Act 2020) and European Law (Article 50, of the Treaty on the Functioning of the European Union) at 11:00pm GMT on the 31st January 2020. At that point we formally withdrew from the institutions of the European Union, including withdrawing our MEPs from the European Parliament, as we were no longer entitled to them, given that we had ceased to be a Member State. The EU thus reduced from 28 Member States to 27, with the UK's departure now also representing a financial loss to Brussels, as it had for many years been the second largest net contributor to the EU budget, after Germany.

Chairman of the ERG

In March 2020, with the UK having successfully exited the EU and the negotiations on the FTA well underway during the Transition Period, Steve Baker contacted me to say that he had decided to stand down as Chairman of the ERG and encouraged me to succeed him.

Steve, who by now (uniquely in the history of the ERG) had been Chairman, not once but twice, represented a seat, Wycombe, in Buckinghamshire, which had narrowly voted Remain in the 2016 Referendum. Moreover, there had been quite a degree of demographic change in the constituency since another friend, Paul Goodman, was first elected as Steve's predecessor back in 2001. At the 2019 General Election, Steve's majority went down rather than up and, as a result of these several factors, Steve decided the time had come to stand down as Chairman.

I initially advised Steve to "sleep on it" and come back to me only if and when he was resolved but, when he did so, almost a fortnight later, I then consulted the other ERG Officers, who were happy for the Deputy Chairman to step up, in line with ERG tradition, which meant that the new Chairman, as subsequently confirmed at the next Plenary meeting of the Group – was me.

Thus, it came to pass, that in March 2020, the boy from Alcatraz became the Chairman of the European Research Group, first founded by Michael Spicer, 28 years previously.

The Battle for Brexit – Combatting the British Establishment

As someone once said: "Hindsight makes geniuses of all of us", but nevertheless, two years or more on from the drama of the Meaningful Votes in the House of Commons in early 2019, it is perhaps possible to look back with at least some degree of distance at what really took place.

This was indeed an epic battle, fought not with bombs or bullets but scraps of paper, Motions and Amendments; on the one hand by the ERG to try and honour the result of the 2016 Referendum and on the other by die-hard Remainers, to do everything possible to frustrate it.

In addition the forces of Remain in Parliament, were given tremendous support by what might be termed "the British Establishment", ranging from the upper echelons of the Civil Service, especially in No 10, the Cabinet Office and HM Treasury, through to powerful forces in the media, in particular large elements (though not all) of the BBC; several other TV channels; the Confederation of British Industry (CBI), the Trade Union Congress (TUC), the Bank of England, and a number of national newspapers to boot.

All of this took place, as many people in the upper echelons of British society consistently refused to accept the democratic verdict of the electorate in the 2016 Referendum. All this, despite the fact that the 17.4 million people who voted Leave, represented the largest vote by far for any proposition in the entire history of British politics. Despite all of this, "the men in Whitehall knew best", and some of them at least, genuinely seemed to believe that the British public were either bigoted or stupid or both and therefore somehow needed to be saved from themselves.

Whilst this view may have been prevalent among the rich and privileged, it was certainly not the view in the pubs and clubs of towns and villages up and down the country, particularly outside of the M25. Rightly or wrongly, a great deal of the British Establishment is centred in and around London and the Home Counties, and the phrase, "the Metropolitan Elite" is not without merit.

It was representatives of this mandarin class, who it has to be said, skilfully negotiated a highly complex Treaty, which had the ultimate aim of keeping us locked into the European Union but then had the brilliant idea of naming it the "Withdrawal Agreement" and thus trying to purvey the image that anyone who had the temerity to oppose it, was ultimately voting to keep us in the EU. Hence

Tony Blair's comment about the brilliance of the drafting and his backhanded compliment to those involved.[354]

The overwhelming flaw in this cunning plan (as Blackadder's Baldrick might have characterised it) was that Members of Parliament, despite whatever the public may think of them, by and large can actually read. And when the "cranks" and "obsessives" within the European Research Group sat down and read through in detail what the Withdrawal Agreement *actually* meant, they realised very clearly what was actually being perpetrated and reacted accordingly.

The forces of Remain had seriously underestimated the determination of a sizeable group of committed MPs, to stand up for British self-Government – fortified by the absolute moral certainty that they were only doing what the British people had democratically voted for in the first place.

The British Public – "Trust the people"

Throughout the three-year Battle for Brexit, in both Parliament and in the media, one of the things that sustained the European Research Group was the unshakable belief that we were acting to try and fulfil the democratic decision of the citizens of the United Kingdom in the 2016 EU Referendum.

While we were up against the full panoply of the British Establishment – let alone the might of the EU itself – many of us felt we were the voice of "the man or woman in the street", who had voted for self-Government but who lacked the position and/or media contacts of the politicians, without which they struggled to make their 17.4 million voices heard.

Even getting to Millbank Studios or College Green, to do media interviews, you often had to run the gauntlet of Steve Bray and his band of EU flag waving fanatics – although only on one occasion, after Boris had just prorogued Parliament – did this hostility almost turn to actual violence.

Nevertheless, many of us were stopped in the street either in Westminster or back in our constituencies (and in a number of London taxi's it has to be said) and urged to "keep going" and "don't give in!" Away from what Dominic Cumming's once accurately described as "the babble in the bubble" – many of us were stopped, again and again, by people we had never met and urged to keep up the fight.

At ERG meetings, we would sometimes exchange anecdotes about completely random encounters with members of the public the previous weekend, in supermarkets, on trains or even at the barbers/hairdressers, who were adamant that we were doing the right thing – and should keep on doing it, whatever was thrown at us and no matter who was throwing it.

It is the 19th century Conservative Prime Minister, Benjamin Disraeli, who is often credited with coining the expression "Trust the People".

Well, whoever it was, in the end, that is exactly what we did.

Fighting the pro-Remain media

While in theory, our media are meant to remain objective, of course, in reality, as any viewer on television or listener to radio can tell you, in practice this is far from the truth. Britain's broadcast media is overwhelmingly London centric and the majority of those who work at it share the pro-Remain tendencies that I have been describing immediately above. This is not to say that every single broadcast journalist was pro-Remain – there were a number of honourable exceptions – but it is to say that the overwhelming ethos of the broadcasters that they work for, including the BBC, Sky, ITV and most blatantly of all Channel 4, were pro-Remain from start to finish and you only needed to watch a few of the interviews, to see the aggressive tone that was adopted towards Eurosceptics and the far more ameliorative questions and "underarm bowling" that was often directed to pro-Remain guests to see just how true this was.[355]

Within the print media, opinion was more balanced. *The Times*, as the organ of the British Establishment, was unsurprisingly firmly behind the Withdrawal Agreement, as to some extent was the *Daily Mail* as well. The *Financial Times*, *The Guardian* and the *Independent* were shamelessly pro-Remain, whereas the *Express* and the *Telegraph* were markedly more Eurosceptic. Among the tabloids, the *Daily Mirror* was clearly opposed to Theresa May as a Tory Prime Minister, whereas *The Sun* was broadly Eurosceptic, (although some of its most prominent journalists were actually instinctively Remainers). However, in practice, people generally tend to buy a newspaper that accords with their own political views and therefore perhaps it could be argued that "bias" in the print media was more "transparent" as it were.

Nevertheless, in the final run in to MV3, even the print media – with the honourable exception of the *Telegraph* group – argued that we should give in. Even the *Daily Express*, hardly a bastion of left-wing Euro-federalism, but by now clearly exasperated with the whole process, sought to argue on the 29th March that the Spartans should finally concede, (see below).

It was against this overall background, that I conducted numerous interviews on television and radio and indeed with the print media over the course of the Battle for Brexit. Up to the point of Theresa May's No Confidence Vote on the 12th December, I had a relatively low media profile (certainly compared to Jacob and Steve) but after that, perhaps in part because of the interview containing the Tom Enders letter on 25th January (which was my idea, if only at the last minute) and the stare off with Will Self on 8th March (which most certainly was not) then suddenly I achieved national prominence in the media, in a way that I had genuinely never expected – certainly not when I was first elected to the House of Commons long ago, back in 2001.

I have been criticised in a number of quarters for having a "combative" or rather punchy interview style, part of which probably relates back to my formative days, on Basildon Council. I can understand that, particularly for pro-Remain supporters, they may have found some of my remarks irritating. Nevertheless, for someone who has now become relatively experienced in dealing with modern 24-hour media, I would say in my defence that if you are anything less than confident or determined, you are likely to be completely steam-rollered within the first 30 seconds of an interview. Without going into individual names, there are a number of prominent national interviewers, who will quite merrily talk all over their guests, for virtually the entire interview, if you allow them to get away with it; so, if you don't fight to get a word in edgeways, you often won't get a chance to say anything meaningful at all.

Similarly, the institutional view of many of these media outlets was quite clearly pro-Remain from the outset, and therefore whilst these broadcasters were sometimes too clever to show outright bias (which people could complain about) there was nevertheless, a constant undercurrent that was pro-Remain, with one interviewer after another always desperately keen to trip up some member of the ERG or force them into a memorable mistake, ideally live on air.

Enoch Powell once said that Politicians who complain about the media are rather akin to sailors who complain about the sea. There is perhaps some truth in this but, nevertheless, on occasions, one really did have to struggle to be heard, not least when you knew full well that the person at the other end of the microphone privately disagreed with almost every word you were saying. What we now call "cancel culture" in many ways began with the media (and certainly including social media) debates over Brexit. In other words, in most interviews you were up against it right from the outset and if you weren't prepared to stand up for yourself, you had very little practical chance of getting your point across at all.[356]

Dark Blue on Dark Blue

It is one thing in politics to fight your opponents – in a way you expect that as part of your trade. Nevertheless, it is infinitely more difficult to fight your friends. When the ERG split, in the run up to Meaningful Vote Three, this was genuinely a very painful experience for all concerned.

Both sides of the argument passionately wanted to leave the European Union but came to strongly disagree on the best tactics for achieving this. This was not just Tory versus Tory, this was Eurosceptic versus Eurosceptic, Brexiteer versus Brexiteer. To put it another way, whilst rows among Tory MPs are sometimes described as "blue on blue", this was "dark blue on dark blue"; with prominent members of the European Research Group publicly disagreeing with each other in March 2019 on how best to achieve the desired aim of Brexit.

As someone who was present at almost all of the key meetings as this parting of the ways took place, I can honestly relate that whilst people felt strongly and indeed arguments were advanced passionately on both sides, with only a few exceptions, this was done without personal rancour. By now everybody knew everybody else pretty well and there was a certain mutual understanding among all present that people were doing what they genuinely believed to be right.

For instance, although Jacob and I were divided in the end about whether or not to vote for the Withdrawal Agreement on MV3, it never became acrimonious. The nearest we got I think was when I texted Jacob to ask him what Winston Churchill would have done in these circumstances (drawing on the obvious analogy of 1940). Jacob rapidly replied that, above all other things, Churchill was a pragmatist and perhaps I could learn from that, to which I responded that there were a number of very important factors in Winston Churchill's life – but perhaps one of the most important of all was that he went to Harrow rather than Eton![357]

In fact, we managed to conduct our business without becoming really aggressive towards each other and indeed in the final run in to MV3 you would be hard pressed to find examples of members of the ERG really tearing into each other in the media, we just didn't do it that way. Nevertheless, it was an extremely stressful period – not least as all concerned knew full well how high the stakes were.

The vital importance of public support

However, throughout the Battle for Brexit, MPs on all sides were bombarded with emails advising us, sometimes rather pointedly, on what to do.

Because I had achieved something of a high media profile, I received a large number of emails from Remainers, some of them politely disagreeing with me and others becoming quite vituperative, up to and including a couple of actual death threats (which we subsequently reported to the Police).

Conversely, however, I also received literally hundreds, indeed breaking into the thousands, of emails from all round the country, the vast bulk of them from people I had never met, encouraging me and my colleagues in the ERG not to give in. Some further examples of emails I received can be found at Appendix 7 however, as just two examples of them:

From: ███████

Sent: 21 November 2018 20:35

To: The office of Mark Francois <mark.francois.mp@parliament.uk>

Subject: Thank You

Dear Mr Francois,

I just wanted to write to thank you for all you are doing for the country. I voted leave and am appalled at the way we have been lied to most atrociously by Teresa May until we have a withdrawal deal which is BRINO.

I really appreciate your comments in and out of Parliament.

Today in Parliament you were speaking and someone called you a twerp. I think this has happened before. I just wanted to thank you for what you are doing against the odds. The majority of Remainers in Parliament are the real twerps in fact. History will prove you are right.

Anyway, I do not think that most people know the awful truth as you do so keep plugging on please.

Kind regards,

███████358

When you are under pressure on all sides, it is difficult to exaggerate the importance of receiving supportive emails like this, from members of the public, some of whom explained that prior to the Referendum they had never voted in any election whatsoever, such was their generally low opinion of Politicians, but who, nevertheless, kept urging us to keep going. I took notice of such emails (from both sides of the argument) just to act as a reminder of what ordinary people were saying about this issue, without the intermediation of the media to tell me "what people were thinking". I knew full well what ordinary people were thinking because they were frequently emailing me and my Brexiteer colleagues, literally in droves. (In fact, Adele estimated that from July 2017, until January 2020 we received almost 10,000 Brexit related emails, some from constituents but the vast majority from people who were not).

Had this been overwhelmingly one way traffic, in essence arguing that I and my colleagues were wrong, perhaps, over time, this might have dented our morale. Nevertheless, the fact that many of the arguments were at least balanced (and if anything, I got far more supportive emails than the other way around), convinced me throughout that what we were doing was right.

I also received a lot of private and personal encouragement from both serving and former MPs. As just one example, one former Essex colleague texted me at the height of the Brexit debates and said:

"Keep fighting! The fact that they keep mocking you so much, just proves how scared they really are".

When I read this, it reminded me of a quote, often attributed to Mahatma Gandhi, which reads:

"First, they ignore you,
Then they laugh at you,
Then they fight you,
Then you win"

The role of the ERG

I suspect it is not an exaggeration to say that in years and perhaps even decades to come, academics and political scientists will debate the role of the ERG in the Battle for Brexit. I doubt anyone will ever want to write a doctoral thesis on individual Brexiteers – although I could be wrong – but I wouldn't be surprised if at least a few are eventually written on the ERG – in which case I hope this book may prove of some small service, to future historians.

After all, this was arguably the most significant and controversial political event in British history since the end of the Second World War, and passionate arguments were exercised on both sides (and as indicated above, sometimes even within sides) on what was best to do for the destiny of our country.

It was thanks to the incredible foresight of Sir Michael Spicer, who had founded the ERG in 1993, supported by others such as Sir Bill Cash, for exactly this kind of eventuality, that throughout this whole debate there was a coterie of well-informed Members of Parliament, who were able to combat the depth of knowledge that lay within the Remain camp, including in the upper echelons of the British Establishment.

Throughout the "Battle for Brexit" the European Research Group did what it said on the tin, and produced detailed research, laying out specifically the issues that were at stake and the likely consequences of various courses of action. As part of this, there was a determined attempt to explain often complex legal concepts and issues, as far as possible in everyday English, so that not just politicians but also members of the public could follow these arguments and understand for themselves what was at stake. The role of the ERG's Senior Researcher, Christopher Howarth, in helping to research and compile much of this information, should never be underestimated.[360]

This perhaps leads on to the counterfactual question – what if the ERG had never existed? It is of course impossible to prove a counterfactual but, nevertheless, it is possible to draw at least some broad conclusions as to what might have happened had the ERG not been there.

When the skilfully contrived Withdrawal Agreement was published, there would not have been a bespoke resource to analyse a 585-page draft Treaty in detail and indeed to point out, in a media savvy way, the flaws in the Government's approach. The sheer weight of paper would have defeated many MPs, a large number of whom to this day will still admit (if only in private) that they never actually read the Withdrawal Agreement at all. It was only because of this bunch of "cranks" and "obsessives" backed up by a superb Researcher, that the ERG was able to expose to other MPs, and through them, to public attention, what the Withdrawal Agreement was really intended to do.

However, the ERG did not have a monopoly on this activity. Some media outlets, such as the *Telegraph* and the *Sun*, conducted their own forensic analysis of the Withdrawal Agreement, and both concluded that it represented in effect "a surrender" to the European Union – as indeed I pointed out to the Prime Minister to her discomfort in the Chamber of the Commons on 26th November 2018.[361]

Nevertheless, it took considerable determination and indeed co-ordination among Eurosceptic Members of Parliament within the ERG in order to successfully prevent the Withdrawal Agreement from passing through the House of Commons. In MV1, 118 Conservative MPs voted against Theresa May's Deal. With the exception of a handful of ardent Europhiles (who voted against the Withdrawal Agreement for their own reasons) the vast bulk of these 118 were Eurosceptically inclined Tory MPs, but by no means all of whom were members of the ERG.

By the time of MV2 on the 15th March, many of these more moderate opponents had effectively been peeled away by the Whips and others and the 75 Tory MPs who voted No, against Theresa May's Deal again that day, were, with a few exceptions, nearly all members or supporters of the ERG.[362]

By the time it came to MV3 on 29th March, that group of ERG members/supporters had itself split, with approximately 2/3 eventually deciding to vote for the Withdrawal Agreement whilst approximately 1/3 (the so-called 28 Spartans) held out to the bitter end. At one plenary meeting of the ERG, prior to the series of Meaningful Votes commencing, the Chief Whip, Julian Smith, memorably stated: "If you really don't like this deal – then don't vote for it!" So, we didn't.[363]

Nevertheless, had a well organised, skilfully informed and determined group of Eurosceptics not existed within the Conservative Party during this period, then the Withdrawal Agreement would have almost certainly passed through the House of Commons and the destiny of our Country would have been altered accordingly, perhaps forever.

The case for the Spartans

Moreover, given the overwhelming success of the Brexit Party in the European Elections barely two months later – when they won 29 MEPs to the Tory Party's 4 and the Conservatives scored their lowest ever vote in a national election, at just 9% - it is not inconceivable that the Conservative Party would have ripped itself to pieces in the ensuing rows about implementing Theresa May's deal – while Nigel Farage and his allies simply cleaned up, amid the smouldering wreckage.

In a nutshell, had the 28 Spartans resolved to give in on MV3, and voted with the Government, then once word of their impending collapse had spread, there would almost undoubtedly have been sufficient Labour MPs who were prepared to break Nick Brown's extremely stern Three Line Whip, in order to get the Withdrawal Agreement over the line. Indeed, we now know that at least eight Labour MPs went to see the Prime Minister less than an hour before the vote but eventually drew back from supporting the Government, because they felt that their votes would not be enough to make the difference – and therefore the consequences which they would have to suffer from their Labour colleagues were not worth it.[364] In other words, they were not prepared to "die on the wire" for Theresa May in 2019, just as their predecessors had been reluctant to do the same for William Hague, during the debates on the Lisbon Treaty more than a decade earlier. In the end, despite literally months of painstaking efforts by some in No 10, only *five* Labour MPs voted with the Government on Meaningful Vote Three.

Nevertheless, had the Government actually won that vote, and thus the Commons had agreed the Withdrawal Agreement in principle, then at that point all resistance would have effectively collapsed; such was the build-up of pressure at that time.

I remain sceptical to this day that if she had won the division on MV3, Theresa May would have actually stood down as Tory Leader. Remember this is a politician who stated repeatedly in the run up to the 2017 General Election that she was not about to call one – and then did exactly that.

It is also the same person who witnessed her Whips enthusiastically urge the entire Party to vote for the Brady Amendment in January 2019, which passed by 16 votes as a result (including with the near unanimous support of the ERG) but, having won this crucial victory, then declined to exploit this opportunity, because she had somehow been convinced during the following week that removing the Backstop, as the Malthouse Compromise/Brady Amendment had intended, would pose a mortal threat to public order in Northern Ireland.

Moreover, even when she appeared at the 1922 Committee on Wednesday 27th March, two days before the critical vote, despite having agreed in advance with Iain Duncan Smith that she would announce the time of her departure, she repeatedly ducked questions about what the precise timing would be and therefore she never gave a cast iron commitment, certainly not one that I heard anyway, that she would undoubtedly step down if the Withdrawal Agreement had passed. Hence her being pressed several times by backbenchers, including Adam Holloway, to name a date – something she repeatedly refused to do. IDS, who as a former Party Leader with some sympathy for the Prime Minister's predicament, had worked hard for several days behind the scenes to negotiate this compromise between No 10 and a sceptical ERG, felt badly let down by her failure to then offer a date to stand down at the '22.[365]

In reality, once she had won, her authority would have been massively enhanced and I have no doubt, that egged on by her mainly Europhile advisors (some of whom effectively depended on her for their jobs), she would have found some pretext on which to nevertheless remain in office and "see the process through". They would then have asked Parliament to Ratify a brilliantly crafted International Treaty, which would have had the practical effect, via the Backstop, of effectively keeping us in the European Union forever.

It is therefore not an exaggeration to say that on the 29th March 2019, those 28 "Spartans" literally saved their country from becoming a vassal state. Some may argue that this is a bold claim, but I believe it to be absolutely true. Had the Spartans folded that day, the battle would effectively have been over, the vote in the Referendum would have been completely betrayed and arguably the democratic process in the United Kingdom would have been irreparably damaged ever after.

On the day that the UK left the European Union, *The Sun* newspaper ran a headline "Our time has come" and accompanied it with the words "Tonight at 11:00pm, after 30 years of resistance to the creeping danger of a European Superstate, the great people of the United Kingdom have at last, finally…Got

Brexit Done". In an accompanying editorial, in which it praised a number of those involved, *The Sun* included the following:

"Jacob Rees-Mogg, Iain Duncan Smith, Steve Baker, Bill Cash and their ERG of Tory backbenchers whose refusal to compromise was admirable, even if *The Sun* did despair of it when it threatened to destroy Brexit entirely. They have been vindicated. As has the ERG's founder, the late ex Tory MP, Michael Spicer".[366]

One and a half years later, in September 2021, 25 of the 28 Spartans gathered for a special reunion dinner at The Carlton Club in London (the commemorative photograph from the event is on the cover of this book). The highlight of the evening was a very moving address by Sir Bill Cash, whose reminded companions of everything that had been at stake and then thanked his fellow Spartans for standing firm, despite the immense pressure which they had all been subjected to in early 2019.

The photograph was subsequently printed in the *Daily Telegraph* who accompanied it with a leading article under the heading "Molon Labe", which translated from the original Ancient Greek (in a way that Boris Johnson might perhaps approve of) means: "Come and take them" – echoing Leonidas' defiant reply to Xerxes demands for his 300 warriors to lay down their weapons and surrender. *The Telegraph's* leader then went on to argue:

"The Spartan group of Tory MPs held a celebratory dinner on Wednesday: their stand against Theresa May's Brexit deal will certainly go down in history. They saved the country from a surrender that might have torn the Tory's apart, so they rescued us from Jeremy Corbyn as well. The Spartans also deserve credit for coming up with an analogy other than the Second World War, and thus confusing Remainers who weren't familiar with the battle of Thermopylae. The odds were against the Greeks; they lost the battle, yet their persistence turned the tide. It goes to show that if you stand by an idea, and that idea is sufficiently logical and just, you can win in the end."[367]

A Battle for the Democratic Principle Itself

Ultimately, the "Battle for Brexit" was therefore not just a question about Europe or indeed even about British self-Government but about upholding the democratic principle itself. In other words, whether or not people voting in a Referendum, would then subsequently be obeyed by Politicians, who had faithfully promised to do their bidding, before the votes were cast.

Remember, the Government booklet, circulated to every household in the UK at the start of the Referendum Campaign, had promised quite unambiguously: "This is your decision. The Government will implement what you decide". Which part of that emphatic promise was unclear? And yet, in fact, when it came to it, they then endeavoured to do precisely the opposite.

Thus, over time, the Battle morphed substantially. It evolved from simply Leave vs Remain, both inside and outside Parliament, to a struggle to uphold the democratic principle itself. The "Metropolitan Elite", having, to their amazement, lost first time around, were determined to win, another way instead.

If the Remainers had won their artful war of attrition, then I really believe it would fatally have undermined public confidence in our entire democratic process, which could, eventually, have led to some extremely ugly outcomes, further down the line. The eventual winners in such a dangerous situation would have only been the likes of the odious BNP. Nevertheless, in the end, The People did triumph over The Establishment and we finally managed to Leave the EU after all.

Historians will have the luxury of arguing over this point for decades and perhaps even centuries to come. Long after I am dead, people will still be debating these matters backwards and forwards but part of the reason for writing this book, if nothing else, is so the case for the ERG and the Spartans, at least as I saw it, as one of their leaders, can stand on the record. If nothing else, it should give all these people something genuinely "meaningful" to argue about.

As it turned out, in the end, Paul Goodman was right. This time round, the Spartans won after all.

A promise kept

As for me, I have always enjoyed being a Member of Parliament and hope that I can continue doing so, as long as my employers in Rayleigh and Wickford are content to renew my contract of employment (as Ken Livingstone might have put it). I intend to continue to work hard on their behalf and hopefully persuade them to do so, at least for a few more years yet.

In truth, I have fought my war and with the aid of many others, we won it. I may have suffered on Twitter, for snapping back at Beth Rigby on *Sky* that "I wasn't trained to lose" but in the end, to put it bluntly, I didn't. I had the great privilege of being part of a group of Members of Parliament who realised instinctively, from the outset, what was at stake and then did everything in their power to defend the country that they loved from vassalage.

Having done that, there is nothing really that I could do in politics to top it. Even serving as a Cabinet Minister now a very remote prospect at best) could not possibly match the excitement and the drama and indeed the salience and overarching importance of those great issues that stood in the balance, in the early part of 2019.

As I explained earlier on in this book, even though many may disbelieve me, when I was a teenager, I had some indefinable sense that one day there would be some threat to my country and that it was my duty to go into politics to help resist it. At the time I had no idea what it might be, I just sensed that there would be "something" and, in the end, there was.

As a ten-year-old boy, sitting at my father's knee, hearing about his experience on D-Day, I had faithfully promised him that "I would never take living in a free country for granted". I had absolutely no idea at that time that within four years he would be dead – but I kept my solemn promise to my father, nonetheless.

I never *did* take living in free country for granted and so, when it mattered, I fought when I considered that freedom to genuinely be at stake, which I ardently believed it was.

I hope I can look back, in the autumn years of my life, and say that, in extremely difficult circumstances, when the pressure was really on, I did the right thing by my country and fought for what I truly believed in, with all my heart.

Or, as Rudyard Kipling once put it, far better than I ever could:

"If you can force your heart and nerve and sinew
To serve your turn long after they are gone,
And so hold on when there is nothing in you
Except the Will which says to them: 'Hold on!'

If you can talk with crowds and keep your virtue,
Or walk with Kings—nor lose the common touch,
If neither foes nor loving friends can hurt you,
If all men count with you, but none too much;

If you can fill the unforgiving minute
With sixty seconds' worth of distance run,
Yours is the Earth and everything that's in it,
And – which is more – you'll be a Man, my son!"[368]

Appendix 1

List of 'The Buddies'

The Brexiteer Whipping Team that defeated Theresa May's so-called Withdrawal Agreement.

Chief Buddy:	Mark Francois MP	Rayleigh and Wickford
Deputy Chief Buddy:	Steve Baker MP	Wycombe
	Simon Clarke MP	Middlesbrough South and East Cleveland
	Charlie Elphicke MP	Dover
	Adam Holloway MP	Gravesham
	David Jones MP	Clwyd West
	Laurence Robertson MP	Tewkesbury
	Ross Thomson MP	Aberdeen South
	Michael Tomlinson MP	Mid Dorset and North Poole
	Anne-Marie Trevelyan MP	Berwick-upon-Tweed
	Theresa Villiers MP	Chipping Barnet
	██████████████*	██████████████*

* The 12th member of 'The Buddies' wished to remain anonymous.

Appendix 2

Enter – or Rather Exit – The Spartans

&conservativehome

By Paul Goodman
Published: March 18, 2019

The battle of Thermopylae is famous in legend for the sacrifice of 300 Spartans. They died in battle, but saved their city. The tale has a modern day Brexit resonance.

As we approach a third "meaningful" vote on Theresa May's Brexit deal, the number of Conservative MPs still willing to oppose it is falling. It was 118 in January, and 75 last week.

Switchers for last Tuesday's second vote included David Davis, Graham Brady, Philip Davies and our columnist, Robert Halfon. Among those who now suggest that they will switch on a third are Esther McVey, Simon Clarke and Daniel Kawczynski.

Which returns us to Thermopylae.

ConservativeHome is told that a hardcore of those determined to hold out now refer to themselves as "the Spartans". These include a significant chunk of the ERG – though calculations are complicated by the fact that not all those who oppose the deal are ERG members.

If the Prime Minister's deal gets through, among the corpses of MPs slain in the pass should be those of: Peter Bone, Bill Cash, Christopher Chope, Mark Francois, Andrea Jenkyns, John Redwood and, we believe, Steve Baker.

Others who died at Thermopylae include Thespians, Helots and Thebans, history tells us.

Readers must decide for themselves which of these labels best describe Dominic Grieve's band of pro-Second Referendum holdouts, but they, too, will surely stick against May's deal – a fact that many of our media colleagues tend to overlook.

Last week, they included Guto Bebb, Damian Collins, Justine Greening, Sam Gyimah, Jo Johnson, and Grieve himself. It is unlikely that many of them will peel off.

As we write, Downing Street is striving to win the DUP over to the deal.

If it succeeds, the calculation for May will be whether enough Opposition MPs will back her deal to cancel out the Spartans who oppose it. We would say that the former are among the Persians, but are in danger of stretching this historical analogy way too far.

Among those well placed to pronounce on the question is Boris Johnson. What will he do when the vote comes? Will he stand with the Spartans, and return "with my shield or on it", as he sometimes likes to write? Or will he swap sides and join the Persians?

His *Daily Telegraph* column today is ambiguous on the point. We are less qualified to pronounce on classical history than the former Foreign Secretary, but can't help questioning whether the analogy holds at all.

For in this case, the city wouldn't be saved if the Spartans are massacred, since a consequence of their defeat would be the deal passing.

And in any case, this time round, the Spartans may actually win.

Appendix 3

List of the 28 'Spartans'

The 28 Brexiteer MPs who voted against the so-called Withdrawal Agreement during 'Meaningful Vote Three' – 29th March 2019

1.	Adam Afriyie	Windsor
2.	Steve Baker	Wycombe
3.	John Baron	Basildon and Billericay
4.	Peter Bone	Wellingborough
5.	The Rt Hon Suella Braverman QC	Fareham
6.	Andrew Bridgen	North West Leicestershire
7.	Sir William Cash	Stone
8.	Sir Christopher Chope OBE	Christchurch
9.	James Duddridge	Rochford and Southend East
10.	The Rt Hon Mark Francois	Rayleigh and Wickford
11.	Marcus Fysh	Yeovil
12.	Philip Hollobone	Kettering
13.	Adam Holloway	Gravesham
14.	Ranil Jayawardena	North East Hampshire
15.	Sir Bernard Jenkin	Harwich and North Essex
16.	Andrea Jenkyns	Morley and Outwood
17.	The Rt Hon David Jones	Clwyd West
18.	The Rt Hon Dr Julian Lewis	New Forest East
19.	Julia Lopez	Hornchurch and Upminster
20.	Craig Mackinlay JP	South Thanet
21.	Anne Marie Morris	Newton Abbot
22.	The Rt Hon Priti Patel	Witham
23.	The Rt Hon Owen Paterson	North Shropshire
24.	The Rt Hon Sir John Redwood	Wokingham
25.	Laurence Robertson	Tewkesbury
26.	Andrew Rosindell	Romford
27.	Lee Rowley	North East Derbyshire
28.	The Rt Hon Theresa Villiers	Chipping Barnet

Appendix 4

'We May be Beaten'

Speech in Committee Room 9 by Steve Baker MP, to the European Research Group, following the 1922 Committee at which Prime Minister Theresa May announced her willingness to leave office earlier than planned – 27th March 2019

I am consumed by a ferocious rage … after that pantomime of sycophancy and bullying next door.

It is a rage I have not felt since the time of the Lisbon Treaty, when I realised that those who govern us care not how we vote.

For what did our forebears fight and die? It was for our liberty. And what is our liberty, if not the right to govern ourselves, peacefully at the ballot box?

Like all of you, I have wrestled with my conscience, with the evidence before me, with the text of the Treaty, and I resolved that I would vote against this deal however often it was presented, come what may, if it meant the fall of the Government and the destruction of the Conservative Party.

By God, right now, if I think of the worthless, ignorant cowards and knaves in the House today, voting for things they do not understand, which would surrender our right to govern ourselves, I would tear this building down and bulldoze the rubble into the river. God help me, I would.

But I know that if we do this, if we insist and we take this all the way, we might find ourselves standing in the rubble of our Party and our constitution and our Government and our country. I am so filled with rage that we should have been deliberately put in this place by people whose addiction to power without accountability has led them to place before this country a choice between Remain or Brexit in Name Only.

I want to destroy, to tear down, to break. I confess to you I do not know what to do.

So, God help me, I am going to look at these votes tonight and see where we stand. As I said in my *Telegraph* article – which I meant and still do – we may yet be beaten by the numbers.

Jacob's case is persuasive. Catherine makes a good point, and I am grateful. But by God this will cost me dear if in the end I go back on what I said to Mark and others, if in the end, because of the consequences of a communist governing this country I have to vote for this deal.

It will cost me dear. I may yet resign the Whip in fury rather than be part of this.

So, I've been honest with you. I have been proud to be your Deputy Chairman, to be your Chairman before, when we made this thing, when we – when I – designed this ERG to be what it is today. I'm proud to have been the Bill Minister for the EU Withdrawal Act.

But I fear today we may be beaten. We shall find out later.

Appendix 5

'We are the Last Line of Defence'

Speech in the Grand Committee Room of the House of Commons by Mark Francois MP – just prior to 'Meaningful Vote Three' – 29th March 2019

Thank you, Jacob,

Can I begin by endorsing your call for mutual respect when this is all over, either one way or another. We in the European Research Group have been through a great deal together and we cannot fall out now, even though some of us in this room now hold opposing views, albeit for honourable reasons, on both sides of the argument.

Our colleague, Dr Julian Lewis, has already made an analogy with May 1940, and the role that our predecessors in this House played then. All I can add is that, when the bells ring about thirty minutes from now, the destiny of this nation, of what Churchill once called our island story, will be decided, quite literally, by the 50 or so of us now sitting in this room.

My father, Reginald Francois, died when I was still a boy. However, as a present he once gave me a copy of Rudyard Kipling's poem "If" and told me if ever I faced a dilemma to read it. Well, I did that again last night and straight away it struck me, that although it was composed over a century ago, it could almost have been written for us in the ERG, today. Remember the famous opening stanza:

If you can keep your head, when all about you
Are losing theirs and blaming it on you
If you can trust yourself, when all men doubt you
Yet make allowance for their doubting too

Well, we must trust ourselves now. If we support this so-called Withdrawal Agreement today and it passes as a result, then before long the Backstop will undoubtedly be activated, by collusion between EU bureaucrats and our own Europhile civil servants and we will rapidly find ourselves trapped in a Customs Union, from which there is no escape without EU consent, which will never be forthcoming. Despite the Referendum, despite the votes of 17.4 million people, despite the democratically and peacefully expressed will of the British people, we will have been imprisoned in The EU's trade policy forever, and thus effectively in the European Union itself.

Remember, the Backstop has no Article 50, no unilateral escape cause – because it was quite deliberately drafted that way, including by some of our own senior officials, who have never accepted the result of the Referendum and probably never will. It falls on us, as elected MPs, sent here by our constituents, who we serve, to prevent this. There is no-one else who can intercede. We are now, just the few of us here today, absolutely our country's last line of defence.

As effectively your Chief Whip throughout this whole process I know full well this has been difficult, sometimes very difficult, for many of us. But we have not come this far, marched all this way, fought so hard and for so long, only to buckle at the last moment. If we do, if we give in now, history will never forgive us for it. But if we hold out, Article 50 cannot be extended forever and eventually we will obtain our liberty, perhaps even as early as next month.

In summary, all I have ever really wanted is to live in a free country, which elects its own Government, makes its own laws – and then lives under them in peace. If that is also what you want, not just in your head but in your heart, then I earnestly appeal to you: walk through the lobbies with me and Steve this afternoon – and don't just save your country but set it free!

Appendix 6

'If' – by Rudyard Kipling

If you can keep your head when all about you
Are losing theirs and blaming it on you,
If you can trust yourself when all men doubt you,
But make allowance for their doubting too;
If you can wait and not be tired by waiting,
Or being lied about, don't deal in lies,
Or being hated, don't give way to hating,
And yet don't look too good, nor talk too wise:

If you can dream – and not make dreams your master;
If you can think – and not make thoughts your aim;
If you can meet with Triumph and Disaster
And treat those two impostors just the same;
If you can bear to hear the truth you've spoken
Twisted by knaves to make a trap for fools,
Or watch the things you gave your life to, broken,
And stoop and build 'em up with worn-out tools:

If you can make one heap of all your winnings
And risk it on one turn of pitch-and-toss,
And lose, and start again at your beginnings
And never breathe a word about your loss;
If you can force your heart and nerve and sinew
To serve your turn long after they are gone,
And so hold on when there is nothing in you
Except the Will which says to them: 'Hold on!'

If you can talk with crowds and keep your virtue,
' Or walk with Kings – nor lose the common touch,
if neither foes nor loving friends can hurt you,
If all men count with you, but none too much;
If you can fill the unforgiving minute
With sixty seconds' worth of distance run,
Yours is the Earth and everything that's in it,
And – which is more – you'll be a Man, my son!

Appendix 7

Sample of genuine emails received by Mark Francois MP during the 'Battle for Brexit'

From: ▓▓▓▓▓
Sent: 15 October 2018 13:31
To: The office of Mark Francois <mark.francois.mp@parliament.uk>
Subject: You

Just heard you on radio. You are a disgrace to your country. When are you idiots going to stop making me ashamed to be British? If you idiots and crooks get your way and we become Cayman Islands in the Cold, I hope you get ▓▓▓▓▓.

From: ▓▓▓▓▓
Sent: 21 November 2018 20:35
To: The office of Mark Francois <mark.francois.mp@parliament.uk>
Subject: Thank You

Dear Mr Francois,

I just wanted to write to thank you for all you are doing for the country. I voted leave and am appalled at the way we have been lied to most atrociously by Teresa May until we have a withdrawal deal which is BRINO.
I really appreciate your comments in and out of Parliament.
Today in Parliament you were speaking and someone called you a twerp. I think this has happened before. I just wanted to thank you for what you are doing against the odds. The majority of Remainers in Parliament are the real twerps in fact. History will prove you are right.
Anyway, I do not think that most people know the awful truth as you do so keep plugging on please.

Kind regards,
▓▓▓▓▓

From: ███████

Sent: 02 December 2018 12:02

To: The office of Mark Francois <mark.francois.mp@parliament.uk>

Subject: Please vote against the Prime Minister's Brexit deal

Dear Mr Francois,

As one of your loyal constituents, you have always had my vote. I write now to urge you to please vote down the Prime Minister's Brexit deal. We need a managed no-deal Brexit. Please do not be swayed, hold your course and we will win this.

Yours sincerely,

███████

From: ███████

Sent: 13 January 2019 23:17

To: The office of Mark Francois <mark.francois.mp@parliament.uk>

Subject: your brilliant Brexit explanations on Sky TV today.

Dear Mr Francois,

Today I was lucky enough to catch your interview about Brexit on Sky news.

Of all the many many people I have heard explaining or discussing Brexit you have, by far, made the most sense. You were so clear and helpful in your explanations and in promoting the very sensible Canadian plan.

It was such a relief to hear someone speaking sense (once the news presenter shut up !) about the situation, and I felt such admiration for your common sense views.

I wonder if it is possible for you to get on to the BBC and ITV news saying the same sort of sensible things , or Newsnight or Andrew Marr. You need more platforms.

Thank you so much for explaining it all so clearly, you did such a great job.

If only we had more MPs of your calibre. I hope your constituents appreciate how lucky they are.

Yours sincerely,

███████

From: ▮▮▮▮▮▮

Sent: 25 January 2019 12:58

To: The office of Mark Francois <mark.francois.mp@parliament.uk>

Subject: Well done from old left, blue collar workers

Mark

We may come from different backgrounds we are all old style labour (maybe a closet ukip or two)voters ,blue collar, skilled manual workers and union members always prepared to strike or fight for our rights mainly leavers .We were watching you in the factory canteen on the TV when you ripped up that piece of paper from Enders and a tremendous cheer went up from everyone not just the leavers. Politics could be changing in this country for a generation.

Keep up the good fight

▮ and the lads(ps we're all the wrong side of 40)

From: ▮▮▮▮▮▮▮▮▮▮▮

Sent: 25 January 2019 18:14

To: The office of Mark Francois <mark.francois.mp@parliament.uk>

Subject: Bluetree contact form

This is an email sent via the Contact form on your Bluetree website. It is not spam.
Please do not reply, but instead copy the email address and compose a new message.

Name: Brit
Email:

Address 1: Brexit Britain
Town:
County:
Postcode: BR1X 1IT
Telephone:

Message: Piss off back to France you ugly foreign French twat. England for the English, no immigrants or foreigners, thank you.

Viva la Britian!

From: ▓▓▓▓▓
Sent: 20 March 2019 23:06
To: The office of Mark Francois <mark.francois.mp@parliament.uk>
Subject:

Hi Mark
Saw you on tv tonight – calm, dignified, polite – well done you!
You are one of the few who talks sense – please don't allow them to browbeat you as they are trying to do…..
God bless you as you try to extricate us from the EU.

▓▓▓▓▓

From: ▓▓▓▓▓
Sent: 25 March 2019 05:16
To: The office of Mark Francois <mark.francois.mp@parliament.uk>
Subject: Deliver Brexit on 29 March

Dear Mark,

Parliament promised that we would leave the European Union on 29 March.

If Parliament breaks this promise, all parties will be letting us down.

Any extension runs the risk of losing Brexit.

> Stick to your manifesto pledge.
> Honour the referendum result.
> Leave on 29 March.

Thank you,

From: ███████

Sent: 29 March 2019 21:22

To: The office of Mark Francois <mark.francois.mp@parliament.uk>

Subject: Brexit

Sent from my iPhone. Hi Mark just a quick thank you for showing great courage along with the others who voted down the May deal .I take great comfort in your efforts and speeches in the House of Commons that we will eventually see the back it the EU as we know it many thanks ███████

From: ███████

Sent: 31 March 2019 10:03

To: The office of Mark Francois <mark.francois.mp@parliament.uk>

Subject: Your stance on Brexit

Dear Mr Francois,

I was at the march to leave demonstration at Parliament Square on Friday and had a number of conversations with others there, one of the topics was our Member of Parliament. When I mentioned you were my MP they told me I was lucky and I agree.

It really annoys me when I am told by a politician or TV pundit that I didn't know what I was voting for and that I was lied to about the facts. I didn't want a deal, I just wanted to leave and anyone who believed any of the propaganda leading up to Brexit was a fool.

I respect your stance on Brexit but it was clear to see during the interviews the pressure you are under to maintain this stance, it's a great pity that some of your colleagues have not shown the same strength of character.

The "indicative votes" that will take place this week are nothing more than a scam to remain in the EU or even revoke it altogether, either of which is unacceptable. I am not sure what can be done to see that the referendum result goes through, I am beginning to think it will never happen.

You will continue to retain my support, should you wish to continue as a politician after this debacle has ended but I will do everything in my power to disrupt this disgraceful political system. Both Labour and Lib-Dem will never ever get my vote again and I will only vote for the Conservatives as long as you are my MP.

I wish you luck in the coming few weeks and sincerely hope your fight is successful. Thank you very much for your time.

Sincerest best wishes

███████

From: ██████████

Sent: 31 October 2019 12:46

To: The office of Mark Francois <mark.francois.mp@parliament.uk>

Subject: Imminent explosion of U.K

Dear Honourable Mr Mark Gino Francois,

I watched in horror when you predicted the U.K would explode today and naturally I took this prediction seriously, like you're never wrong are you.

Can you let me know what time it will happen I need to book a Eurostar.

Thanks,

██████████

Sent from my iPhone

From: ██████████

Sent: 31 October 2019 13:38

To: The office of Mark Francois <mark.francois.mp@parliament.uk>

Subject: Happy Brexit Day!

Dear Mark,

Hope you haven't exploded yet.

P.s. thanks for all your fighting in all the wars through history.

From: ▮▮▮▮▮▮
Sent: 01 February 2020 12:19
To: The office of Mark Francois <mark.francois.mp@parliament.uk>
Subject: Re: Brexit Update from the Rt Hon Mark Francois MP - 4th November 2019

Dear Mr Francois,
Just wanted to say a massive thank you for Getting Brexit Done! Your contribution to this was immeasurable and I applaud you for never giving up 👏. It was great being part of the amazing crowd last night in Parliament Square and an experience I will always remember...Thank you!
Best wishes,
▮▮▮▮▮

From: ▮▮▮▮▮▮▮▮▮▮▮▮▮▮▮▮
Sent: 01 February 2020 11:11
To: The office of Mark Francois <mark.francois.mp@parliament.uk>
Subject: Bluetree contact form

This is an email sent via the Contact form on your Bluetree website. It is not spam.
Please do not reply, but instead copy the email address and compose a new message.
Name: ▮▮▮▮▮
Email:

Submission time: Saturday, February 1, 2020, 11:11:13
Timezone: UTC

Message: Firstly to thank you for fighting for Democracy for the last 3years all your effort has been much appreciated.

I would also like to bring it to your attention the chaotic introduction of new 50mph speed limit on the A127. I would be very upset after 54 years of driving and never receiving a speeding ticket to receive one now, due to the failure of highways to install clear and sufficient signage. Regards ▮▮▮▮▮

419

From: ███████

Sent: 02 February 2020 14:30

To: The office of Mark Francois <mark.francois.mp@parliament.uk>

Subject: Thank you

Dear Mark,

Thank you for all you've done for this country and helping to secure Brexit. The history books should look kindly on your achievements. The people of the world will recognise your contribution to democracy.

I was a fellow Brexit traveller, signed the various business / entrepreneur letters in the press, attended meetings and contributed ideas to the leave campaign.

As someone who led 5 businesses across Europe, led a pan European trade association and lived in Germany and Switzerland I welcome Brexit

Simply – Thank you

With kind regards

███████

Appendix 8

Tribute to the late Sir David Amess MP

Tribute made by the Rt Hon Mark Francois MP in the House of Commons on Monday 18th October 2021

Sir David Amess was my best and oldest friend in politics, so I confess that I am hurting terribly, and I hope the House will forgive me if, because of that, my contribution this afternoon is even more incoherent than usual. I certainly cannot match those two beautiful and, if I may say so, extremely moving tributes from the Prime Minister and the Leader of the Opposition. I thank them.

Everything that I ever learned about how to be a constituency MP, I learned from David Amess. He sponsored me for the candidates list, and he mentored me when I arrived. Without him, I would never have become a Member of Parliament, so some might well argue that he has much to answer for.

I grew up in Basildon when David was the local MP. I grew up on a working-class council estate which even the locals nicknamed Alcatraz. David helped me to campaign in 1991 to win election to Basildon Council—quite a robust place to learn one's trade, and once described as the only local authority in Britain where at council meetings the councillors actively heckled the public gallery. I was there. Trust me: I'm a politician.

In return, I ran David's ground war in his iconic defence of Basildon in 1992. During that campaign, the late Paul Channon came down from Southend to help, and we were out canvassing on a council estate in Pitsea. I will never forget that. We knocked on a door, and a monster of a bloke answered it. He looked at us both, and he looked at the blue rosettes, and he said, "Conservative? Tory? You must be bloody joking, mate— I'm voting for that David Amess!" I said, "I know when I'm beat, sir. Well done."

My partner Olivia and I were due to be on David's table at the Southend West Conservatives' annual dinner on the day he was murdered. But David is now our fallen comrade.

He was a devoted and a loving family man, and our deepest sympathies are with his widow, Julia, and his five children, who produced the most amazingly courageous statement, the essence of which was, I think, that love must conquer hate. I am sure we all agree with that.

He was an animal-lover, a patriot, a Thatcherite, a Eurosceptic, a monarchist, a staunch Roman Catholic whose faith sustained him throughout his life, a truly great friend to those in need—I can vouch for that—and a fine parliamentarian. He was probably the best potential Father of the House we will now never have.

David had a zest for life, a joie de vivre. For him the glass was never half empty; it was three quarters full. He was a doughty champion for Basildon and then for Southend. So thank you, Prime Minister—and I thank Her Majesty and the Privy Council—for making Southend a city after all. It was the right thing to do, and our apologies to Cleethorpes! While you are at it, Prime Minister, perhaps you can help Southend United: they are going through a bit of a sticky patch, and they really need all the help they can get.

You never knew what David was going to do next. That Essex "cheeky chappie" smile, that impish Amess grin, always with a hint of gentle mischief behind it. He once even persuaded His Holiness the Pope to bless a boiled sweet, as my friend and neighbour, my Hon Friend James Duddridge, will explain in a moment.

However, David also had a serious side, and it is that on which I want to focus the rest of my speech. In the last few years, he had become increasingly concerned about what he called the toxic environment in which MPs, particularly female MPs, were having to operate. He was appalled by what he called the vile misogynistic abuse that female MPs had to endure online, and he told me recently that he wanted something done about it. Three years ago, my Right Hon Friend Ms Dorries wrote a powerful article about this on *ConservativeHome* in which she quoted the following social media post:

"I want to see you, trapped in a burning car and watch as the heat from the flames melts the flesh from your face."

I ask you, Mr Speaker, what did she ever do to deserve that? Another fallen comrade, Jo Cox, whose sister now graces this place, said that we have more in common than that which divides us, and I think she was absolutely right.

All of us, wherever we come from, came here to try to help people. We may disagree, sometimes passionately, about how best to help people, but surely we could all agree that we came here to try. For this, we are now systematically vilified day after day, and I simply say to you, ladies and gentlemen, that enough is enough. We all have one thing in common: we are legislators. So I humbly suggest that we get on and do some legislating.

I suggest that if we want to ensure that our colleague did not die in vain, we all collectively pick up the baton, regardless of Party, and take the forthcoming Online Safety Bill and toughen it up markedly. If I may be so presumptuous, let us put "David's law" on to the statute book, the essence of which would be that, while people in public life must remain open to legitimate criticism, they could no longer be vilified or their families subjected to the most horrendous abuse, especially from people who hide behind a cloak of anonymity, with the connivance of the social media companies for profit. The mood I am in, I confess that I would like to drag Mark Zuckerberg of Facebook and Jack Dorsey of Twitter to the Bar of the House, kicking and screaming if necessary, so that they could look us all in the eye and account for their actions, or rather their inactions, which are making them even richer than they already are.

Let us also do that for all our Councillors, who are sick and tired of reading on Facebook after every planning committee meeting the night before, that "it must have been a brown envelope job". Let us do it for all those other people who hold surgeries, including our GPs who have carried on tending to the sick throughout the pandemic but who are now being vilified online, along with their loyal receptionists and staff, just for trying to do their job. If the social media companies do not want to help us to drain the Twitter swamp, let us compel them to do it by law, because they have had more than enough chances to do it voluntarily. Please bring in this Bill, Prime Minister, and if you need any assistance in toughening it up, we are called the Back Benchers of the House of Commons and we are here to help. What better way to ensure that a fine Parliamentarian did not die in vain than to enshrine one of his last wishes in legislation forever, for the benefit of all those in public life?

Many Members wish to pay tribute, so I will end with this: another thing about David was his legendary timekeeping, or rather lack of it. His constituency events always ran late because he was so popular and so many people wanted to speak to him. By the end of a busy constituency Friday, of which he had many, he was sometimes running up to an hour late—he invariably overran, and this afternoon, in his honour, so have I; sorry, Mr Speaker—but what better fault to have than that wonderful trait? Among some of his closest friends, he was known affectionately as the late Sir David Amess.

Well, now he really is the late Sir David Amess. I am absolutely determined—I ask for the House's support in this—that he will not have died in vain. He is now resting in the arms of the God he worshipped devotedly his whole life, so farewell David, my colleague, my great friend—in fact, quite simply the best bloke I ever knew. I thank the House for its indulgence.

Acknowledgements

Apparently, many people who were stuck at home during the Lockdown caused by the Covid-19 pandemic but who had always thought "they had a book in them" decided to use that opportunity to write it – and I was no exception. Nevertheless, there are a number of people without whom this book would never have come to fruition.

I must thank Christopher Howarth, the Senior Researcher of the ERG, for double checking the manuscript for factual accuracy and also for ensuring that my recollections of often complex and fast-moving events were correct. Having fought a Parliamentary seat at the 2019 General Election, I believe that Chris still aspires to be a Conservative MP one day and any Association that needs to pick a future candidate, might do well to bear him in mind, as we might never have succeeded in the Battle for Brexit without him.

I also want to thank my Parliamentary colleagues, for sharing their own recollections of these tumultuous events with me. It would not be practical to mention them all by name here, but they know who they are, and I am very grateful. Similarly, I am indebted to my friend, Steve Baker, for allowing me to use a few of his copious collection of photographs which he took during the whole episode. Also, Mark Garnier, provided me with a quite comprehensive "timeline of events" relating to Brexit, which was very helpful in maintaining the correct order in which things played out, especially in 2019.

I am particularly indebted to five people who took the time and trouble to read through an initial draft of the manuscript, and then provide me with a number of very helpful comments on how the text could be improved. These five people were: the Rt Hon Jacob Rees-Mogg MP (the Leader of the House of Commons); Paul Goodman (the former MP for Wycombe and now Editor of *Conservative Home*); Christopher "Chopper" Hope (the Chief Political Correspondent of *The Daily Telegraph*); Brendan Carlin (the Political Correspondent of *The Mail on Sunday*); and lastly Christopher Howarth (see above). All of them kindly encouraged me to try and get the book published, not least as a historical record and they also made numerous other helpful suggestions along the way.

I am also deeply grateful to Kindle Direct Publishing (Amazon), for allowing me to self-publish this important story and thus helping to uphold the principle of free speech in a publishing industry where "Remain" has very clearly been the orthodoxy throughout.

I must also thank my twenty-seven fellow Spartans, without whom there would be no story to tell. As well as my story, this is in many ways their story too – and I genuinely hope that I have done it justice.

I must also record my gratitude to those members of the Conservative Voluntary Party that I have worked with very closely down the years, including those in both the Basildon and Brent East Conservative Associations, prior to my entering Parliament. However, in the particular context of the Battle for Brexit, I am especially grateful to all those members of the Rayleigh and Wickford Constituency Conservative Association, who stood by me as their local MP throughout, even in the highly pressurised run up to Meaningful Vote Three. Indeed, when Conservative Campaign Headquarters (CCHQ) delivered 10,000 leaflets in support of Theresa May's deal to my Constituency Headquarters – which encouraged constituents to contact their MP and urge them to vote for the deal – my then Chairman, the redoubtable Mr Hilton Brown, told me he was about to put them all in the recycling bin as a contribution to the Association's annual recycling target. When I told him I didn't know we had an annual recycling target, he simply replied: "Well we do now!".

It would be invidious to try and pick out a list of names from among my staunchest supporters in the Association during the Battle for Brexit but again, these people know who they are. Suffice to say that I was (and still am) extremely fortunate to have such a hardworking dedicated team in Rayleigh and Wickford, I am indebted to each and every one of you.

Crucially, I would also like to thank my partner, Olivia, who campaigned actively for Vote Leave during the 2016 Referendum – before we met – and who has shown great patience and understanding while I have been working on this book. She has been my Rock and I treasure her love and support.

Finally, I must reiterate my thanks to my parents, Reginald and Anna Francois, for nurturing me from humble beginnings and for all of their love and encouragement, without which, given where I started out from, I would probably never have got anywhere near Parliament in the first place. They taught me to stand up for what I believed in, and as my father made me promise, never to take living in a free country for granted.

As the reader will have gathered by now, it was that solemn promise that underlay everything that I did throughout the Battle for Brexit.

Job done Dad. May you Rest in Peace.

Bibliography

Sir David Amess, 'Ayes & Ears: A Survivor's Guide to Westminster' (Luath Press, 2020).

Michael Ashcroft & Isobel Oakeshott, 'Call Me Dave': The Unauthorised Biography of David Cameron' (Biteback Publishing, 2015).

Michael Ashcroft, 'Jacob's Ladder: The Unauthorised Biography of Jacob Rees-Mogg' (Biteback Publishing, 2019).

Michael Ashcroft, ' Red Knight: The Unauthorised Biography of Sir Keir Starmer; (Biteback Publishing, 2021).

Aaron Banks, 'The Bad Boys of Brexit: Tales of Mischief, Mayhem & Guerilla Warfare in the EU Referendum Campaign' (Biteback Publishing, 2016).

Gavin Barwell, 'Chief of Staff: Notes from Downing Street' (Atlantic Books 2021).

Anthony Beevor, 'D-Day: The Battle for Normandy' (Penguin / Viking, 2009).

John Bercow, 'Unspeakable', (Weidenfeld & Nicolson 2020).

Tony Blair, 'A Journey', (Hutchinson, 2010).

Tom Bower, 'Gordon Brown' (Harper Collins, 2004).

Tom Bower, 'Boris Johnson: The Gambler' (Penguin/WH Allen, 2020).

John Campbell, 'Edward Heath: A Biography' (Jonathan Cape, 1993).

John Campbell, 'Margaret Thatcher: The Grocer's Daughter' (Jonathan Cape, 2000).

David Cameron, 'For The Record' (William Collins, 2020).

Paul Cartledge, 'The Spartans: An Epic History' (Pan Macmillan, 2002).

Alan Clark, 'Diaries' (Weidenfeld & Nicholson, 1993).

Alan Clark, 'The Tories: Conservatives and the Nation State, 1922 – 1997' (Weidenfeld & Nicholson, 1998).

Bernard Connelly, 'The Rotten Heart of Europe: The Dirty War for Europe's Money' (Faber & Faber, 1995).

Michel Barnier, 'My Secret Brexit Diary – A Glorious Illusion' (Polity, 2021).

Matthew D'Ancona, 'In It Together: The Inside Story of the Coalition Government' (Viking, 2013).

Nick de Bois, 'Confessions of a Recovering MP' (Biteback Publishing, 2019).

Lode Desmet & Edward Stourton, 'Blind Man's Brexit: How the EU Took Control of Brexit' (Simon & Schuster UK, 2019).

Frances Elliot & James Hanning, 'Cameron: The Rise of the New Conservative' (Fourth Estate, 2007).

Kate Fall, 'The Gatekeeper: Life Inside No.10' (HQ/Harper Collins, 2020).

Sir Lawrence Freedman, 'Strategy' (Oxford University Press, 2013).

Martin Gilbert, 'Churchill: A Life' (Book Club Associates Edition, 1991).

Matthew Goodwin & Caitlin Milazzo, 'UKIP: Inside the Campaign to Redraw the Map of British Politics' (Oxford University Press, 2015).

Theresa Gorman MP with Heather Kirby, 'The Bastards: Dirty Tricks and the Challenge to Europe' (Pan/Sidgwick & Jackson, 1993).

Philip Gould, 'The Unfinished Revolution: How the Modernisers Saved the Labour Party' (Little, Brown & Company, 1998).

William Hague, 'William Pitt the Younger' (Harper Collins, 2004).

Morrison Halcrow, 'Keith Joseph: A Single Mind' (Macmillan, 1989).

Daniel Hannan MEP, 'Why Vote Leave' (Head of Zeus Ltd, 2016).

David Heathcoat-Amory, 'Confessions of a Eurosceptic' (Pen & Sword Politics, 2012).

Simon Heffer, 'Like the Roman: The Life of Enoch Powell' (Weidenfeld & Nicholson, 1998).

Roy Jenkins, 'Churchill' (Macmillan, 2001).

Boris Johnson, 'The Churchill Factor: How One Man Made History' (Hodder & Stoughton, 2014).

Rupert Matthews, 'Thermopylae: A Campaign in Context' (Spellmount, 2006).

Charles Moore, 'Not for Turning' / 'Everything She Wants' / 'Herself Alone' – Three Volume Biography of Margaret Thatcher (Penguin / Allen Lane, 2013, 2015 & 2019 respectively).

Jo-Anne Nadler, 'William Hague: In his Own Right' (Politico's Publishing, 2000).

Ben Pimlot, 'The Queen: A Biography of Elizabeth II' (Harper Collins, 1996).

Rosa Prince, 'Theresa May: The Enigmatic Prime Minister' (Biteback Publishing, 2017).

Harvey Proctor, 'Credible and True' (Biteback Publishing, 2016).

John Ramsden, 'An Appetite For Power: The History of the Conservative Party Since 1830' (Harper Collins, 1998).

John Redwood, 'Singing the Blues: The Once and Future Conservatives' (Politico's Publishing, 2004).

Andrew Roberts, 'Eminent Churchillians' (Weidenfeld & Nicholson, 1994).

Andrew Roberts 'Churchill: Walking With Destiny' (Penguin / Allen Lane, 2018).

Anthony Seldon & Peter Snowdon, 'Cameron at 10: The Verdict' (William Collins, 2015).

Anthony Seldon, 'May At 10' (Biteback Publishing, 2019).

Tim Shipman, 'All Out War: The Full Story of How Brexit Sank Britain's Political Class' (William Collins, 2016).

Tim Shipman, 'Fallout: A Year of Political Mayhem' (William Collins, 2017).

FM Viscount Slim, 'Defeat into Victory' (Cassell & Company, 1956).

Michael Spicer, 'The Spicer Diaries' (Biteback Publishing, 2012).

John Sutherland & Diane Canwell, 'Churchill's Pirates: The Royal Naval Patrol Service in World War II' (Pen & Sword Books, 2010).

Margaret Thatcher, 'The Downing Street Years' (Harper Collins, 1993).

'The Times Guide to the House of Commons' 1987, 1992, 1997, 2001, 2005, 2010, 2015 & 2017 Editions (Times Books, dates as given).

Robert Waller & Byron Criddle, 'The Almanac of British Politics' – 5th, 6th, 7th & 8th Editions, (Routledge, 1996, 1999, 2002 & 2007 respectively).

Sebastian Whale, 'John Bercow: Call to Order' (Biteback Publishing, 2020).

Hywell Williams, 'Guilty Men: Conservative Decline and Fall, 1992-1997' (Aurum Press, 1998).

Hugo Young, 'This Blessed Plot: Britain and Europe from Churchill to Blair' (Macmillan, 1998).

Notes on Chapters

Chapter 1: From Alcatraz to Westminster

[1] My birthplace was the City of London Maternity Hospital on Hanley Road, in Crouch End. It no longer exists, and the site is now a block of flats.

[2] Huguenots were French Protestants who fled France after the revocation of the Edict of Nantes in 1685, which led to the widespread persecution of French Protestants by Catholics. See for instance Randolph Vigne and Charles Littleton, (Editors) 'From Strangers to Citizens: The Integration of Immigrant Communities in Britain, Ireland and Colonial America 1550-1750'. (Sussex Academic Press, 2001).

[3] HMS Bressay was subsequently sold to the Belgian Navy, before being given up for scrap, several years later.

[4] The original book, '*Thomas the Tank Engine*' was first published in 1946.

[5] By the late 1970s, Basildon New Town included a number of large, working class housing estates, including Five Links or 'Alcatraz' and Siporex (Laindon), Craylands (Fryerns); The Crockerfords (Vange) and Felmores (Pitsea).

[6] Alastair Campbell quoted in *The Daily Telegraph,* 13th February 2001.

[7] The BBC has commissioned a number of such "Britain's Favourite ...." polls down the years. For instance, Turner's "The Fighting Temeraire" showing a veteran wooden battleship from the Battle of Trafalgar being towed off to be broken up at Rotherhithe circa 1838 was voted Britain's Favourite Painting in 2005, beating Constable's "The Haywain" into second place.

[8] Although the brilliant TV series "*Churchill, the Wilderness Years*" came out in 1981 with Robert Hardy in the lead role.

[9] See for instance Roy Jenkins' "*Churchill*" (Macmillan, 2001).

Chapter 2: Battling Bercow at University

[10] For a good summary of the Falklands War see Max Hastings and Simon Jenkins, "*The Battle for The Falklands*" (Book Club Associates, 1983).

[11] David Amess' 1983 result in Basildon was as follows:

David Amess	Conservative Candidate	17,516
Julian Fulbrook	Labour Co-op	16,137
Sue Slipman	SDP	11,634
Conservative Majority		1,379
Turnout		69%

[12] See also, John Vincent "*Gladstone and Ireland*" (1978) and John Vincent, "*An Intelligent Persons Guide to History*" (2006).

[13] See Sebastian Whale's book *'John Bercow: Call to Order'* (Biteback Publishing, 2020).

[14] Taken from Mark Francois' lecture notes at the time.

[15] The 'Fog of War' is generally attributed to the Prussian military theorist, Carl von Clausewitz, whose famous treatise *'On War'* is still taught in military academies, from Sandhurst to West Point, to this day.

Chapter 3: Working with David Amess – The Basildon Years

[16] In the 1992 General Election, the Basildon Constituency was one of the crucial battlegrounds on the Labour Party's target list.

[17] David Walsh's election result was as follows:

Name	Party	Result
David Walsh	Conservative	1,780
Harold Bruce	Labour	1,360
Simon Wilson	Liberal Democrats	530
Conservative Majority		420

This was all the more remarkable as when the campaign, caused by the untimely death of the sitting councillor began, David had booked an expensive foreign holiday, which he had faithfully promised his wife and children he would not cancel. He then spent most of the campaign abroad, occasionally sending us postcards enquiring about how his campaign was going and exhorting us to work harder on his behalf!

[18] John Smith's 'Shadow Budget'

[19] Our highly detailed canvas returns were the crown jewels of our two-year campaigning operation and after each night's door-knocking were tallied at Liz Frost's home in Billericay, where the Association computer and its Coley software was kept. We figured this was more secure than leaving the computer in the Association Office in Pitsea. During the General Election itself, Liz would produce a print-out each morning, showing the results of each of the canvas team the night before and the overall running total. This print out had a very limited circulation of Barbara Allen, David's redoubtable Election Agent, who has come out of retirement to work on his campaign, the Association Chair, Steve Allen and myself. Labour would have killed to see these hard-won numbers and we tracked them with a reverence akin to the Enigma Code.

[20] Alan Rusbridger, 'The Political Barometer That Brings the House Down', The Guardian, 18th July 1992.

[21] The Labour Party had briefly lost overall control of Basildon Council for a period in the 1980s, when the Council has been run by an anti-Labour coalition of Conservatives, Residents and others but, up to this point, the Conservatives had never controlled the Council outright.

[22] We discovered some years afterwards that the real reason for Labour's overconfidence had been an extremely sloppy canvas, where if one elector in a household said they would vote Labour, their canvassers automatically put all the occupants down as Labour supporters, even in large domains, which were quite common in the New Town. Conversely, our canvassers were trained to ask about each individual elector in the house ("will both your children be voting Tory as well Mrs Bloggs?") so our canvass was far more accurate than theirs. Besides, we had always thought it would be close – and planned accordingly.

[23] Interest rates were hiked substantially in Britain on the day we entered the First World War.

[24] Black Wednesday 20 years on, how the day unfolded, Philip Inman, the Guardian, 13th October 2012

[25] Ibid.

[26] For example, both the Newbury and Christchurch 1993 by-elections saw large Conservative majorities wiped out by the Liberal Democrats.

[27] When challenged on this assertion that he had not read the Maastricht Treaty by Sir Bill Cash during a Commons debate in 2008, Ken Clarke claimed he 'knew more about the Maastricht treaty than most of the Maastricht', Hansard, 20th February 2008, Column 448.

[28] EDM (Early Day Motion)174: tabled on 3rd June 1992, House of Commons.

[29] Ironically, the Whip on the Bill was one David Davis MP.

[30] A very credible account is Theresa Gorman's 'The Bastards'.

[31] Norman Lamont's resignation speech, House of Commons, 9th June 1993.

Chapter 4: Beating Boris to Get a Seat

[32] See Philip Gould, *'The Unfinished Revolution'*, Abacus, 2011.

[33]

Date Conducted	Polling Organisation	Conservative	Labour	Lib Dem
9th January 1995	Gallup/Telegraph	18.5%	62%	14%

[34] Alan Clark, *'Diaries'* (Weidenfield & Nicholson, 1993).

[35] Derek Conway had served as the MP for Shrewsbury and Atcham.

[36] The actual results of the final ballot of Conservative MPs was:

Candidate	1st ballot: 10 July 2001		2nd ballot: 12 July 2001		3rd ballot: 17 July 2001	
	Votes	%	Votes	%	Votes	%
Michael Portillo	49	29.5	50	30.1	53	32.0
Iain Duncan Smith	39	23.5	42	25.3	54	32.5
Kenneth Clarke	36	21.6	39	23.6	59	35.5
David Davis	21	12.7	18	10.8	Withdrew	Withdrew
Michael Ancram	21	12.7	17	10.2	Withdrew	Withdrew

[37] *The Echo* at the time had a political diary column, in which the suggestion appeared.

[38] Planning Policy Guidance Note 3, Department of the Environment, 1992.

Chapter 5: Into Parliament and Working for George

[39] The Father of the House on this occasion was Tam Dalyell, the MP for Linlithgow, first elected in 1962.

[40] Amongst other things, the Treaty of Nice expanded the extent of Qualified Majority Voting (QMV) by which the UK could be outvoted in the European Council without a veto.

[41] This speech, arguably the greatest in Parliamentary history, forms the climax of the wonderful film, '*The Darkest Hour*', which was released in 2019.

[42] *Hansard*, Debate on the European Communities (Amendment) Bill, Second Reading, 4th July 2001, Column 307.

[43] David Blunkett is a remarkable man. He was blind from birth and grew up in a deprived area of Sheffield but still represented his hometown in Parliament for some 28 years, during which time he rose to become Home Secretary, one of the four Great Offices of State (the others being the Prime Minister, Chancellor of the Exchequer and Foreign Secretary). After stepping down from the House of Commons in 2013, he was ennobled as Baron Blunkett of Brightside and Hillsborough in the House of Lords.

[44] "The Kundan" was rather dingy, being located underground at the bottom end of Horseferry Road, less than 10 minutes from the House of Commons., where the waiters were all Indian, and all of the waitresses seemed to be from Eastern Europe, which made for a rather curious mix. Nevertheless, the food was decent and reasonably priced, and we would dine there regularly, until it closed several years later.

[45] The '92 Group (so called because it first met at 92 Cheyne Walk in Chelsea) broadly represents the right-wing of the Conservative backbenches. Its current Chairman is Bill Wiggin MP (Also a member of the 2001 intake).

[46] Stuart Polak served as the Director of the Conservative Friends of Israel for over twenty-five years until 2015.

[47] A number of other Senior potential contenders, such as David Davis, the Shadow Home Secretary, agreed not to stand against Michael Howard, thus obviating a contest among the Parliamentary Party and the Voluntary Party in the country too.

48 The Shadow Treasury Team at that time comprised:

Shadow Chancellor	Oliver Letwin
Shadow Chief Secretary to the Treasury	George Osborne
Shadow Paymaster General	Andrew Tyrie
Shadow Financial Secretary	Mark Hoban
Shadow Economic Secretary	Mark Francois

49 'With you whatever': Tony Blair's letters to George W. Bush, *The Guardian*, 6th July 2016.

50 E.g., *Times* Populus Poll, 2-3 May 2005.

Labour	38%
Conservatives	32%
Liberal Democrats	21%
Others	8%
Lead	6%

51 Labour still won 355 seats in 2005 (down 48 on 2001) whilst the Conservatives increased to 198 (up 33 on 2001). However, Blair's Labour Party only secured 35.2% of the popular vote across the UK, compared to 32.4% for Michael Howard's Conservatives. However, at the time of the 2005 General Election, the electoral boundaries in the UK were drawn very much in Labour's favour.

52 David Cameron, '*On the Record*' (William Collins, 2019).

53 In fact, David Cameron's victory over David Davis in 2005 was even more emphatic than IDS's victory over Ken Clarke in 2001.

54 In fairness to Ed Balls, he apparently really did join all three main parties.

Chapter 6: Working for William – and Fighting the Lisbon Treaty

[55] Perhaps surprisingly, in my experience William is not always eager to be reminded about his 1977 speech, even though it first brought him to the attention of the wider public.

[56] 'It's Neck and Neck', *The Guardian,* 5th October 2007.

[57] David Cameron's pledge to withdraw his MEPs from the EPP and form a new, non-Federalist grouping with likeminded MEPs from other countries, was undoubtedly important in helping him to win support from Right Wing Conservative MPs during the 2005 Leadership Election.

[58] The 1957 Treaty Establishing the European Community contained the objective of "ever closer union" in the following words in the Preamble. In English this is: "Determined to lay the foundations of an ever-closer union among the peoples of Europe …".

[59] See for instance, Hugo Young, '*This Blessed Plot*', Macmillan, 1998.

[60] Margaret Thatcher said at the time in the *Daily Telegraph:* "To come out (of Europe) now, with nowhere else to go, would jeopardise our own and our children's future".

[61] Enoch Powell accused Heath of breaking his promise to secure the 'full-hearted consent of the British Parliament and people' before entry. Tony Benn said that: "The ECC taken together, would in effect make the United Kingdom into one province of a Western European state".

[62] The actual result of the 1975 Referendum was:

	Votes	%
Yes (In)	17,378,581	67.23%
No (Out)	8,470,073	32.77%

[63] The new currency, The Euro, was officially issued on 1st January 1999.

[64] France for instance rejected the original European Constitution in a Referendum in May 2005 by 55% to 45%, on a 69% turnout.

[65] By convention, Treaties such as Lisbon have to be ratified by Parliament, via Primary Legislation i.e., a specific Act of Parliament – for that purpose.

[66] House of Commons, European Scrutiny Committee, The work of the committee, 2007.

[67] *Hansard*, European Union (Amendment) Bill, 21st January 2008.

[68] The Speech of the Year Award, given annually at the Spectator Awards is one of the premier accolades in the world of SW1.

Fellow Eurosceptic, David Heathcott-Amory, in his own account of the time, seems to remember slightly fewer amendments than Bill Cash (Quote from DHA's book, '*Confessions of a Eurosceptic*', Pen and Sword Politics, 2012).

[70] The Czech President, Vaclaw Klaus, a strong Eurosceptic, was by no means keen to ratify the Treaty and, under the Czech constitution, his signature as President was still required.

[71] The state of the main Parties in the House of Commons in 2008 was as follows:

Party	Seats
Labour	355
Conservative	198
Lib Dem	62
SNP	6
DUP	9
Other	14

[72] The 2005 Lib Dem Manifesto said this about Europe:

"MAKE EUROPE MORE EFFECTIVE AND DEMOCRATIC – Membership of the EU has been hugely important for British jobs, environmental protection, equality rights, and Britain's place in the world. But with enlargement to twenty-five Member States, the EU needs reform to become more efficient and more accountable. The new constitution helps to achieve this by improving EU coherence, strengthening the powers of the elected European Parliament compared with the Council of Ministers, allowing proper oversight of the unelected Commission, and enhancing the role of national parliaments. It also more clearly defines and limits the powers of the EU, reflecting diversity and preventing over-centralisation. We are therefore clear in our support for the constitution, which we believe is in Britain's interest – but ratification must be subject to a referendum of the British people."

[73] Gordon Brown was very clear that he didn't want any photographs of him signing the Treaty.

[74] During Commons debates on legislation, amendments on a similar topic are 'grouped' together, with the most important amendment being declared the 'lead amendment', which, crucially, means that it is usually voted on first. Whoever tables the 'lead amendment' thus normally opens and briefly sums up the debate.

[75] Paul Cash MC was killed at the "Battle of Hill 112" in July 1944.

[76] Theresa Gorman MP with Heather Kirby, '*The Bastards: Dirty Tricks and the Challenge to Europe*' (Pan/Sidgwick & Jackson, 1993).

[77] The other MP who tops the table, Michael Spicer, later founded the European Research Group.

[78] Quote from William's speech, *Hansard*, 26th February 2008.

[79] *Hansard*, 5th March 2008, Column 1863.

[80] Ibid. Col 1863.

[81] Under the principle of 'collective responsibility', the Lib Dem spokespersons who defied their own Party line, had to resign their front bench positions.

[82] Powell's actual quote was: "All political lives, unless they are cut off in mid-stream at a happy juncture, end in failure, because that is the nature of politics and of human affairs." (Essay on Joseph Chamberlain, 1977).

[83] UKIP did well in the 2009 European Elections when they increased their number of MEPs and took 16% of the popular vote.

[84] I subsequently wrote a detailed article on this for the Eurosceptic website, Brexit Central. "*The appalling handling of the Lisbon Treaty sowed the seeds of Brexit*", September 2016.

[85] There had been previous abortive attempts, including under the Leadership of Michael Howard.

[86] Oliver had insisted on paying for my train fare to Dorset and I had consistently refused, so to settle the matter, when I attended the next Shadow Cabinet meeting, he had placed a bottle of very good vintage port on the table, in front of my seat – at which point I conceded!

[87] See for instance Volume 2 of Charles Moore's masterful '*Three Volume Biography of Margaret Thatcher*' Thatcher, Penguin, 2015.

[88] Liam Byrne's note has since passed into political legend.

Chapter 7: Working for Her Majesty

[89] There had been several such Shadow Cabinet calls during the General Election Campaign, but these were now obviously in a completely new context.

[90] *The Guardian*, 10th May 2010.

[91] David Cameron, '*On the Record*' (William Collins, 2019).

[92] From private notes, taken at the time.

[93] Dennis Skinner, the 'Beast of Bolsover' was an ex-miner and Labour firebrand, first elected in 1970, who had a reputation for challenging the Prime Minister of the day, regardless of which party they happened to be from, but especially if they were a "bloody Tory!". ·

[94] There are, in fact, well over 2,000 military charities, of varying sizes in the United Kingdom – which is in many ways a testament to the degree of public support for our Armed Forces and Veterans – but which can also sometimes lead to a considerable amount of duplication of effort.

[95] See Help for Heroes Annual Report, 2020.

[96] The 'Tin Hut' was so named as it was effectively a small, corrugated iron building on the garrison, that Bryn had told me they had eventually given him "to shut him up!".

[97] I was also assisted by my then colleague Nick de Bois MP, the MP for Enfield North, whose secretary's son was a severely wounded veteran, see Nick de Bois, '*Confessions of a Recovering MP*', (Biteback, 2018).

[98] Today, PJHQ forms part of the MoD's 'Strategic Command', or STRATCOM, which is headquartered at Northwood, Middlesex.

Chapter 8: Vote Leave and the 2016 EU Referendum

[99] Conversations with Jacob Rees-Mogg MP.

[100] The Parliamentary battle to join the EEC, Michael Cockerell, *The House Magazine*, 5th December 2018.

[101] The UK formally joined the European Economic Community (the EEC) on 1st January 1973.

[102] Charles Moore, '*Not for Turning*' (Allan Lane, 2013).

[103] Ibid.

[104] Ibid.

[105] Ibid.

[106] John Major, '*The Autobiography*' (Harper Collins, 1999).

[107] The result of the 1995 Leadership contest among Conservative MPs was:

John Major	218
John Redwood	89

[108] Beethoven's Symphony No.9 in D Minor, popularly known as "Ode to Joy" after the poem by German poet, Fredrich Shiller, was adopted as the "Anthem of Europe" by the Council of Europe in 1972 and then subsequently by the European Union.

[109] Tony Blair, '*A Journey*' (Hutchinson, 2010).

[110] Author's notes from the conference.

[111] *The Sun*, 26th September 2007.

[112] *Hansard*, 6th November 2009.

[113] Author's note, taken at the time.

[114] Cameron did this in a press conference at the St Stephen's Club in Queen Anne's Gate on 23rd January 2008.

[115] The 2010 Conservative General Election Manifesto promised the following: "In future, the British people must have their say on any transfer of powers to the European Union. We will amend the 1972 European Communities Act so that any proposed future Treaty that transferred areas of power, or competences, would be subject to a referendum – a 'referendum lock'.".

[116] See *Hansard*, 15th May 2013, Column 660.

[117] *Wikipedia*, UKIP.

[118] Result for Putney in the 1997 General Election:

Candidate	Votes	%
Tony Colman (Labour)	20,084	45.6
David Mellor (Conservative)	17,108	38.9
Russell Pyne (Liberal Democrats)	4,739	10.8
James Goldsmith (Referendum)	1,518	3.5
William Jamieson (UKIP)	233	0.5
Lenny Beige (AKA Steve Furst) (Happiness Stan's Freedom to Party)	101	0.2
Michael Yardley (Sportsman's Alliance: Anything but Mellor)	90	0.2
John Small (Natural Law)	66	0.2
Ateeka Poole (Independently Beautiful Party)	49	0.1
Dorian Van Braam (Renaissance Democrat)	7	0.02
Majority	2,976	6.7
Turnout	43.994	73.3

[119] This was still a notable electoral achievement for a political party which, at that time did not have a single MP in the House of Commons.

[120]After the 2013 Local Elections, *The Guardian* wrote that: Out of a total of 1,343 council seats across the regions analysed, UKIP picked up a total of 73. However, in a further 226 seats secured by neither UKIP or the Conservatives, their vote share combined would have been enough to take the seat – meaning the indirect effect of UKIP on the split Tory vote is larger by far than a simple count of the number of council seats won by the Eurosceptic party would suggest.

[121] Cameron's actual quote about UKIP was: "UKIP is sort of a bunch of... fruitcakes and loonies and closet racists mostly", Interview on LBC Radio, April 2006.

[122] See for instance: '*For the Record*', David Cameron, William Collins, 2019.

[123] Results of 2014 Scottish Independence Referendum:

Yes	1,617,989	44.70%
No	**2,001,926**	**55.30%**
Valid Votes	3,619,915	99.91%
Invalid or Blank Votes	3,429	0.09%
Total Votes	3,623,344	100.0%

[124] Conservative Party General Election Manifesto, 2015.

[125] EU speech at Bloomberg, *Gov.uk*, 23rd January 2013.

[126] See for instance Tom Parfitt, *Daily Express*, June 29th 2016.

[127] The Act states that: Paragraph 1(2) of that Schedule (limit on expenses incurred by permitted participants during referendum period) has effect for the purposes of the referendum as if— (a) in paragraph (a) (designated organisations) for "£5 million" there were substituted "£7 million".

[128] HM Government Booklet, 'why the Government believes that voting to remain in the European Union is the best decision for the UK.' April 2016.

[129] The Brussels Broadcasting Corporation?, David Keighley and Andrew Jubb, (Civitas, 2018).

[130] Private information based in part on conversations with Chris Grayling.

[131] Up to this point I had not declared for either side.

[132] Anthony Seldon, '*Cameron at 10*', (William Collins, 2015).

[133] 'Boris Johnson joins campaign to leave EU', Nicholas Watt, *The Guardian,* 21 February 2016.

[134] '*Uncivil War*', Channel 4, first broadcast in 2018.

[135] Mark Francois MP, Constituency leaflet, "Why I'm backing Brexit", June 2016.

[136] George Osborne interviewed on the *Today* Programme, May 2016.

[137] In one scene, during a conference call, Craig Oliver, David Cameron's communications chief berates Labour for Mr Corbyn's repeated failure to meet campaign commitments.

[138] See for instance: Barack Obama says Brexit would leave UK at the 'back of the queue' on trade, BBC, 22nd April 2016.

[139] '*Uncivil War*', Channel 4.

[140] Private information.

[141] Andrea Leadsom's interview in *The Times*, July 9th 2016.

[142] See Statement from the new Prime Minister Theresa May, *Gov.uk*, 13th July 2016.

Chapter 9: The ERG and the Road to Chequers

[143] See for instance Theresa Gorman MP with Heather Kirby's, '*The Bastards: Dirty Tricks and the Challenge to Europe*' (Pan/Sidgwick & Jackson, 1993) for a highly readable account of the Maastricht Rebellion of 1992-93.

[144] Perhaps based on what he discovered, Daniel Hannan later became an MEP and a very articulate advocated of Leaving the EU; see for instance his book '*Why Vote Leave*', (Head of Zeus, 2016).

[145] Other prominent members of the ERG in recent years have included Sajid Javid and David Davis.

[146] Speech at Lancaster House, 17th January 2017.

[147] *The Daily Telegraph*, 18th January 2017, *The Daily Mail* 18th January 2017.

[148] Article 50, Treaty of the European Union. Ironically, this Article was largely drafted by a British Diplomat, Lord Kerr.

[149] Theresa May's letter to Donald Tusk, 20th March 2017.

[150] See R (Miller) v Secretary of State for Exiting the European Union.

[151] Anthony Seldon, '*May at 10*' (Biteback Publishing, 2019).

[152] YouGov/*The Times*, 12-13th April 2017.

[153] According to Nigel Rees in Brewster's Quotations (1994), asked shortly after his retirement in 1977 about the quote, Wilson could not pinpoint the first occasion on which he uttered the words.

[154] 'Nothing has changed': A year on from Theresa May's immortal words, *Sky News*, 22nd May 2018.

[155] The term, 'Maybot' was popularised by *Guardian* sketch writer, John Crace and has now entered the Westminster lexicon.

[156] 24th – 25th May 2017, YouGov/*The Times*, Con 43%, Lab 38%.

[157] The result in Thurrock in the 2017 General Election was as follows:

Candidate	Votes	%
Jackie Doyle Price (Conservative)	19,880	39.5
John Kent (Labour)	19,535	38.8
Tim Aker (UKIP)	10,112	20.1
Kevin McNamara (Liberal Democrats)	798	1.6
Majority	345	0.7
Turnout	50,325	64.4

[158] Jacob's performance was hilarious and also kept provoking Labour backbenchers to intervene, which of course took up even more time.

[159] Private information.

[160] See for instance: No 10 warns taxis on standby for minsters who resign today, Christopher Hope, *the Daily Telegraph,* 6th July 2018.

[161] See for instance: David Davis 'felt he had no choice but resignation', Laura Kuenssberg, BBC, 9th July 2018.

[162] Private Information.

[163] Steve Baker quoted in his resignation letter said: "The policy for our future relationship with the EU agreed by the Cabinet on 6 July will be the centrepiece of DEXEU's work. I acknowledge the Parliamentary opinion and arithmetic which constrain the Government's freedom of action, but I cannot support this policy with the sincerity and resolve which will be necessary. I therefore write with regret to resign from the Government.".

[164] See for instance: *The Financial Times*, Theresa May's Chequers proposal is best route to Brexit, 31st July 2018.

[165] Quote from the White Paper, The Future Relationship Between the United Kingdom and the European Union, 12th July 2018.

[166] Quote from Boris Johnson, *The Guardian*, 9th July 2018.

[167] The last line of Boris Johnson's book on Churchill reads: "When history needed it, in 1940, there was only one man who possessed the Churchill Factor; and having spent quite some time now considering the question, I am finally with those who think there has been no one remotely like him before or since.".

[168] *'How to Win a Marginal Seat: My Year Fighting For My Political Life'*, Gavin Barwell, Biteback, 17th March 2016.

[169] Gavin Barwell's Twitter Account, 24th June 2016.

[170] Agreement on the withdrawal of the United Kingdom of Great Britain and Northern Ireland from the European Union and the European Atomic Energy Community, as endorsed by leaders at a special meeting of the European Council on 25th November 2018.

[171] Extract from The Strand Group website, September 2021.

[172] The Strand Group website (Past events Tony Blair: 'Progressive Politics in an Era of Populism' the 33rd Strand Group lecture, 14th November 2018.

[173] Harry Cole, BLAIR BOAST Tony Blair claims Eurocrats gloated to him about defeating Britain during Brexit talks *The Sun Online*, 14th November 2018.

[174] *UK News* Blair condemns PM's Brexit deal as 'capitulation' to EU, 14th November 2018.

[175] Guido Fawkes website, *www.order-order.com,* Blair: Robbins' Chequers camouflage a 'tribute' to civil service – 14th November 2018.

[176] Article 4 of the Withdrawal Agreement, Clause 1 & 2.

[177] *Hansard*, 12th February 2019, Column 758.

[178] Article 20 of the Protocol on Ireland/Northern Ireland, Withdrawal Agreement.

[179] *The Telegraph,* Britain cannot accept this horrific, humiliating surrender to the EU, 14th November 2018 – *The Sun,* MORE FOOL EU Theresa May is tricking Britain over Brexit 'surrender' as she pretends to talk tough, Boris Johnson blasts, 13th November 2018.

[180] *Hansard*, 26th November 2018, Column 37.

[181] Article 164 of the Withdrawal Agreement, Clause 4.

[182] Article 166 of the Withdrawal Agreement, Clauses 1 & 2.

[183] Annex 8, Rule 9 of the Withdrawal Agreement.

[184] *Hansard*, 20th March 2019, Urgent Question: 'To ask the Secretary of State for Exiting the European Union if he will outline what checks the House of Commons has over the power of the "Joint Committee" contained in the proposed EU withdrawal Agreement, Columns 1061 to 1072.

[185] Article 174 of the Withdrawal Agreement, Clause 1.

Chapter 10: Fighting the Withdrawal Agreement That Did the Opposite

[186] The MP in question has told me that he is "saving this up for his own memoirs", which, as I have now written my story, I fully respect.

[187] As such, the Chairman of the 1922 Committee is responsible for organising the ballot, assisted by other officers of the committee.

[188] In the end, it pretty much came to that anyway.

[189] The Whips office had been aware of this possibility for some time and had already done a lot of work to seek to shore up the PM's position.

[190] 'Stupid Boy', the *Evening Standard,* 20th November 2018.

[191] From one of the Executive of the 1922 Committee – apparently, we were two letters short.

[192] *Today* Programme 10th December 2018.

[193] *Hansard*, 10th December 2018.

[194] I suspect Paul, who is very well connected, had got this from one of the Executive of the 1922 Committee who had probably been told by Sir Graham.

[195] As the Returning Officer, Sir Graham Brady had considerable influence over the timetable of the ballot.

[196] For instance, Margaret Thatcher won such a vote in 1990 but with an unconvincing margin of victory – and was eventually forced to resign, paving the way for John Major to become Prime Minister.

[197] In situations such as this, rapid comment on the result to the media is vitally important.

[198] Interview subsequently broadcast on the *Today* Programme the following morning, 13th December 2018.

[199] A "pyrrhic victory" is one in which the victor effectively loses more in winning, than the opponent they have defeated. The term is named after King Pyrrhus of Epiuus, who suffered crippling losses in defeating the Romans at the battle of Asculum, in 279 BC.

Chapter 11: Meaningful Vote One – The Government are Crushed

200 Private notes.

201 Notes from meeting of The Buddies, January 2019.

202 Only one senior member of the ERG chaffed at this restriction, but he was very much in the minority on that point.

203 This "tradition" of the European issue cutting across party lines goes back a very long way. Ted Heath's Government pulled off something similar in 1972, in persuading Labour rebels to back his controversial motion to take Britain into the European Economic Community in the first place (see Chapter 6).

204 The Confidence and Supply Agreement was signed by Gavin Williamson, the then Government Chief Whip and Sir Jeffrey Donaldson for the DUP on 26th June 2017.

205 Of the Pizza Club, only Andrea Leadsom eventually resigned over the Withdrawal Agreement, and then right at the end. The others determined to remain in the Cabinet and "fight from within".

206 Sebastian Whale, '*John Bercow: Call to Order*' (Biteback Publishing, 2020).

207 *Hansard*, 9th January 2019, Column 367.

208 See for instance: Bercow's unprecedented ruling could change the course of Brexit, Mark D'arcy, BBC, 9th January 2019.

209 Anthony Seldon, '*May at 10*' (Biteback Publishing, 2019).

210 Private note from the plenary meeting.

211 Even allowing for a bit of switching at the margins, virtually every Tory MP who had voted against May's leadership, had seemingly voted against her so-called Withdrawal Agreement as well.

212 The 1924 Division was over the response to the Government's decision to drop criminal proceedings against John Ross Campbell, editor of the Communist newspaper Workers' Weekly. A few weeks afterwards, a General Election was held following a motion of no confidence in the Government, which saw the Tories gain over 150 seats and returned Stanley Baldwin to power.

213 *Hansard*, 16th January 2020, Column 1171.

214 Ibid.

[215] Anthony Seldon, in '*May at 10*' writes that Theresa May's Chief of Staff, Gavin Barwell in particular, consistently believed that a large number of Labour MPs would come to save them, which of course they never did.

Chapter 12: Meaningful Vote Two – Holding the Line

216 Others at the lunch also included Iain Duncan Smith.

217 The creation of the Brexit Party had an important "knock-on effect" within the Conservative Party, which undoubtedly contributed to the eventual downfall of Theresa May.

218 Quote from Nigel Farage's press conference on 12th April 2019.

219 See for instance: General Election 2019: Brexit – where do the parties stand?, BBC, 5th December 2019.

220 'A Better Deal and a Better Future', European Research Group, 15th January 2019.

221 Steve was very enthusiastic, almost messianic, about the benefits of the Malthouse Compromise.

222 By this time, Airbus was being investigated in a number of jurisdictions, including the United States, the United Kingdom and France, regarding accusations of inappropriate business practices, over multiple years, See for instance: Airbus bribery scandal triggers new probes worldwide, Reuters, 3rd February 2020.

223 Letter from Tom Enders, CEO of Airbus, dated 24th January 2019.

224 Two years on, I think Adele has just about forgiven me.

225 The irony in all this was that this was in no way "pre-meditated", the idea only came to me when the BBC invited me on, less than half an hour after I had read Enders' letter.

226 'House of Lords reform halted after largest Tory rebellion of the Parliament', Nicholas Watt, *The Guardian,* 11th July 2012.

227 There were some seven options in total on offer that night.

228 *Hansard*, 29th January 2019.

229 *Hansard*, 29th January 2019.

230 For example, *Hansard*, 13th March 2019.

231 Anthony Seldon, '*May at 10*', (Biteback).

232 Quote from Leo Varadkar, *www.thejournal.ie*, January 30th 2019.

233 Private information from within No 10 at the time.

[234] As part of his rousing address, Cox quoted from Milton as follows: "*Methinks I see in my mind a noble and puissant Nation rousing herself like a strong man after sleep, and shaking her invincible locks: Methinks I see her as an Eagle mewing her mighty youth, and kindling her undazl'd eyes at the full midday beam.*".

[235] *The Guardian*, 12th February 2019.

[236] *Hansard*, 19th February 2019.

[237] Anthony Seldon, '*May at 10*' (Biteback).

[238] Nigel revealed this to me over dinner, after we had both appeared at a 'Brexit Heroes' event (their title, not mine) arranged by the *Daily Telegraph* the following year, just prior to the Covid-19 inspired lockdown.

[239] Excerpt from a transcript of the BBC *Politics Live* show, 8th March 2019.

[240] James Morris, 'Will Self gives Tory MP Mark Francois terrifying death stare during blazing Brexit row', the *Evening Standard*, Friday 8th March 2019.

[241] Will Self, 'The Story behind my stare-off with Mark Francois', *The New European*, 29th March 2019.

[242] A number of friends texted me that night to say "Mark, you've just been on Gogglebox!".

[243] The Attorney General in 2003 was Lord Goldsmith.

[244] Extract from the Attorney General's legal advice in advance of Meaningful Vote Two, 11th March 2019.

[245] This total of 75 does not include several former Conservative MPs, who by now had moved across to form The Independent Group (TIG).

[246] The coordinated signal for the Europhile Ministers to abstain was apparently 'Tally Ho!'.

[247] Private information.

[248] Interview with Beth Rigby, *Sky News*, 13th March 2019.

[249] Interview with Victoria Derbyshire, BBC, 14th March 2019.

[250] See Anthony Sheldon, '*May at 10*', (Biteback).

[251] See for instance: Theresa May requests Brexit extension, *Politico*, 5th April 2019.

[252] *Hansard*, 14th March 2019.

[253] *Hansard*, 14th March 2019, Column 628.

[254] Private information.

[255] EU Referendum: Quitting Europe would make the UK less safe, warns Sir Keir Starmer", Charlie Cooper, *The Independent*, 16th January 2020.

Chapter 13: Meaningful Vote Three – Spartan Victory

256 See Ed Stourton and Lode Desmet, '*Blind Man's Brexit: How the EU took control of Brexit*', (Simon & Schuster) 2019.

257 *Hansard*, 18th March 2019.

258 Kwasi Kwarteng, '*Ghosts of Empire*', (Bloomsbury) 2012.

259 *Hansard*, 20th March 2019.

260 Anthony Seldon, '*May at 10*', (Biteback, 2019).

261 Theresa May's address to the nation, shown on most TV Channels, 19th March 2019 and see also Anthony Seldon, '*May at 10*' (Biteback, 2019).

262 *The Times* and *The Telegraph*, Friday 22nd March 2019.

263 Paul Goodman, 'Enter – or rather exit – the Spartans', *ConHome,* 18th March 2019.

264 Ibid.

265 Private notes of 26th March meeting.

266 See Alex Wickham, *Buzzfeed News*, 23rd March 2019.

267 See *The Sun*, 5th May 2019.

268 Private notes made shortly after the meeting.

269 Steve Baker's speech to the ERG Plenary on 27th March 2019, which he subsequently recorded in writing and from which this extract is taken, is reproduced in full at Appendix 4.

270 Anthony Seldon, '*May at 10*', (Biteback).

271 'The Sun Says', *The Sun*, 29th March 2019.

272 *The Daily Mail*, 29th March 2019.

273 *The Daily Express*, 29th March 2019.

274 *The Daily Telegraph*, 29th March 2019.

275 My account of this meeting is based on a combination of my own notes from the meeting, that of the ERG's Researcher, Christopher Howarth, my own Researcher, Rory Boden, and discussions with several of the other people who were present.

276 'Labour MPs reveal they are ready to rescue Theresa May's Brexit deal in Common's vote', *The Independent,* 3rd October 2019.

277 From notes of the meeting.

---

[278] For the record, these six other Conservative MPs were: Dominic Grieve, Guto Bebb, Justine Greening, Sam Gyimah, Joseph Johnson and Phillip Lee.

Chapter 14: The Fall of the House of May

[279] Laura Kuenssberg, '*The Brexit Storm*', BBC Two, 1st April 2020.

[280] See Tom Bower, '*Dangerous Hero: Corbyn's Ruthless Plot for Power*', (William Collins, 2019).

[281] *The Guardian*, 3rd April 2020.

[282] The long-standing convention is that in the very rare event of a tie, as the House has failed to show a majority for the proposition in question, the Speaker then votes 'No' – so that it does not pass. However, by this stage Bercow had already clearly demonstrated that he refused to be bound by the normal conventions of the House – hence all the speculation at the time.

[283] *Hansard*, 3rd April 2019.

[284] The new deadline was agreed by the European Council, after quite some debate.

[285] Conservative Party 'risks splitting' as storm rages over Philip Hammond's extremist Brexiteers jibe, *Evening Standard,* 13th December 2018.

[286] How 'condescending' Brexiteer Mark Francois met his match in US Speaker Nancy Pelosi, *The Times,* April 18th, 2019.

[287] Anthony Seldon, '*May at 10*' (Biteback Publishing).

[288] See: 'Donald Tusk: Special place in hell for Brexiteers without a plan', BBC, 6th February 2019.

[289] By mid-1995 the Conservative Party controlled barely a dozen councils across the whole of the UK.

[290] *Conservative Home*, 29th March 2019.

[291] '*Behind Closed Doors*' produced by Lode Desmet, broadcast as a BBC Four Documentary, 8th & 9th May 2020.

[292] Ibid.

[293] Ibid.

[294] Lode Desmet & Edward Stourton, '*Blind Man's Brexit: How the EU Took Control of Brexit*' (Simon & Schuster UK, 2019).

[295] Ibid.

[296] In fairness to Verhofstadt, he has always been absolutely consistent in his pro-European views and has often berated the European institutions for lack of progress in European integration.

[297] Mark Francois, 'BBC4's Brexit documentary should be compulsory viewing before voting in the European election', Brexit Central, May 13th 2019.

[298] Lord Archie Hamilton and Lord Michael Spicer, 'If Tory MPs wish to change the 1922 committee no confidence vote rules there is nothing standing in their way', Daily Telegraph, 13th April 2019.

[299] Private Information. See also Christopher Howarth's article, 'Mrs May: My part in her Downfall', The Critic, July 2021.

[300] Private information.

[301] By this stage, even Conservative Party members were telling Tory canvassers that they intended to vote for the Brexit Party.

[302] Theresa May's resignation speech outside Downing Street, 24th May 2020.

Chapter 15: Boris to the Rescue?

[303] By comparison, even in the 1997 General Election, when Tony Blair's 'New Labour' slaughtered John Major's Conservatives by 418 seats to 165, the Conservatives still achieved 30.7% of the popular vote (to Labour's 43.2%).

[304] *BBC European Election Results* programme, BBC 1, 26th May 2016.

[305] The "Election Night" sketch is less well known than the famous "Parrot Sketch" but is nonetheless popular with Monty Python aficionados.

[306] Other colleagues apparently contemplated running too, but these were among the principal contenders, at least at the outset.

[307] Private notes on the meeting.

[308] Private Information.

[309] Conservative Party Leadership debate, BBC.

[310] Debate on the *James Whale Show*, Talk Radio, July 2020.

[311] Result in the Kensington Constituency at the 2019 General Election:

Candidate	Votes	Vote %	Change %
Felicity Buchan (Conservative)	16,768	38.3	-3.9
Emma Dent Coad (Labour)	16,618	38.0	-4.3
Samuel Gyimah (Liberal Democrats)	9,312	21.3	9.1
Vivien Lichtenstein (Green)	535	1.2	-0.8
Jay Aston Colquhoun (BXT)	384	0.9	0.2
Roger Phillips (*CPA)	70	0.2	0.2
Harriet Gore (*Touch Love Worldwide (UK))	47	0.1	0.1
Scott Dore (WRP)	28	0.1	0.1
Conservative Majority	150		

[312] There were some people in the front row wearing prominent pro-EU t-shirts and so I cannot honestly say the whole hall rose to its feet.

[313] *The Guardian*, 23rd July 2019.

[314] Oliver Cromwell's speech to the Rump Parliament, 20th April 1653 (*Britpolitics.co.uk*).

[315] *The Guardian*, August 28th 2019.

[316] I have not been able to ascertain the veracity of these claims, but they were certainly circulating at the time.

[317] BBC *Daily Politics*, BBC 1, 17th September 2019.

[318] R (Miller) v The Prime Minister, 24th September 2019.

[319] Quote from Keir Starmer on the Supreme Court Decision, *The Independent*, 11th September 2019.

[320] Quote from Gina Miller, 11th September 2019.

[321] Boris Johnson Speech to the Conservative Party Conference in Manchester, 2nd October 2019.

[322] Private information.

[323] Vote Leave boss Dominic Cummings blasts Tory Eurosceptics as 'metastasising tumour' in call for new Brexit party, *Politics Home*, 27th March 2019.

[324] Based on MF's notes, taken during and after the meeting.

[325] Government questioned on the powers of the EU Withdrawal Joint Committee, Parliament.uk, 20th March 2019.

[326] Ironically, this majority of 16 was very similar to that for the Brady Amendment, back in January 2019.

Chapter 16: Getting Brexit Done

[327] Page 5 of the Conservative 2019 General Election Manifesto, entitled: Get Brexit Done and Unleash Britain's Potential.

[328] Christopher Howarth's grandfather ran the Matthew Turnbull glassworks in Southwick, Sunderland.

[329] Article from the *Northern Echo*, 25th November 2019.

[330] Appearance on the ITV *Peston Show*, 4th December 2019.

[331] Jonathan Ashworth, quoted in the *Daily Mail,* 10th December 2019.

[332] Nigel Farage Advert, the *Daily Telegraph*, 19th October 2019.

[333] Mark Francois' interview on the *World at One*, 1st November 2019.

[334] Cameron refuses to apologise to UKIP, *The Guardian*, 4th April 2006.

[335] Richard Tice is now the Leader of the Reform Party.

[336] This couldn't have been an easy decision for Nigel Farage to take.

[337] During the 2017 General Election, the Thurrock Conservative Association kept a running list of the number of times in the run-up and the campaign itself, Tory MPs/Candidates had visited the seat to help. I came tied first with my friend and colleague James Brokenshire (12 each): but in view of the number of activists from my seat who helped out as well, the Thurrock Conservative's subsequently found the list and presented it to me, on behalf of my association, where it is regarded as an important campaign memento.

[338] This is a far cry from the simple "Swingometer" of the General Elections in the 1960s & 70s.

[339] In the end, John Curtice and his team got the number of Conservative seats exactly right – 365 – and were only a handful out for Labour, 198, compared to the actual final total of 202.

[340] Mark Francois' interview on the BBC *General Election Results* night programme, 12th December 2019.

[341] In the end, there were over 30 seats where the Brexit Party candidate polled more votes than the eventual Labour majority.

[342] Private information.

[343] Labour 2019 General Election Manifesto.

[344] Lib Dem 2019 General Election Manifesto.

Chapter 17: Sunrise on a Free Country

[345] Palace of Westminster Restoration and Renewal Programme, National Audit Office, 24th April 2020.

[346] *Hansard*, Written Answers, 16th January 2020.

[347] Prime Minister's interview on *BBC Breakfast*, 14th January 2020.

[348] Private information.

[349] Our target was £500k, the estimated cost from the House of Commons authorities to make Big Ben chime on 31st January 2020.

[350] Letter from the CEO of Help for Heroes, February 2020.

[351] I was one of a handful of Conservative MPs, mainly Spartans from memory, who had been invited to Nigel Farage's party.

[352] *Hansard*, 30th December 2019.

[353] John Humphrys, 'The EU row over Covid jabs has destroyed the faith of an old Remainer like me', *The Daily Mail*, 24th March 2021.

Chapter 18: Epilogue – The Case for the Spartans

[354] Tony Blair, Olly Robbins Quote (See Chapter 10).

[355] See again the Civitas Report 'The Brussels Broadcasting Corporation' as one of the best examples of all this.

[356] Simon Heffer, '*Like the Roman: The Life of Enoch Powell*', (Wiedenfield & Nicholson, 1998).

[357] I still have the texts, to this day.

[358] Email from ██████, received 21st November 2018.

[359] Email from ██████, received 20th March 2019.

[360] We were also very ably supported by distinguished legal experts, including Martin Howe QC and Barnabas Reynolds and trade experts, such as Shanker Singham.

[361] *Hansard*, 26th November 2018.

[362] Gavin Barwell, '*Chief of Staff: Notes from Downing Street*' (Atlantic Books, 2021).

[363] From a note of the meeting, taken at the time.

[364] 'Mrs May: My part in her Downfall', Christopher Howarth, *The Critic*, July 2021.

[365] Anthony Seldon, '*May at 10*' (Biteback, 2019). Seldon records that: "When ERG members left the meeting, they were muttering to themselves: 'There you go again, you can't trust the Prime Minister. Ian was gullible, her assurances are valueless'.".

[366] Editorial in *The Sun, 31st January 2021*.

[367] 'Molon Labe', Leader Article in the *Daily Telegraph*, 24th September 2021.

[368] "If" by Rudyard Kipling.